PERSONAL WELLNESS

CONTRIBUTORS

Thomas M. Davis, HSD ◆ **Forrest Dolgener, PhD**

Larry Hensley, EdD ◆ **Sue Joslyn, PhD** ◆ **Susan J. Koch, EdD**

Fred Kolkhorst, PhD

University of Northern Iowa
Cedar Falls, Iowa

Scott W. Roberts, EdD

SUNY College at Buffalo
Buffalo, New York

eb

eddie bowers publishing, inc.

2600 Jackson Street
Dubuque, Iowa 52001-3342

FOREWORD

The Editors would like to extend a very special thank you to Dr. Jeanette Marsh for her extensive review of each chapter. Her comments were most useful to all of the chapter contributors.

Design, Graphic Illustrations, and Production: David Corona Design

Medical Illustrations: pp. 39, 40, 147, 148, 149, 153, 354, 407, 433, 435, 469
LifeART Super Anatomy 1 and Super Anatomy 2 Images
LifeArt Images Copyright © 1989–1997
by TechPool Studios, Inc. USA

eddie bowers publishing, inc.

2600 Jackson Street
Dubuque, Iowa 52001-3342

ISBN 0-945483-85-6

9 8 7 6 5 4 3 2 1

Brief Contents

Jan 26 - 2.8
   28 - 2.7, 3.6 (1/5)

Feb 9 - 3.9
   18 - 3.4
   23 - 2.3, 2.4, 2.10, 2.14

Contents

Cardiorespiratory Endurance 33
Forrest Dolgener

Musculoskeletal Function 145

Forrest Dolgener

4

Assessment of Body Composition   209

Fred Kolkhorst

Weight Management 241

Fred Kolkhorst

Nutrition Principles   283

Sue Joslyn

Lifestyle Diseases   351

Forrest Dolgener

Health Concerns of Psyhoactive Drugs, Tobacco and Alcohol   397

Scott W. Roberts

Healthy Sexual Behavior   431

Susan J. Koch

Coping with Stress   467

Susan J. Koch

Preface

The most recent data from national surveys indicate that more Americans are overweight and obese than ever before. Heart disease and cancer are still the leading causes of death in this country, even though they have been the focus of research for decades. Other lifestyle diseases such as diabetes and osteoporosis afflict many Americans each year. In short, Americans are "living" themselves to premature death and disability at an ever increasing pace.

Even though there has been much time and huge amounts of money spent over several decades in attempts to significantly impact these lifestyle diseases and their devastating social and economic consequences, little progress has been evident. One reason is the failure to reach young adults with the necessary information that would enable them to make healthy decisions from an early age, before behaviors become so entrenched that they are almost impossible to change. In order to positively address this need, a three semester-hour course entitled "Personal Wellness" was adopted as part of the general education requirement of all students at a midwestern university. The primary purpose of the course is to provide the necessary information and experiences that will enable and motivate college students to begin to make appropriate decisions that will significantly enhance the quantity and quality of their lives. Two hours each week are spent in a traditional classroom format and three hours each week are spent in laboratory/activity classes involving exercise, fitness assessments, and lifetime skill acquisition.

At the time the course was initiated, there was not a single textbook that covered all the content areas of the course. To fill this void, the faculty teaching the course began to develop their own material in their areas of expertise. This current text is a culmination of the process.

The basic philosophy incorporated in this text is that regular and appropriate exercise and a nutritious and adequate diet serve as the foundation for a healthy lifestyle. Optimizing behaviors in these two areas provides the biologic foundation that can lead to increased longevity and quality of life.

Although the importance of good nutrition has been generally accepted for some time, recent scientific information has provided even greater confirmation of the role of good nutrition in maintaining good health throughout the lifespan. However, exercise has not been traditionally viewed at the same level of importance by the general population or by the medical community. Recent scientific evidence has confirmed the importance of exercise and this has been further emphasized and supported by a recent *Report of the Surgeon General* which expounded on the importance of an active lifestyle.

Once the foundation of appropriate activity and nutrition has been developed, the text focuses on reducing and eliminating destructive and unhealthy behaviors like drug, alcohol, and tobacco use, risky sexual behavior, and stress. Providing the knowledge-base for wise decision-making in these areas can significantly impact one's health, both acutely and chronically.

The sequence of content of this text follows the order of content presented in the course "Personal Wellness." This sequence has been established and refined over several years and represents, in our opinion, the most logical and effective sequence for presenting the content. The initial chapter introduces the concept of wellness and lays the groundwork for behavior modification. If students are to be successful in changing behaviors, they have to understand the process of behavior-change as well as the attitudes, beliefs, and values which influence behavior, either positively or negatively. Following this introductory chapter, the order of content is as follows: exercise, nutrition, weight management, alcohol, drugs, tobacco, sexual behavior, and stress. Each chapter contains the most recent and valid information available today.

This full-color text contains many illustrations, graphs, and photos which enhance the content of each chapter. Each chapter lists objectives and key terms used in the chapter. There are "Key Concept" boxes located throughout each chapter which are used to expand discussion in areas the authors deem important and/or interesting. To encourage students to expand their knowledge and seek information from other sources, each chapter contains "Exploring Wellness on the Web" boxes that provide information regarding sites on the world wide web pertinent to the content of that chapter. Key terms are defined at the end of each chapter and a cumulative glossary is provided at the end of the text. Lastly, each chapter contains laboratory experiences. Some of the labs are assessments of current status and others are experiences which emphasize and reinforce concepts.

In addition to the features notes above, there is one unique feature of this text that make it different from other text in this area. Seven different authors have contributed their expertise and abilities in writing chapters. Not only does this help ensure an accurate and valid content, it adds diversity of approach and opinion, where warranted, to each content area. Yet, all the chapters are integrated and contribute to the overall broad goal of the text.

ACKNOWLEDGMENTS

The number of individuals that have positively impacted this text are too numerous to list here. There have been multitudes of students in the Personal Wellness course who have challenged us even when we were trying to challenge them. To all the students we say "thank you" and we hope that your experiences in the personal wellness course will help you to a healthy and productive life.

To the many instructors of Personal Wellness course and of the lab sections, who have offered suggestions and critiques, we say thanks. Without your input and your varied experiences, this text would not be a reality.

A special thanks to Jeanette Marsh for her thorough review of content and her many suggestions for labs. We hope that your impending retirement goes well and that you have a healthy, happy, and active retirement.

To Eddie Bowers and the staff at Eddie Bowers Publishing, we extend our gratitude for your efforts in bringing this text to completion. Thanks for keeping us on task and for your guidance through and around the many pitfalls of textbook writing.

And finally, to all our understanding, loving, and patient spouses, thank you. Without your support, this text (and many of the other things that we attempt to do) would not have been successfully completed.

PERSONAL WELLNESS

What Is Wellness?

Thomas M. Davis

- ◆ Understand the nature of wellness; be able to define wellness.

- ◆ Recognize the relationship between behavioral choices and health status.

- ◆ Recognize the indicators of deteriorating or improving health.

- ◆ Understand the difference between intrinsic and extrinsic decisions.

- ◆ Identify positive and negative factors influencing health behaviors.

- ◆ Recognize the common components of wellness.

- ◆ Understand the wholistic nature of wellness.

KEY TERMS

asymptomatic

enabling factors

extrinsic decisions

high level wellness

intrinsic decisions

positive self-concept

premature death

predisposing factors

reinforcing factors

wellness

wellness continuum

wholistic

WHAT IS WELLNESS?

Definition of Wellness

Only a few years ago "wellness" was a term known only to a few, and even today the majority of English dictionaries do not include it. In spite of that circumstance, most people, when asked to define wellness, have an answer that focuses on the quality of one's health. A diverse group of professionals have identified wellness as the province of their professions, including home economists, medical personnel, health and physical educators, business leaders, recreation specialists, community service agency administrators, and others. While each of these disciplines can provide a definition of wellness that varies slightly from the others, one should not conclude that only one definition can be correct. In fact, the wellness definition that suits you best may not be found among any adopted by these groups.

The authors have a friend who collects definitions related to wellness. These definitions are jotted on slips of paper, cut from newspapers, photocopied from books, or found in cartoons, but all of them end up taped to his office door and walls. Among them are many definitions of wellness and a few of them are included here:

1. Wellness is dynamic.
2. Wellness is a social movement.
3. Wellness is more than physical fitness.
4. Wellness is multidimensional.
5. Wellness is available to everyone.
6. Wellness is a lifestyle.

These definitions are included here not to suggest they are the best, or that others are wrong, but to underscore that wellness is many things to many people, and that your own definition of wellness may be better suited to you than any that others will provide. While acknowledging the variability of wellness, the idea that a person's health is determined by behavioral choices is reinforced by the fact that lifestyle choices often contribute more to a person's health than genetics, environmental circumstances, and the quality or availability of health care combined.[1]

It may be that your personal risk of heart disease is elevated due to hereditary factors or environmental circumstances. Certainly the cardiovascular stress of breathing air on a Los Angeles freeway or a postwar Kuwaiti oil field is greater than breathing air on a mid-western prairie. For the person whose life is literally saved by a miracle of modern medicine, lifestyle choices may seem to have limited influence over the quality of that person's health. For most of us, though, the most powerful determinant of our health is our lifestyle.

Just as there are many definitions of wellness, there are many topics that are studied in the pursuit of wellness. These topics will be examined throughout this text. Hopefully, you will be convinced that a healthy lifestyle is a desirable objective.

WHAT IS THE WELLNESS CONTINUUM?

The Wellness Continuum

The wellness continuum is a diagrammatic representation of a concept originated by Dr. Halbert Dunn and popularized by Don Ardell[2] in his book, *High Level Wellness, An Alternative to Doctors, Drugs and Disease*. During your lifetime you will "ride" up and down on the wellness continuum, much as you would an elevator (Figure 1.1). Your health-related choices contribute greatly to your destiny as a passenger on this "wellness elevator." Some people reach the penthouse and others drop to the lowest of subbasements. Whether you go up or down is determined somewhat by things over which you have little or no control. Your genetically predetermined risk of heart disease is something over which you obviously have no control, and your exposure to environmental health risks and your access to health care are, to some degree, outside your control. The good news is that the dominant factor determining whether you go up or down is lifestyle.[1] The health behavior choices you make are the strongest indicators that you will enjoy high level wellness, or be burdened with disease, disability, and even premature death.

Most often your entry point on this "wellness elevator" is going to be "ground level," the point at which you are asymptomatic. Being characterized as being asymptomatic is determined most by what is absent from your life. To be asymptomatic is to be without symptoms of a health problem. If you are asymptomatic you don't currently have any indicators that tell you or a health practitioner that your health is threatened. Some mistakenly believe that being asymptomatic, by itself, is an indicator of good health. In fact, a person who is asymptomatic is not guaranteed of fulfilling her or his health potential. A person may be asymptomatic and still possess limited cardiovascular fitness, be exposed to unnecessary risks, and feel a vague helplessness in the face of life's challenges. The most that can be said for being asymptomatic is that you are without any clear indicators of health problems, but it doesn't mean that you are enjoying your full health potential.

FIGURE 1.1

The Wellness Continuum

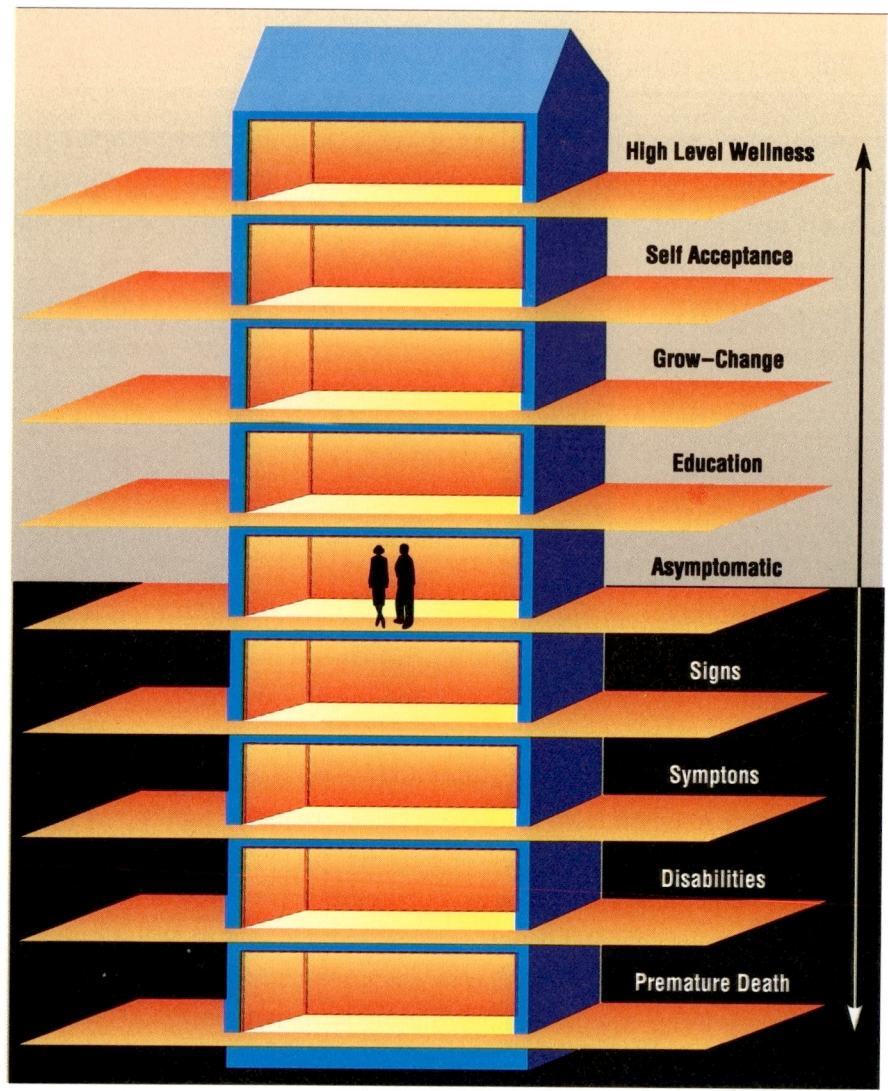

The first indicator that your personal wellness elevator is going down is an assortment of vague signs that may not seem important to you, but given a closer look, reveal that all is not right. Examples of these vague signs may include back pain, indigestion, insomnia, feelings of fatigue or frustration, or feeling overwhelmed by stressful circumstances at school or work. Many people come to accept these signs, believing that stress is something they can do nothing about, assuming that indigestion is a natural product of aging, or not knowing to whom they can turn for help with feelings of frustration or despair.

The next level on our descent on the wellness continuum is symptoms, the definitive signals that a person's health is in jeopardy. These symptoms or signals are what patients report to health care providers seeking relief from a health problem. A skilled diagnostician will use these symptoms to make a determination of the specific threat to the patient's health and to

You and your physician are partners on your personal wellness team.

decide what treatment regimen is in order to help the patient recover from this threat. Acute pain on the lower right side of the abdomen suggests that the patient may need to have her/his appendix surgically removed. Chest pain upon physical exertion suggests that the heart is not getting a satisfactory amount of oxygenated blood to facilitate the work the body is attempting to perform. It may be that this deficiency is the product of arteries being partially blocked by an accumulation of plaque in the circulatory system. Based on the symptoms reported by the patient, a skilled diagnostician can perform additional diagnostic procedures, and, in many cases, make a clear determination of the patient's specific health threat.

As we near the bottom of the wellness continuum, our next stop is disabilities. Disabilities are temporary or permanent serious impairments of a person's health and life. These disabilities are frequently a product of lifestyle decisions. In the early weeks of the 1991 baseball season, Lenny Dykstra, outfielder for the Philadelphia Phillies, was involved in a one-car accident. Following a party he and Philadelphia catcher Darren Daulton attended, he got behind the wheel after drinking and drove his $90,000 Mercedes into a tree. While both players recovered before the end of the season, Daulton spent a few weeks on the National League disabled list and Dykstra's injuries disabled him for much of the season. Another famous sports figure suffered a much more serious outcome from driving while intoxicated. Famous jockey Willie Shoemaker spent a quarter-century career as the toast of the horse racing world, but a few months after his retirement he also was involved in a one-car accident while intoxicated. He is almost totally paralyzed and there is no expectation that he will regain control of his arms and legs.

Another disabling health problem caused by our health behavior is emphysema. Emphysema is nearly always the result of a long smoking history. It reduces the lungs' ability to oxygenate blood and prevents its sufferers from engaging in vigorous activity. For grandparents with emphysema, it means they and their grandchildren may never enjoy tossing a football in the back yard or swimming at the local pool.

The ultimate consequence for those plunging to the depths of negative health is premature death. While a variety of factors determine each person's life expectancy, on average, Americans born in the 1990s can expect to live between 70 and 80 years. The label "premature death" may be applied to the majority of deaths that occur prior to the seventh decade of life. People who die in their 60s from lung cancer after a lifetime of smoking, die in their 40s

---

KEY CONCEPT

THE ECONOMICS OF A HEALTHY LIFESTYLE

Living an optimal wellness lifestyle has many personal benefits including an increased quality and quantity of life. Not only will one probably live longer, but the kinds of activities than can be enjoyed throughout the lifespan can make for happier and more productive lives. In addition to these personal benefits to an optimal wellness lifestyle, there is also a tremendous potential economic benefit to the entire nation if a large segment of the population adopted healthy lifestyles. In 1992, health care costs accounted for 12% of the gross national product and it is projected to reach 18% by 2002. Because living a healthy lifestyle reduces health care costs, the economic burden imposed by health care could be significantly reduced. Health insurance would be cheaper, employers would be better able to provide health insurance as a benefit, and the entire economy would benefit.

Regular exercise plays an important role in preventing disease and maintaining wellness.

from AIDS, or commit suicide in their teen years, all have lost years of life that might have been enjoyable and productive. The cocaine-induced death of University of Maryland basketball player Len Bias, hours after the announcement of his signing to a lucrative professional contract, was mourned across the nation. The grief felt by many when reflecting on this young person's death was a product, in part, of the prematurity of it, coupled with the fact that many perceived it to be preventable.

The steps from the asymptomatic level to premature death (signs, symptoms, disabilities), are only half of the wellness continuum. Fulfilling one's health potential means being more than asymptomatic. Just as there are well-defined indicators to mark our descent toward impaired health and premature death, other indicators reveal our progress toward fulfilling our health potential and attaining high level wellness.

Using the same starting point of being asymptomatic, the ascension to high level wellness is marked first by learning from the planned educational experiences offered to us in school and our community and also learning from the unexpected events that are a part of our life's experiences. These educational opportunities may be formal instructional opportunities like a college course, a nutrition education program offered through Weight Watchers or the YMCA, or participating in a program offered by the American Cancer Society increasing your ability to identify cancer warning signals. There is also the potential to learn from life's coincidental events. It is not uncommon for people who survive near-death experiences to set new priorities in their lives. Several years ago former senator Paul Tsongas of Massachusetts was stricken with life-threatening cancer. At that point in his political career he chose not to run for a second term even though political circumstances guaranteed his re-election. When asked why he would give up such an important and prestigious position he replied "I've heard of people on their death beds saying 'I wish I'd spent more time with my family,' I never heard of anyone saying 'I wish I'd worked harder.'" In the face of his life-threatening illness Senator Tsongas decided to spend more time with his family. He lived for more than 10 years after his original diagnosis and in subsequent interviews he repeatedly affirmed his decision.

Although formal and informal educational opportunities are a part of everyone's life experience, they are not a guarantee that high level wellness will be attained. To move in a positive direction, a person needs to grow and change in response to life's learning opportunities. A tragic national circumstance that, as a result of the O. J. Simpson trial, has received much overdue recognition, is the problem of family violence. Many families disintegrate in the face of this brutal behavior, with all parties feeling the pain of the loss of spouse or parent. The abusing family member sometimes moves on to new relationships, assuming that if other people would just be "better" he wouldn't need to behave in an abusive way. Such a person obviously has not grown or changed much following the disintegration of his family. Others are stimulated by the pain of the loss of family to examine their own behavior, to learn new ways of relating to others, and to eliminate abusive behavior. These people have grown and have changed in positive ways that permits them to more nearly approximate high level wellness.

One of the most valuable lessons learned from life's experience is the development of a positive self-concept. While some people grow up with confidence, respecting others and simultaneously respecting themselves, others arrive at adulthood lacking confidence, devaluing their own opinions and their overall worth. In our model of wellness, the last prerequisite to the achievement of high level wellness is a positive self-concept. Even though there are a variety of forces at work that encourage us to make choices that are not in our own best interests, people who feel good about themselves are more likely to find that healthy choices are the easiest choices. Many students have been encouraged by friends to skip important study time to go out for a pizza. Many advertising messages suggest that alcohol consumption is the key to exceptional sexual relationships. Cultural norms create an environment that burdens students with more stress than is healthy. For people who feel badly about their own self worth, they are commonly guided by the feeling of affirmation that goes with "belonging to the group" that goes out for pizza, even at the expense of academic success. The same people are more likely to seek the promise of social and sexual fulfillment modeled in many alcohol advertisements. Students with a poor self-image are more likely to feel helpless in the face of stress and believe that feeling uncomfortable is a deficiency within themselves instead of an environmental circumstance they may potentially change.

Health behavior decisions might be categorized as intrinsic, extrinsic, or some mixture of the two (Figure 1.2). Intrinsic decisions are those that are made to meet one's own needs. Extrinsic decisions are those that are made primarily to please others. Choosing to spend more time studying because you want to do well on a test is an intrinsic decision. Studying just to please your parents with high grades is an extrinsic decision. Choosing to exercise because it makes you feel good is an intrinsic decision. Choosing to exercise to lose weight because your girlfriend or boyfriend doesn't like to "go out with a fat person" is an example of an extrinsic decision. Most people probably make their decisions based on a blend of intrinsic and extrinsic influences, but people who are primarily extrinsic decision makers are encouraged to reflect on the reasons they seek to serve other's needs instead of their own best interests.

FIGURE 1.2

Most decisions are combinations of intrinsic and extrinsic factors.

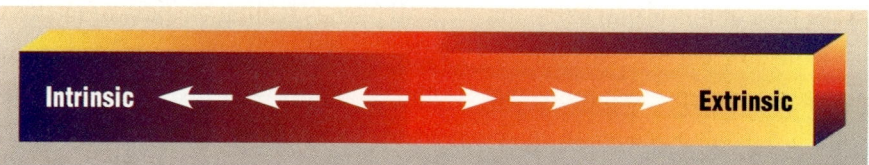

People with a positive self-image are less in need of external approval that confirms their self-worth. People that devalue themselves are more likely to make extrinsic decisions, those decisions that will result in receiving the approval of others. People with a positive self-image are more likely to make intrinsic decisions, those decisions that meet their own needs. Recognizing this ultimate motivation for some of our health decisions makes it easy to see why developing a positive self-image will help us make decisions that are in our own best interests and, consequently, are the healthiest decisions. Not surprisingly, if we want to help others adopt new health behaviors, we probably help them more by encouraging them and underscoring their best qualities, than by criticizing their failings. Encouraging a person to adopt new eating and exercise patterns to lose weight is probably best achieved by congratulating them on the exercise they do undertake, not by reminding them how great they used to look before they got fat.

Once a person has taken advantage of opportunities to grow and change in positive ways, including developing a more positive self-image, a person has set the stage for achieving a higher level of wellness. Unfortunately, some people look at high level wellness as a destination that, once achieved, can be forgotten. In fact, the pursuit of wellness is a lifelong process. It is infrequent that a person reaches a state of perfect wellness, and even when achieved, its enjoyment is usually short-lived. While perfect wellness is not easily attained, the health decisions people make determine the degree to which they fulfill their health potential. The wellness continuum diagramed in Figure 1.1 describes a path along which we may chart the quality of a person's health at any particular time. People tend to live in zones along this line. Some people invite many risks into their lives and, consequently, experience more signs, symptoms, and disabilities, and are at greater risk for premature death. People who take their live's experiences and grow from them, and in the process feel better about themselves, set the stage for choosing health behaviors that are the healthiest choices.

WHAT ARE THE BENEFITS OF LIVING A HEALTHY LIFESTYLE?

Most people, when asked "Why live a healthy life?" might list some of the following reasons:

- ◆ to live longer.
- ◆ to improve quality of life.
- ◆ to have more fun.
- ◆ to sleep better and have more energy.

At the same time, every day's news seems to bring a conflicting report about what is good for our health and what behaviors are risky. That may leave students wondering "What is the right answer?" or "Why should I try to live a healthy life?" Let there be no doubt, there is abundant evidence that wellness has its payoffs. The body of evidence documenting the benefits of a healthy lifestyle has been building for decades. More than 30 years ago the *Surgeon General's Report on Smoking* was published, providing the first widely publicized evidence of the link between smoking and premature death, and in 1996 the Surgeon General has published another report *(Physical Activity and Health, A Report of the Surgeon General)* that documents the benefits of an active lifestyle, including reducing the risk of overall premature mortality, coronary heart disease, hypertension, colon cancer, and diabetes mellitus. Physical activity also improves mental health, and is important for the health of muscles, bones, and joints.[12]

Louis Sullivan, M.D., former Secretary of Health and Human Services wrote in the forward to *Healthy People 2000* [11] "Health promotion and disease prevention comprise perhaps the best opportunity to reduce the ever-increasing portion of resources that we spend to treat preventable illness and functional impairment" and can " . . . dramatically cut health care costs, . . . prevent the premature onset of disease and disability, and help all Americans achieve healthier, more productive lives." While individuals may not feel the personal impact of reducing the percentage of the gross national product spent on health care, each can more easily appreciate the increased years of healthy life that can be expected among those who chose to live a healthy, low-risk life. Additional evidence of the value of a healthy lifestyle is reported by the National Center of Health Statistics.[9] Exercise reduces the risk for premature death for three of the ten leading causes of death for all Americans, (heart disease, stroke, diabetes mellitus), a healthy diet reduces risk of premature death of four (heart disease, cancer, stroke, diabetes mellitus), limiting alcohol consumption reduces the risk of four (cancer, accidents, AIDS, and homicide) and choosing not to smoke reduces the risk of six (heart disease, cancer, stroke, accidents, obstructive lung diseases, and pneumonia)!

We are a nation that has developed great dependence on our health care system to restore lost health. Many who read this book know someone who has undergone coronary bypass surgery to repair the damage of years of smoking, poor dietary choices, and a sedentary life. More than 280,000 such surgical procedures are performed every year in the U.S.[11] Unfortunately, some who read this book will, one day, need the same operation or, worse, suffer premature death due to heart disease. The reality is that, while good health care is invaluable to the person whose life is saved by a medical miracle, far more premature deaths are prevented by prudent health behavior choices than by medical intervention. In fact, heredity, environmental influences, and health care *combined,* contribute less to premature death than health behaviors alone.[1] In response to the question *What are the benefits of a healthy lifestyle?* the answer is clear. A longer, happier, more enjoyable life can be expected by those who adopt low-risk behaviors and achieve high level wellness.

MAKING HEALTHY CHOICES THE EASY CHOICES

The Determinants of Health Behavior

Feeling good about one's self certainly "sets the stage" for making healthy choices, but it is not a guarantee that a person will make the healthiest choices. When it comes to health behaviors, it has become popular in our society to "blame the victim" when things go wrong. Many assume that if a person really wanted to stop smoking they would stop; if they really wanted to start an exercise program they, in the words of Nike advertisements, would "Just Do It." As popular as this attitude is, it doesn't fit with experiences many of us have had or observed in others. We either know someone who has tried unsuccessfully, or we have tried unsuccessfully, to change some behavior. We may have known people who sincerely wished they could be more assertive, control their appetite, or stop smoking. In many of those cases there is no doubt the person wanted to make the change even though they were still unsuccessful. What explains this lack of success? Is it merely

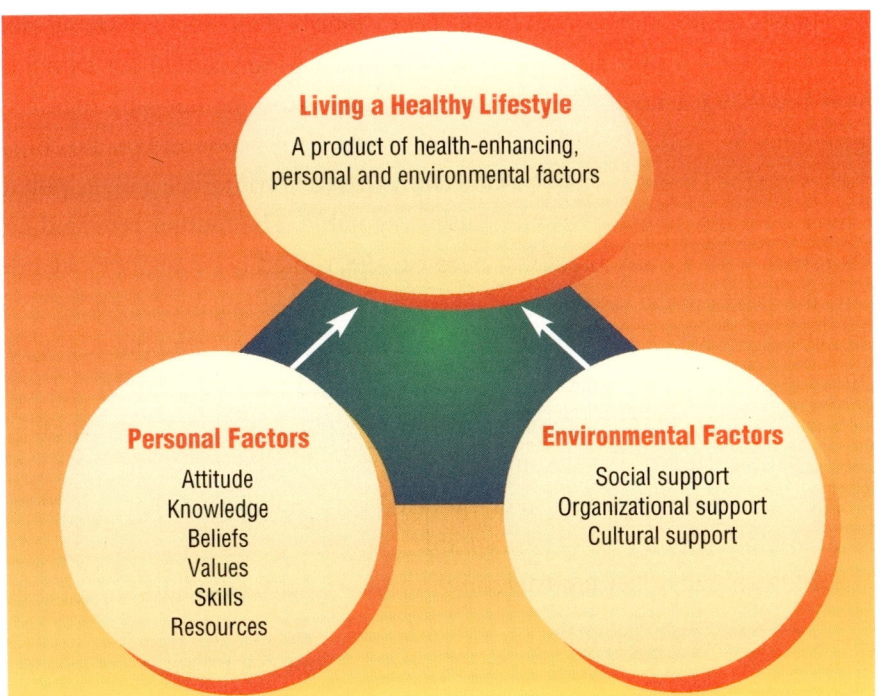

Many different factors influence the decisions that determine your health and wellness.

a lack of willpower? Are only those possessing an iron will going to be successful in making important health behavior changes? The answer is an emphatic "No!"

Making the healthy choice become the easy choice is not the result of cultivating a tough-mindedness about health behaviors. Many think that becoming healthy involves great sacrifice, including hours of painful exercise and self-denial at the dinner table, and that achieving wellness includes a feeling of pride at overcoming great obstacles. Self-congratulations are certainly in order for the person who makes positive change, but it is possible to chart a path to wellness that has fewer barriers and, for some, is the easiest of all possible pathways. Several personal and environmental factors collectively determine whether healthy choices are easy or difficult. In a model for understanding health behavior and planning health promotion programs, Green and Kreuter[5] label the personal factors that determine health behavior as predisposing and enabling factors. Personal factors include attitudes, beliefs, values, and knowledge that trigger our desires to follow one behavioral path or another and skills and resources that make it possible for people to act on their health behavior desires.

Personal Factors that Influence Our Health Behavior Choices

Our attitudes, beliefs, values, and knowledge can push us toward, or away, from a desirable health behavior. The author once had the opportunity to listen to public health nutritionists talk about their interactions with mothers in a public health nutrition program. They described one mother who valued her daughter's health and voiced her commitment to see that her daughter was receiving a healthy breakfast every day. This mother was regularly providing her child with a breakfast of Orange Crush soda and potato chips, believing the Orange Crush was the equivalent of a fruit juice and the potato chips were the equivalent of a healthy vegetable. The mother provided her daughter with a daily breakfast because she valued her daughter's health, but she failed in the provision of a healthy breakfast because she held false beliefs about what constituted good nutrition. Another example of the influence of personal factors is college students who are inclined to exercise regularly if they believe possessing a fit body will make them more popular among their friends. Those same students may risk their health by following a starvation diet if they feel so dissatisfied with their bodies that only quick and dramatic weight loss is acceptable.

Knowing what fast foods are high in fat content, believing that regular exercise will make you feel better about yourself, and valuing one's health, all make it easier to follow a healthy path. Conversely, false beliefs and inadequate knowledge may be barriers to healthy choices. Believing it is impolite to discuss condom usage with a potential sexual partner, not knowing that latex condoms provide the best protection against sexually-transmitted diseases, or believing you can identify a person with HIV by the person's appearance, all increase the likelihood that a person will make a risky sexual choice. The challenge for each person is to cultivate the prerequisite knowledge and accurate beliefs, and activate one's health-promoting values and attitudes.

While knowledge, beliefs, and attitudes set the stage for the types of health behaviors people choose, other personal factors make it possible for people to act on their health behavior desires. All health behaviors have essential skills and most behaviors require some prerequisite resource necessary to act out the behavior. Certainly many people possess the attitudes, beliefs, and knowledge that result in a wish to pursue a healthy lifestyle but it is sometimes not possible to act on these wishes without the necessary resources or skills. The desire to reduce risks by always wearing a seatbelt is not very helpful if the seatbelts in a person's car don't work. A prospective mother may want the very best in prenatal care but if she doesn't have reliable transportation to the doctor, lives 75 miles from a physician, or doesn't have insurance or personal financial resources to pay for care, it is unlikely she will get all the care she desires. Fortunately, for college students that wish to exercise regularly, most universities have facilities and recreational programs that facilitate participation. Such students have the personal factors in place (a personal wish to exercise and a place to exercise comfortably and regularly) to lead active lifestyles, reduce their health risks and enhance their health.

Sometimes the personal factors in students' lives seem to conspire to defeat students' pursuit of a wellness lifestyle. If students' nutritional health beliefs come from advertising that misrepresents favorite foods as "low in fat" and if students eat in dining halls that provide unlimited ice cream, soda, highly sugared breakfast cereals and other high fat foods, it will not be surprising if they have difficulty controlling body weight. Another important and more long term consequence is that these false beliefs and high fat diet may contribute to the development of lifelong eating habits that will increase the likelihood of developing cardiovascular disease. One of the challenges in developing a wellness lifestyle is the cultivation of the health enhancing personal factors (attitudes, beliefs, knowledge, skills, and resources) that are prerequisite to living a healthy life and making healthy choices easier.

Environmental Factors

While personal factors are a measure of the personal control people have over their health behavior, other circumstances are also play a part in determining our behaviors. Green and Kreuter[5] identify these other circumstances as elements that reinforce our health behavior decisions. They are elements in the environment that provide organizational and social support for health behaviors. These environmental factors may complement or conflict with our attitudes and beliefs about our preferred health behaviors.

Environmental reinforcers include the encouragement we receive for the behaviors we adopt. Encouragement comes to us through support from our friends, the health norms of our culture, and by the health practices we observe in others at school, in dormitories, at the worksite, and at home. Just like personal factors (knowledge, attitudes, skills), environmental reinforcers can encourage us to adopt behaviors that either protect our health or endanger it. Many students have been to parties where even the most intoxicated person was "reinforced" to risk their well-being by being encouraged to "just have one more drink for the road." Movie actor Gary Busey suffered a serious head injury as a result of a motorcycle accident that happened while he was not wearing a helmet. For weeks following his accident he remained an advocate of free choice regarding helmet use until he discovered his "reinforcing" message was encouraging many young motorcycle riders to ride without helmets, resulting in some riders suffering serious head injuries.

Instead of focusing on negative environmental messages, people seeking to improve and maintain health enhancing behaviors should recognize the positive environmental circumstances that surround them. The change in smoking behaviors nationally is an example of how positive behavioral norms are encouraging current smokers to become non-smokers. An increasing number of restaurants and government buildings have been designated "smoke-free" environments and passengers are now prohibited from smoking on U.S. flights that are shorter than six hours. Some airlines have become totally smoke free. The combination of these regulations, omnipresent messages related to the risks of smoking, and a decreasing frequency of smoking among the American population have collectively provided a positive environment to help people stop smoking

The challenge for the person attempting to change health behaviors is not to depend on willpower to prevent a "slip" back to former risky behaviors. The challenge is to simultaneously cultivate the necessary personal factors (knowledge, beliefs, attitudes, skills, resources) that push us toward our desired behaviors and the environmental factors (social, organizational, cultural reinforcement) that encourages us to maintain those desired behaviors.

The author knew a person who, as a child, was teased with the nickname "Bucky" because of his severely protruding front teeth. The child lived in a family with limited financial resources and no dental insurance, and could not afford orthodontic care (negative personal factors). The child was not encouraged by his family to plan on getting such care (negative environmental factor) because of the financial barriers. As an adult this same person visited an orthodontist's office with his daughter and saw a brochure regarding orthodontic care for adults. Reading the brochure immediately made him realize he was a candidate for orthodontic care. At that time in his life he was then able to afford to pay for orthodontic treatment (positive personal factor) and was encouraged to get orthodontic care (positive environmental factor) by his family and two adult friends who were also orthodontic patients. For him, deciding to get orthodontic care became the easy choice when the personal and environmental factors all pushed him toward that decision. The challenge for people seeking to adopt a healthy lifestyle is to create an environment in which they simultaneously possess the positive personal factors and are surrounded by an environment that encourages healthy choices. In this positive environment, making the healthy choice really does become the easy choice.

THE COMPONENTS OF WELLNESS—THE WELLNESS PIE

At the outset of this chapter several definitions of wellness were proposed to the reader, including its characterization as dynamic and multidimensional. Wellness is also wholistic (Figure 1.3). The incorporation of many elements in wellness is affirmed by the nation's national health objectives. *Healthy People 2000, The National Health Promotion and Disease Prevention Objectives*[11] sets targets for preventing disease and creating a more health-promoting environment. Consistent with the multidimensional

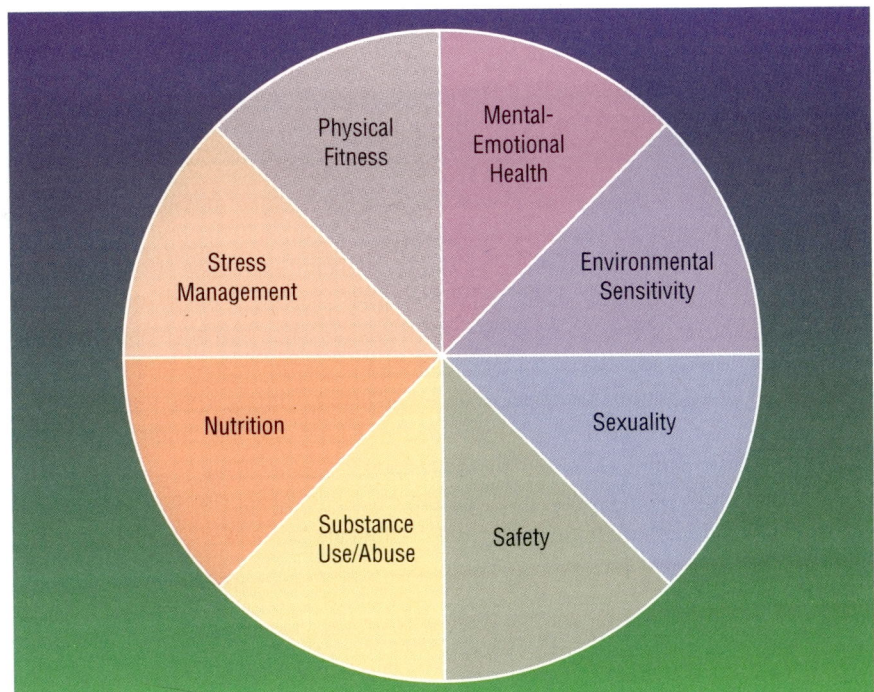

FIGURE 1.3

Wholistic wellness is comprised of eight major categories.

The Surgeon-General has determined that inactivity is bad for your health.

A wide variety of activities can significantly reduce the risk of disease and improve fitness.

nature of wellness and health promotion, the national health objectives are organized under 22 headings in four major categories (health promotion, health protection, preventive services, and surveillance and data systems). Just as there is no absolute definition for wellness, there is no universally accepted grouping of wellness topics. The following section introduces the major wellness topics along with national health promotion and disease prevention objectives demonstrating the importance of these health issues within the framework of America's national health policy.

Physical Fitness

National Health Objective: Reduce sedentary lifestyles to less than 15% of population (a 38% decrease).

While physical fitness is not the only element of wellness, it is certainly an important part. In times past, vigorous activity was a regular part of work, but as machines have replaced human toil in the workplace, the pursuit of physical fitness has required the inclusion of vigorous activity as a part of one's recreational patterns, or it has been necessary to engage in fitness activities for their own sake. Many of our great grandparents could honestly report that, as children, they had to walk miles to school, even on the coldest days of winter, whereas our parents might claim that when kids their burden was not having remote control for the television and they had to walk across the room to change the channel. Today, many young people develop television viewing patterns that result in spending more time in front of the TV than in school or sleeping. While television is not inherently

KEY CONCEPT

JUST DO SOMETHING

Recent scientific evidence has confirmed that the greatest health benefit incurred from being physically active occurs in those individuals that have been in a chronic sedentary condition and they then begin to exercise at a relatively low level. In other words, just doing a "minimal" amount of exercise can produce significant health benefits in those individuals who have been chronically sedentary. Increasing the activity level above this minimal threshold will continue to improve health, but to a lesser degree than the improvement occurring from doing just "minimal" exercise. Activities falling into the "minimal" exercise categories would be any activity that expends around 1000 kcals of energy per week. Brisk walking, gardening, various recreational sports and even some occupational tasks could easily expend 1000 kcals per week.

bad, such huge investments of time in TV viewing makes it impossible to spend much time in active pursuits.

To be physically fit requires regular participation in vigorous physical activity.[3, 8] Later in this book the concepts of training heart rate, and frequency, intensity, and duration of physical activity will be described, and the minimal requirements for fitness will be defined. For now it is sufficient to know that fitness requires activity and these activity requirements can be met through cycling, jogging, swimming, or other aerobic activities that elevate the heart rate into the training heart rate zone and, under certain circumstances, can also be fulfilled by activities such as racquetball, tennis, gardening or regular walks with your dog.

Nutrition

National Health Objective: Reduce overweight to a prevalence of no more than 20% of population (a 23% decrease).

Americans eat too much fat, sugar, and salt and far too many Americans are overfat. Simultaneously, and partly because of our overfatness, our nation seems obsessed with being slim and with the many pieces of equipment and diets that provide the promise of the slim bodies seen in advertisements for the Easyglider, Soloflex, and Thighmaster. Examining the magazines on display at the checkout stands at almost any supermarket in America will reveal numerous diet articles promising quick results.

Much of the eating that people do is not done with the intent of satisfying hunger. Some people eat as a means of resolving stress. Some eat as a means of making social contact with others. For many, eating is an integral part of other activities. For some, seeing a movie in a theater just doesn't seem complete without a big container of popcorn, and, for others, a baseball game isn't complete without a hotdog or a bag of peanuts. Developing the knowledge necessary to make sound nutrition decisions, creating an environment in which sound nutrition decisions can be enacted, and cultivating the support systems to reinforce those healthful decisions are all a part of wellness.

Over one-third of Americans are overweight. Overweight increases the risk of several chronic diseases.

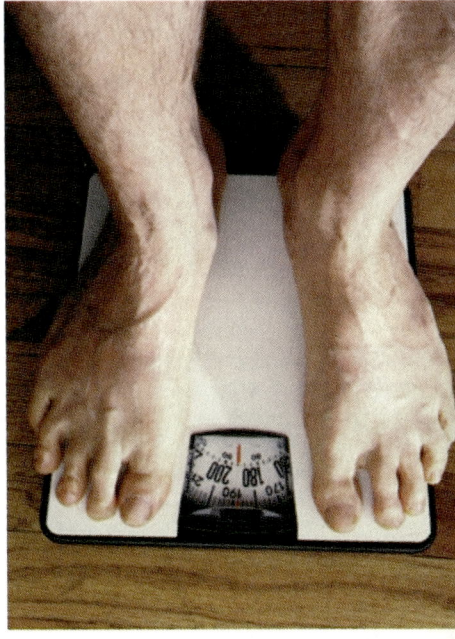

Stress Management

National Health Objective: Reduce adverse effects of stress to less than 35% of population (an 18% decrease).

People not currently in college, including the parents of many college students, often believe that the college years must be an easy time in one's life. They know that students have to do some studying, but they often assume that people who are spending only approximately 15 hours a week

Participating in relaxing and enjoyable activities can reduce the impact of daily stress.

in class, live in a dormitory where all the food is prepared by a dietary staff, and have on-campus intramural sports leagues, musical performances, famous speakers, and health services provided can't be feeling too much stress.

In fact, the college years are a period of extraordinary stress and change. For most students the college years combine several changes of residence, forming and often ending intimate relationships, the pressure of academic competition, widely varying sleep patterns, and anxiety about the future. In fact, Thomas Holmes, M.D., psychiatrist and member of the faculty at the University of Washington School of Medicine found, through the use of the Holmes Readjustment Rating Scale, that college students are among the groups that experience the most change of all, and the feelings of stress that accompany that change.[6]

Substance Use and Abuse

National Health Objective: Reduce alcohol-related motor vehicle crash deaths to no more than 8.5 per 100,000 people (age adjusted) (a 12% decrease)

It seems that every day's newspaper carries stories about drug related violence or the flood of illegal drugs that are penetrating our borders from foreign lands. Government at every level has made the fight against drugs a top priority. Leaders in both amateur and professional sports have instituted widespread drug testing, and in the process, have provided the evidence to confirm our suspicions that many of our sporting heroes have enhanced their performances through the use of drugs. In the face of these circumstances it would be easy to conclude that cocaine, steroids, and amphetamines are the most serious problems facing all of America, including college students. In fact, while college campuses are not without their drug problems, it is not the aforementioned drugs that are the most serious drug threats. Alcohol is a far more serious health problem in high schools and colleges than any other drug. In March of 1991, Surgeon General Antonia Novello released data indicating that more than 40% of all college students are intoxicated at least once in every two-week period.[10] Students drink to resolve stress, as a social bridge, and as a way of "fitting in" with other students. College students' per capita alcohol consumption is more than the rest of the American population, including people of traditional college-age who do not go on to college after high school graduation.

Considering the tremendous amount of social support for drinking, including drinking to the point of intoxication, some would say it is surprising that consumption and intoxication rates are not higher. One example of the omnipresent social support for alcohol consumption is alcohol advertising that characterizes drinking as a prerequisite to being attractive and chic. Some ads associate drinking with activities that can only be considered as high risk when done in combination with alcohol consumption, including surfing, ski jumping, and sky diving. Other ads communicate the promise of sexual fulfillment for the consumers of each advertiser's beverage.

Sexuality

National Health Objective: Reduce unintended pregnancies to no more than 30% of pregnancies (a 46% decrease)

The 1960s were for the "baby boomers" and the '70s were for "YUPPIES." The '80s were the "me" generation. Unfortunately the '90s appears to be the AIDS generation. Acquired Immune Deficiency Syndrome has triggered a national dialogue on sexual mores and considerable reflection on sex behavior norms. At the same time, apparently, the threat of HIV infection has not put the brakes on the sexual activity of young people, including colleges students. Approximately 70% of American high school students have engaged in sexual intercourse by the time of their graduation. An equal or greater number of college students are sexually active, many with more than one partner in any given year.

No cure exists for AIDS and none appears to be presenting itself on the immediate scientific horizon. The best protection against HIV infection for the sexually active person is the use of a condom (with a lubricant or spermicide that includes nonoxynol-9) during every act of intercourse.[7] Public education campaigns and regular news stories about AIDS have raised the

Alcohol is the number 1 drug problem in colleges.

KEY CONCEPT

THE BAD NEWS ABOUT BINGE DRINKING

The relationship of drinking alcohol to heart disease has been studied for several decades. It turns out to be a "good news-bad news" relationship. The good news is that drinking a modest amount of alcohol (defined as the equivalent amount of alcohol in two beers) on a daily basis is actually protective against heart disease. The bad news is that binge drinking, or drinking large quantities of alcohol on an irregular basis substantially increases the risk of heart disease. Unfortunately, the kind of drinking behavior most often exhibited by college students is of the binge variety and can lead to long-term negative consequences.

Responsible relationships consider the consequences of dangerous and irresponsible sexual behavior.

public awareness about the preventive value of condom usage. In spite of that increased awareness, many sexually-active college students (a substantial percentage of college students continue to abstain from becoming sexually active) never use a condom and only a small percentage use condoms every time they engage in intercourse.

HIV infection is not the only health issue associated with sexual activity. Chalmydia, herpes, gonorrhea, syphilis, are among several diseases that are a threat to a youthful, sexually-active population. The threat of unwanted pregnancy, and subsequent consideration to undergo an abortion are also issues to be weighed by the person contemplating becoming sexually active.

Environmental Health

National Health Objective: Increase protection from air pollutants so that at least 85% of people live in counties that meet EPA standards (a 71% increase).

Of all the pieces of the wellness pie, the environmental slice is the one over which people feel they have the least personal control. Although there are multiple determinants of our nutritional choices, our drinking patterns, and the frequency with which we exercise, these are all activities about which we ultimately make personal decisions.

It is hard to imagine that any single, personal act can contribute significantly to the depletion of the ozone, the contamination of a lake or river, or increasing the average temperature around the world. Were it not for the communications systems that bring us up-to-the-minute news from every part of the world, most American college students might not even know about the wreck of the Exxon Valdez that destroyed a portion of the Alaska shoreline, or the air pollution that was produced by the oil well fires set during the Gulf war.

Collectively though, our decisions make a tremendous difference, and some experts even believe the world has reached a stage in its environmental history when its literal survival is threatened.[7]

Safety

National Health Objective: Reduce unintentional injury deaths to no more than 29.3 per 100,000 population (a 15% decrease).

Safety is not often thought of as a component of wellness but accidents are a leading cause of death among young people, including college students. Some accident-risk-related behaviors are relatively easy to change, possibly because there is not as much negative reinforcement for these

You would never consider rock climbing without appropriate safety equipment. What about when you ride your bicycle?

behaviors. An example is seat belt utilization. While there is considerable social support for the risky behaviors of over eating and over drinking, there is very little encouragement for seatbelt users to increase their risks by taking off their seat belts. In fact, seat belt utilization is one of the few behaviors that can be modified merely by pointing out the risks associated with non use, without any other educational intervention.[4]

Mental/Emotional Health

National Health Objective: Reduce suicides to no more than 10.5 per 100,000 people (a 10% decrease).

Are you satisfied with yourself as a person? Are you optimistic about your future? Do you respect others while simultaneously respecting yourself? Are you able to maintain comfortable relationships with your friends and classmates? These are the kinds of questions that are asked and answered in an examination of one's mental and emotional health.

While each of the aforementioned components of wellness are important, some would argue that emotional wellbeing is the primary prerequisite to high level wellness. Feeling good about one's self provides a degree of freedom from the manipulative forces that surround us, including friends who want us to join them in high risk behaviors, or advertising messages that affirm our negative perceptions of self while simultaneously offering a "solution" to those negative perceptions.

The Wholistic Nature of Wellness

The preceding pages identify the components that are commonly thought to be a part of wellness. While each of them can be examined individually, it is important to understand that wellness is wholistic (sometimes spelled "holistic"), that the wellness concept is a concept of integration and each of the pieces of the wellness pie are related to one another. For example, it would be impossible to make a thorough examination of the topic of physical fitness without identifying the relationship of fitness to nutrition. Physical activity is also used by many as a means of resolving stress, and that reduction of stress may result in a reduced risk of becoming involved in substance abuse behaviors. In turn, students who do not drink frequently and heavily, are at lower risk for injury or death due to accidents.

As a way of demonstrating your understanding of the integrated nature of wellness, you may want to list as many different relationships between the different pieces of the wellness pie in Figure 1.3. As you continue to read the text, refer to this diagram from time to time to remind yourself of the relationships between all the pieces of wellness, and, in your pursuit of wellness, remember that wellness is dynamic. There may be days when all the elements of your life are operating at the optimum level, but that is unusual. Living a wellness lifestyle is a process, and a part of that process is aspiring to fulfill your potential.

Strategies for Changing Your Health Behavior

Your lifestyle, whether it be risky or healthy, is a collection of all your health-related behaviors. Hopefully as a result of reading this book you will want to make a fuller commitment to reducing your risks and living the healthiest life that is possible for you. Making such a commitment is a start toward achieving a healthy lifestyle, but as this chapter has revealed, a person's health behaviors are determined by a collection of personal and environmental factors. The following strategies may assist you in setting the stage for adopting a healthier lifestyle and creating the environment in which that lifestyle is possible for you.

1. Make a list of all the behaviors you think you might like to change. Possible changes may include reducing the amount of fat in your diet, increasing your use of seatbelts, stopping smoking or chewing tobacco, or never riding with an intoxicated person or driving while drunk.

2. Examine the list of behaviors you are contemplating changing. You are encouraged to select one behavior to change instead of trying to change many things simultaneously. Stopping smoking, losing weight, commencing a daily exercise program

and more effectively managing the stress in your life are all admirable goals, but trying to achieve all of them at once may make your goals seem overwhelming. Pick one change that you feel strongly about and that may seem easier than others. It will probably be easier to increase your seat belt use than to terminate a long-term smoking habit. Start with easier goals first and after you gain confidence with these changes move on to more difficult goals.

3. Set a specific target for achieving your goal. This target should allow you to determine if you have achieved your goal. For example you may set as your target "wearing seatbelts 100% of the time I am riding or driving during the month of January" or "limiting fast food meals to twice per week for the semester."

4. Analyze the personal and environmental factors related to your goal. Cultivate those factors that will help you achieve your goal and try to eliminate those factors that are barriers to your success. Figure 1.4 provides a sample analysis of personal and environmental factors related to seat belt use. Remember, the task is not to depend on will power to change your behavior. Instead, you should try to create an environment where the desired behavior actually becomes the easy choice. If you can create an environment in which all the personal and environmental factors support your desired behavior, you may discover making change is easier than you anticipated.

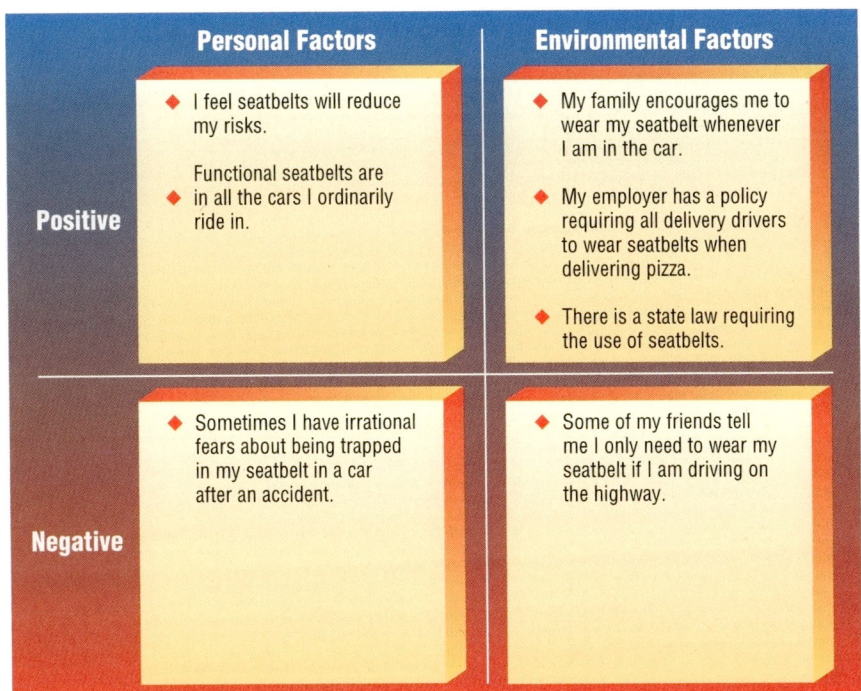

Personal Factors

Positive
- ◆ I feel seatbelts will reduce my risks.
- ◆ Functional seatbelts are in all the cars I ordinarily ride in.

Negative
- ◆ Sometimes I have irrational fears about being trapped in my seatbelt in a car after an accident.

Environmental Factors

Positive
- ◆ My family encourages me to wear my seatbelt whenever I am in the car.
- ◆ My employer has a policy requiring all delivery drivers to wear seatbelts when delivering pizza.
- ◆ There is a state law requiring the use of seatbelts.

Negative
- ◆ Some of my friends tell me I only need to wear my seatbelt if I am driving on the highway.

FIGURE 1.4

Personal and environmental factors interact on your decision-making, whether it is about wearing seatbelts or some other area that affects your health and wellness.

EXPLORING WELLNESS ON THE WEB

Many resources are available on the World Wide Web. You can reinforce, expand and enhance the information presented in this chapter by accessing the following sites.

http://www.columbia.edu/cu/healthwise/alice.html — a web site from Columbia University that answers all types of questions related to health and wellness.

http://www.wellweb.com — A highly regarded web site connecting you to other resources and addressing contemporary topics across the spectrum of health and wellness.

http://www.wellnessweb.org/teachers/ — operated by the West Virginia Department of Health and sponsored by Bell Atlantic South, this web site is for teachers of wellness in elementary schools, but provides great resources for anyone interested in wellness issues. Covers the spectrum of wellness topics.

http://www.living-well-today.com — an on-line magazine with a primary focus on achieving health while balancing family and work/school expectations.

REFERENCES

1. Amler, R. W. & Dull, H. B. (1987). *Closing the gap: The burden of unnecessary illness*. New York. Oxford University Press.

2. Ardell, D. B. (1981). *High level wellness*. New York. Bantam Books.

3. Corbin, C. B. & Lindsey, R. (1991). *Concepts of physical fitness*. Dubuque, IA. Wm. C. Brown.

4. Eberhard, J. W. (1988). Health risk appraisal programs and safety belt use. *Research notes*. Washington, D. C. U.S. Department of Transportation. Office of Driver and Pedestrian Research.

5. Green, L. W. & Kreuter, M. W. (1991). *Health promotion planning: An educational and environmental approach*. Mountain View, CA., London, Mayfield Publishing.

6. Holmes, T. H. & Rahe, R. H. (1967). The social readjustment rating scale. *Journal of Psychomatic Research*. 11, 213.

7. Insel, P. M. & Roth, W. T. (1991). *Core concepts in health*. Mountain View, Ca., London, Mayfield Publishing.

8. Miller, D. K. & Allen, T. E. (1990). *Fitness: A Lifetime commitment*. New York. Macmillian Publishing.

9. National Center for Health Statistics. (1992, September 30). *Monthly vital statistics report. 40, 13*

10. Novello, A.C. (1993, June 30). Beer: Teens drug of choice. *U.S.A. Today*. pp 11A.

11. U. S. Department of Health and Human Services. (1990). Healthy people 2000: National health promotion and disease prevention objectives. (DHHS Publication No. [PHS] 91-50213). Washington, D. C: U.S. Government Printing Office.

12. U. S. Department of Health and Human Services. (1996). Physical activity and health: A report of the surgeon general. (DHHS Publication No. S/N 017-023-00196-5). Washington, D. C: U.S. Government Printing Office.

DEFINITIONS OF KEY TERMS

asymptomatic — the absence of indicators that suggest the individual may need to seek medical care.

enabling factors — skills, resources, or access to resources that make it possible for a person to act out health related behaviors

extrinsic decisions — decisions motivated primarily by forces outside of one's self. Advertising or the persuasiveness of others are examples.

high level wellness — an optimal level of health; a dynamic, not static state.

intrinsic decisions — decisions made to meet one's personal needs and provide personal satisfaction

positive self-concept — a positive view of self

premature death — death that occurs before the average age of death, roughly 75 years of age for American men and 80 years of age for American women.

predisposing factors — knowledge, attitudes, beliefs, values, perceptions that underpin behavioral desires

reinforcing factors — support (organizational, cultural, social) to adopt or continue certain behaviors

wellness — a standard of health based on the interaction of physical fitness, nutrition, stress management, sexual decision making substance use patterns, emotional health, safety, environmental considerations, and other factors.

wellness continuum — a scale for assessing fulfillment of one's wellness potential.

wholistic — (also spelled "holistic") identifies the potential influence on health of integrating the multiple dimensions of physical fitness, nutrition, stress management, sexual decision making, substance abuse patterns, emotional health, safety, environmental considerations, and other factors.

LAB 1.1

BEHAVIOR CHANGE PLAN

Name _____ ID _____ Sect _____ Time _____ Date _____

Purposes

1. To identify the negative health behaviors that can increase your risk of disease.

2. To prioritize the health behaviors you wish to change.

3. To develop a strategy for making the changes that will be beneficial to your health.

Directions

1. In the chart below, list three health behaviors or characteristics that you want to change.

2. In the **Priority** column, list your priority for changing the behaviors. Place a 1 in the space next to the behavior/characteristic you want to change most, 2 for the second priority behavior, and 3 for the third priority.

3. In the **Ease** column, place a 1 next to the behavior you feel is the <u>easiest</u> to change, place a 2 next to the behavior you feel is next easiest, and 3 next to the behavior least easy to change.

4. In the **Support** column, place a 1 next to the behavior you feel you have the most support for changing, a 2 for the behavior with the next most support, and 3 next to the least supported behavior.

Behavior or Characteristic	Priority	Ease	Support
_____	_____	_____	_____
_____			
_____			
_____	_____	_____	_____
_____			
_____			
_____	_____	_____	_____
_____			
_____			

(Continued)

5. For the behavior or characteristic that you indicated as your highest priority, write a specific goal statement which describes the behavior/characteristics/habit as you wish it to be. For example, if you want to loose, weight, identify how much you want to loose and how long you want to take. Under the goal, list 2 factors which could help you (positive) to reach your goal and 2 factors which may prevent you (negative) from reaching your goal.

Goal: _____

_____

_____

_____

Positive Factors: _____

_____

_____

_____

_____

Negative Factors: _____

_____

_____

_____

_____

NOTES

Cardiorespiratory Endurance

FORREST DOLGENER

CHAPTER OBJECTIVES

◆ Understand the basic concept of aerobic and anaerobic energy systems.

◆ Understand how the cardiorespiratory system functions to deliver oxygen to exercising muscles.

◆ Understand how cardiorespiratory endurance is developed.

◆ Be able to determine target heart rates using two methods.

◆ Understand the benefits of cardiorespiratory exercise.

◆ Be able to select appropriate exercise that will improve cardiorespiratory endurance.

◆ Understand how the environment affects exercise capacity.

◆ Be able to measure and evaluate cardiorespiratory endurance.

◆ Be able to plan and implement an exercise program that will improve cardiorespiratory endurance.

KEY TERMS

adenosine triphosphate (ATP)

aerobic

anaerobic

atria

cardiac output

cardiorespiratory endurance

duration

energy systems

exercise prescription

frequency

hemoglobin

intensity

latic acid

overload principle

maximal oxygen uptake (VO_2max)

mode

overuse injuries

physical fitness

rating of perceived exertion (RPE)

specificity principle

standard error of estimate (SEE)

stroke volume

ventricles

INTRODUCTION

Prior to 1900, the major causes of death in this country were infectious diseases such as pneumonia, influenza, and tuberculosis. Diseases of the heart, cancer, and stroke accounted for less than 22 percent of all deaths.[11] Today, lifestyle diseases such as heart disease, cancer, stroke, and HIV account for about 64 percent of all deaths (Figure 2.1). Why has there been such a change? One reason is that most of the infectious diseases have been controlled by antibiotics and other medications. A second reason is that as America became more technologically advanced and more affluent, Americans ate more of the wrong kinds of food and exercised less. This led to sedentary lifestyles, obesity, and the beginnings of the chronic disease epidemic that has plagued this country for decades.

A recent report from the Office of the Surgeon General[6] emphasizes the importance of regular exercise. Among the major findings of the report were the following:

1. People who are usually inactive can improve their health and well-being by becoming even moderately active on a regular basis.

FIGURE 2.1A

Major Causes of Death in the U.S. in 1900. Infectious diseases accounted for a high percentage of deaths in the U.S. in 1900.

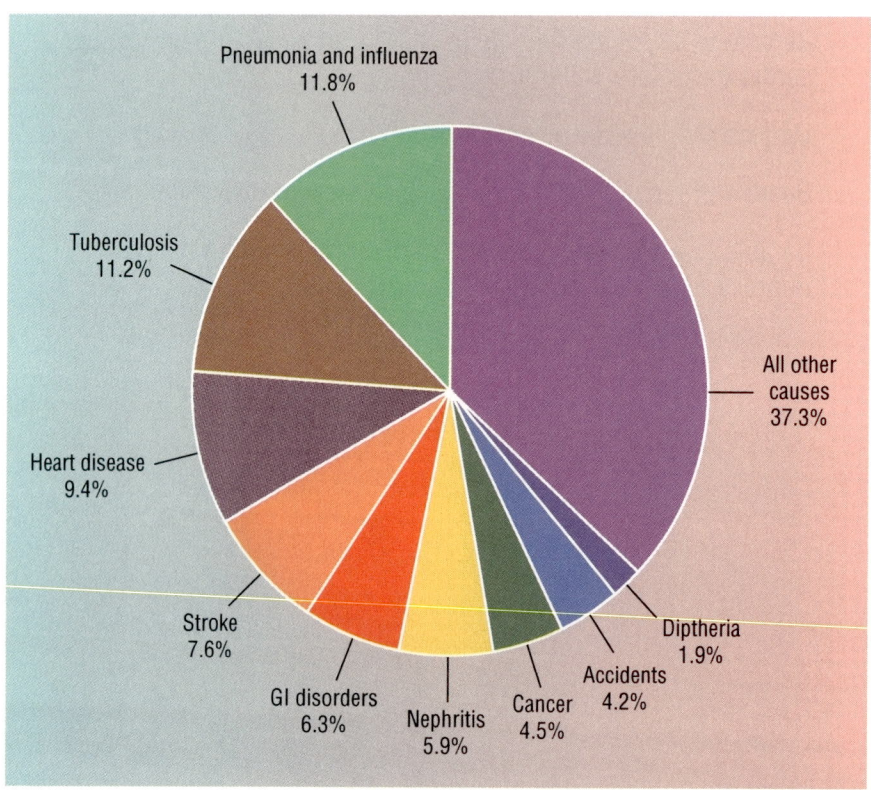

2. Physical activity need not be strenuous to achieve health benefits.

3. Greater health benefits can be achieved by increasing the amount of physical activity.

Public awareness campaigns have been launched in hopes of making the majority of Americans aware of the importance of a healthy lifestyle which should include regular exercise to maintain a healthy level of cardiorespiratory endurance. A lifestyle of inactivity leads to low cardiorespiratory endurance. One recent important study identified low cardiorespiratory endurance resulting from inactivity as being more important in the prevention of heart disease than the traditional three major risk factors of smoking, high blood pressure, and high cholesterol.[3] This study, conducted at the Aerobics Institute in Dallas, concluded that regular exercise was every bit as important in preventing heart disease as the other major risk factors.

You will have many choices to make as you go through life. Some of the choices will directly affect your health and well-being. Making appropriate choices will allow you to have a longer, more enjoyable and more fulfilling life. Choosing to be a regular exerciser will be beneficial and rewarding and will enable you to fulfill the potential you have. In the remainder of this chapter the concept of cardiorespiratory endurance will be discussed. Why

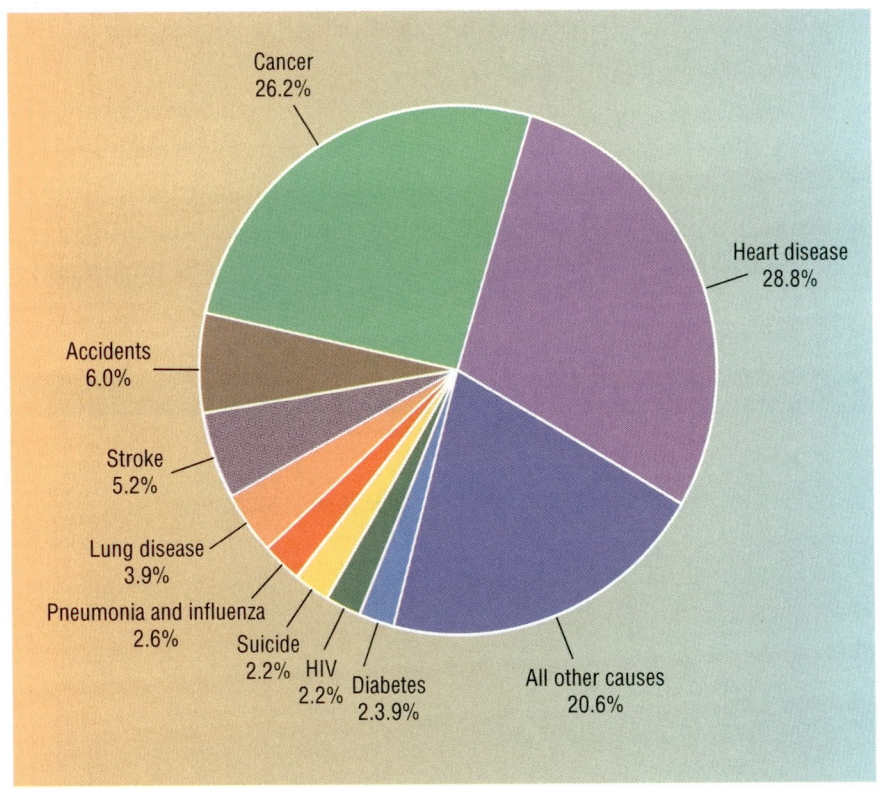

Cancer
26.2%

Heart disease
28.8%

Accidents
6.0%

Stroke
5.2%

Lung disease
3.9%

Pneumonia and influenza
2.6%

Suicide
2.2%

HIV
2.2%

Diabetes
2.3.9%

All other causes
20.6%

FIGURE 2.1B

Major Causes of Death in the U.S. in 1991. Today, lifestyle diseases account for the majority of deaths in this country.

may it be the most important risk factor for heart disease? What are the benefits of regular cardiorespiratory exercise? What is the best type of cardiorespiratory exercise? It is hoped that this information will enable you to develop and implement a personal exercise program that will lead to a lifetime of physical activity and good health.

PHYSICAL FITNESS: FOR WHAT PURPOSE?

Before we begin to specifically discuss cardiorespiratory endurance, it is useful to consider briefly the general concept of **physical fitness**. Physical fitness is the ability to perform one's daily task without becoming fatigued while having enough energy in reserve for situations requiring higher levels of energy, such as for exercise or emergencies. There are two major "types" of physical fitness: **performance-** or **skill-related fitness** and **health-related fitness**. Each type of physical fitness has several key components which are illustrated in Table 2.1.

The specific components of performance- or skill-related fitness include agility, balance, coordination, speed, power and reaction time. All of these components contribute to one's ability to perform at high levels or in competitive situations. It would be highly desirable for competitive athletes to develop all of these components because they would help the athlete perform at higher levels. However, these components of performance-related fitness have very little impact on one's health. They are not detrimental, they just don't improve health.

The older you get, the less you will probably be concerned about performance fitness and the more you should be concerned with health-related fitness. The components of health-related fitness are **cardiorespiratory endurance, muscular strength, muscular endurance, flexibility, and body composition**. Although these components can also be important for

TABLE 2.1	
The Components of Physical Fitness	
Skill-Related Fitness	**Health-Related Fitness**
1. Agility	1. Cardiorespiratory Endurance
2. Balance	2. Body Composition
3. Coordination	3. Musculoskeletal
4. Speed	a. Flexibility
5. Power	b. Muscular Strength
6. Reaction Time	c. Muscular Endurance

performance fitness, we are primarily interested in them because they contribute to one's health. Each will be discussed in detail in this text, but each will be discussed relative to their health impact, not their impact on performance. As each component is discussed, the discussion will focus on how you can best develop the component to positively affect your health. For example, a training program that develops cardiorespiratory endurance optimally for performance is different from a training program that develops cardiorespiratory endurance optimally for health. The same is true of muscular strength, muscular endurance, and flexibility.

The components of performance-related fitness are important to the competitive athlete but not to the average adult.

CARDIORESPIRATORY ENDURANCE

Let's start by clarifying a few terms which you hear about and read about all the time— **cardiorespiratory endurance**, **cardiovascular endurance**, and **aerobic endurance**. Although these three terms are technically a little different, they are used interchangeably by most authors. All three terms are referring to the ability of the heart and lungs to supply oxygen to skeletal muscle and other tissues of the body. If our heart and lungs can continually supply an adequate amount of oxygen to skeletal muscle, the muscles can continue to contract. Therefore, the fundamental essence of cardiorespiratory endurance is the ability of the heart to supply large amounts of oxygen to the skeletal muscles. In order for the heart and lungs to be able to meet the potential demand of the skeletal muscles for oxygen, the heart and lungs have to be trained, just like the skeletal muscles have to be trained. But let's not get too far ahead without looking a little more specifically at why it is necessary to supply oxygen to skeletal muscle.

Developing the components of health-related fitness, such as cardiorespiratory endurance, will add quantity and quality to your life.

Energy Systems

In order for muscles to contract, chemical fuel for the contraction process must be supplied to the muscles. This fuel, or energy, is called **Adenosine Triphosphate (ATP)** and is produced inside the muscle cell by different biochemical processes referred to as **energy systems**. The ability of muscle to develop tension, both in quantity and duration, is directly proportional to the ability to manufacture adequate amounts of ATP.

There are two major energy systems in muscle cells, the **anaerobic** and **aerobic energy systems**. Anaerobic means "without oxygen" and aerobic means "with oxygen." Simply put, the anaerobic system is a series of chemical reactions taking place in the cells that has the capacity to produce ATP without using oxygen. On the other hand, the aerobic system must use oxygen when making ATP and inadequate supplies of oxygen means inadequate production of ATP.

Anaerobic Energy System

On the surface it may seem desirable to be able to produce ATP without using oxygen and, indeed, this is an important energy producing process for many types of activities. The anaerobic energy system is the primary system used whenever we do activities or exercise that require heavy muscular contractions, such as weight lifting, sprinting, or high jumping. On the negative side, as a result of making a lot of ATP anaerobically, a by-product of this biochemical process is formed which is detrimental to the muscle. This by-product is **lactic acid**.

Lactic acid, if produced in great enough quantity, inhibits the muscle cell from making and using ATP. For example, if you start sprinting as fast as you can, you will soon reach a point where you begin to fatigue very rapidly and you will have to slow down or stop. If you are truly sprinting as fast as you can, you will probably only be able to continue for 45—60 seconds before you have to abruptly slow down. One thing that makes you fatigue and slow down is the inability to continue to make and use ATP due to the production and accumulation of lactic acid.

Aerobic Energy System

In contrast to the anaerobic energy system, the aerobic energy system makes ATP for activities that require low to medium muscular contractions for periods of time exceeding several minutes, such as when you are resting or even jogging easily. The aerobic energy pathways producing the energy can only function when there is oxygen present in the muscle cells. Where does this oxygen come from? It originally comes from the air you breathe and it gets to the muscle as a result of the activity of the lungs and heart.

Cardiorespiratory System

The heart and lungs are referred to as the **cardiorespiratory system**. Their ability to deliver oxygen to the muscles is critical to the ability to continue muscular effort that lasts longer than about 2 minutes. The lungs function to bring air from the atmosphere into the body and eventually to get oxygen into the blood. Once oxygen gets into the blood it combines with hemoglobin, and is pumped around the circulatory system by the heart.

The primary factor that characterizes individuals at different levels of cardiorespiratory endurance is how much blood their heart can pump. Let's look more closely at the function of the heart and lungs.

SYNERGY OF THE HEART AND LUNGS

The heart and lungs function as a team. One is not much good without the other. If the lungs did not get oxygen into the blood, it would not do any good for the heart to pump the blood. Likewise, if the oxygen got into the blood but the heart did not circulate it, it would do no good. Various diseases can specifically affect the lungs or the heart, but the end consequence is the same. For example, chronic obstructive lung disease (COPD) prevents oxygen from reaching the blood in adequate quantity and the end result is constant fatigue and poor exercise capacity. Likewise, ischemic heart disease decreases the ability of the heart to pump blood to the muscles and the end result is constant fatigue and poor exercise capacity.

Function of the Heart and Lungs

The heart, illustrated in Figure 2.2, is a hollow, four-chambered muscle about the size of your fist and located in the center of the chest just under the sternum or breastbone. The upper two chambers are called **atria** and the bottom two chambers are called **ventricles**. The primary function of the heart is to pump the blood around the circulatory system. The pumping of blood is a never-ending task. Even at rest, each time the heart beats about 70 milliliters (about 1/3 cup) of blood is pumped into the circulation. The volume of blood ejected from the heart each beat is called the **stroke volume**. The total volume of blood pumped by the heart in one minute is the

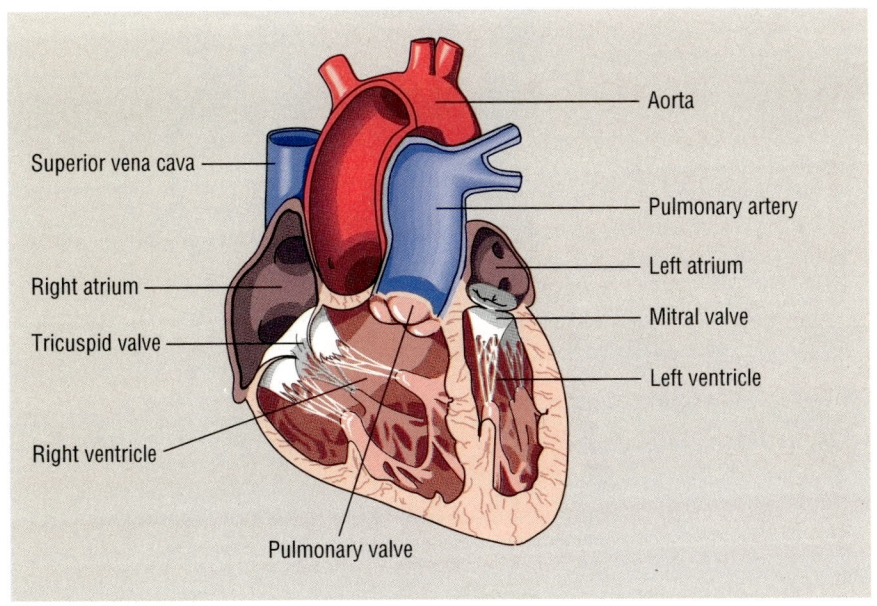

Superior vena cava

Right atrium

Tricuspid valve

Right ventricle

Pulmonary valve

Aorta

Pulmonary artery

Left atrium

Mitral valve

Left ventricle

FIGURE 2.2

The heart is a four-chamber pump that can pump as much as 3–4 gallons of blood per minute.

cardiac output. The relationship between the heart rate, the stroke volume, and the cardiac output can be expressed mathematically as

Cardiac Output = Heart Rate x Stroke Volume

From this relationship, it is obvious that the cardiac output can be increased by either increasing the heart rate, increasing the stroke volume, or a combination of both. When the exercise effort is low to moderate, the heart increases the cardiac output by increasing both the heart rate and stroke volume. However, when the workload becomes greater than about 50% of an individual's capacity, the cardiac output increases only by increasing the heart rate.

The lungs are the other half of the cardiorespiratory system (Figure 2.3). The function of the lungs is to exchange oxygen and carbon dioxide with the blood. The air we breathe contains about 21% oxygen with the remainder being primarily nitrogen. When we take in a breath, air containing oxygen is drawn down into tiny air sacks called **alveoli**, located deep within the lungs. In the alveoli, the oxygen in the air is transferred into the blood and carbon dioxide in the blood is transferred into the alveoli, to be breathed out with the next expiration. The oxygen that is transferred from the alveoli into the blood attaches to a special protein compound in the blood called

FIGURE 2.3

The lungs oxygenate the blood in order that oxygen can be pumped throughout the body.

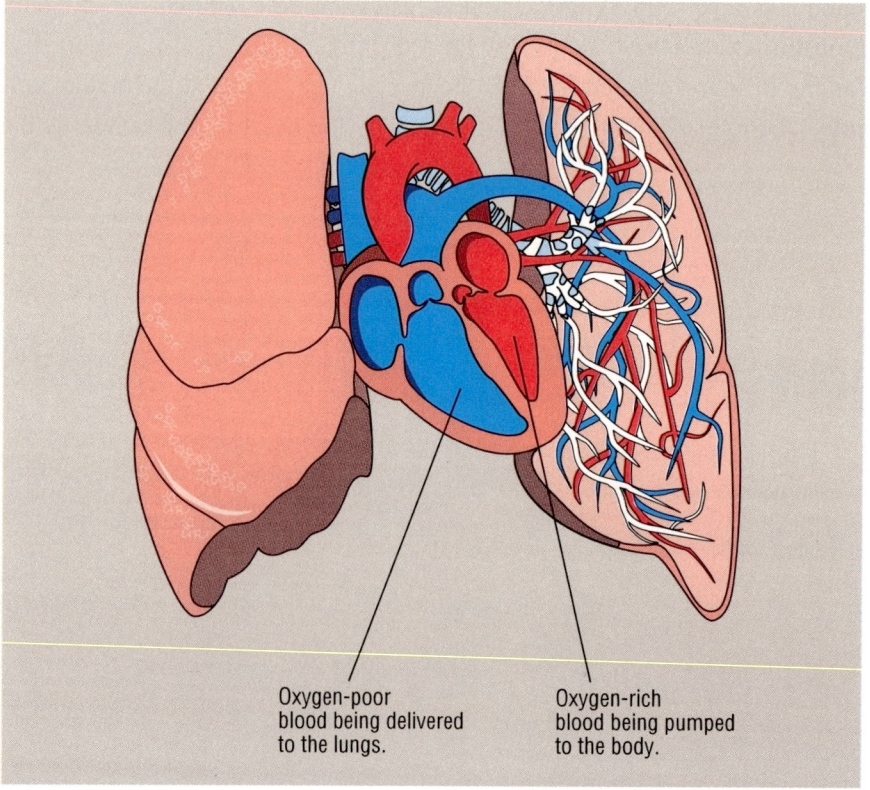

Oxygen-poor blood being delivered to the lungs.

Oxygen-rich blood being pumped to the body.

hemoglobin. The vast majority of oxygen is transported in the blood by joining with hemoglobin and is pumped through the blood vessels to the muscles and other tissues.

The Effects of Training The Heart

Because cardiac output is determined by the stroke volume and heart rate, if cardiac output improves with training, either the stroke volume, or the heart rate, or both must change. What actually happens is that the stroke volume increases and the heart rate decreases at any level of effort below maximal effort. At maximal effort, the maximal heart rate does not change but because the maximal stroke volume is greater, the maximal cardiac output is greater. So, a sign of a conditioned heart is one with a large stroke volume which, in turns, produces a large cardiac output.

Table 2.2 illustrates this relationship by showing typical values for cardiac output, stroke volume, and heart rate for an untrained college-aged male and female, the same individuals after participating in an aerobic training program, and, finally, an elite level athlete. Note that if the heart rate goes down as the level of fitness goes up, the stroke volume must go up in order for the cardiac output to stay constant or increase. One of the most consistent changes as you become more aerobically fit is that your resting heart rate and the heart rate at any submaximal effort declines as a result of the stroke volume increasing. Also notice that the maximal cardiac output and stroke volume of the female is less than the male, which explains why females, on the average, have lower aerobic capacities than males.

TABLE 2.2				
Effects of Gender, Tranining, and Genetics on Cardiorespirtory Variables				
Variable	**Gender**	**Untrained**	**Trained**	**Elite Athlete**
Maximal Heart Rate	Male	190	190	190
(beats per minute)	Female	190	190	190
Maximal Stroke Volume	Male	79	105	184
(milliliters)	Female	60	75	150
Maximal Cardiac Output	Male	15	20	35
(liters)	Female	11.4	14.2	28.5
VO_2max	Male	35	43	75
(ml/kg/min)	Female	30	38	68

Note: 1 liter =1.057 quarts; 100 milliliters = 3.3 fluid ounces or about 1/2 cup

Maximal Oxygen Uptake

Another variable that is highly related to cardiorespiratory endurance is **maximal oxygen uptake (VO_2max)**. VO_2max, defined as the greatest amount of oxygen a person can consume while performing exhaustive aerobic exercise, is the single best indicator of aerobic capacity and the one most often measured in the exercise laboratory.

Maximal cardiac output and VO_2max are directly related and are measures of the same functional capacity of the cardiorespiratory system. The reason is that if the heart can supply more oxygen to the muscles, the muscles usually have the capacity to use the oxygen to make ATP. What limits the capacity of the muscles to make ATP is the ability of the heart to supply oxygen to the muscles, not the ability of the muscle to use oxygen to make ATP. Remember, the reason the muscle is consuming the oxygen is to make ATP. The higher the cardiac output, the more oxygen is delivered to the muscles, and the more ATP the muscles can make. The result is that you have a higher capacity for aerobic exercise.

The units for VO_2max values are ml/kg/min (read mililiters per kilogram per minute). The units express the amount of oxygen being used (to make ATP) for every kilogram of body weight for one minute. Because the units are expressed per kilogram of body weight, VO_2max values are comparable across individuals. The higher the value the better because it indicates more oxygen can be used to make ATP. VO_2max values range from 30 ml/kg/min for sedentary young adults to 85 ml/kg/min for elite endurance athletes.

VO_2max is routinely measured in the exercise laboratory but it requires expensive equipment and a maximal effort from the individual being measured. The reason VO_2max is measured instead of cardiac output is because VO_2max is technically much easier to measure. Knowledge of either would provide the same type of information regarding cardiorespiratory fitness but cardiac output is extremely difficult to measure. In a later section in this chapter, methods of estimating VO_2max will be discussed.

BENEFITS OF CARDIORESPIRATORY EXERCISE

If the primary factor that characterizes a person with high cardiorespiratory endurance is the ability of the heart to pump blood, then the heart's pumping ability must improve in response to training. Table 2.2 illustrates the type of change in the heart's pumping ability in response to training. On the average, the heart will improve it's capacity to pump blood by about 25% when optimally trained.[2, 10] Also, as was indicated earlier, most of this increase is due an increase in stroke volume. This improved ability to pump blood translates into a greater exercise capacity for performing exercise lasting longer than several minutes, such as in jogging two or three miles.

KEY CONCEPT

GENETICS AND CARDIORESPIRATORY ENDURANCE

There is a limitation on how much the pumping capacity of the heart can improve. For example, the hearts of high level endurance athletes, such as marathoners, can pump as much as 40 quarts of blood per minute during maximal exercise.[10] The heart of the average college male can maximally pump about 20 quarts of blood per minute and the average college female can pump about 17 quarts or 15 percent less than the average male. The difference in the heart's pumping ability between the elite athlete and the average individual is primarily explained by genetics, not by training. Most of us could never train long and hard enough to become elite endurance athletes. We have to have the right parents.

Not only does cardiorespiratory exercise increase your capacity to exercise but, more importantly, it improves your health. Table 2.3 lists the major benefits of cardiorespiratory exercise as outlined by the recent report from the Surgeon General of the United States. The incidence of these lifestyle diseases can be substantially decreased by engaging in an aerobic exercise program on a regular basis.

The physiologic and health benefits listed in Table 2.3 are likely to result in two additional benefits that can be broadly classified as personal benefits and industrial or economic benefits. The personal benefits are a longer life

TABLE 2.3

Benefits of Cardiorespiratory Exercise

Regular cardiorespiratory activity that is performed on most days of the week reduces the risk of developing or dying from some of the leading causes of illness and death in the United States. Regular physical activity improves health in the following ways:

- Reduces the risk of dying prematurely
- Reduces the risk of dying from heart disease
- Reduces the risk of developing diabetes
- Reduces the risks of developing high blood pressure
- Helps reduce blood pressure in people who already have high blood pressure
- Reduces feelings of depression and anxiety
- Helps control weight
- Helps build and maintain healthy bones, muscles, and joints
- Helps older adults become stronger and better able to move about without falling
- Promotes psychological well-being

Source: Centers for Disease Control (1996). A Report of the Surgeon General: Physical Activity and Health. U.S. Department of Health and Human Services.

and a more enjoyable life. Projections have been made that a person who maintains regular exercise throughout the life-span can add 2-3 years to their life.[14] Also, perhaps more importantly, the quality of life can be significantly enhanced. Being able to do the types of things one enjoys and not being limited by poor health or poor fitness, will enable one to enjoy life to the fullest.

The industrial or economic benefits will result from lower health care costs and greater worker productivity. As noted above, cardiorespiratory exercise can reduce the incidence of many chronic diseases. This, in turn, will reduce the need for expensive health care. A more healthy and physically fit employee will be a more productive employee. Studies[14] have shown that lower absenteeism, employee turnover, and industrial injury rate can result from greater fitness. As health care costs are lowered, business and industry will have greater profits and employees will reap the economic benefits.

GETTING READY TO EXERCISE

Prior to engaging in exercise that stresses the cardiorespiratory system, you should determine your readiness for such exercise. In most cases, especially with young adults, all that is required is answering a few questions assessing risk. In other cases it may require a complete physical examination and maximal exercise test under the supervision of a physician. All individuals who have not recently been active should use some type of assessment to determine their readiness to exercise.

The simplest assessment of readiness is a short questionnaire such as the **Physical Activity Readiness Questionnaire (PAR-Q).** This questionnaire (Table 2.4) assesses general risk for starting an exercise program. For young adults who are apparently healthy, this is all that is necessary. For older adults and those who have various risk factors, the American College of Sports Medicine (ACSM)[1] has published guidelines concerning the need for pre-evaluation before participating in exercise. The need for a pre-evaluation is determined by categorizing your risk level into one of three risk categories identified by the ACSM (Table 2.5).

The first category, **Apparently Healthy,** is defined as having no symptoms of disease and having no more than one major risk factor for coronary artery disease. The second category, **Higher Risk**, is defined as having symptoms suggesting possible cardiorespiratory or metabolic disease and having two or more major risk factors for coronary artery disease. The third category, **Diseased,** is defined as having known heart, lung or metabolic disease. Table 2.5 contains the ACSM categories and criteria and a list of the major coronary risk factors are in Table 2.6.

TABLE 2.4

Physical Activity Readiness Questionnaire (PAR-Q)

PAR-Q is designed to help you help yourself. Many health benefits are associated with regular exercise, and the completion of PAR-Q is a sensible first step to take if you are planning to increase the amount of physical activity in your life.

For most people physical activity should not pose any problem or hazard. PAR-Q has been designed to identify the small number of adults for whom physical activity might be inappropriate or those who should have medical advice concerning the type of activity most suitable for them.

Common sense is your best guide in answering these few questions. Please read them carefully and check YES or NO opposite the question.

Question	Yes	No
1. Has your doctor ever said you have heart trouble?	_____	_____
2. Do you frequently have pains in your heart and chest?	_____	_____
3. Do you often feel faint or have spells of severe dizziness?	_____	_____
4. Has a doctor ever said your blood pressure was too high?	_____	_____
5. Has your doctor ever told you that you have a bone or joint problem such as arthritis that has been aggravated by exercise, or might be made worse with exercise?	_____	_____
6. Is there a good physical reason not mentioned here why you should not follow an activity program even if you wanted to?	_____	_____
7. Are you over age 65 and not accustomed to vigorous exercise?	_____	_____

If you answered **YES** to one or more questions, then

If you have not recently done so, consult with your personal physician by telephone or in person BEFORE increasing your physical activity and/or taking a fitness evaluation. Tell your physician what questions you answered YES to on PAR-Q or present your PAR-Q copy.

After medical evaluation, seek advice from your physician as to your suitability for:

- unrestricted physical activity starting off easily and progressing gradually

- restricted or supervised activity to meet your specific needs, as least on an initial basis. Check in your community for special programs or services.

If you answered **NO** to all questions, then If you answered PAR-Q accurately, you have reasonable assurance of your present suitability for:

- a GRADUATED EXERCISE PROGRAM—a gradual increase in proper exercise promotes good fitness development while minimizing or eliminating discomfort;

- A FITNESS APPRAISAL such as the Rockport Walking Test, the 1-Mile Jog Test, or the Bench Stepping Test.

Source: Government of Canada, Fitness and Amateur Sport. *Canadian Standardized Test of Fitness*, Operations Manual, 1886.

TABLE 2.5

ACSM Risk Categories and Criteria for Medical Exam Before Starting Exercise

Risk Category	Criteria	Is a Medical Exam Before Exercise Necessary?
Apparently Healthy	No symptoms and no more than 1 major risk factor.	For moderate* exercise, then NO. For vigorous exercise**: If male and >41 or female >51, then YES
Higher Risk	Two or more major risk factors without symptoms. Two or more major risk factors with symptoms.	If moderate exercise, then NO. If moderate or vigorous exercise, then YES
Diseased	Diagnosed cardiovascular or metabolic disease.	For any level of exercise, YES

*Moderate exercise (exercise intensity 40% to 60% of VO_2 max) is exercise well within the individual's current capacity and can be comfortably sustained for a prolonged period of time.

**Vigorous exercise (exercise > 60% of VO_2 max) is exercise intense enough to be a substantial challenge and resulting in fatigue in 20 minutes or less.

TABLE 2.6

Major Coronary Risk Factors

1. High blood pressure of >159 mmHg systolic and/or >89 mmHg diastolic.
2. High blood cholesterol of >239 mg/dl.
3. Tobacco smoking
4. Diabetes Mellitus
5. History of heart disease in parents or siblings prior to age 55.
6. Lack of exercise

The vast majority of college students fall into the "Apparently Healthy" category and a medical exam is not necessary. However, if you are in a risk category in which a medical exam is recommended, it is important to get your physician's approval prior to starting an exercise program. In some cases, a comprehensive medical exam may be warranted including a graded exercise test to determine how your heart functions during exercise. Only your physician can determine this.

Although following these guidelines does not guarantee that you will not have some sort of medical problem while exercising, it does substantially reduce the risk of something significant occurring. In all cases, the simple rule of "start low and progress slowly," which is explained in more detail in a later section of this chapter, is the best policy to follow. When in doubt, always consult your physician.

MEASURING CARDIORESPIRATORY ENDURANCE

Once you have determined to start a cardiorespiratory exercise program, determining your starting level of fitness can be quite helpful. By knowing your current level of cardiorespiratory endurance, an accurate determination of how much exercise and how hard it should be can be made. This is important because too little or too much exercise can be, at best, useless and, at worst, detrimental and actually cause problems. Periodically measuring cardiorespiratory endurance allows you to determine the effectiveness of an exercise program and it can be a motivational tool. You can actually see the amount of improvement. This enables adjustments in the program to be made when necessary in order to maintain the effectiveness of the program.

There are several ways to measure cardiorespiratory endurance. These methods range all the way from a simple walking test to sophisticated laboratory procedures using equipment costing thousands of dollars. As previously mentioned, the best method of measuring cardiorespiratory endurance, is to measure **maximal oxygen uptake** or **VO$_2$max**. Although other factors contribute to cardiorespiratory endurance, VO$_2$max gives you the most information. Remember that VO$_2$max is primarily determined by how much blood the heart can pump over time (i.e. the cardiac output). The greater the heart's ability to pump blood, the higher the VO$_2$max. Regular aerobic exercise increases the hearts ability to pump blood and thereby increases VO$_2$max.

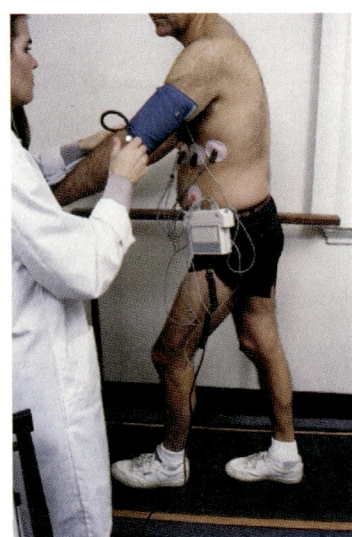

Individuals at risk for heart disease may require a graded exercise test to determine the condition of their heart before starting an exercise program.

Measuring VO$_2$max in the Lab

In the exercise laboratory, cardiorespiratory endurance is determined by directly measuring how much oxygen a person uses (oxygen uptake or VO$_2$) while performing some type of aerobic exercise, like running or riding a bicycle. While riding or running, the subject breathes into a special apparatus that allows all their expired air to be collected in instruments that actually measure how much oxygen is being used. When the subject is not working maximally, the amount of oxygen being used is termed **oxygen uptake or VO$_2$**. If the amount of work the subject is doing is gradually increased until the subject is exhausted, the greatest amount of oxygen consumed at or near the point of exhaustion is called the **maximal oxygen uptake or VO$_2$max** . Although this method is very accurate, it is also time consuming and expensive and usually only available at universities and medical facilities.

Estimating VO$_2$max

Due to the cost and inaccessibility of the laboratory method, several methods of estimating cardiorespiratory endurance have been developed. These methods use some type of easy-to-administer test such as a walk test, a run test, a step test or a stationary bicycle test and VO$_2$max is estimated based on how you performed on the test. The test can either be a maximal test, requiring a maximal effort, or it can be a submaximal test, requiring only a moderate effort.

The maximal exertion tests are generally more accurate, but are not as safe to administer to the general population because maximal exercise would be contraindicated in individuals with various diseases or at risk for diseases, especially heart disease. Submaximal tests are more useful for screening large populations and cause little safety risk for participants.

Submaximal tests assess an individual's heart rate response to a known amount of work. The individual works at approximately 50-75% of their maximal capacity for several minutes and their heart rate is determined. Because the normal relationship between the heart rate and oxygen uptake is known, the maximal oxygen consumption can be estimated based on the submaximal heart rate response to the workload. Three popular submaximal tests used to estimate VO$_2$max are the Rockport Walking Test,[9] a 1-mile jog test,[8] and a bench-step test.[10]

Rockport Walking Test

In performing the Rockport Walking Test, an individual walks a mile as fast as they can. The time it takes them to walk the mile, their heart rate at the end of the walk, their age and gender are put into a formula and the VO$_2$max is computed. This test is simple to administer to large groups and provides a reasonably accurate estimation of VO$_2$max . A complete description of the test can be found in the **Lab 2.12** at the end of this chapter.

One-Mile Jog Test

The submaximal 1-mile jog test is similar in may ways to the Rockport Walking Test except, instead of walking, you jog at a comfortable pace. Gender, body weight, jog time, and heart rate at the end of the jog are put into a formula and the VO$_2$max is computed. Like the Rockport Walking Test, this test is simple to administer but it does require a higher level of effort. Normal college-aged individuals usually have no difficulty in performing the test. A complete description of the test can be found in **Lab 2.13** at the end of this chapter.

Bench-Step Test

The third type of submaximal test is a bench-step test. In this type of test, an individual steps up and down on a bench to a rhythmical beat at a pre-determined stepping rate. At the end of the stepping period a heart rate is taken and VO_2max is computed from a formula or taken from a chart. This type of assessment is a little more difficult to administer because it requires individuals to step at a constant stepping rate. This requires that some type of timing device, like a metronome or prerecorded audio tape, be used to maintain the appropriate stepping rate. A complete description of the test can be found in **Lab 2.11** at the end of this chapter.

All three of the submaximal test mentioned above have about the same accuracy so the determination of which test to use is just personal preference and ease of administration. None of the tests require any special equipment, except a 16" step for the bench-step test. You can even perform more than one test and compare the results. The results will probably not be identical but should be in the same ballpark. If there is more than a 15-20% difference in the results, do the third test and then average the results of all the test.

Interpreting Estimations of VO_2max

Recognizing that these estimation tests have a certain amount of error is important to making a valid interpretation of the results. Two values from these test are important: the estimated VO_2max value and the standard error of the estimate (SEE). All estimation tests will have an associated SEE value for that test. The SEE is a measure of how close the estimated VO_2max value is to the true VO_2max value. An example of how the SEE is interpreted is shown in Table 2.7.

TABLE 2.7
Interpreting the Standard Error of Estimate (SEE)

Assume a 1-mile jog test was performed and the estimated VO_2 max is 40 ml/kg/min and the SEE for the test is 3.0 ml/kg/min. The correct interpretation of the test result would be as follows.

- There is a 68% probability (68 chances out of 100) that the true VO_2max is between 37-43 ml/kg/min, or the estimated VO_2max ± 1 SEE, (40 ± 3).

- There is a 95% probability (95 chances out of 100) that the true VO_2max is between 34-46 ml/kg/min, or the estimated VO_2max ± 2 SEE (The 95% probability level is known as the 95% Confidence Interval, i.e. you are 95% confident that the true VO_2max is within the range of 34-46.

- There is a 99.5% probability (99.5 chances out of 100) that the true VO_2max is between 31-49 ml/kg/min, or the estimated VO_2max ± 3 SEE.

- The probability levels used (68%, 95%, 99.5%) are always the same. The value for the SEE will vary in different tests. All estimation tests will have an associated SEE value.

The amount of error in estimating VO_2max can be as low as 10% or as high as 25%. Unfortunately, you cannot predict the error for any specific individual so you are forced to make interpretations based on probability. However, these tests are useful for screening purposes and for tracking changes in fitness over time.

Fitness classification tables have been developed that allow you to compare your level of cardiorespiratory fitness to that of others your age and gender (Table 2.8). After you perform any of the assessment tests in this chapter, compare your level of cardiorespiratory fitness to the classifications in Table 2.8. It is desirable to be at least at the moderate level but, in general, higher is better.

One cautionary note is necessary. Most research available on the subject suggests that the absolute value for VO_2max may not be as important as the exercise program that you are participating in. The bottom line is this- **the important thing is to be a regular exerciser**. As mentioned previously, the prediction of VO_2max is not always as accurate as we would like it to be. Therefore, regardless of your value for VO_2max, if you are exercising in an appropriate way on a regular basis, the health benefits will result. Don't worry too much about the value for your VO_2max as long as you are engaging in regular aerobic exercise.

TABLE 2.8

Fitness and Risk Classification for Cardiorespiratory Endurance as Measured by VO₂max (ml/kg/min)

		Fitness Classification				
		Very Low	Low	Moderate	High	Very High
		Risk Classification				
Gender	Age	High	Average	Low	Very Low	Very Low
Males	<29	<25	25-33	34-42	43-52	>52
	30-39	<23	23-30	31-38	39-48	>48
	40-49	<20	20-26	27-35	36-44	>44
	50-59	<18	18-24	25-33	34-42	>43
	60-69	<16	16-22	23-30	31-40	>40
Females	<29	<24	24-30	31-37	38-48	>48
	30-39	<20	20-27	28-33	34-44	>44
	40-49	<17	17-23	24-30	31-41	>41
	50-59	<15	15-20	21-27	28-37	>37
	60-69	<13	13-17	18-23	24-34	>34

TRAINING THE CARDIORESPIRATORY SYSTEM

Training the cardiorespiratory system results in a stronger and more efficient heart. The heart is able to pump more blood with less relative effort and less energy cost. A stronger heart makes the heart more resistant to disease and improves the supply of blood and oxygen to all the tissues of the body. Regardless of the type of aerobic exercise you engage in, the health benefits will occur if you exercise at the appropriate level over the long haul.

Training Principles

There are two general principles of training that apply to any training program—the **overload principle** and the **specificity principle**. The proper application of these principles to training programs helps insure that significant training effects will result.

Overload Principle

The overload principle states that in order for a biologic system, like the cardiorespiratory system, to improve, the system must be regularly "overloaded" or forced to work harder than it normally works. Overloading the cardiorespiratory system forces the heart to pump more blood and the lungs to move more air. If the overload is applied at regular intervals, the system adapts and gets better at what it does, in this case pumping blood and moving air. An overload of the cardiorespiratory system is achieved by doing some type of aerobic activity such as walking, running, swimming, bicycling, or aerobic dance which forces the heart to pump more blood than it normally pumps. The specifics of applying the overload are discussed in the next section.

When any biologic system is overloaded, that system responds by getting better at doing what it does.

Specificity Principle

The specificity principle states that the changes caused by overloading a system will be specific to the system being overloaded. In other words, if you only overload the cardiorespiratory system, improvement only occurs in that system. Overloading the cardiorespiratory system does not automatically improve muscular strength. The specificity principle says that in order to develop all the components of fitness you need to do different kinds of exercise to overload each system. You need one type of exercise to improve cardiorespiratory endurance, a different type of exercise to improve muscular strength and endurance, and a third type of exercise to improve flexibility.

Rollerblading and biking both improve cardiorespiratory fitness but each trains the specific muscles used in that activity.

There are some types of exercises that will produce some, but not optimal, changes in two or more systems simultaneously. Unfortunately, there is not a single exercise that will optimally develop the cardiorespiratory system, muscular system, and flexibility at the same time. For example, bicycling is primarily a cardiorespiratory or aerobic exercise and it primarily affects the cardiorespiratory system. However, bicycling can also improve muscular strength in the quadriceps because these muscles are heavily used in bicycling. Nevertheless, if you wanted to optimally strengthen the quadriceps, specific resistance exercises would be much better than bicycling.

COMPONENTS OF THE EXERCISE SESSION

Once you decide to begin an exercise program, safety and effectiveness should be primary considerations. There are three key components that should be included in any exercise session if the exercise is to be safe and effective. These components are the warm-up, the primary exercise to develop the component(s) of interest, and the cool-down. Each exercise session should begin with a warm-up, progress to the primary exercise, and end with a cool-down.

Warm-Up

A cardiorespiratory exercise session should be preceded by a warm-up and ended with a cool-down. Warm-up consists of 5-10 minutes of low level activity, possibly including flexibility exercises. The low level of activity should be sufficient to raise the body's metabolic rate gradually toward the level the cardiorespiratory endurance exercise will be performed at. For example, if your cardiorespiratory exercise will be jogging at a 6 mph pace, then a warm-up might start with a couple of minutes of moderate walking followed by a couple of minutes of brisk walking. This will gradually raise the functioning of the body near the level used for the jogging. This is beneficial because it allows the body to gradually adapt to the increasing demands. The heart, lungs, and muscles will function more efficiently once the jogging starts if they have had some time to adapt. The importance of warm-up is greater when the cardiorespiratory exercise is to be performed at a high intensity.

Whether or not flexibility exercise or stretching exercise should be included as part of the warm-up or cool-down is a matter of debate. Ideally, flexibility exercises should probably be included before and after the cardiovascular exercise but this would be too time consuming for most individuals. Physiologically, flexibility exercise is most beneficial when performed after the muscles have been warmed-up by some light to moderate aerobic activity such as walking or jogging. Muscles stretch better when they are warm and the flexibility exercise can be more beneficial when performed following aerobic warm-up. For this reason, some recommend that the flexibility exercises not be done until after the cardiorespiratory exercise. This would be appropriate only if the cardiorespiratory exercise was not at or near maximal effort. You should always stretch the involved muscles before doing maximal or near maximal exercise requiring forceful muscular contractions, such as in sprinting. Specific flexibility exercises are discussed in Chapter 3.

Primary Exercise

The primary exercise mode(s) should follow the warm-up. In some cases the primary exercise may just be cardiorespiratory exercise but it would not be unusual that strength exercises would be included in a well-rounded program. If cardiorespiratory and strength exercises are both performed, should one necessarily be performed first? If the purpose of the training is just general fitness/health development, it probably doesn't matter which is performed first. Some prefer to do the strength training first while others prefer to do the cardiorespiratory exercise first. Try it and see what feels better to you. The only precaution is that you do a warm-up appropriate for each type of exercise you are doing.

If a person is specifically concerned about optimal development of either the cardiorespiratory system or of muscular strength, then the type of exercise of primary concern should be performed first so that higher intensity training can be used without residual fatigue resulting from the exercise mode of secondary concern. For example, a competitive weight lifter should do strength training prior to doing a cardiovascular workout.

Cool-Down

Following the cardiorespiratory exercise, a cool-down should be done. A cool-down is the reverse of a warm-up. During a cool-down, the level of activity is gradually lowered toward rest. After jogging at 6 mph, an appropriate cool-down would be to ease into a brisk walk for a couple of minutes and then into a slower walk for a couple of minutes. It is also at this point of the exercise session that flexibility exercise is most appropriate.

The best time to stretch is during the cool-down following aerobic activity.

The major benefit of a cool-down is that it prevents pooling of blood in the lower extremities following exercise. During cardiorespiratory exercise, the vessels of the body which transport blood to the working muscles are enlarged and filled with blood. The contraction of the muscles of the legs when exercising helps to force the blood back to the heart by squeezing on the vessels. This function of the muscles is important for maintaining an adequate return of blood to the heart so the blood can then be recirculated.

If you suddenly stop exercising and stand still, the squeezing action of the muscles ceases and the blood begins to pool in the leg vessels and return of blood to the heart is drastically reduced. The result is the heart doesn't get enough blood back to pump out to the tissues which can result in inadequate blood flow to vital organs, particularly the brain. Light-headedness or even fainting can result but can be prevented by cooling-down and slowly returning back down to rest.

CARDIORESPIRATORY EXERCISE PRESCRIPTION

In order to determine how much and what kind of exercise is necessary to produce desired benefits, the purpose of the exercise program needs to be defined. There is a major difference in the amount of exercise necessary for producing changes in an individual's performance capacity versus the amount of exercise necessary for producing health benefits.

The younger you are, the more important the performance aspect usually is. This is especially true if one is an athlete and participates in competitive situations. The older you get, the more important the health benefits become. Following graduation from college and entry into the workforce, you are likely to loose interest in competitive athletics and the focus should shift to exercise for the health benefits. Generally speaking, it takes less exercise to produce benefits that will result in improved health and decrease in the risk for disease, especially heart disease.[1, 2] Therefore, the focus of this section will be on the amount of exercise necessary to produce long-term health benefits.

The effectiveness of any exercise program will depend primarily on five factors—**mode** or **type of exercise**, the **frequency, duration, intensity** of the exercise program, and the **initial level of fitness**. The mode of exercise determines the application of the specificity principle. The frequency, duration, and intensity quantifies the amount of overload being imposed. The initial level of fitness determines how much overload is necessary to achieve the desired results.

Mode of Exercise

The mode of exercise is the type of exercise performed. Examples of different modes of aerobic exercise are running, cycling, swimming, cross-country skiing, and aerobic dance. Different types of exercise modes produce specific changes in different body systems. Exercise using any of the modes listed above will train the heart to be a better pump because they are all "aerobic" exercises. An aerobic exercise is characterized by the use

KEY CONCEPT

THE BEST AEROBIC EXERCISE

One of the ways to rate the various aerobic exercises is by determining the greatest VO_2 max that can be produced by the exercise. This has been done for many of the aerobic exercises and based on this criteria, the best type of aerobic exercise is cross-country skiing. Highly conditioned elite cross-country skiers have the highest VO_2 max values for any group of athletes. But, for the average person it doesn't really matter which aerobic exercise is done because all the aerobic exercises will provide sufficient stimulus to improve VO_2 max in all but the elite athlete.

The mode of exercise also affects the muscular system, but only those muscles used in a particular type of exercise will be trained. For example, cycling uses different muscles than running. Cycling will cause desirable changes in the muscles used in cycling, but not in the non-used muscles. After a person has become trained doing one mode of exercise and they then switch to a different mode of exercise, their exercise capacity will be diminished until the muscles used in the new mode of exercise become trained. It must be emphasized that all aerobic exercise modes have the ability to train the heart but each mode will train only the specific muscles used in that mode of exercise.

of larger muscle groups in rhythmical, repetitive movements. Such activities require a constant flow of blood to the muscles involved and thereby require the heart to pump a lot of blood. Activities that require you to propel your body in some fashion (cross-country skiing, running, walking, skating, rollerblading, cycling, etc.) for a prolonged period of time will be good aerobic exercises. **Forcing the heart to pump a lot of blood is the stimulus that trains the heart to be a better pump.**

Given the fact that all aerobic exercise modes have the ability to train the cardiovascular system, there are several considerations when selecting a particular mode. Probably of utmost importance is that you enjoy the activity you select. Not many people will continue doing an activity they really don't like to do. The more enjoyable the activity, the more likely you will continue exercising over the long haul. It would be even better if you enjoyed two or three different modes because you could alternate modes and further decrease the chance of getting bored.

Another consideration is the amount of musculoskeletal trauma you are able to endure from the activity. Some modes are more traumatic than others. For example, running is probably the most traumatic aerobic exercise you can do. There is a much greater potential for injury from running than from any other aerobic exercise. Swimming and biking are very non-traumatic activities and would be good choices if you have a history of musculoskeletal injury or if you are overweight.

Other considerations include such things as convenience, the need for special equipment or facilities, and the need of having someone to do the activity with. Although running scores high in the trauma category, it is a very convenient exercise, requires little equipment or special facilities, and can be done alone. Try a variety of activities and weed out those that are inconvenient, likely to cause injury, or not enjoyable.

Frequency of Exercise

The frequency of exercise is the number of times per week that the exercise is done. In order to improve cardiorespiratory endurance, the frequency of exercise should be a minimum of 3 days per week.[2] Usually, 2 days per week is not sufficient to increase cardiorespiratory fitness unless the fitness level is very low to begin with. However, 2 days per week may be sufficient to maintain a level of cardiorespiratory fitness already achieved. Performing exercise more than 3 days per week usually does not produce significant results beyond what 3 days per week will produce. Exercise is more beneficial when done every other day as opposed to 3 days in succession.

It should be also understood that the frequencies recommended are for improving the capacity and health of the cardiorespiratory system. There are some situations in which more frequent exercise would be beneficial.

For example, if one were exercising primarily to lose weight, exercising six days per week would be twice as beneficial as exercising 3 days per week because twice as many calories are burned. Also, if one were a competitive athlete and every bit of improvement was important, then exercising 5-7 days per week would probably be important.

For the typical individual who is primarily interested in maintaining an adequate level of cardiorespiratory endurance for the health benefits, exercising 3 days per week using an every-other-day program would be very adequate. For the amount of time spent, such a program would result in good improvement and would maintain a level of cardiorespiratory endurance that would be optimal for good health.

Duration of Exercise

The duration of exercise is the length of time the exercise is performed in a single exercise session. For example, if you jogged for 30 minutes for 3 days per week, then the duration of exercise is 30 minutes. To develop adequate cardiorespiratory endurance, exercise duration should be a minimum of 15 minutes. The maximum beneficial duration is about 60 minutes. Exercising longer than 60 minutes does not seem to provide any further significant improvement in health unless the objective is weight reduction.[2] There is also evidence suggesting that it does not matter if you break the duration of exercise into multiple shorter sessions. For example, exercising 10 minutes 3 time per day may produce the same results as exercising 30 minutes once per day.

Intensity of Exercise

The intensity of exercise is the "hardness" of the exercise and it quantifies how hard the heart has to work to pump blood during the exercise. When using an aerobic exercise mode, the intensity can be determined from either the heart rate or the rate of perceived exertion (RPE). Using heart rate is more accurate but using the RPE is easier.

Heart Rate as a Measure of Intensity

The heart rate is an indirect measure of how much blood the heart is pumping. Remember, the stimulus that makes the heart stronger and more healthy is the pumping of large quantities of blood. The more blood the heart pumps, the better the heart is able to pump blood and the more healthy it becomes. This is because the heart acts just like a skeletal muscle—when forced to work hard it adapts by becoming better at what it is doing.

As long as an aerobic activity is being performed, the heart rate will be a good measure of the amount of blood the heart is pumping. The range of heart rates at which significant benefits begin to occur differs depending on the method chosen to compute the training heart rate. There are two methods for computing the training heart rate—the **heart rate reserve (HRR) method** and the **percentage of maximal heart rate (PMHR) method**. When using the HRR method the appropriate heart rate intensity is 40 to 85%. When using the PMHR method the appropriate heart rate intensity is 55 to 90%.[2] These two heart rate intensity ranges are equivalent when using each with the corresponding method of calculating the training heart rate.

Calculating the Training Heart Rate

The HRR method is considered to be the most accurate method but it requires a little more computation than the PMHR method. To use the HRR method, the maximal heart rate (HR_{max}) and the resting heart rate (HR_{rest}) must be known. To use the PMHR method, only the HR_{max} has to be known. Examples of how to use both methods are detailed in Tables 2.9 and 2.10.

The HR_{max} is the greatest number of times the heart will contract in one minute. The HR_{max} is most accurately determined by doing maximal work for 3-5 minutes and measuring the heart rate at the end of the work period.

TABLE 2.9

Calculating the Training Heart Rate Using the Heart Rate Reserve (HRR) Method

Example: Calculate the training heart rates for a 20-year old female representing 40-85% intensity using the HRR method. Her HR_{rest} = 70 bpm

- The estimated HR_{max} is **220 − 20 = 200 bpm**
- The heart rate reserve is $HR_{max} − HR_{rest}$ or **200 − 70 = 130 bpm**
- Multiply the HRR by both the low (40%) and high (85%) intensity values

  130 x 0.40 = 52 bpm; 130 x 0.85 = 111 bpm (rounded-up)
- Add the HR_{rest} to each of the values determined in the above step

  70 + 52 = 122 bpm (this is the training heart rate for the low end of the range)

  70 + 111 = 181 bpm (this is the training heart rate for the high end of the range)

Conceptually, the heart rate reserve range ($HR_{max} − HR_{rest}$) represents the ability of the heart to increase its pumping capacity, i.e. it can increase from a resting rate of 70 to a maximal rate of 200. Multiplying the percentage for the low intensity (40%) and the percentage for the high intensity (85%) times the heart rate reserve merely determines the percentage of the heart's capacity to pump. Finally, the HR_{rest} has to be added onto the heart rate reserve percentage value because the HR_{rest} is the "zero" point—the heart rate can't be any lower than the HR_{rest}.

TABLE 2.10
Calculating The Training Heartrate Using the Percentage of Maximal Heart Rate (PMHR) Method

Example: Calculate the training heart rate for a 20-year old male representing the 55-90% intensity range using the PMHR method. His HR_{rest} = 70 bpm

- The estimated HR_{max} is **220 – 20 = 200 bpm**
- Multiply the HR_{max} times the low (55%) and high (90%) intensity values

  200 x 0.55 = 110 bpm (this is the training heart rate at the low end of the range)

  200 x 0.90 = 180 bpm (this is the training heart rate at the high end of the range)

In this method, the HR_{rest} has no relevancy. Even if the HR_{rest} were 40 bpm, it would not have an effect on calculating the training heart rate using the PMHR method but it would have an effect on the actual training response. This is the major weakness of this method.

Because there is some danger in certain populations (middle-aged or older adults) in doing maximal work without a thorough medical evaluation, an estimation of the HR_{max} is typically used in place of an actually measured value. The maximal heart rate can be estimated by the formula:

$$HR_{max} = 220 - age$$

As indicated by the above formula, the primary factor that affects HR_{max} is age. The older one is, the lower is the HR_{max}, on average. There will be exceptions to this general rule, but it will hold true for the majority of individuals.

The HR_{rest} can be easily determined by taking the heart rate after 15-30 minutes of rest or inactivity. The lowest heart rate would be found just after awaking in the morning, but the difference between the heart rate just after awaking and that after 15-30 minutes of supine rest will not significantly affect the computation of the training heart rate.

The results from the two methods of computing the training heart rate in Tables 2.9 and 2.10 indicate that using either method of computing the training heart rate gives results that are very similar as long as the appropriate training heart rate intensities for each method are used. In Table 2.9, if the resting heart rate were a lot different than 70, the results using the HRR method would have been slightly different. These examples really emphasize the difference and similarity of the two methods. The HR_{max} will be the same for each method and it is the HR_{rest} that changes the calculated training heart rates.

Figures 2.4 and 2.5 are handy charts that can be used to determine the training heart rate based on the HRR and PMHR methods. Whether using these charts or calculating the training heart rates, one major precaution

KEY CONCEPT

THE ERROR IN ESTIMATING HR$_{MAX}$

Like all physiologic estimates, there is error in estimating HR$_{max}$. The interpretation of an estimated HR$_{max}$ is exactly like the interpretation of an estimated VO$_2$max or an estimated %fat. The SEE for estimating HR$_{max}$ is 10 beats per minute. What does this mean? For example, the estimated HR$_{max}$ for a 20 year old would be 200. Because the SEE is 10 beats per minute, there is a 68% probability that the true HR$_{max}$ is between 200 plus and minus 10 or (1 x SEE) on either side of the estimated HR$_{max}$. There is a 95% probability that the true HR$_{max}$ is between 200 plus and minus 20 or (2 x SEE) on either side of the estimated HR$_{max}$. Finally, there is a 99.5% probability that the true HR$_{max}$ is between 200 plus and minus 30 or (3 x SEE) on either side of the estimated HR$_{max}$. For this example the probabilities and ranges for HR$_{max}$ would be:

68% probability that the true HR$_{max}$ is 190–200.

95% probability that the true HR$_{max}$ is 180–220.

99.5% probability that the true HR$_{max}$ is 170–230.

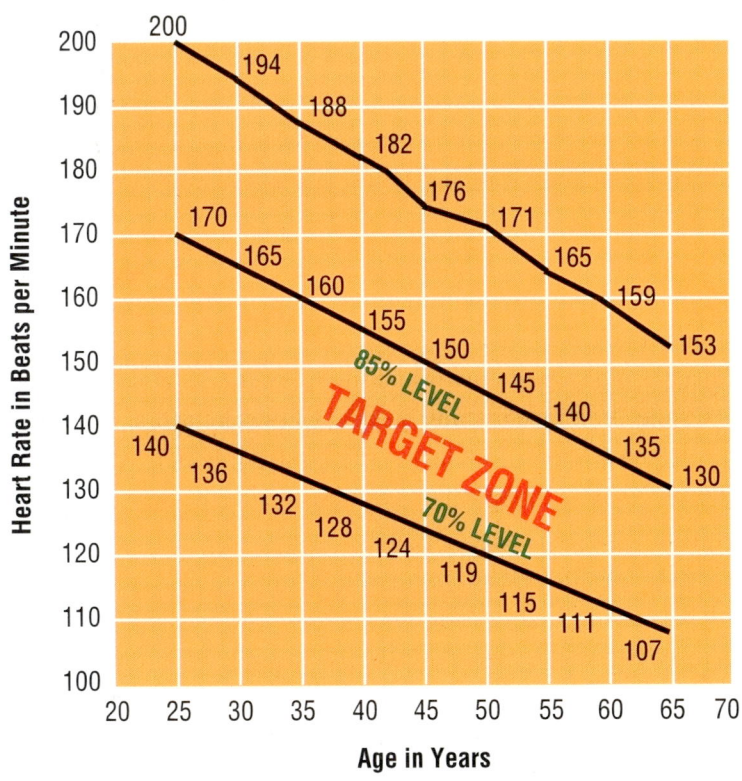

FIGURE 2.4

Target Heart Rates: Percentage of Maximum Method. This chart can be used to determine the target heart rate using the percentage of maximum heart rate method.

* Heart rates are based on 70 percent (minimum) and 85 percent (maximum) of the maximal attainable heart rate.

FIGURE 2.5

Target Heart Rates: Karvonen Method. This chart can be used to determine the target heart rate using the heart rate reserve or Karvonen method. The heart rates in the chart are based on a maximal heart rate of 220-age and a resting heart rate of 70. The values in the chart would change if the resting heart rate were different than 70.

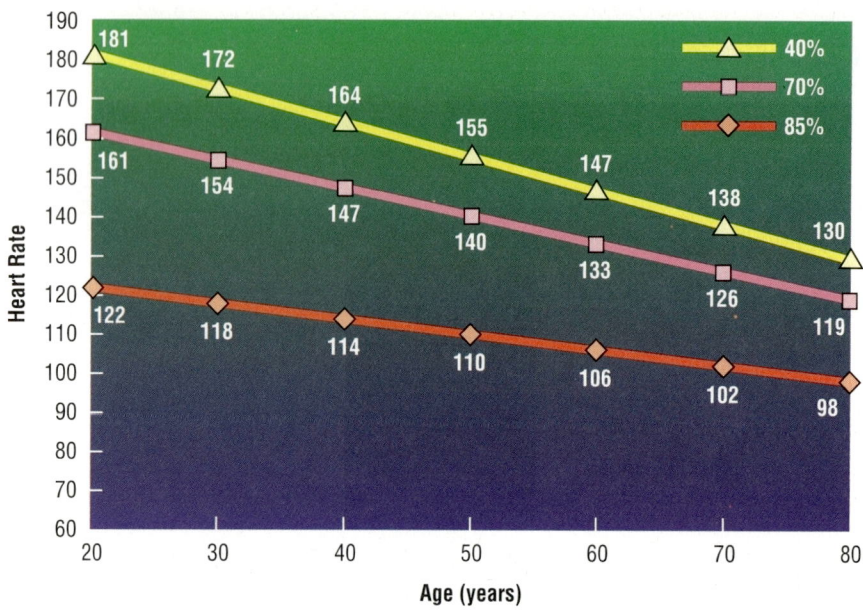

should be remembered. If the HR_{max} is estimated based on age, there is the potential for considerable error, as previously explained. If the estimated HR_{max} is 15-20 beats wrong, the training heart rate will also be wrong. To help rectify this potential error, use a RPE rating as a check on your calculated training heart rate. If your training heart rate is at a level that should be moderate exertion but your RPE is 9-10, then there is a problem. The problem is likely that your true HRmax is significantly lower than your estimated HR_{max}.

Exercising at the higher end of the intensity zone will improve performance more than exercising at the lower end, but exercising at the higher end is not necessary and usually not appropriate. A person just beginning to exercise should start gradually and should exercise at the lower end of the intensity zone. In a recent study, people who exercised at this lower level (40% using the HRR or 55% using the PMHR) demonstrated significant health benefits even though the aerobic capacity was not that high.[3] For most college students, exercising between 60-70% using the HRR or 70-80% using the PMHR will be appropriate. If you are interested in increasing your VO_2max as high as possible, then periodically training at the upper end of the intensity zone is necessary. Table 2.11 gives appropriate ranges for training heart rates for different age groups and training status.

If you do choose to exercise at the higher intensities, you should still start slowly. Exercise at the lower end of the training heart rate zone for 4-6 weeks before gradually increasing the intensity. This will allow adaptation of the muscles and joints and will reduce the risk of injury. Also, exercise will be psychologically easier to perform at this lower end and will be more likely to be continued. As you become more conditioned, the intensity can be gradually increased toward the higher end of the intensity zone without changing how hard the exercise feels to you.

TABLE 2.11

Recommended Exercise Intensity for Training Status and Training Objective

Objective	Heart Rate Method	Fitness Status		
		Low Fit	Moderate Fit	High Fit
Health	HRR	40-50%	50-55%	55-70%
Health	PMHR	55-60%	60-70%	70-80%
Performance	HRR	55-65%	50-75%	75-85%
Performance	PMHR	60-70%	60-80%	80-90%

RPE as a Measure of Intensity

A second way to determine the intensity of exercise is by using the **Rating of Perceived Exertion Scale (RPE)**.[4] The RPE scale (Figure 2.6) is used to rate how hard a person feels they are working. A scale from 0-10 is used, with 0 being equivalent to no effort and 10 being equivalent to maximal effort. Descriptors are used at the indicated numbers to make it easier to relate the numbered scale to more familiar terms. This makes the use of the scale more consistent when used by different individuals.

Initially, the RPE scale should be used simultaneously with a heart rate to facilitate the association of how one feels while exercising at a certain heart rate. After using the RPE scale for a while, one learns that exercising at a certain heart rate feels a certain way. After this association is made, the RPE scale can be used in place of the heart rate. Periodic heart rate checks are still advised, but most of the time the RPE scale can be used to rate the intensity of effort.

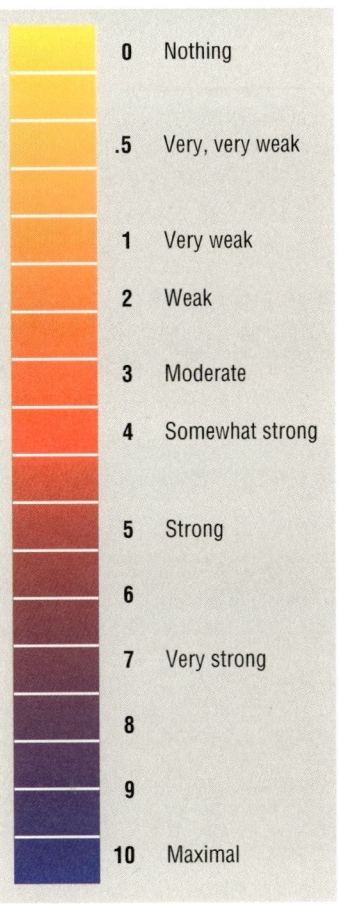

FIGURE 2.6

The RPE scale can be used to determine the intensity of exercise.

0	Nothing
.5	Very, very weak
1	Very weak
2	Weak
3	Moderate
4	Somewhat strong
5	Strong
6	
7	Very strong
8	
9	
10	Maximal

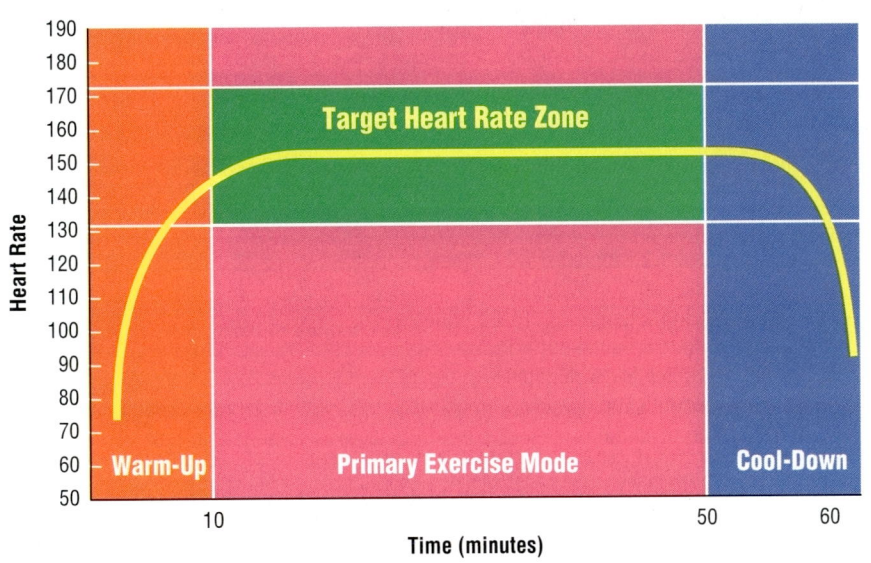

Composition of Typical Exercise Session. An exercise session should consist of a warm-up, a primary exercise mode, which raises the heart rate into the appropriate training zone and a cool-down.

How Hard Do You Have To Exercise?

This question can only be answered by identifying the objectives of the exercise. If the objective is to gain the majority of the health benefits of the exercise, then the answer is that you need to exercise at least at 40% using the HRR method or 55% using the PMHR method. Expressing it a little differently, the Surgeon General of the United States has recently issued a report in which it is suggested that the health benefits of exercise will result from performing **moderate** amounts of physical activity on a regular basis.[6] This report defines moderate physical activity as activity that uses approximately 150 kcal of energy per day, or 1,000 kcal per week. Table 2.12 lists some activities that would typically meet this moderate exercise goal.

Notice in Table 2.12 that as the exercise gets more vigorous, the time requirement decreases. This is an illustration of the interaction between intensity and duration. In general, this principle says that as long as you meet the minimal intensity requirements, as the duration increases the intensity can decrease or visa versa. This training concept is also built into the recommendations that 1,000 kcal per week be expended in activity. To expend 1,000 kcal per week, you could perform an exercise that expended 10 kcal per minute for 100 minutes or you could perform an exercise that expend 15 kcal per minute for 67 minutes.

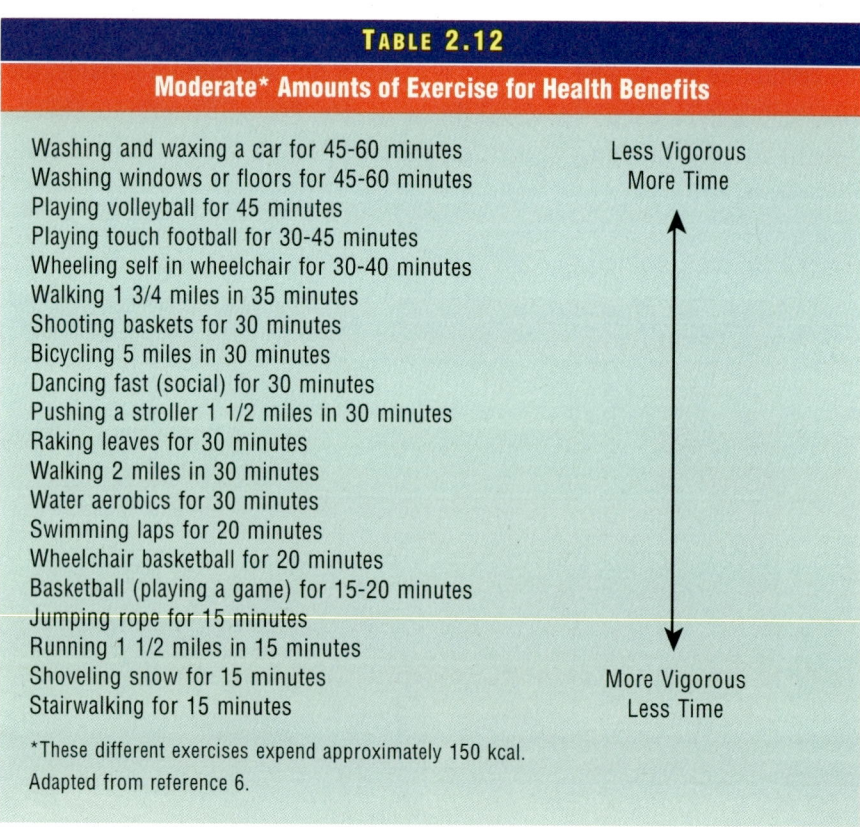

TABLE 2.12
Moderate* Amounts of Exercise for Health Benefits

Washing and waxing a car for 45-60 minutes
Washing windows or floors for 45-60 minutes
Playing volleyball for 45 minutes
Playing touch football for 30-45 minutes
Wheeling self in wheelchair for 30-40 minutes
Walking 1 3/4 miles in 35 minutes
Shooting baskets for 30 minutes
Bicycling 5 miles in 30 minutes
Dancing fast (social) for 30 minutes
Pushing a stroller 1 1/2 miles in 30 minutes
Raking leaves for 30 minutes
Walking 2 miles in 30 minutes
Water aerobics for 30 minutes
Swimming laps for 20 minutes
Wheelchair basketball for 20 minutes
Basketball (playing a game) for 15-20 minutes
Jumping rope for 15 minutes
Running 1 1/2 miles in 15 minutes
Shoveling snow for 15 minutes
Stairwalking for 15 minutes

Less Vigorous
More Time

More Vigorous
Less Time

*These different exercises expend approximately 150 kcal.
Adapted from reference 6.

Table 2.13 contains a more extensive listing of exercises and their approximate caloric expenditures. Based on your weight and the activity selected, you can easily determine how long you have to do an exercise to expend 150 kcal per day or 1,000 kcal per week.

TABLE 2.13

Caloric Expenditure (kcal·lb⁻¹·min⁻¹) of Selected Physical Activities

Caloric Expenditure kcal/lb/min	Activity	Description	Caloric Expenditure kcal/lb/min	Activity	Description
0.0636	Basketball	Competitive, full court	0.0636	Running	5 mph, level
0.0676	Bicycling	BMX or mountain	0.0795	Running	6 mph, level
0.0318	Bicycling	<10 mph, leisure, level	0.0914	Running	7 mph, level
0.0477	Bicycling	10-11.9 mph. leisure, level	0.1074	Running	8 mph, level
0.0636	Bicycling	12-13.9 mph, leisure, level	0.1193	Running	9 mph, level
0.0795	Bicycling	14-15.9 mph, fast, level	0.1272	Running	10 mph, level
0.0955	Bicycling	16-19 mph, racing/not drafting or >19 mph drafting,			
0.0557	Skating, ice	recreational, moderate			
0.1273	Bicycling	>20 mph, racing/not drafting	0.0517	Stair Stepper	Stairmaster, level 5, 60 steps·min⁻¹
0.0438	Bicycling	stationary, 50 Watts, light	0.0636	Stair Stepper	Stairmaster, level 7, 77 steps·min⁻¹
0.0557	Bicycling	stationary, 100 watts, moderate	0.0756	Stair Stepper	Stairmaster, level 9, 95 steps·min⁻¹
0.0835	Bicycling	stationary, 200 watts, heavy	0.0636	Skiing, snow	X-country, 4-5 mph
0.0239	Bowling	recreational	0.0716	Skiing, snow	X-country, 5-8 mph
0.0636	Calisthenics	pushups, pullups, situps- vigorous effort	0.1114	Skiing, snow	X-country, >8mph, racing
0.0636	Circuit Training	upper and lower body	0.0398	Skiing,snow	downhill, light effort
0.0477	Dancing	aerobic, general	0.0478	Skiing, snow	downhill, moderate effort
0.0398	Dancing	aerobic, low impact	0.0636	Skiing, snow	downhill, vigorous effort
0.0557	Dancing	aerobic, high impact	0.0795	Soccer	competitive
0.0636	Football	competitive touch or flag	0.0398	Softball	recreational
0.0437	Golf	walking, carrying clubs	0.0795	Swimming	freestyle, fast
0.0398	Golf	walking, pulling clubs	0.0636	Swimming	freestyle, slow
0.0278	Golf	riding cart	0.0478	Tennis	doubles
0.0636	Hockey	ice	0.0636	Tennis	singles
0.0795	Racquetball	competitive	0.0318	Volleyball	competitive
0.0398	Rollerblading	5 mph, level	0.0238	Volleyball	recreational
0.0795	Rollerblading	10 mph, level	0.0199	Walking	<2mph, leisurely
0.1193	Rollerblading	15 mph, level	0.0238	Walking	2-3mph
0.0955	Rope Jumping	fast	0.0398	Walking	3-4 mph
0.0795	Rope Jumping	moderate	0.0318	Water aerobics	moderate effort
0.0636	Rope Jumping	slow			

Directions: To compute the energy expenditure in kilocalories for any activity listed, multiply the caloric expenditure listed in the left column times body weight times the minutes the activity is performed. For example, if a 150 lb runner runs at 6 mph for 30 minutes, the caloric expenditure would be computed in the following way: 0.0795 x 150 x 30 = 358 kilocalories Values are from various research studies in the literature.

In actuality, there is a dose-response relationship between the quantity of exercise and health benefits. As the quantity of exercise increases from 1,000-2,000 kcal per week the health benefits increase from good benefits to optimal benefits. Of course, the exercise has to meet the minimal intensity requirement of 40% using the HRR method or 55% using the PMHR method. Another way of expressing the relationship is to say that you get 70-75% of the benefit by exercising at the recommended minimal level but you get 100% of the benefit by exercising at the higher intensity and duration levels.

If the objective in exercising is to maximize both the health benefits and the performance benefits, then the exercise needs to periodically be close to the upper end of the recommended training zone. Exercising at 70-85% using the HRR method or 80-90% using the PMHR method two to three times per week will optimize both the health and performance benefits. This is the type of exercise intensity necessary to produce larger increases in VO_2max.

Initial Level of Fitness

The fifth factor that determines the effectiveness of exercise is the initial level of cardiorespiratory fitness that one has. A person who has been sedentary for years and is at a low level of fitness will show improvement with lower intensity, less frequent and shorter duration of exercise. This type of individual may get significant benefit with relatively low levels of exercise such as walking.

On the other hand, if an individual is already fit, it takes a higher intensity, and a greater frequency and duration to cause further improvement. This is because the farther away from our maximal potential we are, the less we have to do to improve. But, as we get closer to our maximal potential, we have to do more and more to continue to improve. That is why competitive athletes have to train so hard to gain a slight improvement. Therefore, the exact amount and intensity of exercise necessary to produce changes in the cardiorespiratory system will vary with the initial fitness level. The less fit to start with, the less exercise and the lower the intensity necessary to produce changes.

MEASURING THE HEART RATE

Periodically measuring the heart rate during exercise provides information regarding the appropriateness of the exercise intensity. In some cases, it may be a safety issue. In an ideal world, you would like to progress from measuring heart rates to using RPE, but for some this transition will never occur and measuring heart rate will always be necessary. How exactly do

There are several steps you can take to help prevent the potential ill-effects of exercising in the heat. First and foremost is drinking adequate amounts of fluid. If you know you are going to be exercising in the heat, make sure you drink lots of fluid for several days before you are to exercise in the heat. Secondly, make sure that fluid is consumed frequently during the exercise bout. This will help ensure an adequate amount of fluid is replaced as fluid is lost through sweating. Thirdly, expose as much skin surface to the air as feasible. This helps by getting rid of heat through a secondary method called convection and allows for more efficient evaporation of the sweat.

For every pound of water lost through sweating, approximately 2 cups of fluid needs to be replaced. You actually need to drink more than the amount to be replaced because not all of the fluid consumed will be retained in the body. If you vigorously exercise in the heat for longer than 1 hour, drink approximately 6 ounces of fluid every 15-20 minutes. Start replacing the fluid early in the exercise session even if you don't feel thirsty. If you wait until you feel thirsty, you may already have a fluid deficit.

You often see commercially available "**sport drinks**" like Gatorade advertised on TV and in magazines. Are these sports drinks better than water for fluid replacement? There has been considerable research looking at this issue. Most of the research has concluded that these sport drinks are somewhat better than plain water for fluid replacement when exercising in the heat, especially when the duration of exercise is longer than 60 minutes. These sport drinks contain electrolytes like sodium, potassium, and chlorine which help replace the electrolytes lost in the sweat. They also contain carbohydrate, usually glucose or fructose. The carbohydrate will provide some energy which may be important during long duration exercise. However, even though these drinks may provide an advantage, the most critical component is the fluid, i.e.. water. If you drink plain water to replace fluid, the electrolytes will usually be replaced when you eat. In most situations, the important aspect is making sure you replace the water by using either plain water or a sport drink.

There are many commercially available sport drinks. The contents of all these sport drinks is very similar.

Exercise in the Cold

Exercising in the cold does not present as much a problem as exercising in the heat. Since exercise produces heat, we normally have a higher tolerance for exercise in the cold. In addition, when we exercise in the cold protective clothing can be added and removed as necessary but, when we exercise in the heat, only so much clothing can be removed.

Whenever the rate of heat loss exceeds that of heat production, a decrease in body temperature called **hypothermia** can result. If the internal temperature drops too low, loss of consciousness and even death can result. The best preventive measure is to wear adequate clothing. When exercising in the cold, it is best to wear layers of lighter clothing so that it can be removed as the body heats up and put back on as the body cools down or as the weather changes. The inside layer or layers should optimally be made of the newer types of synthetics that can wick sweat away from the skin, such as polypropylene. The outside layer should be made of material that does not allow wind or water to penetrate. Material like Gortex (or similar) provides both a wind and water barrier and also allows sweat to be wicked away from the body.

The fingers, ears, toes and face are the most susceptible to frostbite, a condition in which the fluids around the skin turn to ice crystals. Whenever you exercise in the cold, care should be taken to protect these sensitive areas. Gloves should be worn to protect the fingers and a head covering should be worn to protect the ears since a considerable amount of heat is lost through the head. Table 2.15 can be used to identify when the danger of frostbite is greatest.

TABLE 2.15
Wind Chill Chart

Wind MPH	Temperature (Fahrenheit)																				
Calm	40°	35°	30°	25°	20°	15°	10°	5°	0°	−5°	−10°	−15°	−20°	−25°	−30°	−35°	−40°	−45°	−50°	−55°	−60°
5	35°	30°	25°	20°	15°	10°	5°	0°	−5°	−10°	−15°	−20°	−25°	−30°	−35°	−40°	−45°	−50°	−55°	−65°	−70°
10	30°	20°	15°	10°	5°	0°	−10°	−15°	−20°	−25°	−35°	−40°	−45°	−50°	−60°	−65°	−70°	−75°	−80°	−90°	−95°
15	25°	15°	10°	0°	−5°	−10°	−20°	−25°	−30°	−40°	−45°	−50°	−60°	−65°	−70°	−80°	−85°	−90°	−100°	−105°	−110°
20	20°	10°	5°	0°	−10°	−15°	−25°	−30°	−35°	−45°	−50°	−60°	−65°	−75°	−80°	−85°	−95°	−100°	−110°	−115°	−120°
25	15°	10°	0°	−5°	−15°	−20°	−30°	−35°	−45°	−50°	−60°	−65°	−75°	−80°	−90°	−95°	−105°	−110°	−120°	−125°	−135°
30	10°	5°	0°	−10°	−20°	−25°	−30°	−40°	−50°	−55°	−65°	−70°	−80°	−85°	−95°	−100°	−105°	−115°	−120°	−130°	−140°
35	10°	5°	−5°	−10°	−20°	−25°	−35°	−40°	−50°	−60°	−65°	−75°	−80°	−90°	−100°	−105°	−115°	−120°	−130°	−135°	−145°
40*	10°	0°	−5°	−15°	−20°	−30°	−35°	−45°	−55°	−60°	−70°	−75°	−85°	−95°	−100°	−110°	−115°	−125°	−130°	−140°	−150°

Little Danger	Increasing Danger (Flesh may freeze within one minute)	Great Danger (Flesh may freeze within 30 seconds)

* Winds above 40 mph have little additional effect.

Source: National Oceanic and Atmospheric Administration.

Layers of light clothing are the best way to dress for exercise in the cold.

Exercise at Altitude

Another environmental factor which can affect exercise is altitude. As you go to higher altitudes, changes in the environment make it more difficult to transport oxygen to the muscles. The result is that aerobic exercise capacity is reduced. The altitude effect begins to become apparent at about 5,000 feet and gets more pronounced as you go to higher altitudes. If you stay at altitude, adaptations begin to occur that improve exercise capacity. However, the exercise capacity usually does not increase to what it was at sea level.[15]

Table 2.16 lists recommendations to follow if you are going to be exercising at an altitude you are not accustomed to. Although it may be impractical to follow all the recommendations each time you go to altitude, follow as many as you can. These recommendations become more important for individuals that have a compromised cardiorespiratory system, such as those with heart disease or lung disease.

TABLE 2.16
Recommendations for Exercising at Altitude
The following suggestions can help reduce the effect of higher altitudes on exercise capacity and general well-being.
1. Exert little for the first 24 hours.
2. Avoid or minimize alcohol consumption for the first 48 hours.
3. Keep the daily rate of ascent below 1,000 feet.
4. Keep well-hydrated and avoid sedatives.

Exercise and Air Pollution

Air pollutants can cause considerable problems to the exerciser. The pollutants of concern are ozone, sulfur dioxide and carbon monoxide. Ozone is produced primarily from automobile emissions and concentrations depend on such factors as weather conditions, traffic density and industrial output. Effects of exercising while exposed to 0.20 ppm of ozone (the concentration in Los Angles basin over 100 times per year) include decreases in lung function and inflammatory responses and cellular damage to the lung tissue.[7, 12]

Sulfur dioxide is emitted primarily from smelters and refineries and would be most concentrated in areas that have concentrations of these types of heavy industry. Sulfur dioxide does not seem to have significant effects on normal healthy individuals but it is a potent bronchoconstrictor in asthmatics. If you are asthmatic, you should not exercise in conditions of heavy sulfur dioxide emissions.

Carbon monoxide is an air pollutant emitted from automobiles and from tobacco smoke. Carbon monoxide combines easily with hemoglobin in the blood and reduces the oxygen transport capacity of blood. Subsequently, maximal work capacity decreases and exercise performance suffers. Such effects can be prolonged for several hours following exposure, like being in a smoked-filled room before exercising. The effect of carbon monoxide on submaximal exercise capacity should be minimal at exercise intensities below 70% of maximum.

EXERCISE-RELATED TOPICS

There are three additional factors that can affect participation in exercise—injuries, shoes, and clothing. Each will be generally discussed in this section, but it is beyond the scope of this text to treat each topic fully.

Exercise Injuries

Most persistent exercisers will eventually have some type of exercise-related injury. Injury can take the fun and motivation out of exercise and result in permanently discontinuing exercise. Most injuries resulting from fitness-type exercises are not from pulls, strains or sprains. They are not injuries that the exerciser can say "opps, I just injured myself." They are injuries that creep up on you and appear almost out of nowhere. They are called **overuse injuries** and they result from the accumulation of trauma and repetitive motion from the exercise you have been doing. Sometimes, biomechanical abnormalities increase the likelihood for overuse injury.

Certain individuals are going to be more susceptible to injuries than others and some types of exercise are more likely to cause injury. Unfortunately, it is difficult to determine who will be most susceptible. Some structural factors that may make it more likely an injury will occur from weight-bearing exercise like running are body weight, hip width, the angle of the lower leg at the knee, and the mobility of the feet. The only one of these structural factors you can directly manage is the body weight. The others you just have to live with, but you can do things that will diminish their contribution to injury. Prevention is the best way to deal with overuse injuries but, when injury strikes, early detection and treatment are extremely important in resolving the injury with minimal down time.

Most overuse injuries begin with minor, annoying symptoms, most commonly some degree of noticeable discomfort or slight pain, often occurring around a joint. The pain is rarely described as a sharp pain, but is most often a dull, achy pain. Initially the pain may only be evident at the beginning of an exercise session or just when getting out of bed in the mornings. If the exercise is continued, the pain often progresses and becomes more intense and lasts for longer periods of time. Some exercise injuries are self-limiting in that they eventually will either go away or become so painful that you will have to discontinue or limit exercise. However, some injuries, like Achilles tendinitis and stress fractures, can lead to more severe consequences if not properly diagnosed and treated.

One thing consistent about exercise injuries is that higher intensity and longer duration exercise increases the injury risk. Exercising at lower intensities, particularly at the beginning of a newly initiated exercise program, will decrease the chance of injuries. Progressing slowly to higher intensities will also minimize injury risk.

Exercise in the water, whether it be swimming or water aerobics, reduces the risk of injury from overuse.

As already indicated, the best way of dealing with exercise injuries is to try to prevent them, but, if you do begin to have symptoms, early treatment is critical to early recovery. There are specific treatments for specific overuse injuries, but there is a general protocol to decrease symptoms and start the healing process for just about any overuse injury. Sometimes, this general protocol will be all that is necessary to solve the problem. In other cases, you need to determine and eliminate the cause of the injury.

The following are suggestions for preventing exercise injuries. If you utilize these suggestions as much as possible, you may never have a serious exercise injury.

1. Stretch on a regular basis. For details, see Chapter 3.

2. Start your training program slowly and progress slowly, as indicated earlier in this chapter.

3. When possible, exercise on appropriate surfaces. It is especially beneficial for runners to run on soft surfaces like grass or dirt trails. If you have to run on concrete or pavement, stay out of the gutter as much as possible and run on a level surface.

4. Wear good shoes that are made for your type of foot. For details, see the next section.

At the first sign of an impending injury, begin the treatment protocol in Table 2.17. Continue until the symptoms have resolved or until additional medical advice is sought.

TABLE 2.17
Injury Treatment Protocol
• Apply ice to the affected area after exercise and 3-4 times throughout the day. The best way to do this is to use an ice massage. Fill a paper cup with water and freeze it. After it is frozen, tear or cut away part of the cup to expose the ice. Rub the ice on the affected area for about 10-15 minutes, constantly moving the ice around. If you want to use an ice pack and just leave it on the area, put a towel or washcloth between the skin and the ice pack. This will prevent the possibility of damaging the area with too much cold. • Take over-the-counter anti-inflammatory drugs like **ibuprofen**. Over-the-counter ibuprofen is Advil, Motrin, and Nuprin. Ibuprofen should be taken with food because it can be hard on the stomach in some individuals and it should not be taken for longer than 1 week without consulting a physician. Appropriate dosage for treating overuse injuries is 1200-1600 mg per 24 hours. If you cannot tolerate ibuprofen, you can utilize other anti-inflammatory drugs like acetaminophen. When in doubt, consult your physician. • Try to determine what the cause of the injury may be. Try exercising on softer surfaces, make sure you are using correct form, check your shoes for wear, and reduce your intensity and duration.

Exercise Shoes

Good shoes can be the exerciser's best friend and their value should not be underestimated. Shoes have the greatest potential impact on injury prevention in weight-bearing activities, like running and aerobics. Since there are so many shoe manufacturers today with an almost endless selection, it is almost a crime for poor shoes to be the cause of an exercise injury.

In weight-bearing activities, shoes act as shock absorbers for the forces that are developed when the feet contact the ground. Activities like running and aerobics are "traumatic" exercises because of the constant pounding that occurs each time the foot strikes the ground. The bigger you are and the faster you move, the more important good shoes become. It is the constant pounding each time the foot strikes the ground that eventually causes injuries. Good shoes can eliminate or reduce the incidence of many exercise injuries.

Fortunately, the exerciser has a wide selection of good exercise shoes from which to choose. There are shoes made specifically for running, walking, hiking, tennis, cycling, aerobics, and basketball, just to name the most common. All of the different types of shoes are made to provide the greatest support and shock absorption for that particular activity. However, there are some general considerations regarding shoe types and biomechanics of the foot that can help in shoe selection, especially for runners.

There are three primary categories of shoes (primarily running shoes) produced by most manufacturers and made for running on roadways, sidewalks and smooth tracks and trails. The three types are motion-control shoes, stability shoes, and cushioned shoes. Because shoe types have some overlapping characteristics, more than one shoe type may be appropriate for any given person. Experience and a little "trial and error" will help you to eventually select the best shoe type for you.

Motion control shoes are designed to control excessive or uncontrolled movement in the joints of the foot. These shoes are constructed to be relatively rigid, and offer stability and maximum support along the inside border of the shoe. These shoes are particularly appropriate for heavy individuals with flat feet in need of extra durability and control of foot movement.

Stability shoes, characterized by a good blend of cushioning, good support along the inside border of the shoe, and durability, are made for normal sized individuals who do not need a lot of motion control.

Cushioned shoes have the most cushioned mid-soles and the least support along the inside border of the shoe. They are for individuals who have stiff, rigid feet who underpronate. They are good shoes for individuals with high arches who do not overpronate.

The selection of sport shoes is almost endless.

What is Your Foot Type?

In order to know which of the three categories of shoes would be best for you, you should determine your basic foot type. Foot types fall into three categories, **normal, flat, and high-arched**. To understand the relationship of the various foot types and the appropriate type of shoe for each, a brief description of foot mechanics during running is helpful.

Part of the role of the foot in running is to act as a shock absorber to the tremendous forces developed as each foot strikes the ground. In order for the foot to be a good shock absorber, there must be some movement in the foot as it strikes the ground. Normally, the foot should strike the ground at the heel or mid-foot and then roll inward toward the inside margin of the foot. This is called pronation and the movement helps to distribute the landing forces over more of the foot's surface area. If the foot does not pronate sufficiently (called a supinated foot), the forces are focused on a smaller area of the outside portion of the foot. In some cases, the foot overpronates, rolling inward too much. This puts strain on the muscles, joints, and tendons of the lower leg.

Normal feet have a normal-sized arch. When a normal foot lands on the ground, the foot rolls inward (pronates) in order to absorb and distribute the landing forces over more of the foot. Normal-weighted individuals with a normal foot usually do best in a stability shoe with moderate control features. Individuals with normal feet and normal biomechanics usually show shoe wear on the outer edge of the heel, under the ball of the foot, and at the front of the sole.

The flat foot is characterized by a low arch which causes over-pronation when the foot lands on the ground. This excessive motion can lead to various overuse injuries and one should attempt to control the motion by wearing motion-control or stability shoes with firm mid-soles and control features. If you have flat feet, do not wear highly cushioned shoes with little stability and control. Individuals with over-pronation problems show shoe wear along the inside edge to the heel and forefoot.

The high-arched foot doesn't pronate enough when it strikes the ground resulting in poor shock absorption characteristics. The best type of shoe for the runner with a high-arch is a cushioned shoe. The idea is to encourage more foot motion so this runner should stay away from motion-control or stability shoes. Runners with high-arch feet show shoe wear along the outer portion of the heel and forefoot.

Replacing Exercise Shoes

Exercise shoes are very much like the tires on a car—they wear out after they have accumulated sufficient mileage. The need to replace exercise shoes should be determined primarily by the accumulated mileage or equivalent hours of use. Most quality running shoes are good for about 500 miles. This will vary somewhat according to your size and running mechanics with smaller, efficient runners getting more mileage out of their shoes. Unfortunately, it is difficult to tell by looking at a running shoe if it is time to replace it. Running shoes can look pretty good on the outside but their shock absorbing qualities can be all used up. Wearing running shoes too long increases the chance of injury. Shoes used in other weight-bearing activities like step/dance aerobics can be gauged by the number of hours of wear. For aerobic shoes, the equivalent to 500 miles is about 75-100 hours of vigorous exercise. If you vigorously exercise 1 hour, three times a week, aerobic shoes should last about 6 months (don't count the time you are doing stretching and similar activities that don't develop high forces on the feet). Obviously the intensity of the exercise will have some effect on this as well as your body weight. The important thing is to not wait until a problem develops before you replace your shoes.

Which Brand is Best?

There is no one best brand of shoe. All major manufacturers like Nike, Saucony, Reebok, Adidas, Avia, Mizuno, Etonic, Brooks, and Asics make excellent shoes. A good shoe will usually have a retail price of $50-$200. A $200 shoe is not necessarily better than a $50 shoe, but it usually has more bells and whistles. Most exercisers can get along just fine with $50- $80 shoes.

The major criteria used to judge shoe selection should be how the shoes fit your feet. Exercise shoes should feel comfortable when you first put them on and should also be slightly larger (1/2 size) than normal shoes because the foot swells about half a size when exercising. Some space should be left between the longest toe and the front of the shoe. The heel should fit snugly into the heel counter. The shoe should be wide enough to allow the foot to move upwards. Some experimentation with different types and brands of shoes may be necessary before you find the one just right for you. However, too frequent experimentation can be expensive. Once you have found a shoe that feels comfortable and hasn't caused any significant discomforts or injuries, stick with it. Do not be overly swayed by the tremendous amount of advertising for shoes. You are the only one that knows what shoe feels the best.

Exercise Clothing

The importance of appropriate clothing varies with the seasonal changes in temperature and humidity. When exercising outside in neutral to hot weather, the major concern is getting rid of the enormous amounts of body heat that can be produced by activities like running, biking and rollerblading and the general rule is the lesser the amount of clothing and the looser the clothing the better. The more skin surface exposed, the easier it is to get rid of the heat produced when exercising. Loose clothing allows more optimal heat removal because it is easier for air currents to reach the skin and for sweat to evaporate.

In cold weather, the problem is keeping too much heat from escaping to the environment. The goal is to provide adequate insulation while avoiding accumulation of sweat in the garments. Multiple layers of clothing are ideal because air is trapped between layers and acts as insulation. The innermost layer should be made of a moisture-wicking material like polypropylene, so that moisture is carried away from the skin. You want the layer of clothing next to the skin to remain as dry as possible because this reduces heat loss. In windy and rainy weather, the outer layer should be water and wind resistant.

The tendency is for the novice to overdress when exercising in cold weather. If you dress so that you are comfortable while you are not exercising, you will overheat when you start to exercise. Theoretically, you should be cool at the beginning of the exercise session but as you produce more and more heat, you warm up and remain comfortable for the remainder of the session. Perhaps a better way to allow for this warm-up effect is to wear an outer layer that can be easily removed when you get warmed up and reapplied should it be necessary.

Another factor that can dramatically affect the type and amount of clothing that should be worn is the wind. For example, if you run an out and back course, the wind may be in your face for half the distance and at your back for the other half. More clothing may be necessary when the wind is in your face than when it is at your back. The ability to remove and add a layer of clothing will easily solve this problem. Some runners prefer to run out with the wind at their backs and return with the wind in their face once they are producing maximal heat. This would be more a matter of preference since adding and removing clothing would have the same effect.

SUMMARY

You can't control everything that happens to you in life but you can have considerable control over factors that can increase both your longevity and quality of life. One of the choices you can make is to be a regular exerciser. Make it a priority in your daily routine. Schedule in into your day just like any other appointment.

Visualize yourself 20, 30 or 40 years from now. If you are asked the question today "When you are 50 years old, do you want to have a heart attack, or cancer, or diabetes?" your answer would undoubtedly be "No!" No one wants to have chronic diseases. Well, now is the time to start a lifestyle that will decrease the chances of chronic diseases when you get older while allowing the maximal enjoyment out of life. Don't wait, start now!

EXPLORING WELLNESS ON THE WEB

Many resources are available on the World Wide Web. You can reinforce, expand and enhance the information presented in this chapter by accessing the following sites.

http://rampages.onramp.net/%7Echaz/links.html — fitness, nutrition, and wellness resource page that includes lots of resources covering many topics.

http://www.gssiweb.com — this is the Gatorade Sport Science Institute site. There is a great deal of information on various topics related to exercise and sport.

http://www.fi.edu/biosci/healthy/exercise.html — provides information on appropriate types of exercise, how to select a fitness center, exercise equipment, and exercise guidelines.

http://www.1adventure.com/HealthandFitness/Programs/index.htm — this is the American Council on Exercise site. It provides a lot of information on fitness including information from the President's Council on Physical Fitness and the recent Surgeon General Report.

REFERENCES

1. American College of Sports Medicine. (1995). *ACSM,s Guidelines for exercise testing and prescription*. 5th ed., Baltimore: Williams & Wilkins.

2. American College of Sports Medicine. (1990). *The recommended quantity and quality of exercise for developing and maintaining cardiorespiratory and muscular fitness in healthy adults (A Position Stand)*. 5th Ed. Indianapolis: IN.

3. Blair, S. N., Kohl, H. W., Paffenbargr, R. S., Clark, D. G., Cooper, K. H., & Gibbons, L. W. (1989). Physical fitness and all-cause mortality. *Journal of the American Medical Association, 262*(17), 2395-2401.

4. Borg, G. A. (1982). Psychophysical bases of perceived exertion. *Medicine and Science in Sports and Exercise, 14*(4), 377-387.

5. Bouchard, C. (1992). Genetic determinants of endurance performance. In R. J. Shephard & P. O. Astrand (Ed.), *Endurance in sport*, (pp. 149-159). London: Blackwell Scientific.

6. Centers for Disease Control. (1996). A Report of the Surgeon General: Physical Activity and Health. U.S. Department of Health and Human Services.

7. Folinsbee, L. J. (1990). Discussion: Exercise and the environment. In C. Bouchard, R. J. Sutton, T. Stephens, J. R. Sutton, & B. D. McPherson (Ed.), *Exercise, fitness, and health* (pp. 179-183). Champaign, IL: Human Kinetics.

8. George, J.D., Vehrs, P. R., Allsen, P. E. Fellingham, G. W. & Fisher, A. G. VO_{2max} estimation from a submaximal 1-mile track jog for fit college-age individuals. *Medicine and Science in Sports and Exercise*, 25, 401-406.

9. Kline, G. M., Porcari, J. P., Hintermeister, R., Freedson, P. S., Ward, A., McCarron, R. F., Ross, J., & Rippe, J. M. (1987). Estimation of VO_{2max} from a one-mile track walk, gender, age and body weight. *Medicine and Science in Sports and Exercise, 19*(3), 253-259.

10. McArdle, W. D., Katch, F. I., & Katch, V. L. (1991). *Exercise physiology*, Malvern, PA: Lea & Febiger.

11. Nieman, D. C. (1990). *Fitness and sports medicine. An introduction.* Palo Alto, CA: Bull Publishing.

12. Nieman, D. C., & Nehlsen-Cannarella, S. L. (1992). Effects of endurance exercise on the immune response. In R. J. Shephard & P. O. Astrand (Ed.), *Endurance in sport*, (pp. 487-504). London: Blackwell Scientific.

13. Savard, G., Kiens, B., & Saltin, B. (1987). Central cardiovascular factors as limits to endurance; with a note on the distinction between maximal oxygen uptake and endurance fitness. In D. Macleod, R. Maughan, M. Nimmo, T. Reilly, & C. Williams (Ed), *Exercise: Benefits, limits and adaptations*, (pp. 162-180). London: E. & F. N. Spon.

14. Shephard, R. J. (1990). Costs and benefits of an exercising versus a non exercising society. In C. Bouchard, R. J. Sutton, T. Stephens, J. R. Sutton, & B. D. McPherson (Ed.), *Exercise, fitness, and health* (pp. 49-60). Champaign, IL: Human Kinetics.

15. Sutton, J. R. (1987). Exercise at extreme altitude. In D. Macleod, R. Maughan, M. Nimmo, T. Reilly, & C. Williams (Ed), *Exercise: Benefits, limits and adaptations*, (pp. 313-323). London: E. & F. N. Spon.

DEFINITIONS OF KEY TERMS

adenosine triphosphate (ATP) — a high-energy chemical compound that supplies the energy the cells of the body need to function.

aerobic — literally means with oxygen. Usually refers to energy systems in the body which use oxygen to make ATP.

anaerobic — literally means without oxygen. Usually refers to energy systems in the body which make ATP without using oxygen.

atria — the upper two chambers of the heart that act as temporary holding reservoirs for blood coming back to the heart from the body.

cardiac output — the volume of blood pumped out of the heart in one minute.

cardiorespiratory endurance — the ability of the heart and lungs to supply oxygen to the skeletal muscles. Interchangeable terms are aerobic endurance and cardiovascular endurance.

duration — how long you exercise in a single exercise session.

energy system — a series of biochemical reactions in the cells that produce ATP

exercise prescription — the amount of exercise that it is appropriate for an individual to perform. The exercise prescription usually identifies the mode, frequency, duration, and intensity of exercise

frequency — how many times per week you exercise.

hemoglobin — an iron-containing protein in the blood that attaches to oxygen to facilitate oxygen transport.

intensity — how hard you exercise. Intensity may be measured by heart rate or rate of perceived exertion.

lactic acid — a by-product of anaerobic energy production which interfers with muscle contraction.

overload principle — states that in order for a biologic system, like the cardiorespiratory system, to improve, the system must be regularly "overloaded" or forced to work harder than it normally works.

maximal oxygen uptake (VO$_2$max) — the maximal volume of oxygen that can be utilized by the body.

mode — the type of exercise performed, such as bicycling, running, walking, or swimming.

overuse injuries — exercise injuries caused by repetitive motion and accumulated trauma.

physical fitness — the ability to perform one's daily task without becoming fatigued while having enough energy reserve for situations requiring higher levels of energy, such as exercise.

rating of perceived exertion (RPE) — a rating of how hard you are exercising. Usually a scale of 1–10 is used to indicate no work (1) to maximal work (10)

specificity principle — states that the effects of overload are specific to the system being overloaded.

standard error of estimate (SEE) — a measure of accuracy of prediction formula. The SEE identifies how close you can expect the predicted value to be to the true value.

stroke volume — the volume of blood pumped out of the heart each heart beat.

ventricles — the two lower chambers if the heart that are responsible for pumping blood around the circulatory system.

18:15   HR 110

38

45

LAB 2.4 (CONTINUED)

KEEPING AN EXERCISE LOG: WEEK 3

Name _____ ID _____ Sect _____ Time _____ Date _____

Date	Exercise Mode	Warm-Up Activities and Duration	Exercise Duration	Exercise Heart Rate and RPE	Cool-Down Activities and Duration	Calories Expended	Comments
Sunday				HR: _____ RPE: _____			
Monday				HR: _____ RPE: _____			
Tuesday				HR: _____ RPE: _____			
Wednesday				HR: _____ RPE: _____			
Thursday				HR: _____ RPE: _____			
Friday				HR: _____ RPE: _____			
Saturday				HR: _____ RPE: _____			

(Continued)

LAB 2.4 (CONTINUED)

KEEPING AN EXERCISE LOG: WEEK 4

Name _____ ID _____ Sect _____ Time _____ Date _____

Date	Exercise Mode	Warm-Up Activities and Duration	Exercise Duration	Exercise Heart Rate and RPE	Cool-Down Activities and Duration	Calories Expended	Comments
Sunday				HR: _____ RPE: _____			
Monday				HR: _____ RPE: _____			
Tuesday				HR: _____ RPE: _____			
Wednesday				HR: _____ RPE: _____			
Thursday				HR: _____ RPE: _____			
Friday				HR: _____ RPE: _____			
Saturday				HR: _____ RPE: _____			

(Continued)

NOTES

LAB 2.4 (CONTINUED)

KEEPING AN EXERCISE LOG: WEEK 5

Name _____ ID _____ Sect _____ Time _____ Date _____

Date	Exercise Mode	Warm-Up Activities and Duration	Exercise Duration	Exercise Heart Rate and RPE	Cool-Down Activities and Duration	Calories Expended	Comments
Sunday				HR: _____ RPE: _____			
Monday				HR: _____ RPE: _____			
Tuesday				HR: _____ RPE: _____			
Wednesday				HR: _____ RPE: _____			
Thursday				HR: _____ RPE: _____			
Friday				HR: _____ RPE: _____			
Saturday				HR: _____ RPE: _____			

(Continued)

NOTES

LAB 2.4 (CONTINUED)

KEEPING AN EXERCISE LOG: WEEK 6

Name _____ ID _____ Sect _____ Time _____ Date _____

Date	Exercise Mode	Warm-Up Activities and Duration	Exercise Duration	Exercise Heart Rate and RPE	Cool-Down Activities and Duration	Calories Expended	Comments
Sunday				HR: _____ RPE: _____			
Monday				HR: _____ RPE: _____			
Tuesday				HR: _____ RPE: _____			
Wednesday				HR: _____ RPE: _____			
Thursday				HR: _____ RPE: _____			
Friday				HR: _____ RPE: _____			
Saturday				HR: _____ RPE: _____			

(Continued)

NOTES

KEEPING AN EXERCISE LOG: WEEK 7

Name _____ ID _____ Sect _____ Time _____ Date _____

Date	Exercise Mode	Warm-Up Activities and Duration	Exercise Duration	Exercise Heart Rate and RPE	Cool-Down Activities and Duration	Calories Expended	Comments
Sunday							
_____	_____	_____	_____	HR: _____	_____	_____	_____
	_____	_____		RPE: _____	_____		_____
	_____	_____			_____		_____
	_____	_____			_____		_____
Monday							
_____	_____	_____	_____	HR: _____	_____	_____	_____
	_____	_____		RPE: _____	_____		_____
	_____	_____			_____		_____
	_____	_____			_____		_____
Tuesday							
_____	_____	_____	_____	HR: _____	_____	_____	_____
	_____	_____		RPE: _____	_____		_____
	_____	_____			_____		_____
	_____	_____			_____		_____
Wednesday							
_____	_____	_____	_____	HR: _____	_____	_____	_____
	_____	_____		RPE: _____	_____		_____
	_____	_____			_____		_____
	_____	_____			_____		_____
Thursday							
_____	_____	_____	_____	HR: _____	_____	_____	_____
	_____	_____		RPE: _____	_____		_____
	_____	_____			_____		_____
	_____	_____			_____		_____
Friday							
_____	_____	_____	_____	HR: _____	_____	_____	_____
	_____	_____		RPE: _____	_____		_____
	_____	_____			_____		_____
	_____	_____			_____		_____
Saturday							
_____	_____	_____	_____	HR: _____	_____	_____	_____
	_____	_____		RPE: _____	_____		_____
	_____	_____			_____		_____
	_____	_____			_____		_____

(Continued)

NOTES

LAB 2.4 (CONCLUDED)

KEEPING AN EXERCISE LOG: WEEK 8

Name _____ ID _____ Sect _____ Time _____ Date _____

Date	Exercise Mode	Warm-Up Activities and Duration	Exercise Duration	Exercise Heart Rate and RPE	Cool-Down Activities and Duration	Calories Expended	Comments
Sunday				HR: _____ RPE: _____			
Monday				HR: _____ RPE: _____			
Tuesday				HR: _____ RPE: _____			
Wednesday				HR: _____ RPE: _____			
Thursday				HR: _____ RPE: _____			
Friday				HR: _____ RPE: _____			
Saturday				HR: _____ RPE: _____			

NOTES

LAB 2.6

THE EFFECT OF TRAINING ON RESTING HEART RATE

Name _____ ID _____ Sect _____ Time _____ Date _____

Purposes

1. To understand the effect of aerobic training on resting heart rate.
2. To understand the relationship of heart rate, stroke volume, and cardiac output.

Directions

Define each of the variables listed.

heart rate —

stroke volume —

cardiac output —

What is the mathematical formula that describes the relationship between heart rate, stroke volume and cardiac output? Write the formula in the form of A = B × C.

Using the units of **beats/min** for heart rate, **ml/beat** for stroke volume, and **ml/min** for cardiac output, substitute the units in the equation above to verify that both sides of the equation are equal and that the equation is correct.

In the following table there are spaces for values for resting heart rate, stroke volume and cardiac output for a typical 20 year old college student in an untrained state and then after 6 months of aerobic training. Some of the values are filled in and some are blank. Calculate the appropriate values for each variable that is blank and fill in the missing values in the table.

(Continued)

THE EFFECT OF TRAINING ON RESTING HEART RATE

	Cardiac Output (ml/min)	Heart Rate (beats/min)	Stroke Volume (ml/beat)
Rest Untrained	5250	70	_____
Rest Trained	5250	55	_____

In the table below there are spaces for values for maximal heart rate, stroke volume and cardiac output for a typical 20 year old college student in an untrained state and then after 6 months of aerobic training. Some to the values are filled in and some are blank. Calculate the appropriate values for each variable that is blank and fill in the missing values in the table.

	Cardiac Output (ml/min)	Heart Rate (beats/min)	Stroke Volume (ml/beat)
Maximal Untrained	14,000	200	_____
Maximal Trained	20,000	200	_____

Answer each of the following questions.

1. The expected response of the resting heart rate to aerobic training is that the resting heart rate goes down. Why does the resting heart rate go down in response to aerobic training? (hint: look at the relationship between the three variables)

2. In contrast to the resting heart rate, the maximal heart rate does not change in response to aerobic training while the maximal cardiac output increases 20-25%. How can the maximal cardiac output increase 20-25% if the maximal heart rate is unchanged?

DETERMINING YOUR TRAINING HEART RATE USING THE PERCENTAGE OF MAXIMUM METHOD

Name _Gabe Peasley_   ID _346709_ Sect _82_ _03_ Time _9:30_   Date _1/28/98_

Purposes

1. To understand the concept of training heart rate.

2. To learn how to determine your training heart rate using the percentage of maximum method.

3. To understand the effect of age and fitness level on training heart rate.

Directions

Compute your estimated maximal heart rate (HR_{max} = 220 − age): ___200___ bpm

Compute the low end of the training heart rate zone using 60% intensity. This is the minimal training heart rate and is the lowest heart rate at which significant improvements in the cardiorespiratory system occur.

Minimal Training Heart Rate = (HR_{max}) ___200___ × 0.60 = ___120___ bpm

Compute the high end of the training heart rate zone using 90% intensity. This is the maximal training heart rate and is the highest heart rate at which significant improvements in the cardiorespiratory system occur.

Maximal Training Heart Rate = (HR_{max}) ___200___ × 0.90 = ___180___ bpm

Your Training Heart Rate Zone = ___120___ (minimal) to ___180___ (maximal)

(Continued)

DETERMINING YOUR TRAINING HEART RATE USING THE PERCENTAGE OF MAXIMUM METHOD

After calculating your training heart rate zone, determine the level of aerobic exercise necessary to achieve your minimal and maximal training heart rates. Start by performing a level of exercise that you estimate will be near the minimal training heart rate. After 2-3 minutes, take your heart rate and increase or decrease the exercise to adjust your heart rate to the level necessary. Once you achieve the level of exercise to raise the heart rate to the desired level, continue exercising at that level for a total of 10 minutes. In the space below, explain how you subjectively felt exercising at this level. Could you have continued this exercise for 30 minutes?

After 10 minutes at the minimal training heart rate, use the same procedure to determine the level of aerobic exercise necessary to raise your heart rate to the maximal training heart rate. Exercise at this level for a total of 10 minutes. In the space below, explain how you subjectively felt exercising at this level. Could you have continued this exercise for 30 minutes?

LEARNING TO TAKE AN ACCURATE HEART RATE

2. Were the pulse counts for 10 sec or 15 sec the most accurate? Should the 10-sec or 15-sec count be the most accurate at reflecting what your heart rate was during the exercise bout? Explain.

3. The general recommendation for taking pulse rates to determine an exercise heart rate is to take either a 10-sec or 15-sec pulse count. However, if you are taking a "resting" pulse, the recommendation is to take a 30-sec or 60-sec count. Why should you take a 30-sec or 60-sec count at rest but only a 10-sec or 15-sec count following exercise?

NOTES

LAB 2.9

LEARNING TO USE THE RPE SCALE

Name _____ ID _____ Sect _____ Time _____ Date _____

Purposes

1. To learn how to use the RPE scale to rate the intensity of exercise.

2. To understand the relationship between the amount of physiologic effort and how you perceive that effort.

Directions

1. This lab is designed to be done on two days. On Day 1, the lab is done in partners. On Day 2, the lab is done individually. This lab is designed to be able to be done using any mode of aerobic exercise (walking, jogging, swimming, biking, stepping, etc.). Each set of partners should have one electronic heart monitor for Day 1 but each needs a monitor for Day 2. If heart monitors are not available, heart rates can be checked by counting the pulse.

2. To begin the activity, one partner is the **"exerciser"** and the other is the **"checker."** After the **exerciser** has completed each exercise bout, the responsibilities are switched.

3. For this lab, it is best to use an electronic heart monitor. If the lab is done without a heart monitor, the **checker** verifies the heart rate by counting the pulse. On Day 1, the **exerciser** wears the sending unit (the part that goes on the chest) of the heart monitor and the **checker** wears/holds the receiving unit (the watch)

4. On Day 1, the **exerciser** performs each exercise bout listed in the table on the next page. At the completion of each bout, the **exerciser** rates the intensity of the exercise by using the RPE Scale. The **checker** uses the heart monitor to get the heart rate. The RPE and the heart rate are recorded in the data table for Day 1.

5. On Day 1, the **exerciser** and **checker** should perform the exercise bouts together and as the bout is completed, the checker should put the receiving watch next to the exercisers chest in order to get the heart rate.

6. On Day 2, the exercise bouts are done individually.

The RPE Scale.

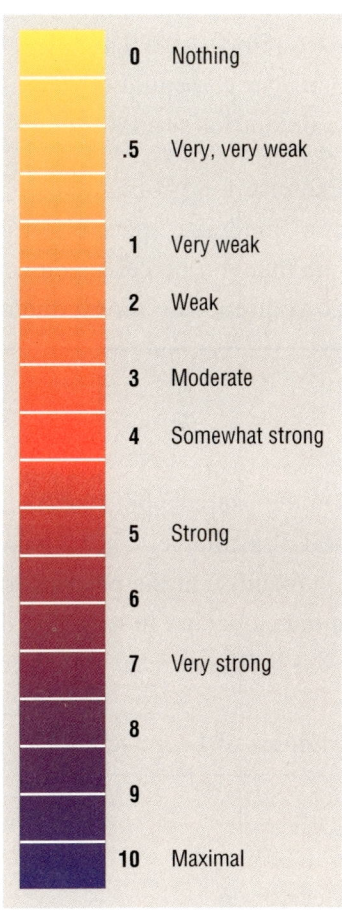

0	Nothing
.5	Very, very weak
1	Very weak
2	Weak
3	Moderate
4	Somewhat strong
5	Strong
6	
7	Very strong
8	
9	
10	Maximal

(Continued)

Day 1.

Do the exercise bouts listed in the table below on Day 1.

Exercise Bout	RPE from Exerciser	Heart Rate From Monitor
Pre-exercise RPE	_____	_____
Exercise for 3-4 minutes at an "easy" or "leisurely" pace/effort—one that you perceive you could easily maintain for several hours.	_____	_____
Exercise for 3-4 minutes at a "moderate" pace/effort— one that you perceive you could do continuously for 60 minutes.	_____	_____

Day 2.

Do the exercise bout in the table below on Day 2. On Day 2, the exercise bouts are done individually and, if available, a heart monitor is worn by each individual.

   Exercise at the pace/effort you used at the "moderate" level on Day 1. Exercise for a total of 30 minutes, trying to maintain the same pace/effort your used on Day 1 at the "moderate" level. Record your RPE and heart rate every 5 minutes during the exercise bout.

Minutes of Exercise ⇒	Pre-exercise	5 min	10 min	15 min	20 min	25 min	30 min
RPE	0	2.5	2	4	5	6	7
Heart Rate	52	95	126	153	164	176	185

(Continued)

Answer the following questions.

1. On Day 2, did your RPE and heart rate stay constant during the 30-min exercise bout or did they vary? Explain.

2. On the RPE Scale, certain percentage of maximal heart rates should approximately correspond to the RPE numbers. The correspondence between the RPE numbers and the percentage of maximal heart rate are given the table below. In the row labeled "**Your Heart Rate**" record your heart rate that corresponds to that same percentage of estimated maximum heart rate (based on 220-age) for you. For example, if you were 20 years old, your estimated maximal heart rate would be 220-20 = 200. Your heart rate corresponding to 40% of maximum would be 200 x 0.40 = 80. Your heart rate corresponding to 50% of maximum would be 200 x .50 = 100, and so on.

RPE Value ⇒	0	.5	1	2	3	4	5	6	7	8	9	10
%HRmax ⇒	Resting HR	40	45	50	60	70	80	85	90	95	100	100
Your Heart Rate ⇒	52	80	90	100	120	140	160	170	180	190	200	200

3. How did your RPE ratings and heart rates from the exercise on Day 2 compare to the RPE ratings and the heart rates in the table above? Explain.

Mine all compared pretty well.
They were all really close to matching up with the table

3
52
4 98
126
158
169
176
185
951

118
8/951
8
15
8
71

Notes

LAB 2.11

ESTIMATING VO₂MAX USING A STEP TEST

Name _____ ID _____ Sect _____ Time _____ Date _____

Purpose

1. To estimate VO₂max using a step test.

2. To compare your cardiorespiratory fitness to norms for a similar population.

3. Understand the error in estimating VO₂max with this type of test.

Directions

1. The test is performed on a bench that is approximately 16 inches high. Most gymnasium bleachers are approximately 16 inches high.

2. The stepping is easiest when performed to some type of cadence, like a cassette tape with the proper cadence on it. The stepping rate is 24 steps per minute for males and 22 steps per minute for females. The stepping sequence is "up with one foot, up with the other foot, down with the first foot, down with the second foot." If using a metronome, set the rate at 96 bpm for males and 88 bpm for females and change a foot position each beat.

3. Step for a total of 3 minutes.

4. At the end of 3 minutes, remain standing and take your pulse using one of the following methods:

   a. If using a heart monitor, take you heart rate off the monitor at 10 seconds after you have stopped stepping.

   b. If counting your pulse, start taking your pulse as soon as possible and count for 15 seconds. Multiply the pulse count by 4 to get a minute heart rate.

Fill in the following data: **Heart rate from heart monitor _____ bpm**

or

15-second pulse rate _____ × 4 = _____ bpm

To Compute VO₂max if MALE: $VO_2max = 111.3 - (heart\ rate \times 0.42)$

VO₂max = _____ ml·kg⁻¹·min⁻¹

To Compute VO₂max if FEMALE: $VO_2max = 65.8 - (heart\ rate \times 0.18)$

VO₂max = _____ ml·kg⁻¹·min⁻¹

(Continued)

ESTIMATING VO₂MAX USING A STEP TEST

Error: The SEE for this test is 8% of the estimated VO_2max. Therefore, you are 95% confident that your true VO_2max is between your estimated value and $\pm$ 16%. This is called the **95% Confidence Interval**.

Your **95% Confidence Interval** is _____ ml·kg⁻¹·min⁻¹ to _____ ml·kg⁻¹·min⁻¹.

Your **Fitness Classification** using Table 2.8 is _____ .

Your **Risk Classification** from Table 2.8 is _____ .

LAB 2.13

ESTIMATING VO₂MAX USING A JOG TEST

Name _____ ID _____ Sect _____ Time _____ Date _____

Purposes

1. To estimate VO_2max using a jog test.

2. To compare your cardiorespiratory fitness to norms for a similar population.

3. Understand the error in estimating VO_2max with this type of test.

Directions

1. The test is performed over a flat 1-mile distance. The use of an indoor or outdoor track is ideal.

2. The objective is to jog one mile at a comfortable and even pace. The pace should be comfortable, constant and sustainable for the entire mile. **Males should not jog any faster than an 8-min mile and females should not jog any faster than a 9-min mile**.

3. The 1-mile jog must be timed and a heart rate at the finish of the mile must be obtained. If using a heart monitor, determine the heart rate within 10 seconds of finishing the jog. If taking a pulse to get the heart rate, take a 15-second pulse immediately upon completing the jog.

Record the following: Time to complete the mile: _____ min _____ sec   Heart rate: _____

Time to complete the mile: _____ minutes*   Age: _____

* You must convert the time for the mile walk into minutes and fractions of minutes by dividing the seconds by 60. For example 13 min 45 sec would convert into 13 min and 45/60 sec or 13.75 minutes.

Compute Your VO₂max:

Multiply your weight (lb) × 0.074   _____ lb × 0.074 = _____

Multiply your mile time × 1.44   _____ min × 1.44 = _____

Multiply your heart rate × 0.19   _____ bpm × 0.19 = _____

Add all the above to get SUM   SUM = _____

(Continued)

ESTIMATING VO₂MAX USING A JOG TEST

If FEMALE: $VO_2max = 100.5 - SUM =$ _____ $ml \cdot kg^{-1} \cdot min^{-1}$

If MALE: $VO_2max = 108.8 - SUM =$ _____ $ml \cdot kg^{-1} \cdot min^{-1}$

The SEE for this test is 3 $ml \cdot kg^{-1} \cdot min^{-1}$. Therefore, you are 95% confident that your estimated VO_2max is between your computed value ± 6 $ml \cdot kg^{-1} \cdot min^{-1}$. This is called the **95% Confidence Interval**.

Your **95% Confidence Interval** for $VO_2max =$ _____ to _____ $ml \cdot kg^{-1} \cdot min^{-1}$.

Your **Fitness Classification** from Table 2.8 is _____.

Your **Risk Classification** from Table 2.8 is _____.

NOTES

Musculoskeletal Function

FORREST DOLGENER

CHAPTER OBJECTIVES

◆ Understand the relationship between musculoskeletal function and health.

◆ Be able to develop a program to enhance muscular strength, muscular endurance, and flexibility to meet individual needs.

◆ Be able to identify specific exercises for preventing and rehabilitating low-back problems.

◆ Understand differences between genders with respect to muscular strength, muscular endurance, and flexibility.

KEY TERMS

circuit weight training

concentric contraction

eccentric contraction

HDL Cholesterol

hyperplasia

hypertrophy

isometric contraction

isotonic contraction

muscular strength

muscular endurance

osteoporosis

PNF stretching

progressive resistance

repetition maximum

set

skeletal muscle

testosterone

valsalva

INTRODUCTION

Muscular strength, muscular endurance and flexibility are important and often neglected components of total fitness. Not only are they important for athletes and others engaged in sport activities on a regular basis, they are also important for the average office worker, housewife, teacher and student. Adequate muscular strength and endurance are important in carrying out many day-to-day tasks like walking, climbing stairs, lifting and carrying objects, and doing housework. Higher levels of strength, endurance and flexibility may be required for specific occupations such as being a firefighter or police officer, working in construction, or being a farmer. Possessing adequate muscular strength and endurance can also be an important factor in how a person feels about himself or herself.

From a health perspective, muscular strength, muscular endurance and flexibility are directly related to low-back problems, the number one cause of disability and loss of work time in this country.[5, 8] One of the major problems faced by older individuals is the loss of mobility due to poor strength and flexibility. As we get older and become progressively more inactive, muscular strength and flexibility start declining. Over a period of 30 years, say from age 30 to 60, it would not be unusual to loose 50% of your strength if you are not physically active. Maintaining good strength and flexibility will make it easier to do simple tasks of daily living, not to mention recreational and occupational activities.

Developing and maintaining adequate muscular strength, endurance and flexibility, like everything else that is beneficial, requires some effort on your part. It doesn't just happen. You have to be willing to work for it. Exercising on a regular basis with a well-rounded program will produce many health benefits in addition to enhanced muscular strength, muscular endurance, and flexibility. As a result of a well-rounded fitness program, you will look better, feel better, and be more healthy. It is your choice, and no one else can make the choice or perform the necessary exercise for you.

In this chapter, the concepts of muscular strength, muscular endurance, and flexibility will be introduced. The types of exercise programs necessary to adequately develop these components will be discussed as well as the benefits of maintaining adequate levels of strength, endurance and flexibility. Methods of evaluating these components will be identified.

MUSCULAR STRENGTH AND ENDURANCE

Muscular strength and endurance are two components of both health-related fitness and performance-related fitness. In athletics, muscular strength and endurance are critical for optimal performance. For the average person, muscular strength and endurance are important for being able to participate in many recreational activities, and for some, occupational activities. For all of us, muscular strength and endurance will be major contributors to our quality of life as we age, not only from the standpoint of being able to do the types of activities we want to do, but by decreasing the risk of several chronic diseases.

Muscular strength is defined as the ability of muscle to develop maximal force one time. Muscular endurance is defined as the ability of a muscle to repeatedly develop submaximal forces or to sustain a submaximal force. Muscular strength is exemplified by the maximal weight that can be lifted one time while muscular endurance is exemplified by the number of repetitions performed when lifting a weight that is less than maximal. However, as will be discussed in a later section, in the practical world muscular strength and endurance interact so often that it is hard to functionally separate them.

Before discussing muscular strength and endurance in more detail, a brief discussion of muscle in general will help reinforce some of the principles of developing muscular strength and endurance.

Types of Muscle

There are three types of muscle in the body: **smooth muscle, cardiac muscle, and skeletal muscle**. Smooth muscle is found in blood vessels and other organs, especially in the gastrointestinal system, and functions to produce many of the involuntary functions like passage of food through the GI tract and decreasing the size of blood vessels. Cardiac muscle is the type of muscle in the heart and its function is to pump blood. Most of the function of cardiac muscle, like that of smooth muscle, is not under our conscious control but occurs automatically.

Although all three types of muscle have many structural similarities, skeletal muscle has several major functional differences. Skeletal muscles attach to the bones and when muscles contract movement is produced (Figure 3.1). Without skeletal muscle, you would not be able to walk, run, jump, or move about in any manner. The critical function of our skeletal muscles in producing movement can be exemplified by the inability of paralyzed individuals to move about. Almost all of the functions of skeletal muscle are normally under our conscious control and we can voluntarily cause muscle to contract or relax.

There are over 600 skeletal muscles in the body ranging in size from muscles that are difficult to see with the naked eye to the large superficial muscles located throughout the body. Most of these muscles are in pairs, one on each side of the body. Figures 3.2 and 3.3 are diagrams of the superficial skeletal muscles of the body and Table 3.1 identifies the primary movements produced by each muscle and exercises to develop each muscle.

FIGURE 3.1

Muscles attached to bones provide the mechanism for movement.

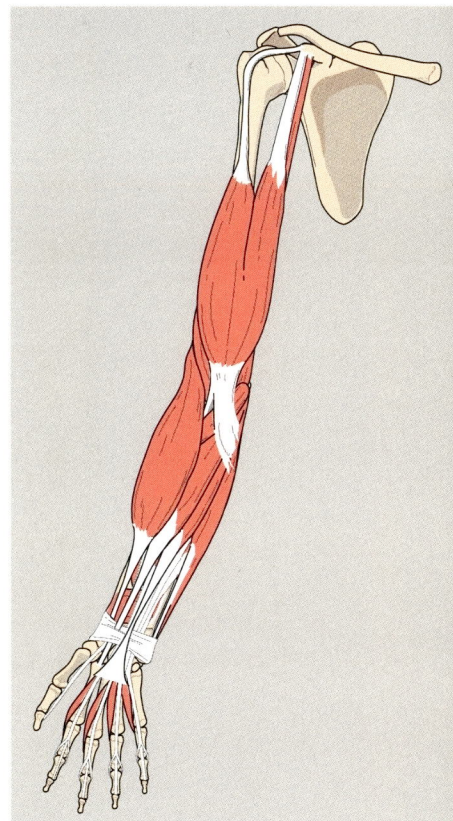

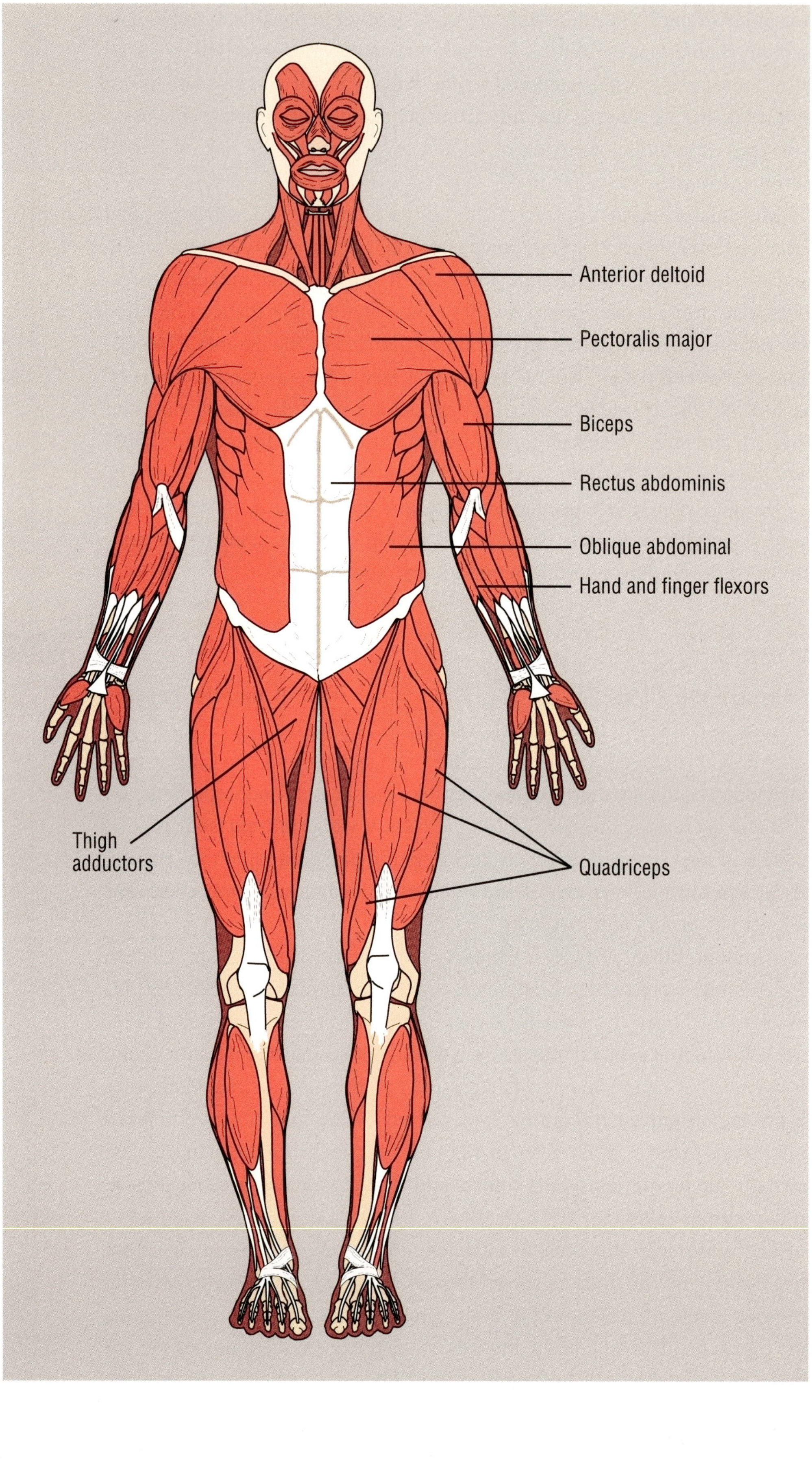

FIGURE 3.2

The superficial skeletal muscles, front view.

Anterior deltoid

Pectoralis major

Biceps

Rectus abdominis

Oblique abdominal

Hand and finger flexors

Thigh adductors

Quadriceps

FIGURE 3.3

The superficial skeletal muscles, back view.

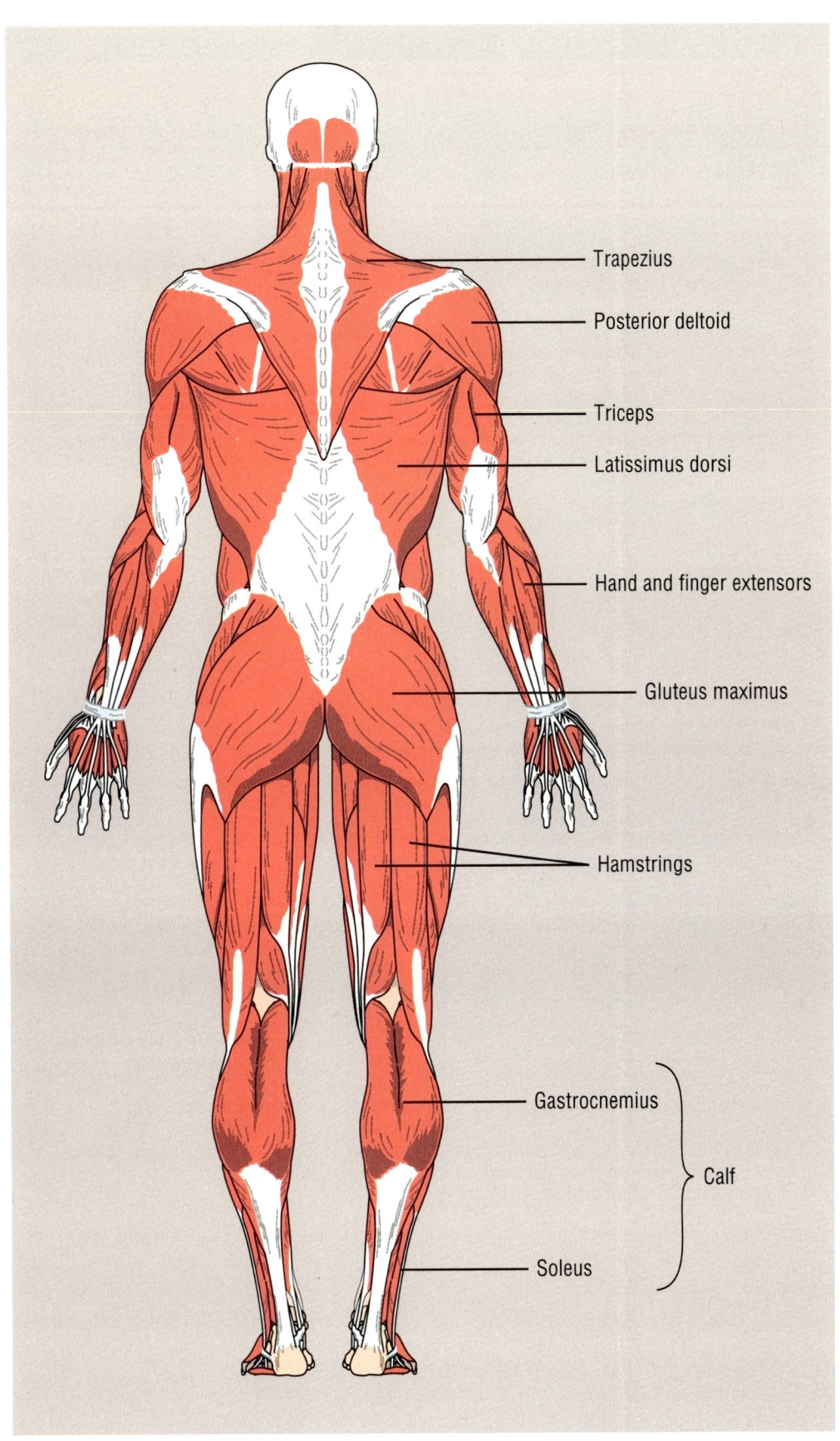

Trapezius

Posterior deltoid

Triceps

Latissimus dorsi

Hand and finger extensors

Gluteus maximus

Hamstrings

Gastrocnemius

Calf

Soleus

TABLE 3.1
Major Superficial Muscles, Movements, and Exercises

Muscle	Primary Movement Produced	Exercise to Develop
Biceps	Bends (flexes) the forearm at the elbow joint.	Biceps curls
Triceps	Straightens (extends) the forearm at the elbow joint.	Triceps extensions
Pectoralis Major	When the upper arm is at the side, it moves the upper arm towards the front of the body (flexion), as in a pushing-type motion.	Bench press, push-ups
Deltoid	The deltoid can act as one muscle or as three separate muscles. If the entire muscle contracts, it moves the arm away from the side (abduction). If just the front portion of the muscle contracts, it performs the same movement as the pectoralis major (arm flexion). If just the back portion of the muscle contracts, it pulls the upper arm back down from a flexed position (extension), as in a pulling-type motion.	Arm abductions with dumbbells. Bench press for the anterior deltoid. Pull-ups or lat exercises for the posterior deltoid.
Latissimus Dorsi	When the upper arm is extended above the shoulder, the latissimus dorsi pulls the upper arm back down (extension) as in doing a pull-up.	Pull-ups; any pulling type motion, in particular with the upper arm initially extended above the head.
Trapezius	Raises the tip of the shoulders (elevation).	Shoulder shrugs with barbell or dumbbells.
Forearm Flexors	This group of muscles, located on the inside of the forearm, aids in flexing the forearm at the elbow and in bending the palm of the hand and fingers into a fist (flexion of hand and fingers).	Any exercise requiring a hard grip, biceps curls, and wrist curls.
Forearm Extensors	This group of muscles, located on the outside of the forearm, extends the hand and fingers and aids in extending the forearm.	Reverse forearm curls and reverse wrist curls
Rectus Abdominis	Bends the trunk forward (flexion) at the hip and bends the vertebral column forward (flexion).	Curl-ups, sit-ups
Oblique Abdominal	Rotates the trunk or causes side-ways bending of the trunk.	Curl-ups or sit-ups with a trunk rotation at the end. Sideward trunk-bending with dumbbells
Erector Spinae	Extends the trunk. Helps maintain upright posture.	Back extension
Gluteus Maximus	When the thigh is raised straight out in front of the body, the gluteus maximus pulls the thigh back down (extension), as in stepping up on a bench or step.	Stair climbing, squats
Hamstrings	Same movement as the gluteus maximus plus bending the lower leg at the knee (flexion).	Hamstring curls, squats
Quadriceps	Moves the thigh to a horizontal position in front of the body; straightens the lower leg (extension).	Lower leg extensions, squats
Gastrocnemius and Soleus	Raises the heel off the ground (plantar flexion) as in raising up on the balls of the feet.	Heel/Toe raises

Types of Muscle Contraction

The primary function of skeletal muscle is to develop tension or to "contract." Although most people interpret the term "contraction" to imply that the muscle shortens, this is not always the case. The term "tension development" is a better term to describe the function of muscle because the muscle can either lengthen or shorten while developing tension.

Muscle contraction is generally classified as either **isometric or isotonic**. An isometric contraction (Figure 3.4) is one during which the muscle develops tension but does not lengthen or shorten. It stays at the same length. This is because the resistance you are attempting to lift or move is too great. An example would be trying to lift a weight that is heavier than you can lift. You can strain and grimace, and the muscles develop tension, but no movement occurs. Isometric contractions are used in various situations involved in sports and general movements, but are used most often in maintaining a posture like sitting and standing.

The majority of the time that movement occurs in sports and everyday tasks, the skeletal muscles are contracting isotonically (Figure 3.5). Most movements results from repetitive isotonic contractions and relaxations of skeletal muscle. In an isotonic contraction the muscle changes length. It either shortens or lengthens. If the muscle shortens, it is termed a **concentric isotonic contraction.** If the muscle lengthens, it is termed an **eccentric isotonic contraction.** It is probably easy to relate to a concentric isotonic contraction because this is what most of us think of when thinking of muscle contraction.

An eccentric isotonic contraction is a bit more difficult to understand but an example will help clarify the concept. Think about doing a push-up. When you start in the down position with your chest next to the floor and then push up, the muscles in the chest and back of the arms are shortening and thereby moving the arms so that you are able to push up. During this portion of the movement, the muscles are doing a concentric isotonic contraction. Now, from the up position, you slowly lower your body to the down position. During this movement, the same muscles that allowed you to push up are now lowering you down by eccentrically contracting. The muscles are resisting the force of gravity trying to push you down, but you are letting gravity win. As a result, you lower yourself slowly and under control.

Another way to distinguish between the two types of contractions is anytime you move a weight or your body against gravity the muscles responsible for that movement are doing concentric isotonic contractions. Anytime you resist the effect of gravity by slowing down the rate at which gravity accelerates an object, including your body, the muscles are doing eccentric isotonic contractions. In weight training, the concentric part of the lift occurs when you move the weight away from the floor and the eccentric contraction occurs when the weight is returned to the starting position of the lift.

FIGURE 3.4

During an isometric contraction, the muscles produce force but no movement occurs.

FIGURE 3.5

During an isotonic contraction, the muscles shorten and lengthen and produce movement.

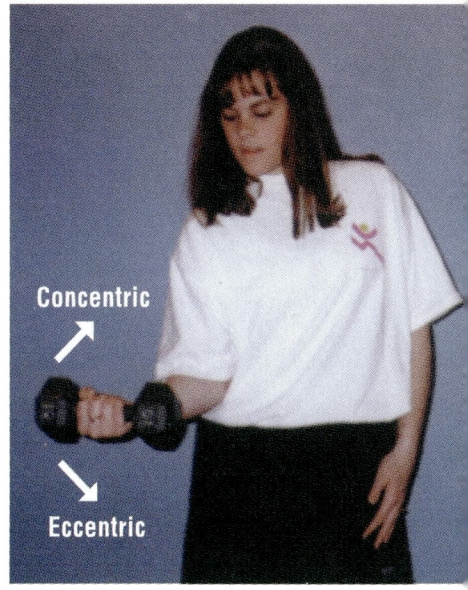

BENEFITS OF RESISTANCE EXERCISE

The type of exercise which results in increases in muscular strength and endurance is called **resistance exercise** because some type of resistance, usually a weight, is lifted, pushed or pulled. There are numerous beneficial changes that result from regular resistance exercise. Some are changes that will improve physical performance in athletic and sport endeavors while others change the way we look. Still other changes improve our health and should be of greatest concern as we get older.

The most obvious benefit of resistance exercise is that it increases muscular strength and endurance. Acquiring and maintaining adequate levels of muscular strength and endurance will enable you to do all the things you need to do throughout the day which are dependent on muscular contraction. When you think about it, just about everything you do requires some level of muscular contraction. No matter how much muscular strength your recreational or occupational activities require, the more strength and endurance you have, the less will be the relative strain on your body, resulting in less fatigue throughout the day.

As we age, our muscular strength and endurance decreases. It is not unusual to loose 50% or more of your strength by the time you are 60 years old. This dramatic decline in strength contributes to may of the problems older individuals experience in performing the tasks of daily living, not to mention more vigorous activities. The increase incidence of injuries resulting from falls can be attributed, in part, to a decrease in muscular strength which decreases stability.

Fortunately, much of the decline in muscular strength seen with aging can be prevented or reversed by maintaining an active lifestyle which includes resistance exercises. Not only will resistance exercise maintain good levels of muscular strength and endurance, but several chronic diseases can be positively impacted.

Low-back problems are a serious medical concern in this country. A major contributing cause of low-back problems is poor muscular strength of the abdominal and spinal muscles that support good posture.[14, 20] In addition, when your stoop, bend, and lift, the stronger the muscles, the less likely injury will result. Good muscular strength combined with good flexibility and lifting mechanics will reduce your chances of having low-back problems. Specific exercises for developing and maintaining good back health will be discussed in a later section of this chapter.

Osteoporosis, a condition in which the mineral content of the bone is reduced and the bones become weak and brittle, is often considered a disease of the elderly. However, part of the cause of osteoporosis is poor bone development during the first three decades of life. Because resistance training increases the forces on the bones, it improves bone development and helps maintain adequate bone mineral in the later decades when everyone starts to lose some bone mineral.[4]

There has been a lot of media coverage lately concerning cholesterol. High cholesterol is recognized as a major risk factor for coronary heart disease, the number one killer in this country. Strength training has been shown to increase the level of the good cholesterol, called **high density or HDL cholesterol**. Higher levels of HDL cholesterol will lower the risk for coronary heart disease and improve the overall health status of the individual.

Because we typically become less active as we get older, our muscle mass declines. The declining muscle mass not only explains most of the loss in strength that occurs, but is also one reason we usually get fatter as we get older. Because the amount of muscle we have is the major determinant of how much energy we expend throughout the day, as muscle mass decreases so does energy expenditure. The end result of the decrease in muscle mass is an increase in fat mass and an increase likelihood of developing obesity and all the health problems that go along with it.

The Physiological Nature of Muscular Strength

One of the most consistent changes that results from resistance exercise is an increase in muscular strength. As indicated previously, muscular strength is the ability of muscle to develop maximal tension one time. An example of muscular strength would be the greatest weight you could lift one time in a particular weight lifting exercise, such as the bench press. As the muscles increase their ability to develop maximal tension, they get bigger in the process. Since many sport skills and performances are directly related to muscular strength, increasing strength is likely to improve athletic performance.

In order to understand how a muscle increases strength, the basic microscopic anatomy of muscle needs to be briefly discussed. If you were to take a muscle like the biceps and cross-section it and look inside the muscle, you would find that the muscle is composed of a large number of small structures called muscle cells or muscle fibers (Figure 3.6). When the muscle fibers are wrapped in a clump with connective tissue, you have a gross muscle like the biceps. The process of developing tension actually occurs in each of the muscle fibers individually. Not all the muscle fibers develop tension at one time but only enough contract at once to produce the amount of force necessary to carry out the desired task.

Two mechanisms are responsible for increased strength. The first is an improved ability to use the muscle fibers already present.[9, 15] Before skeletal muscle can develop tension, a signal must first be sent from the nervous system to the muscle. The nervous signal stimulates the muscle fibers and sets into motion a series of events that concludes with the muscle fibers

FIGURE 3.6

Skeletal muscles are composed of hundreds of muscle fibers which are responsible for producing tension.

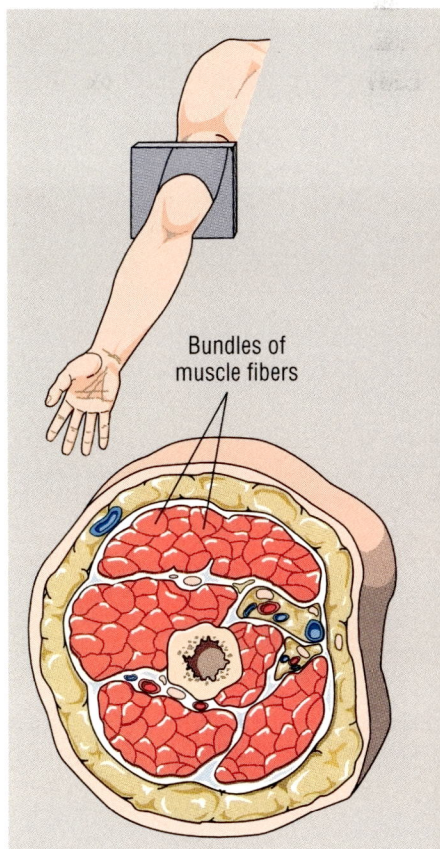

Bundles of muscle fibers

developing tension. If you do not send appropriate signals from the nervous system to develop high levels of tension on a regular basis, you never learn how to activate all the muscle fibers you have. You only learn to activate as many of the muscle fibers as you need. During the early phases of strength training, when you are exposing the muscle to higher levels of tension development, your nervous system learns to better stimulate the muscle fibers. This "learning" by the nervous system results in maximal use of the muscle tissue already present and functionally increases the strength without increasing the size of the muscle.

This increased ability to use existing muscle tissue can be a very desirable result, especially for females. There has traditionally been an aversion on the part of females to do resistance training for fear of developing large muscles. But, because improved strength is very advantageous and can be accomplished without significant muscle size increase, there is no legitimate reason females should not participate in resistance exercises.

The second mechanism by which the muscle increases strength is by increasing size.[12] When the muscle is required to develop more tension than it is normally used to, and after the nervous system has learned how to maximally stimulate the muscle fibers present, the muscle fibers begin to get bigger in diameter, a phenomena called **hypertrophy**. The increase in size is primarily due to the increase of the two proteins (actin and myosin)

KEY CONCEPT

MUSCLE HYPERTROPHY, GENETICS, AND GENDER

Just about everyone could increase their muscle size some by doing appropriate resistance training and consuming an adequate diet. However, everyone has an upper limit for muscle size increase. The two major factors that determine the upper limit are genetics and gender. Females have a much smaller capacity to increase muscle size than males due to the influence of the respective sex hormones. The male sex hormone testosterone promotes muscle mass increase and the female sex hormones promote fat mass increase. Although females produce some testosterone (about one-tenth of males' production), the levels in the average female are not sufficient to produce large muscles. However some females have larger quantities of testosterone (which may be a genetic factor) and can increase muscle size considerably.

Given that one has sufficient testosterone, genetics then limits the potential for muscle hypertrophy in both males and females. Some males have a tremendous capacity for muscle hypertrophy and the difference in muscle size potential between males appears to be highly related to their genetic limit.

Most individuals do not ever reach their genetic potential because they never train long enough or hard enough. If a person were to train optimally with resistance training, it appears to take as long as a decade or more to reach genetic potential.

responsible for the tension development process. How big the muscle will eventually get depends on how much and how often the muscle is used and on genetics. Some individuals have a much greater genetic capacity to increase muscle size than others. In general, males have a greater capacity to increase muscle size than do females.

There has been an ongoing controversy as to whether or not the muscle also gets bigger by increasing the number of muscle fibers, a process called **hyperplasia.** There is some evidence that the number of muscle fibers may increase due to strenuous and long term resistance training.[10] However, if muscle fibers do increase in number, this contributes little to the overall size increase in muscle in the normal individual. The vast majority of the size increase is due to the muscle fibers getting bigger.

The Physiological Nature of Muscular Endurance

A second type of training effect that occurs with resistance training is an increase in muscular endurance. As previously indicated, muscular endurance is the ability of the muscle to repeat submaximal levels of tension or to sustain submaximal levels of isometric strength. Many of the activities in sports and manual occupations require the repetition of movements. These movements usually require less than maximal tension development, but they may require the tension development process to be repeated many times throughout the course of a competition or work day.

Running is a good example of an activity that requires repeated tension development of the muscles. In running, the amount of tension developed in the muscles is fairly low compared to the maximal ability of the muscle, but the muscles have to contract repeatedly. During a 5-mile run, the muscles may have to contract and relax over 8000 times in a rhythmical fashion.

Another example of muscular endurance is maintaining the upright posture throughout the day. Whenever you stand, muscles in your back and abdomen are contracting at a low percentage of their maximal strength level but they may have to contract for hours. Good muscular endurance makes it easier for you to maintain a standing posture without getting fatigued.

In addition to being partly due to an increase in strength, increased muscular endurance is due to an improved ability to deliver oxygen to the muscle and for the muscle fiber to be able to use the oxygen to make ATP. The changes that occur in the muscle are changes that promote better delivery and use of oxygen by the muscle similar to the changes that occur in response to aerobic training. The easier it is to get oxygen and nutrients to the muscles, the easier the muscle can make ATP for the contraction process.

There are two major changes accounting for the increased ability to get oxygen to the muscle. First, there is an increase in the number of vessels (capillaries) supplying a muscle.[17, 21] This decreases the distance oxygen has to travel to reach the muscle fiber. The second change is an increase in the size and number of mitochondria in the muscle cell.[19] Since the mitochondria is where aerobic energy production occurs, more and larger mitochondria improves aerobic metabolism.

Interaction of Muscular Strength and Endurance

Muscular strength and muscular endurance are not totally separate and unrelated components. If absolute muscular strength is increased, muscular endurance will also improve. If a muscle is stronger, any level of absolute tension development below the maximal level will require a lower percentage of the maximal ability of the muscle. For example, let's say you can bench press a maximum of 150 lb one time. This would be a measure of your strength. Now take 50% of the 150 lb (i.e. 75 lb) and do as many repetitions of the bench press as possible. Let's say you could do 10 repetitions. This is a measure of muscular endurance. Now, you train and increase your strength so you are able to bench press 200 lb one time. You now attempt to do as many repetitions as possible with 75 lb (remember you did 10 repetitions before). This time you do 15 repetitions. Your muscular endurance at the same absolute level of resistance has improved about 33%. Although muscular strength and endurance are related, the type of training program necessary to develop each component optimally is different. These specific training programs will be discussed later in this chapter.

RESISTANCE TRAINING PRINCIPLES

In many ways, resistance training is similar to training the cardiorespiratory system. The same basic principles of progressive overload and specificity also apply to resistance training. By following these basic principles, you can develop adequate muscular strength and endurance which will contribute to a healthier life and make it easier to do the things you enjoy doing.

Overload Principle

Just as was true for cardiorespiratory endurance, the fundamental principle used in resistance training, whether for strength or endurance, is the overload principle. The overload principle applied to resistance training simply says that in order for a muscle to increase its capacity to develop tension, it must be worked harder than it is used to working. If an overload is regularly applied, the muscle will adapt and increase its strength and/or endurance. In resistance training, the principle of progressive resistance is used to maintain an overload on the muscle.

OVERLOADING IN RESISTANCE TRAINING

Changing the overload in resistance training can be accomplished by altering several factors. The factor most often altered is the resistance lifted. By increasing or decreasing the resistance, all other factors held constant, the overload is changed.

Another factor that can be altered to change the overload is the number of sets and reps performed. You can think of the total overload as being equivalent to the total amount of weight lifted in an exercise session. If you increase either the number of reps in a set or the number of sets in a session, without changing the resistance, then the overload is changed.

The third factor that can be altered to change the overload is the speed at which the resistance is moved during a repetition. By increasing or decreasing the speed of movement, without changing the resistance, the overload is changed.

It is probably a good idea to use a combination of all three methods to change the overload throughout the training year. It has been found that muscle responds better to variety than to doing the same thing all the time.

Progressive Resistance Principle

The progressive resistance principle is an extension of the overload principle and says that in order to continue to improve muscular strength and endurance, you must periodically increase the resistance you lift in order to maintain an overload. This is necessary because as the muscle gets stronger, the amount of weight that was once a sufficient overload is no longer an overload. The idea is to keep applying an overload over a prolonged period of time and as the muscle continues to adapt, the overload should be increased.

For example, if you are using a program in which you are lifting a weight 8-12 times, the principles of overload and progressive resistance dictates that when you could do 13 or more reps, the resistance should be increased enough to reduce the number of times you can lift the weight back to 8 times. If the principle of progressive resistance is applied over a long period of time, the muscles will continue to adapt and become stronger.

Unfortunately, this adaptation process will not continue forever. Eventually, if you work hard enough, you will reach a plateau and no further increases will occur. Exactly when this plateau will occur is variable and depends on factors such as genetics, nutrition, and the intensity and duration of workouts. In most individuals, this plateau will occur after several years of intensive and prolonged training. Fortunately, the health benefits of resistance training occur a long time before the plateau is reached so, unless you are a competitive lifter or bodybuilder, you will not have to worry about reaching a plateau.

Specificity Principle

A third important principle is the specificity principle that states the effects of resistance training are specific to the muscles trained. Another way of stating it is to say that to strengthen a particular muscle or muscle group, you must do exercises that overload that muscle or muscle group. There is no single exercise you can do to simultaneously strengthen all the muscles of the body. Many different exercises must be done.

The specificity principle can also be applied to developing either muscular strength or muscular endurance. In order to develop optimal strength, a program specifically designed to improve strength must be used. To develop optimal muscular endurance, a specific program designed to improve muscular endurance must be used. There is not a single program that will optimally develop both muscular strength and endurance simultaneously. As discussed in a later section, most people will benefit from a hybrid program that develops both adequate, but not optimal, muscular strength and endurance.

DESIGNING RESISTANCE TRAINING PROGRAMS

The type of program that will be most beneficial for developing muscular strength or endurance will depend on your specific objectives. As mentioned in the preceding section, muscular strength and muscular endurance are optimally developed with different types of programs. In order to understand program design and prescription, three key terms must be defined.

Repetition (Rep)

A repetition or rep is one full range of movement of a particular exercise. If you do a movement 10 times without stopping, you have done 10 reps of that movement.

Repetition Max (RM)

A repetition max or RM is the performance of continuous repetitions such that the final repetition is the last that could have been completed. In other words, you do the repetitions until you cannot do any more. For example, if you can do 10 repetitions of a bench press with 150 pounds but you could not do the 11th repetition, then you have done 10 RM with 150 pounds. In this example, the 150 pounds is a 10 RM weight in the bench press.

Set

A set is a continuous number of repetitions performed without rest or recovery. If you perform 10 reps of an exercise, one rep after the other with no rest in between, you will have done 1 set of 10 reps. If, after a couple of minutes of rest you perform 10 more reps without rest in between, you will have done a second set of 10 reps.

Program Variables for Developing Muscular Strength

Similar to other programs for developing components of fitness, the components of intensity, duration, and frequency must be considered when developing resistance programs. These variables can be manipulated to increase the training load in many different ways and the specific program that will be best for you may be different than what is best for someone else. Part of program design is trial and error but there are some basic principles that can be used to lay a solid foundation for a fundamentally sound program.

Intensity

In strength programs, intensity is a function of the amount of weight lifted and the number of reps and sets performed. If developing muscular strength is the primary objective, a program consisting primarily of low numbers of repetitions and high resistance should be used. It has been scientifically determined that using a resistance that you can do only 4-7 RM with will optimally increase strength.[1,7] It has also been determined that strength continues to increase the more sets you do up to a maximum of about eight. Therefore, optimal strength increases should result from resistance training consisting of 3-8 sets of 4-7 RM.

Even though strength may continue to improve by doing as many as 8 sets, most of the improvement occurs during the first 3 sets. The last 5 of the 8 sets only results in a small percentage of improvement. This means that, unless the objective is to get as much improvement as possible, doing 3 sets will produce the majority of the improvement at less than half the time and effort. It is recommended that 3 sets be done for a general conditioning program.

Frequency

The frequency of training should be 3 days per week with at least 1 day of recovery between training sessions.[1,7] This is especially important for novice resistance exercisers. The muscles need a day of recovery in order to adapt to the overload. The every-other-day type of training can be accomplished by training Monday, Wednesday, and Friday and resting on the other days or by training Tuesday, Thursday, and Saturday with rest on the other days. When using this type of every-other-day training, exercises for each muscle group you wish to train should be performed each training day.

Duration

The duration of a training session will be determined by the total numbers of sets and reps performed and the number of muscle groups exercised. The more muscle groups you attempt to exercise, the longer it will take. Doing exercises that work several muscle groups at one time will save time but will not be as specific as doing exercises that work more specific muscle groups. The duration will also depend on the type of equipment you use. Using free weights is the most time consuming while weight machines can significantly reduce the time spent. With all things considered, a person would normally spend between 30-60 minutes for a well-rounded strength workout although athletes and bodybuilders may spend several hours in a workout.

Recovery

If developing muscular strength is the primary objective of a program, then the recovery time between sets should be 3-5 minutes. It takes 3-5 minutes for the energy systems used to do the training to fully recover. If the energy systems do not fully recover with each successive set, then the ability of the muscle to exert tension will be compromised and the overload will be reduced. Also, real heavy and/or explosive resistance training fatigues the nervous system and the nervous system takes about 5 minutes to recover.

Program Variables for Developing Muscular Endurance

Although muscular strength and endurance are both used in most exercise situations, they are optimally developed using very different programs. Whereas the focus of strength programs is on using high resistance, the focus of muscular endurance programs is on using high repetitions.

Intensity

If developing muscular endurance is the primary objective, a program consisting of higher numbers of repetitions and lower resistance should be used.[1] It has been much more difficult to identify a optimal number of repetitions and sets for developing muscular endurance than for muscular strength. Much of this difficulty results from the almost infinite different combinations of sets and reps. It is appropriate to treat the relationship between strength and endurance as a continuum, rather than as having discrete break points. Using this concept, as you begin to use lighter weights and do more reps, you move away from optimal strength development and begin to develop more endurance. The specific number of sets and reps performed will depend on what your primary objective is and how much time you have to spend.

Frequency

The frequency for training muscular endurance should initially follow the same pattern as for training muscular strength, either M-W-F or T-Th-S. However, as the muscles adapt to the training over time and if the reps exceed 20, the frequency of training can be increased to four or five times per week. This is possible because the resistances used are not as stressful to the muscles compared to doing primarily strength exercises. In fact, as the number of repetitions are increased, the exercise becomes more like an aerobic exercise.

Duration

The duration will depend on the numbers of sets, reps, and muscle groups exercised. Because muscular endurance programs consists of more sets and reps than muscular strength programs, the time involvement is usually greater.

Recovery

When attempting to primarily develop muscular endurance, the recovery time should be shortened to about 1-2 minutes. These shorter recovery periods combined with performing higher numbers of repetitions produces greater lactate accumulation in the muscle and forces the muscle to adapt to handling the lactate more efficiently. Part of this adaptation are changes that enhance muscular endurance.

IS THERE AN OPTIMAL PROGRAM FOR GENERAL MUSCULAR FITNESS?

Unless you are training for some specific type of competitive event or sport, most would be best served by a program that promotes both good muscular strength and endurance, rather than one that would optimize either component. Such a "compromise" program would provide good general muscular fitness and confer the many health benefits discussed earlier in this chapter. Figure 3.7 depicts the relationship between programs for

FIGURE 3.7

Muscular strength and muscular endurance are developed with different programs. The progression of strength to endurance is along a continuum. The recommended combination for general muscular fitness is in the area of the rectangle.

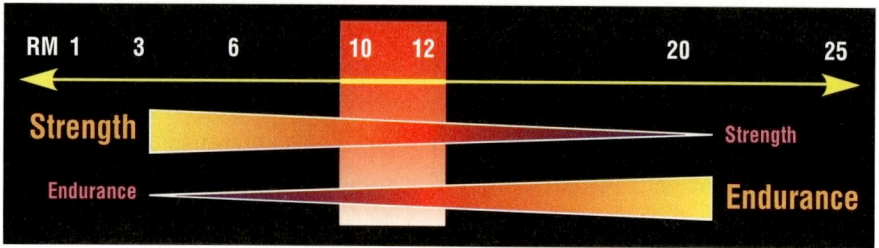

KEY CONCEPT

HOW TO DEVELOP LARGE MUSCLES

In order to develop large muscles like bodybuilders, you have to have the right combination of program, nutrition, and genetics. You can't do anything about the genetics, but you can maximize the influence of the program and nutrition.

The best type of program for developing muscle hypertrophy primarily focuses on doing a large volume of training. This means lifting a lot of total poundage. Bodybuilders usually utilize between 8-12 RM and perform 6-8 sets for each exercise. This combination increases the total volume of training and appears to be the primary stimulus for muscle hypertrophy.

Regardless of the type of training performed, there has to be adequate nutrition in order to increase muscle size. There has to be an adequate protein intake since a primary function of protein is to support tissue growth. The maximal amount of protein required for even the most strenuous program is about 1 gm of protein per pound of body weight. Many individuals consume close to this amount in their normal diet so a protein increase may not even be necessary. The often neglected aspect of nutrition for muscle hypertrophy is an adequate carbohydrate intake. Carbohydrates are the fuel that is used to support the muscular activity. As was discussed in Chapter 6, >55 % of the diet of an active individual should be from carbohydrates.

developing muscular strength and muscular endurance. As the diagram depicts, the strength-endurance relationship is really a continuum that extends from 1 RM to 25 RM or even more than 25 RM. Theoretically, the arrow in the direction of increasing muscular endurance could go indefinitely. As in the example used earlier, running several miles would be an example of extending the endurance end of the continuum far to the right.

A good "compromise" program for developing muscular strength and muscular endurance should consist of 3 sets of 10-12 RM and would take between 30-60 minutes depending on the type of equipment used. Training frequency should be either M-W-F or T-Th-S with a day of rest between each training session. This will provide for optimal recovery and adaptation to the training program. Unless a person had a specific reason to move toward greater strength or greater muscular endurance, this type of program would suffice for a lifetime of conditioning.

Advanced Programs

When the objective is to improve performance in competitive athletics, maximizing muscular strength should be a priority. It is beyond the scope of this text to discuss programs for maximizing muscular strength but it should be noted, that like in every other area of training, there is no one best program. There are almost as many advanced programs as there are athletic teams using them. But, even the advanced programs rely on the same basic principles of overload, progressive resistance and specificity. Table 3.2 lists some advanced programs of resistance training commonly used by athletes.

As discussed in Chapter 2, the closer you get to your maximum potential in any area, the harder it is to continue to improve. This principle is certainly true of resistance training and is the reason athletes have to work so hard to continue to get stronger and bigger. It should be of considerable comfort that the health benefits of resistance training accrue from far less effort than is necessary to maximize muscular strength and endurance.

TABLE 3.2	
Advanced Resistance Programs	
Program	**Description**
Multiple Set	A minimum of 3 sets and a maximum of 8 sets are performed for all exercises. The resistance used varies according to the specific objectives of the program.
Light-to-Heavy	Sets progress from light to heavy resistance. Initial sets use resistances that can be lifted for 10-12 reps and the resistance is progressively increased toward resistances that can be lifted for only 3-4 reps.
Heavy-to-Light	This program reverses the order of the light-to-heavy program. However, before starting the heavy resistance lifts, be sure and warm-up appropriately.
Triangle Program	This program is a combination of the light-to-heavy followed by the heavy-to-light program. In order not to double the number of sets required, bigger jumps in reps are used in each set.
Super Set	Super sets generally use 8-10 RM and utilize several exercises for the same muscle with little or not rest between sets. The idea is to overload the muscle(s) with different lifts in order to maximize the total overload on the muscle.
Split Routine	In a split routine program, different body parts are exercised on different days. For example, the upper body muscles may be exercised on Mondays and Wednesdays, and the lower body muscles on Tuesdays and Thursdays. Usually multiple exercises for each muscle group is performed.

KEY CONCEPT

RESISTANCE TRAINING AND BREATHING

Proper breathing technique is essential to resistance training. The breathing technique helps in the lift but can also pose some physiologic problems if not performed appropriately. Inhalation should occur during the eccentric part of the lift as the weight descends from the ending position of the lift. During the initial phase of the concentric portion of the lift (when the weight is being lifted to the finishing position), the breath is held which helps to stabilize the chest area. This stabilization is important in many lifts because it provides the muscles a stable foundation from which they exert their forces. As the weight nears the end of the range of motion for that lift, the breath is exhaled and the cycle is repeated for the next repetition. A new breathing cycle should be started on each repetition during heavy lifting. When the resistance is light and the effort is low, more than one repetition can be accomplished during one breathing cycle.

RESISTANCE TRAINING EQUIPMENT

There are many types of resistance or strength training equipment on the market today, ranging all the way from traditional free weights to expensive computerized equipment that constantly monitor progress. Does it matter which type of equipment you use? Does some equipment produce greater benefits than others? The truth of the matter is that the type of equipment used is not nearly as important as commitment to exercising on a regular basis using an appropriate program. Some equipment may be better than others for specific purposes or situations, but in general, most equipment will provide the necessary stimulus for improvement.

Regardless of the type of equipment used, the most important part of any training program is consistency and using appropriate intensity, frequency and duration. Just using something as simple as the body weight for resistance, as in doing sit-ups, push-ups and pull-ups, can be very effective when done consistently and appropriately. For the purpose of developing and maintaining good overall muscular fitness, any type of equipment will work if the training methods are appropriate and consistent. The two most common types of equipment are free weights (Figure 3.8) and weight machines (Figure 3.9).

Free Weights

Free weights consist of barbells, weight plates, and dumbbells. There are two major advantages of free weights compared to weight machines. First, free weights are relatively inexpensive. A barbell and weight plates can be

FIGURE 3.8

Using free weights, the most traditional form of resistance exercise, remains a popular method of developing muscular strength and endurance.

purchased for as little as $50 to several hundred dollars depending on how much weight you get. Weight machines will cost anywhere from $500—$10,000, depending on the complexity of the equipment. The second major advantage of free weights is that a greater variety and more specific exercises can be done with free weights. Weight machines limit you to specific exercises and ranges of motion.

Weight Machines

The two major advantages of weight machines are their greater safety and convenience of use. Because weight machines are manufactured as a unit and the weights are secured, there are no weights to fall off bars or bars to fall off racks. This makes for a safer exercise environment with less chance for injury. Secondly, to change the amount of resistance normally requires the placing of a small pin into a weight stack, in contrast to the necessity of changing weight plates with free weights. When time is a factor, and it usually is, the speed at which the resistances can be changed on a weight machines makes a big difference. Females often find weight machines less intimidating and will use them when they would not use free weights.

For the individual wanting to increase muscular strength and endurance in order to be generally physically fit, it will really make no difference which type of equipment is used.[7] The most important aspect will be the consistency and appropriateness of the training program. Using either type of equipment with a good program will produce good results.

FIGURE 3.9
Weight machines provide a convenient method of resistance training.

CIRCUIT WEIGHT TRAINING

There is a special type of weight training that is kind of a hybrid mode. It is called **circuit weight training (CWT)** and it is a combination of strength training, muscular endurance training, and cardiorespiratory endurance training. CWT trains each of these three components, but does not train any one of them optimally.[16] It is a compromise mode which produces many of the benefits of all the components concurrently without having to train each component separately. Because all components are trained concurrently, significant time can be saved.

CWT uses a series of exercises that are repeated over a 30-45 minute exercise session. The exercises are often the same as those used in more traditional modes of weight training or they can be simple calisthenics exercises like push-ups, sit-ups, pull-ups, etc. In CWT, the resistance is reduced to 40-60% of the 1RM in order to perform 15-20 repetitions of each lift. The objective is to move from exercise to exercise, performing 15-20 repetitions, usually taking 20-30 seconds at each station, and continuing the process until three to four sets of each exercise are performed.

Ideally, one moves from one exercise to the next without any rest or recovery but , as in most situations, you should start slowly and progressively increase the number of stations and decrease the length of the recovery periods. Although continuous repetitions train the cardiorespiratory system, beginners will require periodic rest periods until becoming more trained. The circuit can be adjusted to have an even greater benefit to the cardiorespiratory system by alternating a lift with a more aerobic form of exercise such as jumping rope or running in place. Making every other station an aerobic station will enhance the aerobic training of the overall circuit.

SPECIAL CONSIDERATIONS IN RESISTANCE TRAINING

Females and Resistance Training

In general, females are not as strong as males. This differences between the genders is more pronounced in the arms and shoulders than in the legs. In fact, when strength is expressed per amount of muscle, there is little difference in leg strength between males and females.[11, 18] Although there are several biological reasons that females are not as absolutely strong as males, females can improve strength levels in a similar fashion as males.

Most females do not respond to resistance training to the same absolute degree as males because most females lack significant levels of the male sex hormone **testosterone** which promotes muscle growth. However, females can, and do, get stronger when resistance training is appropriately used. Some of the increase in strength can be accounted for by increases in the neuromuscular function of the muscular and nervous system, a concept discussed earlier in this chapter. Some of the increase results from an increase in muscle hypertrophy, but not to the extent seen in males. Female athletes can especially benefit from strength training as performance often improves as strength increases.

Traditionally, there has been a reluctance on the part of females to participate in resistance training. This stemmed from the misconception that resistance training would have a masculinizing effect on females. Most females do not want large muscles, but most would like to have increased levels of strength and muscular endurance, often referred to as "muscle tone." Muscle tone gives the appearance of a firm and attractive body, but more importantly, developing muscle tone will also promote the health benefits discussed earlier in this chapter.

The type of program used by females should be the same as used by males. If the overload principle is applied consistently, females will improve muscular strength and endurance, look and feel better, and, most importantly, receive the health benefits.

Resistance Training and Aging

The average individual will lose about 30-50% of their muscle strength and 40% of their muscle size between the ages of 25 to 70. Much of the reduction in muscular strength is due to loss of muscle tissue. The loss of muscle tissue results from both a decrease in the number of muscle fibers and a decrease in the size of muscle fibers. Although some of this loss in muscle tissue is probably a function of aging, most is thought to be due to the decrease in muscular activity that normally accompanies aging.

If inactivity results in the loss of muscle size and strength, a phenomena referred to as **reversibility**, then what happens if activity is maintained throughout the life-span? The answer is that much of the muscle's size and strength can be maintained. Since the innate ability of muscle fibers to develop tension is maintained fairly well as you get older, you can stay strong and healthy if you prevent muscle tissue loss.

By maintaining muscular activity throughout your life, you maintain much your muscular strength and endurance. You will be able to do the kinds of activities you need or like to do throughout your life-span. When you get to be 60 or 70 years old, you will be able to enjoy the benefits of a lifestyle that promoted the maintenance of muscular strength and endurance.

There is even hope for individuals in their 70's and 80's who have already lost much of their muscle mass. It has also been found that even adults in their 70's and 80's can substantially increase muscular strength and endurance by beginning a resistance training program. The message is clear—**it is never too late to begin an exercise program that can significantly improve your muscular strength and endurance.**

Safety Issues

As with any type of exercise, resistance training has the potential for producing muscular, skeletal and other soft tissue injury. The potential can be kept to a minimum by following recommended safety practices when using resistance equipment. Although free weights are inherently more dangerous than weight machines, any form of resistance equipment will be safer when the routine safety rules listed in Table 3.3 are followed.

TABLE 3.3

Safety Tips for Resistance Training

1. A warm-up should be done prior to resistance training. The warm-up should consist of both flexibility exercises and muscle warming. The flexibility exercises should stretch the muscles and joints that will be used in the resistance exercise. The muscle warm-up can be accomplished most specifically by using the same lifts you will use during the training program but lower the resistance to less than 50% of 1RM. Ideally, the muscles should be warmed-up first followed by flexibility exercise since muscles stretch more easily after they are warmed-up.

2. Correct mechanical lifting technique should be used for each lift. Avoid hyperextending the back and keep the spine as straight as possible in all lifts. Bend at the waist, not in the spine and use your legs to lift all weights off the floor. When lifting weights overhead, keep the weight in alignment with the body so the spine is not hyperextended or flexed excessively. It is highly recommended that a weight belt be worn whenever lifting overhead or off the floor.

3. Try not to hold your breath when lifting. Trying to lift a heavy weight while holding your breath produces a **Valsalva** which may increase blood pressure to very high levels. The proper breathing technique is to breathe out as you push the weight up and breathe in as you bring the weight down.

4. Use collars to secure the weight plates on the bar so accidental movement of the weights cannot occur.

5. When performing lifts with heavy weights, use spotters to help with the weight in case you cannot control it. Spotters are especially needed when doing the bench press and the squat.

KEY CONCEPT

RESISTANCE TRAINING AND MUSCLE SORENESS

When an overload is first applied to a muscle, the muscle will typically develop soreness approximately 24-48 hours following the workout. This type of soreness is called **delayed onset muscle soreness** or **DOMS**. DOMS is due to microtrauma and inflammation occurring in the muscle in response to the overload. The soreness normally disappears within about 72 hours. Once DOMS has occurred in muscle, it usually does not reappear each workout unless a very large overload is again applied. It is perfectly normal to get DOMS periodically in response to a resistance workout that is substantially different than your "typical" workout (like new exercises, substantially changing the intensity or duration of the workout, or resuming a workout after 2 or more weeks of not working out). However, if you get sore after every workout so that you are sore all the time, you are using too much overload. Constant soreness is a warning that you need to decrease your volume and/or intensity of training or improvement will diminish.

Because resistance exercise consists of a lot of repetitive motions, overuse injuries will occur periodically. At the first sign of injury, begin the self-treatment protocol in Table 2.17 in Chapter 2.

Anabolic Drugs

Anabolic drugs such as steroids and human growth hormone are protein-building (muscle building) drugs used in an effort to increase muscle size and strength. Their use is becoming more prevalent, by both athletes and non-athletes. Unfortunately, besides being illegal, these drugs can have extremely harmful side-effects. Potential side-effects of steroids use for both genders are increased risk for heart disease, liver tumors, acne, painful and tender breasts, reduced fertility, and the various diseases associated with injections, such as hepatitis and AIDS. Specific side-effects in males include baldness, reduced testicular size, and the development of breast tissue. Specific side-effects in females include development of a male physique, increased body hair, failure to ovulate, and deepening of the voice. In adolescents, there is risk of premature closure of the long bones resulting in a shorter-than-predicted adult height. Potential side-effects of growth hormone are production of antibodies against themselves.

The use of anabolic drugs for the purpose of increasing muscle size and strength is strongly discouraged on the basis of it being illegal and the potential side-effects from their use. These drugs do have legitimate medical uses and may be prescribed by a physician but it is still illegal for a physician to prescribe these drugs for the purpose of increasing muscle size and strength. The athlete or fitness enthusiasts should rely on proven and reliable strength training methods.

RESISTANCE EXERCISES

Common resistance training exercises are shown in Figures 3.10–3.19. The starting and ending position for each exercise is shown. Figures 3.10–3.14 show exercises for the same muscles using weight machines and dumbells. This is certainly not an exhaustive listing, but it does contain the most popular exercises for developing the major muscle of the body. By picking exercises for specific muscles or muscle groups, you can design your own training program. The application of the principles described earlier along with the specific exercises will provide the information necessary to develop a well-rounded resistance training program. Specificity can be applied by selecting different exercises and by using different frequencies, duration and intensities of training. Remember, the most important component is consistency. You must do it to get the benefit.

COMMON RESISTANCE EXERCISES

FIGURE 3.10

Bench Press. Primary muscles: pectoralis major, anterior deltoid, triceps.

COMMON RESISTANCE EXERCISES

FIGURE 3.11

Forearm Curl. Primary muscles: biceps.

COMMON RESISTANCE EXERCISES

FIGURE 3.12

Upright or Military Press. Primary muscles: deltoids, triceps.

Common Resistance Exercises

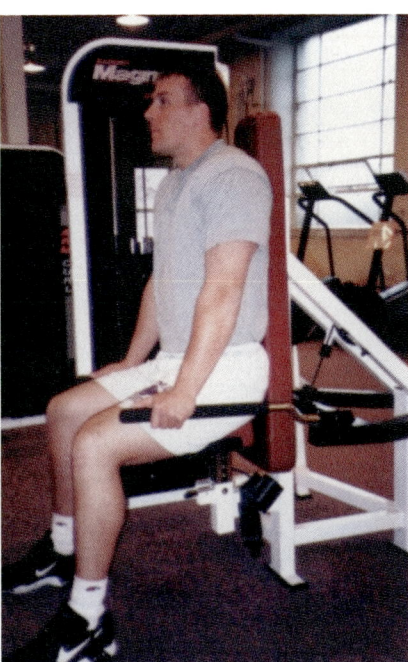

Figure 3.13

Triceps Extension. Primary muscles: triceps.

FIGURE 3.14

Lat Pull. Primary muscles: latissimus dorsi, teres major.

COMMON RESISTANCE EXERCISES

FIGURE 3.15

Leg Press. Primary muscles: quadriceps, gluteus major, hamstrings.

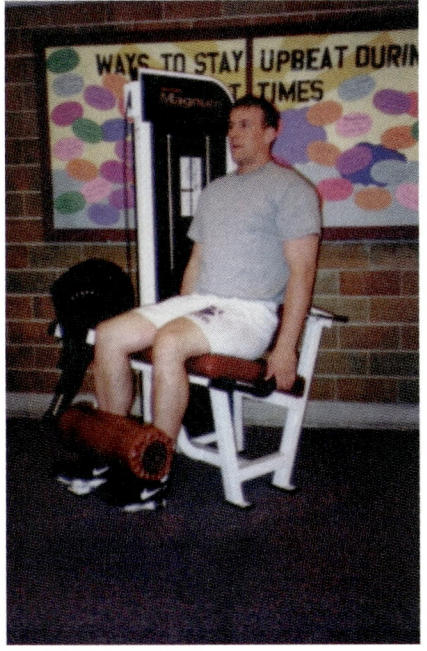
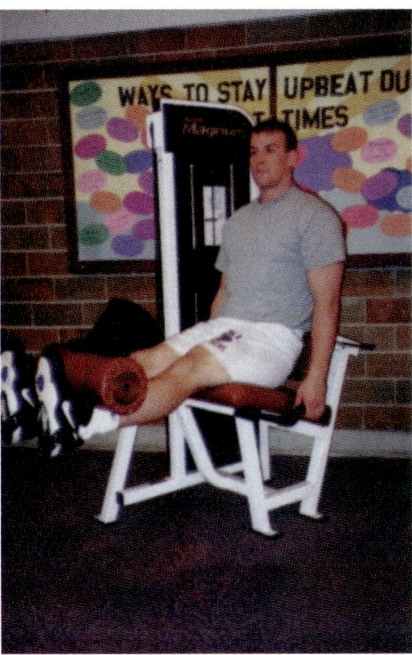

FIGURE 3.16

Leg Extension. Primary muscles: quadriceps.

COMMON RESISTANCE EXERCISES

FIGURE 3.17

Lat Flexion. Primary muscles: hamstrings.

FIGURE 3.18

Back Extension. Primary muscles: back exstensors.

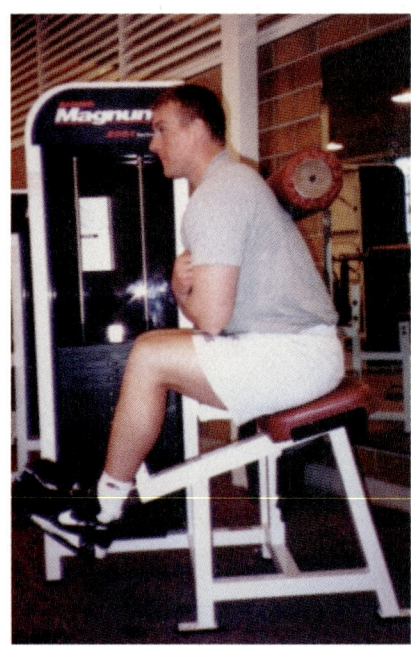 

COMMON RESISTANCE EXERCISES

FIGURE 3.19

Abdominal Crunch. Primary muscles: rectus abdominis.

ASSESSMENT OF MUSCULAR STRENGTH AND ENDURANCE

Muscular strength and endurance can be assessed using calisthenics-type exercises like sit-ups and push-ups, or using free weights or exercise machines. There are two major purposes for assessing muscular strength and endurance. First, assessment will determine your current strength level and will allow comparison to norms to see how you stack up against a typical person your age and sex. Secondly, strength assessment can be used to determine progress resulting from a training program. Periodic assessments during a training program will allow you to determine if the program is effective or whether the program needs to be changed.

The 1 RM Test

Muscular strength can be effectively measured with relatively simple procedures and without expensive equipment. One method is to determine the maximum amount of weight that can be lifted for one repetition (1RM) in a series of lifts which measure the strength of the arms, shoulders, back, abdomen and legs. In this procedure, the lift is performed with progressively increasing resistance until a maximum is reached. The amount of weight lifted can be evaluated on an absolute basis determined by the pounds lifted or on a relative basis by forming a ratio between the weight lifted and the body weight of the lifter. Because larger people are generally stronger, forming a ratio between the weight lifted and the body weight allows for comparison between individuals of different sizes.

For example, say a person weighing 150 lb and a person weighing 200 lb each do a 1RM on the bench press and the person weighing 150 lb is able to lift 150 lb and the person weighing 200 lb is able to do a 1RM with 175 lb. Who is stronger? On an absolute basis the person weighing 200 lb is stronger because he can do a 1RM with 175 lb. However, if a ratio is formed between the weight lifted and the body weights, the person weighing 150 can lift 1.0 times their body weight, while the person weighing 200 lb can only lift 0.85 times their body weight.

Arguments can be made as to which method is the best assessment of strength. In the area of competitive athletics, the absolute strength assessment is probably the best measure. However, from a health standpoint, the ratio is probably better because it indicates a person's strength in relation to their size. Labs 3.1 and 3.2 located at the end of this chapter provide detalis for assessing muscular strength using a bench press and leg press. Norms for gender and age are provided for determining your performance in comparison to the population.

Muscular Endurance Tests

Muscular endurance can be measured by using different exercises performed with the body weight or it can be measured by performing exercises with a certain percentage of a person's 1RM. Performing different exercises with the body weight will measure muscular endurance in relationship to your weight . On the other hand, performing exercises with a percentage of 1RM measures muscular endurance in relation to your maximal strength. In both cases, as many repetitions as can be done, with or without a time limit, are performed.

Any of the specific resistance training exercises depicted in this chapter can be used to test muscular endurance. Each test measures the muscular endurance of the muscles used in that specific exercise. In performing this test, a percentage of the 1RM for each exercise is determined and a percentage of that 1RM is taken as the resistance for the endurance test. Commonly, 75% is used but any percentage between 50-75% can be used. The subject then performs as many repetitions as possible with the percentage of 1RM that has been selected. The advantage of this type of test is that it allows the measurement of many specific muscle groups. The disadvantages are that it requires determining the 1RM for each lift making mass testing more difficult.

Labs 3.3 and 3.4 located at the end of this chapter provide details for assessing muscular endurance using push-ups and sit-ups. Norms for gender and age are provided for determining your performance in comparison with a similar population.

FLEXIBILITY

Flexibility is defined as the range of motion possible at joints in the body. Flexibility tends not to be a general characteristic but is specific to each joint. In other words, a person may be flexible at the shoulder joint, but not flexible at the hip joint. Because of this specific nature of flexibility, programs designed to improve flexibility must work all the joints and segments you wish to improve.

Maintaining good flexibility is important from a health perspective for two primary reasons. First, flexibility of the low back and hamstrings plays a significant role in prevention of low-back problems, one of the most costly medical conditions in this country. Approximately 80% of the population will have some type of back problem during their lifetime.[13] Of these, 50-60% will miss work due to the back pain and 40-60% will have recurrences within 1 year after their initial episode.[3] Maintaining good hamstring and low-back flexibility is a good preventive measure, especially for individuals prone to low-back problems.

The second reason maintaining flexibility is important to health is that loss of flexibility is normally a natural consequence of aging. As one ages and becomes less physically active, flexibility decreases because muscles and joints are used less.[2] Like other components of fitness, if you don't use flexibility, you loose it. For example, sitting at a desk all day for years and years can shorten the hamstring muscles, cause a loss of flexibility in the hip and cause low-back problems. Loss of flexibility can significantly decrease one's ability to perform activities of daily living, restrict recreational activities, and promote accidents due to loss of mobility. It is therefore important for everyone, especially the elderly, to maintain sufficient flexibility and range of motion to counter these potential problems.

Limitations to Flexibility

Flexibility is primarily limited by the bony structure that forms the joint and by the muscles and soft tissues (tendons, ligaments, joint capsule, etc.) that surround and stabilize the joint. For example, the elbow is called a hinge joint because the two bones that form the joint fit together like a hinge. When you extend or straighten out your forearm at the elbow as far as you can, the bones that form the joint are actually prevented from further movement by physical contact with each other. Conversely, when you flex your forearm, range of motion is limited by the front of the forearm contacting the biceps muscle on the front of the upper arm.

Another example of the muscle surrounding a joint primarily limiting flexibility is in the bending over at the waist, called trunk flexion. When you try to bend over at the waist and touch your toes while keeping your legs straight, the limitation is usually imposed by the hamstring muscles on the back of the thigh because the hamstring muscles will not stretch far enough. Stretching the hamstring muscles will improve flexibility in this movement. Of the factors which limit range of motion, the muscle is the most modifiable structure and therefore, most flexibility programs attempt to reduce the restrictions of the muscles to movement, i.e.. they stretch the muscles in an attempt to lengthen them.

It is quite clear that females tend to be more flexible than males. Specific anatomic or physiologic reasons for this are unclear, although the bony structure in some joints is a factor. Regardless of this inherent difference between the sexes, both males and females can improve and maintain good flexibility with a regular flexibility program.

Flexibility Training Programs

Fortunately, flexibility can be improved and maintained with regular flexibility training. In fact, less time needs to be spent in flexibility training than either cardiorespiratory endurance or muscular strength and endurance.

Mode

There are three basic types of flexibility exercises that can improve range of motion. They are (a) **ballistic** or **dynamic stretching**, (b) **static stretching**, and (c) **proprioceptive neuromuscular facilitation (PNF) stretching**. Although all three can improve range of motion, ballistic stretching is generally not recommended because of some potential dangerous side-effects of the stretching procedure.

Ballistic or **dynamic stretching** uses the momentum of the body to produce bouncy and jerky movements in order to force the joints and body segments into greater ranges of motion. For example, the bouncing or bobbing when trying to touch the toes by bending at the waist is ballistic stretching. The weight and momentum of the torso is used to force a stretch of the hamstrings each time you bend at the waist. The hamstrings are temporarily stretched, the stretch is relieved, and then repeated in several cycles.

The problem with ballistic stretching is that there is greater potential for injury as a consequence of performing the stretch. The rapid and relatively uncontrolled nature of the stretch can cause over-stretching of the muscles and joint structures, causing small ruptures and tears in the soft tissue. Because of this injury potential, this technique is not recommended.

Static stretching uses slow, sustained stretches in contrast to the ballistic type of stretching. A joint is taken through its full range of motion and then held at the point of stretch for 10-30 seconds. For example, using the torso flexion movement or touching the toes, you would bend at the waist until a stretch was felt. This stretched position would be held for the required time and then released. This sequence would be repeated several times for maximum benefit. Static stretching has much less potential for causing injury to the soft tissues of the joint compared to dynamic stretching. It is also more comfortable to perform because the soft tissues are not being overstretched.

Proprioceptive neuromuscular facilitation (PNF stretching) is used primarily by athletes. It is a combination of static stretching and active muscular contraction and usually requires a partner to be performed correctly. PNF stretching has been shown to be very effective in producing improved flexibility[22] but it also requires more time.

PNF stretching begins with a static contraction that is held for 10-30 seconds. Immediately following the static stretch, a partner provides resistance to an attempt to move the limb in the opposite direction by isometrically contracting the muscles being stretched. In other words, the same muscles stretched are isometrically contracted, but because of the resistance being applied by a partner, the limb does not move. Following the isometric contraction, the partner moves the limb to a greater stretched position than previously able to do. This type of stretch-contract-stretch cycle can be repeated up to three times and with each repetition the stretch can be increased. A common type of PNF stretch using the hamstrings muscles is illustrated in Figure 3.20.

Intensity

Intensity in flexibility exercise refers to the amount of stretch imposed. When using static or PNF stretching, the muscles should be taken to the point of moderate stretch or mild discomfort. There should not be pain. Persistent pain indicates too much stretch or some other underlying problem perhaps unrelated to the stretching. Applying too much stretch can cause injury to the muscle fibers or elicit a muscle reflex which will impede further increases in flexibility.[6]

(a) In PNF stretching, the partner applies a constant force for a static stretch of the hamstrings. (b) Following the static stretch, the partner provides resistance as the individual attempts to lower the leg by contracting the hamstrings. Isometric contraction should be held for 6–8 seconds. (c) The subject now relaxes the hamstrings and the partner reapplies a constant force for a second static stretch of the hamstrings.

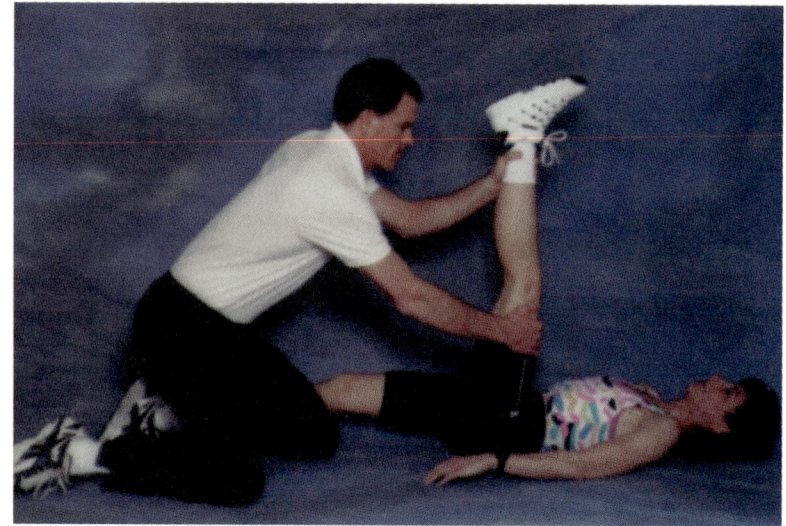

(a)

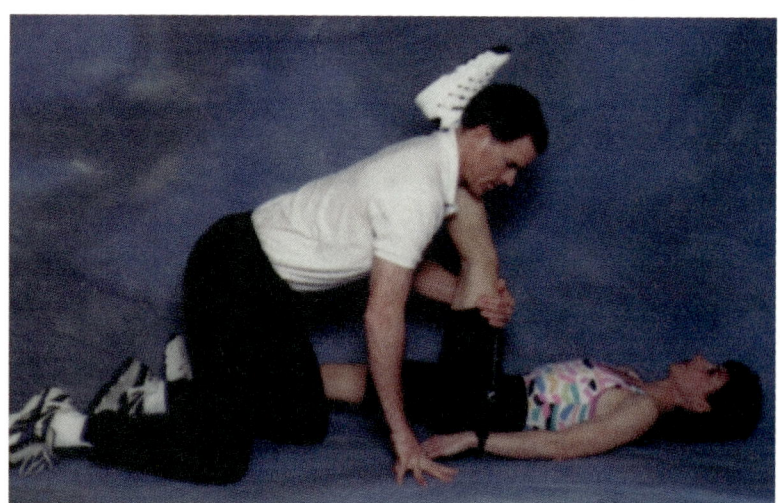

(b)

(c)

Duration

Static stretching should begin with a 5-10 second stretch. For optimal results, the time the stretch is held should be gradually lengthened over several weeks to a maximum of about 30-60 seconds. Each stretch should be repeated 3-5 repetitions, depending on the time available. During the early phases of the program, the duration should be only about 10 seconds for 3 repetitions for a total of 30 seconds of stretch. As improvement and tolerance to the stretch improve, increase the time of the stretch until it can be maintained the for 30-60 seconds continuously. After a 30-60-second continuous stretch is possible, begin doing up to 3 repetitions as time permits.

Frequency

Frequency of stretching will depend on how rapid you wish to progress. During the early phases of a program, progress will be most rapid with daily stretching. However, progress will occur with only 3 days per week, but not at the same rate as with more frequent stretching. Once you become satisfied with your flexibility, it can normally be maintained with 2 to 3 days per week of maintenance stretching.

When To Stretch?

The best time to perform flexibility exercise is somewhat controversial. Stretching should always be done prior to activities that require explosive muscular contractions such as basketball, volleyball, football, softball/baseball and sprinting. But what about before going on a 5-mile run or just as part of a daily flexibility program? Physiologically, a muscle stretches easier when the muscle is warmed up. Stretching a cold muscle has greater potential for causing injury to that muscle.

Ideally, some type of light muscular activity should be done prior to stretching in order to warm-up or increase the temperature of the muscles. Based on muscle physiology, the best time to stretch is after the cardiorespiratory workout since this is when the muscles will be optimally warmed up. This would be a prudent approach as long as the cardiorespiratory workout did not involve powerful muscular contractions, such as sprinting. If fast running is to be done, stretching should be done before the running and, for optimal flexibility effect, after the running as well.

Flexibility Exercises

Common and effective flexibility exercises for the major muscles of the body are shown in Figures 3.21—3.26. Performance of these exercises will result in a well-rounded flexibility program. It is simple to develop a personalized flexibility program to meet individual needs. All you need to do is identify the muscles you want to increase the flexibility of and then stretch those muscles. Different recreational activities like golf and tennis require stretching of different muscles so specificity for the type of movements involved is important and should be built into any stretching program.

FIGURE 3.21

Hamstrings Stretch. Sit with the bottom of one foot against the inner thigh of the straight opposite leg. Bend at the waist and attempt to touch your nose to the knee of the straight leg.

FIGURE 3.22

Groin (inner thigh) Stretch. Sit with the bottom of both feet touching. Using your hands or elbows, gengly press your knees toward the floor.

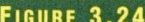

FIGURE 3.23

Quadriceps Stretch. Lay on your side with the top leg bent up behind. Pull the bent leg as far toward your rear as possible.

FIGURE 3.24

Outside Thigh, Low Back. Sit with one leg crossed over the top of the opposite leg. Twist your torso in the direction of the straight leg.

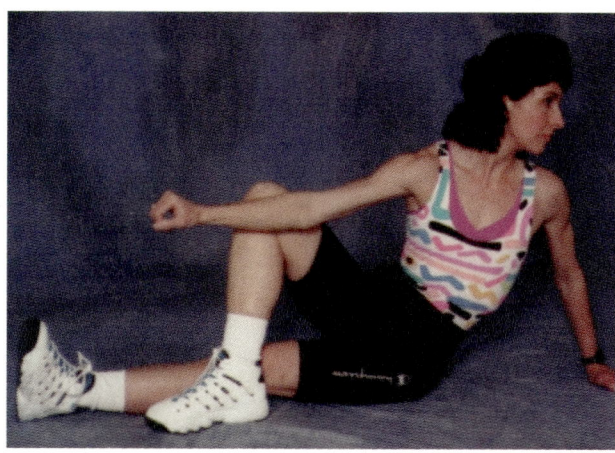

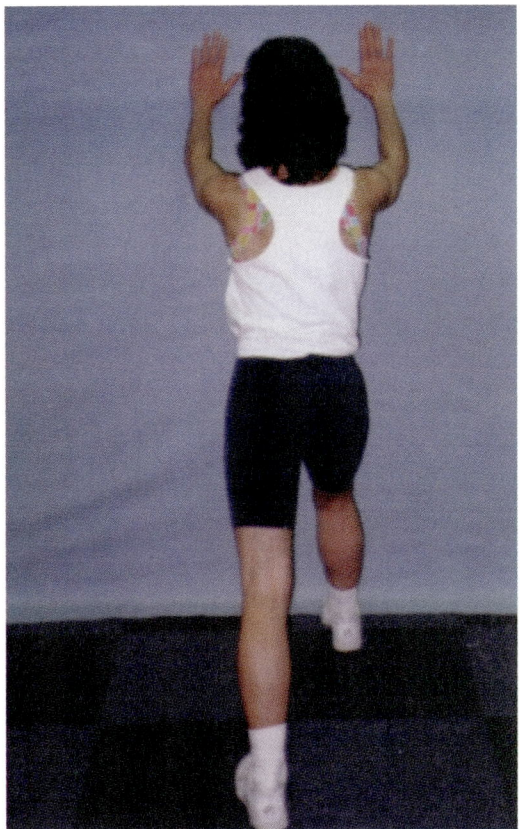

FIGURE 3.25

Calf and Achilles Tendon Stretch.
Lean against a wall with the feet staggered and the heels flat on the ground. for more stretch, move the foot of the back leg further from the wall.

(a)

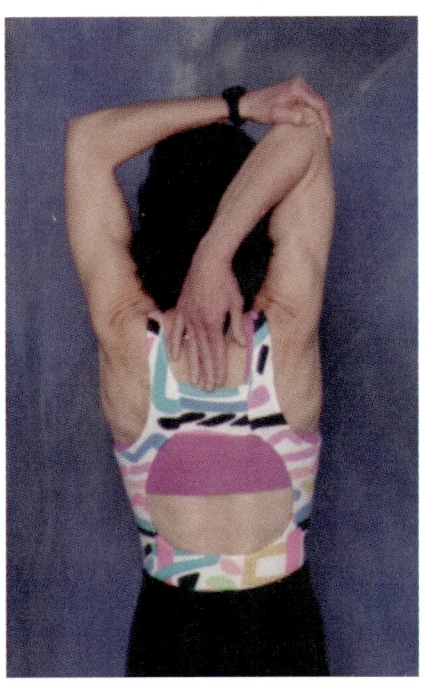

(b)

FIGURE 3.26

Shoulder and Triceps Stretch.
(a) Grasp the back of the arm and pull the arm across the front of the chest. (b) Grasp the elbow and pull toward the back of the opposite shoulder.

Assessment of Flexibility

Flexibility can be assessed in a variety of ways ranging from simple self-testing movements to the use of expensive state-of-the-art electronic instruments. From a practical perspective, simple measures obtained by a sit-and-reach test or through the use of simple instruments to measure angles (called goniometers) are sufficient to tell someone whether or not they are improving. Lab 3.5 located at the end of this chapter provides a description of a simple test for measuring hip, low-back and hamstring flexibility. Because the type of flexibility measured by this test is significantly related to the incidence of low-back problems, this is a good measure of flexibility from a health perspective.

Exercises for the Low-Back

As mentioned in an earlier section in this chapter, low-back problems will afflict a majority of adult Americans at some point in their lives. The economic impact in terms of medical cost and lost productivity is tremendous. As with most chronic diseases, prevention is much easier and effective than dealing with the problem once it develops.

Low-back pain is often the result of physical inactivity, poor posture, inappropriate lifting and carrying mechanics, and excessive body weight. Muscle strengthening and flexibility exercises can play a major role in low-back pain prevention and rehabilitation.[5, 8]

The best type of exercise for abdominal strength and low-back health is the curl-up shown in Figure 3.27. The curl-up is very specific to the rectus abdominis, the abdominal muscle that has the greatest impact on back health. Both muscular strength and muscular endurance should be developed so attention to the resistance and reps used is important. An abdominal program for back health should include sets of 20 or more repetitions for

FIGURE 3.27

The curl-up is the most effective exercise for the rectus abdominis muscle.

endurance and sets of 8-12 repetitions for strength. Initially your should work on being able to do at least 20 repetitions of the curl-up. Once this level of muscular endurace and strength has been achieved, you should begin to work on strength at least twice a week by increasing the resistance to the torso in order to reduce the repetitions to around 8-12. Use a weight plate or dumbbell to add resistance to the torso (Figure 3.28).

In addition to strength, flexibility exercise for the low back and hamstrings are important components of a healthy back program. Figures 3.29 and 3.30 illustrate two good low back stretches. An excellent hamstring stretch is illustrated in Figure 3.18. The exercise prescription should follow the guidelines in the strengthening and flexibility section in this chapter.

FIGURE 3.28

Additional resistance can be added to the torso to reduce the number of repetitions that can be done which improves strength better.

FIGURE 3.29

This is an excellent stretch for the lower back. It can be done one leg at a time or with both legs together. Pull the thigh(s) toward the chest and maintain the position like any static stretch.

FIGURE 3.30

This is another excellent stretch for the lower back. In the all-fours position, raise the upper-back as high as possible and hold.

Lifting Mechanics

Unusual stresses on the muscles and ligaments that support the spine increases the risk for low-back problems. This is compounded when the muscles and supporting structures of the back are weak. Muscles can be strengthened by appropriate exercise but we constantly have to be aware of appropriate lifting mechanics in order to reduce the stresses placed on the back. Even in situations where the muscles are quite strong, a bit of a wrong bend or twist can be enough to cause an acute bout of low-back pain.

Certain occupations are at significantly higher risk than the normal population. Occupational tasks that increase risk include heavy lifting, lifting with bending and twisting motions, pushing and pulling, and long periods of sitting as in driving. Individuals involved in these types of activities need to be especially aware of using proper lifting, standing, and sitting mechanics. Proper lifting mechanics are illustrated in Figures 3.31 and 3.32 while Table 3.4 contains recommendations for lifting and posture maintenance.

FIGURE 3.31

When lifting an object from the ground or floor, bend at the knees and keep the back straight. Lift with the legs.

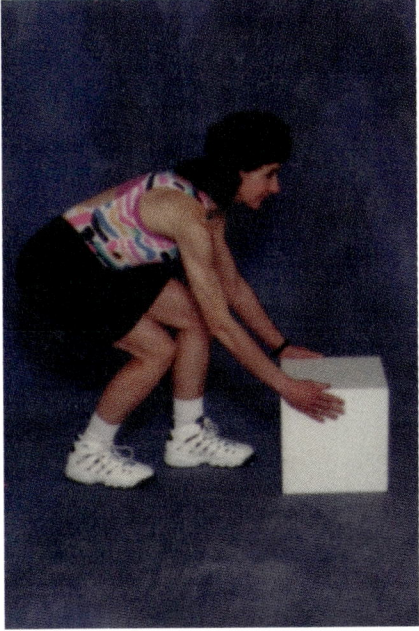

FIGURE 3.32

When carrying a heavy object, carry the object against the body.

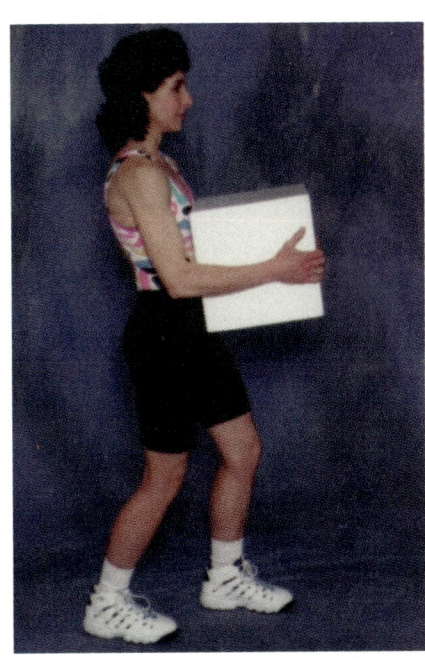

TABLE 3.4

Recommendations of Proper Lifting, Sitting and Standing Mechanics

- Always lift with the legs, not with the back. Keep your back as straight as possible and bend at the knees instead of at the waist.

- When bending at the waist is necessary, maintain a straight back from the waist to the neck. When lifting objects off of shelves or tables, stand as close to the object as possible. Keeping the object close to the body reduces the forces your muscles have to develop. If you have to transfer the object to another location, rotate the entire body as opposed to rotating just the trunk while maintaining the feet stationary.

- If you have to stand or sit for long periods of time, take periodic breaks. When standing for long periods, stand with one leg on an elevated step or platform.

- While sitting or standing, maintain a efficient posture. Keep your back straight, and the abdominal muscles tight to maintain the pelvis tilted forward.

- Sleep on a firm mattress. The most back-efficient position is a side-lying semi-fetal position.

- When lying supine on a hard surface, keep the feet flat on the floor with the knees bent or elevated on a chair.

EXPLORING WELLNESS ON THE WEB

Many resources are available on the World Wide Web. You can reinforce, expand and enhance the information presented in this chapter by accessing the following sites.

http://www.worldguide.com/Fitness/hf.html — recommendations on strength training exercises as well as other topics on exercise.

http://www.ipf.com/fredhome.htm — you can ask questions regarding strength training and get responses from an expert in strength training.

http://www.1adventure.com/HealthandFitness — provides information on many different lifts for various body parts. This information will help add variety to your workouts.

REFERENCES

1. Atha, J. (1981). Strengthening muscle. *Exercise and Sport Science Reviews, 9,* 1-73.

2. Bassey, E. J., Morgan, K., Dallosso, H. M., Ebrahim, S. B. J. (1989). Flexibility of the shoulder joint measured as range of abduction in a large representative sample of men and women over 65 years of age. *European Journal of Applied Physiology,* 58, 353-360.

3. Biering-Sorenson, F. (1984). Physical measurements as risk indicators for low-back trouble over a one-year period. *Spine,* 9, 106-119.

4. Brewer, V., Meyer, B. M., Keele, M. S., Upton, S. J., & Hagan, R. D. (1983). Role of exercise in preventing involutional bone loss. *Medicine and Science in Exercise and Sports,* 15(6), 445-449.

5. Calliet, R. (1987). *Low Back Pain Syndrome.* Philadelphia: F. A. Davis Co.

6. de Vries, H. (1962). Evaluation of static stretching procedures for improvement of flexibility. *Research Quarterly for Exercise and Sport,* 33, 222-.

7. Fleck, S. J., & Kraemer, W. J. (1988). Resistance Training: Basic principles (Part 1 of 4). Physician and Sports Medicine. 16(2), 160-171.

8. Kelsey, J. & White, A. A. (1980). Epidemiology and impact of low backpain. *Spine,* 5, 133.

9. Komi, P. V. (1986). Training of muscle strength and power: interaction of neuromotoric, hypertrophic and mechanical factors. *International Journal of Sports Medicine,* 7(Suppl.), 10-16.

10. Larsson, L. & Tesch, P. A. (1986). Motor unit fiber density in extremely hypertrophied skeletal muscles in man. *European Journal of Applied Physiology,* 55, 130-136.

11. Levine, L., Falkel, J. E., & Sawka, M. N. (1984). Upper to lower body strength ratio comparisons between men and women. *Medicine and Science in Sports and Exercise,* 16(2), 125.

12. MacDougall, J. Hypertrophy or hyperplasia. In P. V. Komi (Ed.), *Strength and Power in Sport* (pp. 230-238). London: Blackwell Scientific.

13. Mayer, G., Gatchel, R. J., Kishino, N., Keeley, J., Capra, P., Mayer, H., Barnett, J., & Mooney, V. (1985). Objective assessment of spine function following industrial injury. A prospective study with comparison group and one-year follow-up. *Spine,* 10, 482-493.

14. Mc Neill, T., Warwick, D., Andersson, G., & Schultz, A. (1980). Trunk strengths in attempted flexion, extension and lateral bending in healthy subjects and patients with low back disorders. *Spine,* 5, 529-538.

15. Moritani, T., & de Vries, H. A. (1979). Neural factors vs hypertrophy in time course of muscle strength gain. *American Journal of Physical Medicine and Rehabilitation,* 58, 115-130.

16. Petersen, S. R., Belcastro, A. N., Quinney, H. A., Haennel, R. G., Reid, D. C., Happagoda, C. T., & Wenger, H. A. (1989). The influence of high-velocity circuit resistance training on VO$_2$max and cardiac output. *Canadian Journal of Sport Sciences,* 14(3), 158-163.

17. Schantz, P. (1982). Capillary supply in hypertrophied human skeletal muscle. *Acta Physiologica Scandinavica,* 114, 635-637.

18. Schantz, P., Randall-Fox, E., Hutchinson, W., Tyden, A., & Astrand, P. O. (1983). Muscle fiber type distribution, muscle cross-sectional area and maximal voluntary strength in humans. *Acta Physiologica Scandinavica,* 117, 219-226.

19. Staron, R. S., Hikida, R. S., Hagerman, F. C., Dudley, G. A., & Murray, T. F. (1984). Human skeletal muscle fiber type adaptability to various workloads. *Journal of Histochemistry and Cytochemistry,* 32, 146-152.

20. Suzuki, N. , & Endo, S. (1983). A quantitative study of trunk muscle strength and fatigability in the low back pain syndrome. *Spine,* 8, 69-74.

21. Tesch, P. A., Hjort, H., & Balldin, U. (1983). Effects of strength training on G tolerance. *Aviation and Space Environmental Medicine,* 54, 691-695.

22. Wallin, D., Ekblom, B., Grahn, R., & Nordenborg, T. (1985). Improvement of muscle flexibility. *American Journal of Sports Medicine,* 13, 263.

DEFINITION OF TERMS

circuit weight training — a method of resistance training characterized by multiple stations or exercises, performed in sequence with little or no rest between each exercise. The general objective is to maintain rhythmical contractions for an extended duration in order to gain some aerobic benefit.

concentric contraction — developing muscular tension during which the muscle shortens

eccentric contraction — developing muscular tension during which the muscle lengthens.

HDL cholesterol — high density lipoprotein cholesterol. HDL-C is the "good" cholesterol because it is involved in reducing the level of cholesterol in vascular cells.

hyperplasia — an increase in the number of muscle fibers.

hypertrophy — an increase in muscle size due to an increase in the size of individual muscle fibers.

isometric contraction — developing muscular tension without the muscle shortening, resulting in no movement. Sometimes referred to as a static contraction.

isotonic contraction — developing muscular tension with either a shortening or lengthening of the muscle which results in movement.

muscular strength — the ability of a muscle to develop maximal tension one time.

muscular endurance — the ability of a muscle to repeat or maintain tension development.

osteoporosis — a complex disease process resulting in a decrease in the strength of the skeletal system and characterized by bone fractures and skeletal deformity.

PNF stretching — a method of stretching that utilizes static stretching combined with isometric contractions of the muscles being stretched.

progressive resistance — a method of continuing to overload the muscular system as the muscles get stronger.

repetition maximum — the greatest weight than can be lifted in a specific movement one time.

set — a series of repetitions of an exercise without rest between repetitions.

skeletal muscle — the type of muscle that attaches to the bones and causes movment when the muscle shortens or lengthens.

testosterone — a male sex hormone which promotes the increase in muscle size and strength during puberty.

valsalva — an increase in intrathoracic pressure by forcible exhalation against the closed glottis.

LAB 3.1

ASSESSING SHOULDER-ARM STRENGTH AND ENDURANCE WITH THE PUSH-UP TEST

Name _____ ID _____ Sect _____ Time _____ Date _____

Purposes

1. To determine your current level of shoulder-arm (pectoralis major, anterior deltoid, triceps) strength and endurance as measured by the push-up test.

2. To compare your shoulder-arm strength and endurance with population norms.

Directions

1. For this assessment, males perform the traditional push-up from the toes and females perform the push-up from the knees (see the figures below). The correct starting position is with the palms placed directly under the shoulders (shoulder-width apart). Males should have their toes contacting the floor and females should have their knees contacting the floor. The chest should be no higher than a fist-width from the floor.

2. A partner assumes a position directly to the side of the one doing the push-up and places their fist directly under the sternum (breast bone) of the one performing the push-ups.

3. From the starting position, push directly up from the floor until the arms are fully extended, keeping the back and hips straight throughout the movement. (A male's body should form a straight line from the neck to the heels; a female's body should form a straight line from the neck to the knees). After full extension of the arms, return to the starting position, making contact with the fist of the partner. The push-up does not count unless contact of the chest to the fist is made.

4. The score is as many repetitions as can be performed without resting. A pause of longer than 2 seconds between push-ups or in the up position terminates the test.

5. The fitness and risk classification is determined from the table on the back side of this lab..

(Continued)

Gender	Age	Fitness Classification				
		Very Low	Low	Moderate	High	Very High
		Risk Classification				
		High	Moderate	Low	Very Low	
Males	<30	<23	23-32	33-39	40-50	>50
	30-39	<19	19-28	29-34	35-43	>43
	40-49	<15	15-24	25-31	31-37	>37
	≥50	<10	10-14	15-21	22-28	>28
Females	<30	<14	14-21	22-27	28-34	>34
	30-39	<10	10-17	18-23	24-30	>30
	40-49	<7	7-14	15-20	21-26	>26
	≥50	<4	4-10	11-16	17-21	>21

Record the number of push-ups performed: _____.

From the above table, record your **Fitness Classification**: _____

From the above table, record your **Risk Classification**: _____

LAB 3.2

ASSESSING ABDOMINAL STRENGTH AND ENDURANCE WITH THE CURL-UP TEST

Name _____ ID _____ Sect _____ Time _____ Date _____

Purposes

1. To determine your current level of abdominal strength and endurance as measured by the abdominal curl-up test.

2. To compare your abdominal strength and endurance with population norms.

Directions

1. In order to perform this assessment, it is necessary to have a 3-inch wide line approximately 36 inches long on the floor.

2. The person being tested sits in the starting position (see the figure) on the floor perpendicular to the 3-inch wide line. The knees should be bent to about 90° and the feet are flat on the floor about 12-15 inches from the buttocks. The arms should be fully extended at the sides in a palm-down position such that the tips of the longest finger is just touching the edge of the 3-inch wide line nearest the head.

3. The person then curls the head and upper back upward, keeping the arms straight and the palms on the floor. The curl-up should be continued until the longest finger crosses the 3-inch wide line. The shoulders should then return to a flat position on the floor following each repetition. Anchoring the feet is not allowed.

4. The score is the total number of curl-ups performed in 30 seconds. The fitness classification is obtained from the table on the back side of this lab.

(Continued)

ASSESSING ABDOMINAL STRENGTH AND ENDURANCE WITH THE CURL-UP TEST

Gender	Age	Fitness Classification				
		Very Low	Low	Moderate	High	Very High
		Risk Classification				
		High	Moderate	Low	Very Low	
Males	<30	<15	15-20	21-29	30-40	>40
	≥30	<13	13-18	19-27	27-36	>36
Females	<30	<15	15-20	21-27	28-34	>34
	≥30	<12	12-16	17-23	24-30	>30

Record the number of curl-ups in 30 seconds: _____.

From the above table, record your **Fitness Classification**: _____

From the above table, record your **Risk Classification**: _____

LAB 3.3

ASSESSING LOW-BACK AND HIP FLEXIBILITY WITH THE SIT-AND-REACH TEST

Name _____ ID _____ Sect _____ Time _____ Date _____

Purposes

1. To determine your current low-back and hip flexibility (hamstring muscles) using the sit-and-reach test.

2. To compare your low-back and hip flexibility with population norms.

Directions

1. To properly perform the sit-and-reach test, a box with an attached ruler or yardstick is necessary (shown below).

2. Prior to testing, good warm-up and stretching of the hamstrings and low-back muscles is necessary for accurate results. Perform light aerobic warm-up followed by static stretching of the hamstrings and low-back muscles prior to performing the sit-and-reach test.

3. The starting position is with in a straight-leg sitting position with the feet flat against the testing box. The back of the knees should be against the floor and the legs together with inner thighs touching.

4. From the starting position, the arms are extended as far forward as possible with palms down, as in trying to touch the toes. The motion should be smooth and continuous, not jerky and fast. The most distant point on the ruler that can be reached with the fingers should be noted and recorded. Three trials are performed and the greatest reach is the score.

5. The scoring and classification system depends on how the ruler/yardstick is placed on the box. The classification system in the table on the back side of this lab is based on the foot line (where the ruler/yardstick is in relationship to where the feet contact the box) being at the 10-inch mark on the ruler/yardstick. If the ruler/yardstick is at some point other than the 10-inch mark, appropriate adjustment can easily be made on the norms.

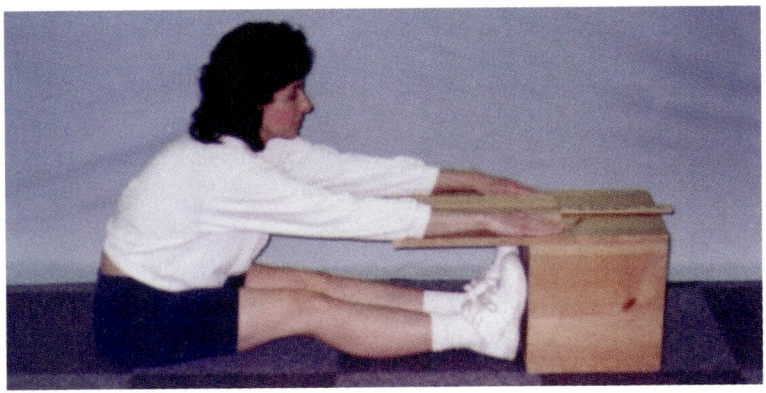

(Continued)

ASSESSING LOW-BACK AND HIP FLEXIBILITY WITH THE SIT-AND-REACH TEST

Gender	Age	Fitness Classification				
		Very Low	Low	Moderate	High	Very High
		Risk Classification				
		High	Moderate	Low	Very Low	
Males	<30	<23	23-32	33-39	40-50	>50
	30-39	<19	19-28	29-34	35-43	>43
	40-49	<15	15-24	25-31	31-37	>37
	≥50	<10	10-14	15-21	22-28	>28
Females	<30	<14	14-21	22-27	28-34	>34
	30-39	<10	10-17	18-23	24-30	>30
	40-49	<7	7-14	15-20	21-26	>26
	≥50	<4	4-10	11-16	17-21	>21

Your Score: _____.

From the above table, record your **Fitness Classification**: _____

From the above table, record your **Risk Classification**: _____

Answer the following questions.

1. What is the primary chronic disease that adult Americans suffer that is related to lack of flexibility as measured by the sit-and-reach test ?

2. Other than affecting the disease indicated in #1 above, what are two other good reasons to maintain good flexibility in all the joints of the body?

DETERMINING APPROPRIATE RESISTANCE

Name _____ ID _____ Sect _____ Time _____ Date _____

Gender _____ Body Weight _____ lb

Purposes

1. To be able to properly perform basic resistance exercises.

2. To know which muscles are being strengthened with each resistance exercise.

3. To determine the appropriate beginning weight for each resistance exercise.

Directions

1. Determine the amount of resistance required for you to do 10 repetitions max (RM) for each of the listed exercises. The percentages listed in the left column for males and females are average percentages of body weight that will result in 10 RM for that lift. These percentages are a good starting point for you to use to determine your 10 RM resistance. After determining the 10 RM resistance for each exercise, record the absolute weight (in pounds) in the right column in the blank opposite **Weight**. Then determine the percentage that this weight is of your body weight and record that percentage in the blank opposite **% Body Weight**.

2. In the center column (**Exercise Mode**) indicate the type of equipment used to perform the test (either free weights or weight machine).

Resistance Exercise	Exercise Mode	Appropriate Weight for 10 RM
Bench Press		Weight _176_
Males — 75%	_____	% Body Weight _132_
Females — 45%	_____	
Lat Pull-Down		Weight _176_
Males — 70%	_____	% Body Weight _123_
Females — 45%	_____	
Overhead Press (Military Press)		Weight _176_
Males — 50%	_____	% Body Weight _88_
Females — 30%	_____	

(Continued)

DETERMINING APPROPRIATE RESISTANCE

Resistance Exercise	Exercise Mode	Appropriate Weight for 10 RM
Forearm Curl Males — 35% Females — 20%		Weight 176 % Body Weight 62
Forearm Extension Males — 35% Females — 20%		Weight 176 % Body Weight 62
Leg Curls Males — 35% Females — 25%		Weight 176 % Body Weight 62
Leg Extensions Males — 65% Females — 50%		Weight 176 % Body Weight 115
Abdominal Crunch Males — 20% Females — 20%		Weight 176 % Body Weight 35

(Continued)

Answer each of the following questions:

1. How would you **subjectively** (based on your general feeling about your strength/endurance)
   describe your current level of muscular strength and endurance for each of the body areas listed
   below.

   Front of the arms (biceps) — *good*

   Back of the arms (triceps) — *good*

   Front of the chest (pects, deltoids) — *needs work*

   Back of torso (lats, deltoids) — *pretty good*

   Abdominal — *good*

   Front of the thighs (quadriceps) — *needs work*

   Back of the thighs (hamstrings) — *needs work*

2. Compare the % Body Weight values you recorded for each lift to the average percentages listed in
   the left column in the table. How does this **"objective"** information compare with your
   "subjective" evaluation from #1 above?

3. Which body area would you most like to change relative to muscular strength and endurance?
   Why would you like to change this area?

   my legs because they are very weak

   leg extensions, leg curls,

LAB 3.5
DESIGNING A MUSCULAR STRENGTH/ENDURANCE PROGRAM

Name _____ ID _____ Sect _____ Time _____ Date _____

Purposes

1. To select appropriate resistance exercises to accomplish the identified goals.
2. To select appropriate intensity, frequency and progression to accomplish the identified goals.

Directions

1. In the chart below, place a check in the boxes under your personal goals for developing muscular strength, endurance, size, and/or firmness for each of the areas listed. Check as many as apply.

	Goals			
Body Part	**High Strength**	**High Endurance**	**Large Size**	**Good Tone, Firmness, and Shape**
Front of Upper Arm	☐	☐	☐	☐
Back of Upper Arm	☐	☐	☐	☐
Chest	☐	☐	☐	☐
Upper Back	☐	☐	☐	☐
Lower Back	☐	☐	☐	☐
Front of Abdomen	☐	☐	☐	☐
Side of Abdomen	☐	☐	☐	☐
Front of Thigh	☐	☐	☐	☐
Back of Thigh	☐	☐	☐	☐
Calf	☐	☐	☐	☐
Buttock	☐	☐	☐	☐

(Continued)

DESIGNING A MUSCULAR STRENGTH/ENDURANCE PROGRAM

2. Design a resistance program to accomplish the goals checked. In the chart on the reverse side, fill in the specific exercises, the muscles developed, the intensity in repetitions RM, the number of sets, and the frequency of exercise.

Exercise	Muscle(s) Developed	Resistance (RM)	Sets	Frequency

NOTES

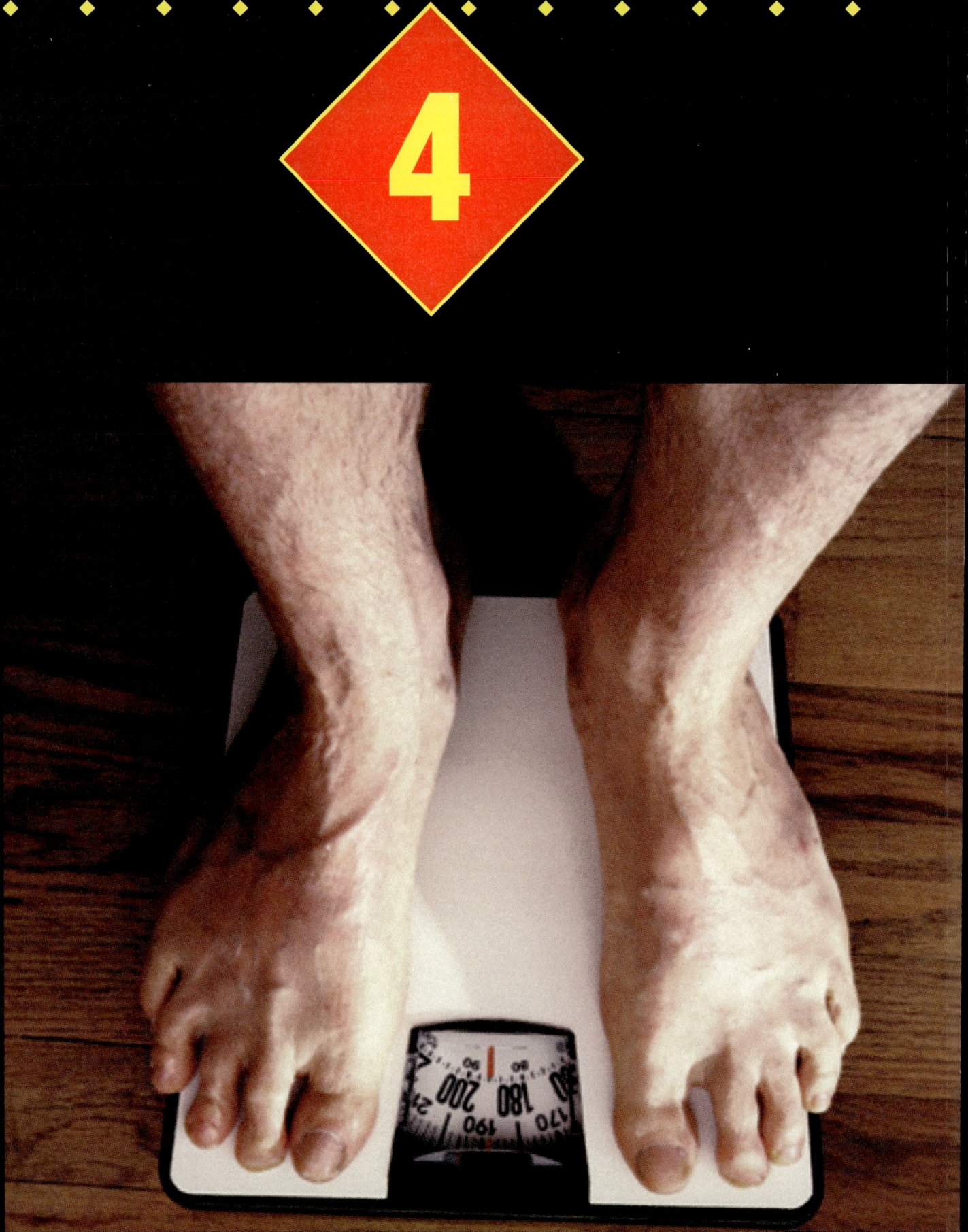

Assessment of Body Composition

Fred Kolkhorst

CHAPTER OBJECTIVES

- ◆ Understand the rationale for the use of body composition for determining ideal body weight,

- ◆ Understand the components of body composition,

- ◆ Understand the concept of percent fat and know acceptable ranges,

- ◆ Understand the principles of estimating body composition by underwater weighing, skinfold measurements, bioelectrical impedance, and near-infrared interactance.

KEY TERMS

ideal body weight

bioelectrical impedance analysis (BIA)

body mass index

essential fat

fat component

fat-free component

generalized equations

near- infrared interactance

percent body fat

standard error of estimate (SEE)

storage fat

underwater weighing

INTRODUCTION

What is an Ideal Body Weight?

Most of us are interested in knowing our *ideal body weight*. But what exactly is an ideal body weight? There are varying opinions as to what constitutes an ideal body weight but we will define it as the body weight when you have the "ideal" amount of body fat and the "ideal" amount of fat-free tissue. In other words, an ideal body weight is dependent on what is determined to be an ideal ratio of the amount of fat to fat-free tissue in the body. The concepts of ideal fat weight and fat-free weight will be discussed in detail later in this chapter.

The first major attempt at determining ideal weight was made by the Metropolitan Life Insurance Company in 1905. They produced a table of desirable weights based on height for adult men and women. The desirable weights were determined from the lowest death rates from their policy holders. The Metropolitan Life Insurance Company continued to revise and update their tables, releasing their latest version in 1983.

Unfortunately, their most recent tables were based on information collected in 1959 and has led numerous health agencies and experts to criticize the tables for a variety of reasons. Among the criticisms is the fact that the desirable weight values are based on a large, but select, population of life insurance policy holders. Non-Caucasians are underrepresented in this population of life insurance policyholders so the data may not be representative of the American population as a whole. Furthermore, while the tables purport to represent adults from 25 to 59 years of age, one report has suggested that the desirable weight values are too high for younger adults and too low for older adults.

In spite of the problems in relying on these tables to determine ideal body weight, they do have some value as a screening device. Individuals who are 10% or more below their desirable weight are considered to be underweight. Those individuals who are 10% or greater above their desirable weight are considered overweight, while those greater than 20% above their desirable weight are classified as obese.

A fundamental problem with the height-weight tables was noted in the 1940s by Dr. Albert Behnke, a U.S. Navy physician, who analyzed 25 professional football players. These players ranged in weight from 170 to 260 pounds. According to the height-weight tables, 17 of these players were above 15% of their "average weight-for-height," classifying them as being too fat for military duty. Yet, a more detailed analysis of these players revealed that 11 of 17 players actually had below average amounts of body fat.[1]

These football player illustrated a fundamental problem with the height-weight tables. The height-weight tables tell us nothing about the amount of fat on our body. Two individuals may be the same height and weight and classified as normal weight by the height-weight tables yet, one of the individuals might be very lean and muscular and have little body fat while the other might have less muscle and excessive body fat.

In order to better determine body composition, researchers developed a model that considers the body to be made up of two components, a **fat component** *and* a **fat-free component**. The fat component, termed fat weight, is comprised of all the fat in the body. The fat-free component, termed fat-free weight, is everything excluding the fat weight. Body composition is most often quantified using the term **percent fat** which is the weight of the fat component divided by the total body weight (or the percentage of the total body weight that is fat). For example, a female who weighs 100 pounds and is 18% body fat has a body composition of 18 pounds of fat and 82 pounds of fat-free weight.

Not all of the fat in our body is excess or unneeded. Some fat actually is a necessary body component in such areas as the brain, bone marrow, cell membranes, heart, and as a storage depot for some reserve energy. This necessary type of fat is termed **essential fat** and it varies somewhat in amount, especially between the genders. Males have approximately 3% essential fat while females have approximately 12%.[1] Females have larger quantities of essential fat because of their reproductive function. While we all require a certain amount of essential fat on our body, any additional fat is considered as **storage fat** and is simply a reservoir of extra energy. When this storage fat gets to be too much, it can cause serious health problems.

We now return to the original question: What is an appropriate ideal body weight? The best answer is that body weight alone is not a good measure of whether or not a person is overweight. You really need to know how fat a person is, not how much they weigh. It is the degree of fatness that is related to health, not the weight.

KEY CONCEPT

FAT PERCENTAGE OR FAT-FREE PERCENTAGE?

We could just as easily quantify the body composition by using the term **percent fat-free** but use of this term is not as common as using percent fat. In the two-component model of body composition, there is always a constant relationship between the percent fat and the percent fat-free (percent fat + percent fat-free = 100%). By knowing either, you can calculate the other.

GENDER DIFFERENCES IN BODY COMPOSITION

As already indicated, males and females have different levels of fatness dictated by biology. On the average, females have a higher percentage of body fat than males. The higher percentage of body fat in females is due to the reproductive function of the female. Prior to puberty, males and females are similar in percentage of fat.

During puberty, females get more body fat due to the influence of the female sex hormones, estrogen and progesterone. During puberty in the male, lean body mass increases primarily due to the influence of the male sex hormone, testosterone. It is during this phase of growth and development that males and females begin to diverge in their levels of body fatness. This difference in body fatness between the genders remains throughout the lifespan.

Table 4.1 depicts the body composition of the average college male and female. Even though the female is close to twice as fat when expressed as a percentage of total body weight, the majority of the difference is due to the difference in essential fat. In fact, the storage fat is very similar (12% vs 13%) for both genders. This simply emphasizes that the difference in fatness is due largely to the biological differences related to the reproductive function in the female.

Certainly, there are some males who have a higher percentage of fat than some females. But, if you look at the average percent fat of males and females at the same age and level of sport participation, from athlete to non-athlete, from young to old, there is always a gender difference. This is illustrated in Table 4.2 which lists some typical values for percent fat for athletes. Within each sport, the males are lower than the females on average, but if you were to look at some of the athletes individually, there would probably be a few females that would be lower in percent fat than the fattest males.

TABLE 4.1

Gender Differences in Body Composition for Average College Student

Gender	Body Weight (pounds)	Total Fat		Essential Fat		Storage Fat	
		%	Pounds	%	Pounds	%	Pounds
Male	150	15	22.5	3	4.5	12	18
Female	115	25	28.75	12	13.8	13	14.95

TABLE 4.2
Percent Fat of Males and Females Athletes in Selected Sports

Sport	Male	Female
Basketball	10	24
Gymnastics	5	15
Skiing	10	18
Swimming	9	26
Tennis	15	20
Distance Running	6	19
Body Building	6	10

Note: Values are averages of studies reported in the literature.
Athletes are college level or better.

AGING AND BODY COMPOSITION

As we increase in age beyond about 25 years, the tendency is that we get fatter. This is unfortunate because it contributes to chronic diseases so prevalent in later life. There are two major causes for this tendency to become fatter as we age. First, we become less active and don't adjust our caloric intake to match the decrease in activity. Secondly, our muscle mass decreases primarily due to inactivity, and muscle mass is the major contributor to resting energy expenditure. Because resting energy expenditure is lower, daily energy expenditure is lower. The relationship between body composition and age is discussed in more detail in Chapter 5 in relationship to weight loss.

METHODS OF MEASURING BODY COMPOSITION

Even though knowing the degree of fatness is the best way to determine a desirable weight, it is substantially more difficult to obtain a measure of fatness compared to simply measuring weight. Methods to assess body composition range from highly sophisticated techniques to relatively easy to administer techniques. The highly sophisticated techniques are generally inaccessible and cost-prohibitive for the general public and are used primarily in research environments. Only the most commonly available techniques of measuring body composition will be described here. When interpreting the results of body composition tests, it is important to recognize that all of these procedures are subject to some error and provide only an estimate of the actual percent fat.

Height-Weight Tables

Using the body dimensions of height and weight are not technically methods of determining body composition because body fatness is not quantified using height-weight relationships. However, body fatness is implied from the height-weight relationship. Also, most of the scientific literature that has attempted to relate disease to body composition have used height-weight relationships as the measures that have been evaluated. Most definitions of obesity use a height-weight relationship because of the ease of measuring height and weight versus fat percentage.

As indicated earlier, the original height-weight table, published in 1959 by the Metropolitan Life Insurance Company, was the first attempt at standardizing a method of determining how much a person should weigh. The most recent version of the tables was constructed in 1983 and this table was adapted by a panel of experts at the National Institutes of Health in 1985 in order to make them easier to use[5] (Table 4.3). This table depicts the weight range for each height that is associated with the lowest mortality. However, it does not consider other health problems that may be related to different weight ranges.

TABLE 4.3		
NIH Consensus Conference Height-Weight Table		
Height (inches)	Weight (pounds)	
	Males	Females
58		100-131
59		101-134
60		103-137
61	123-145	105-140
62	125-148	108-144
63	127-151	111-148
64	129-155	114-152
65	131-159	117-156
66	133-163	120-160
67	135-167	123-164
68	137-171	126-167
69	139-175	129-170
70	141-179	132-173
71	144-183	135-176
72	147-187	
73	150-192	
74	153-197	
75	157-202	

Note: Height without shoes, weight without clothing.

Source: National Institutes of Health. Consensus Development Conference Statement. Health Implications of Obesity. Annals of Internal Medicine, 103:981-1077, 1985

TABLE 4.4

1990 US Department of Agriculture Suggested Weights for Adults

Height (inches)	Weight (pounds)	
	19-34 years	>34 years
60	97-128	108-138
61	101-132	111-143
62	104-137	115-148
63	107-141	119-152
64	111-146	122-157
65	114-150	126-162
66	118-155	130-167
67	121-160	134-172
68	125-164	138-178
69	129-169	142-183
70	132-174	146-188
71	136-179	151-194
72	140-184	155-199
73	144-189	159-205
74	148-195	164-210
75	152-200	168-216
76	156-205	173-222
77	160-211	177-228
78	164-216	182-234

Note: Height without shoes, weight without clothing

Source: U.S. Department of Agriculture. "Nutrition and Your Health: Dietary Guidelines for Americans." Third Edition. Home and Garden Bulletin No. 232, 1990.

In 1990 the US Department of Agriculture published another height-weight table (Table 4.4) for adults which allowed for an increase in weight as one got older. This table has been criticized by health experts for allowing an increase in weight with age because there is no good physiologic reason we should get heavier as we get older.[4]

Body Mass Index

A more precise and informative measure of body composition that still uses height and weight is the **body mass index (BMI)**, also known as the **Quetelet Index**. The BMI is computed by the following formula:

BMI = weight ÷ height²

where: **weight** is in kilograms (kg = pounds x 0.4545)

height is in meters (meters = inches x 0.0254)

This formula can be simplified in the following way:

BMI = (704.4 x weight in pounds) ÷ (height in inches)²

The BMI has been used in many epidemiologic studies because it is simple to obtain and provides considerable more information than obtained from just height-weight tables. In fact, almost everything we know about the relationship of body composition and disease is based on the BMI as the measure of body composition.

Table 4.5 lists the standards for assessing the BMI. The health risks associated with obesity begin to increase as the BMI exceeds 25. The higher the BMI is above 25, the greater the incidence and severity of health problems. Figures 4.1 and 4.2 show the relationship between BMI and mortality

TABLE 4.5
Standards for Body Mass Index

<16	=	Too lean (may indicate an eating disorder), increased risk
16-19.9	=	Lean, underweight
20-24.9	=	Healthy range
25-29.9	=	Grade 1 obesity, increased risk
30-40	=	Grade 2 obesity, moderate risk
>40	=	Grade 3 obesity, serious risk

Adapted from Nieman, D.C. (1995). *Fitness and Sports Medicine: A Health-Related Approach*, Bull Publishing, Palo Alto, CA.; Simopoulos, A.P. (1995). "Body Weight Reference Standards. In VanItallie, T.B. and Simopoulos, A.P. *Obesity*. The Charles Press, Publishers, Philadelphia.

FIGURE 4.1

As BMI, a measure of body fatness, increases in females, the risk of dying increases. There is a 300% increase in risk with a BMI>32 compared to a BMI<19.

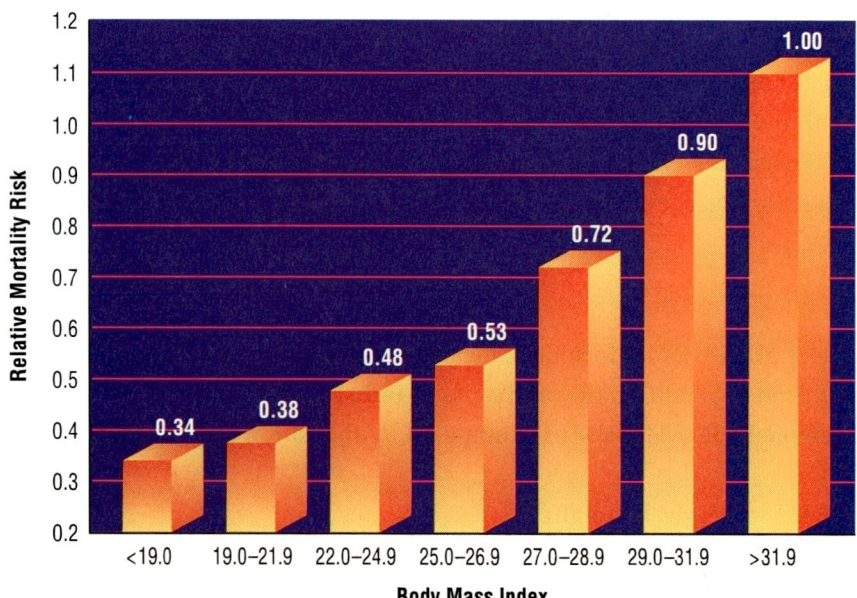

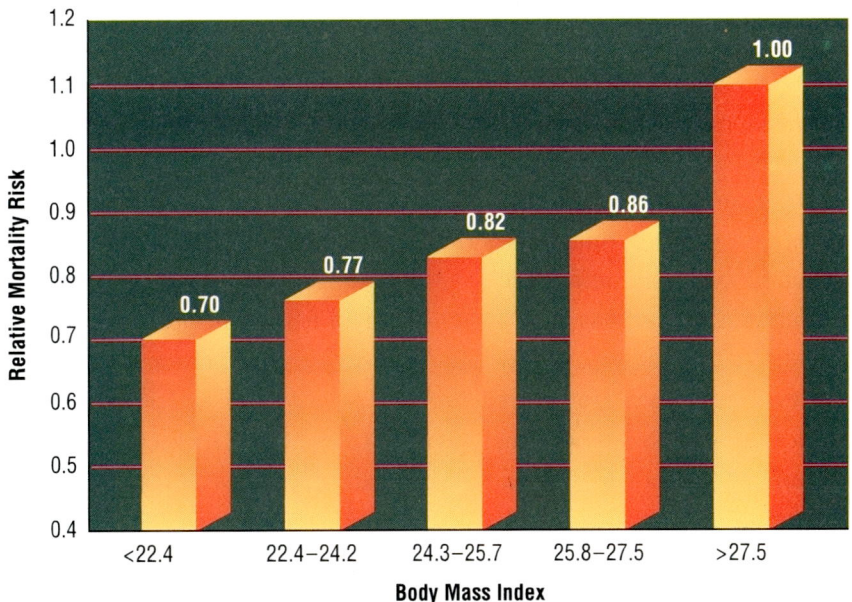

FIGURE 4.2

The risk of dying increases about 43% in males with a BMI>27.5 compared to a BMI<22.4.

in females and males, respectively. It should be noted that individuals with a large amount of muscle, like football players and body builders, generally score poorly on the BMI even though they may not have much body fat. This is only because of their relatively large muscle weight for their height and does not reflect increased risk.

Underwater (Hydrostatic) Weighing

Generally regarded as one of the most accurate methods for body composition assessment, the underwater weighing procedure is based on Archimedes' Principle. In essence, this principle states that a mass less dense than water will float in water, while a mass more dense than water will sink. Because body fat weighs less than water, it increases one's buoyancy while the fat-free mass, which weighs more than water, makes one sink.

To illustrate this principle, think of two women who both weigh 135 pounds. One woman is very lean and muscular with little body fat while the other has more body fat but less muscle. The fat-free weight of the lean woman constitutes a greater percentage of her weight than of the overweight women. The higher fat-free weight and lower fat weight of the lean woman combine to make her heavier when each is weighed underwater.

After correcting for air in the lungs, which increases buoyancy and decreases underwater weight, percent body fat can be calculated based on the underwater weight. However, in spite of being considered as the gold standard, underwater weighing still is only an estimate of body composition.

Skinfold (Anthropometric) Measurements

To find a simpler and less expensive method for determining body composition, scientists have investigated the use of anthropometry, defined as the taking of measurements of circumferences and skinfold thicknesses from different parts of the body. The instruments required are a skinfold caliper to measure skinfold thicknesses (Figure 4.3), and a cloth tape measure to determine body circumferences.

Numerous equations have been developed from anthropometric data to provide an estimation of body composition. Among the most commonly employed equations are the *generalized equations* for males and females developed by Jackson and associates in 1978 and 1980, respectively.[2,3] They are termed "generalized" because they can be used with a more diverse population than most skinfold equations due to a built-in age factor in the equation. Other equations have been developed for specific populations such as athletes, the very thin, and the obese. Lab 4.1 at the end of this chapter uses the Jackson and Pollack skinfold equations to compute percent fat. Tables 4.6 and 4.7 show the percent body fat conversion from the sum of three skinfolds for females and males using these generalized equations.

A major source of error in anthropometry lies not with the imprecision of the skinfold calipers or tape measure but in the actual technique of taking of the measurements. Making accurate skinfold measurements is more involved than pinching the skin somewhere around a particular area and measuring the thickness. There are precise sites on which the measurements are to be taken. Obtaining consistently accurate skinfold measurements requires training and experience (Figures 4.4 and 4.5).

A definite advantage of using the skinfold method is that the skinfold caliper costs as little as $20 up to $250 for a research-quality caliper. With little financial investment, body composition can be easily performed by a trained technician.

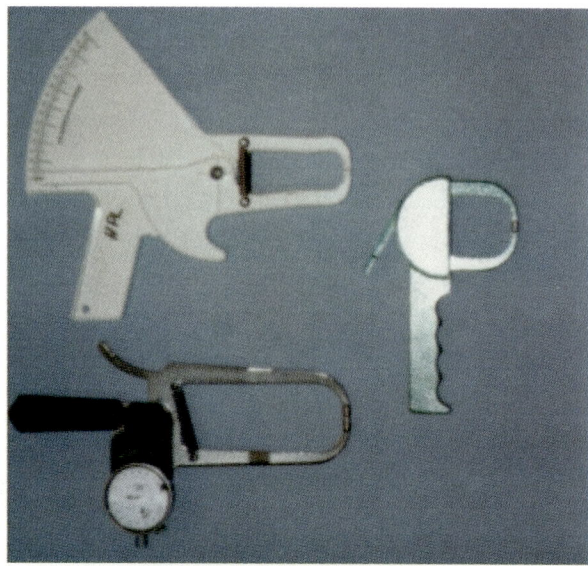

FIGURE 4.3

There are a variety of skinfold calipers available ranging in price from $20–$250.

TABLE 4.6

Female Percent Body Fat Conversion from the Sum of Three Skinfolds

Sum of 3 Skinfolds (mm)	18–22	23–27	28–32	33–37	Age in Years 38–42	43–47	48–52	53–57	58–62
16	7.8	8.1	8.4	8.7	8.9	9.2	9.5	9.8	10.1
18	8.5	8.8	9.1	9.4	9.7	10.0	10.3	10.6	10.9
20	**9.3**	**9.6**	**9.9**	**10.2**	**10.5**	**10.8**	**11.1**	**11.4**	**11.7**
22	10.1	10.4	10.7	11.0	11.3	11.6	11.9	12.2	12.5
24	10.8	11.1	11.4	11.7	12.0	12.3	12.6	12.9	13.2
26	11.6	11.9	12.2	12.5	12.8	13.1	13.4	13.7	14.0
28	12.3	12.6	12.9	13.2	13.5	13.8	14.2	14.5	14.8
30	**13.1**	**13.4**	**13.7**	**14.0**	**14.3**	**14.6**	**14.9**	**15.2**	**15.5**
32	13.8	14.1	14.4	14.7	15.0	15.3	15.6	15.9	16.3
34	14.6	14.9	15.2	15.5	15.8	16.1	16.4	16.7	17.0
36	15.3	15.6	15.9	16.2	16.5	16.8	17.1	17.4	17.7
38	16.0	16.3	16.3	16.9	17.2	17.5	17.8	13.1	18.5
40	**16.7**	**17.0**	**17.3**	**17.6**	**17.9**	**18.3**	**18.8**	**18.9**	**19.2**
42	17.4	17.7	18.0	18.3	18.7	19.0	19.3	19.6	19.9
44	18.1	18.4	18.7	19.1	19.4	19.7	20.0	20.3	20.6
46	18.8	19.1	19.4	19.8	20.1	20.4	20.7	21.0	21.3
48	19.5	19.8	20.1	20.4	20.8	21.1	21.4	21.7	22.0
50	**20.2**	**20.5**	**20.8**	**21.1**	**21.4**	**21.8**	**22.1**	**22.4**	**22.7**
52	20.9	21.2	21.5	21.8	22.1	22.4	22.8	23.1	23.4
54	21.6	21.9	22.2	22.5	22.8	23.1	23.4	23.7	24.1
56	22.2	22.5	22.8	23.2	23.5	23.8	24.1	24.4	24.7
58	22.9	23.2	23.5	23.8	24.1	24.5	24.8	25.1	25.4
60	**23.5**	**23.8**	**24.2**	**24.5**	**24.8**	**25.1**	**26.1**	**26.4**	**26.7**
62	24.2	24.5	24.8	25.1	25.4	25.8	26.1	26.4	26.7
64	24.8	25.1	25.4	25.8	26.1	26.4	26.7	27.0	27.4
66	25.4	25.8	26.1	26.4	26.7	27.0	27.4	27.7	28.0
68	26.1	26.4	26.7	27.0	27.4	27.7	28.0	28.3	28.6
70	**26.7**	**27.0**	**27.3**	**27.7**	**28.0**	**28.3**	**28.6**	**28.9**	**29.3**
72	27.3	27.6	27.9	28.3	28.6	28.9	29.2	29.6	29.9
74	27.9	28.2	28.6	28.9	29.2	29.5	29.8	30.2	30.5
76	28.5	28.8	29.2	29.5	29.8	30.1	30.4	30.8	31.1
78	29.1	29.4	29.7	30.1	30.4	30.7	31.0	31.4	31.7
80	**29.7**	**30.0**	**30.3**	**30.7**	**31.0**	**31.3**	**31.6**	**32.0**	**32.3**
82	30.3	30.6	30.9	31.2	31.6	31.9	32.2	32.5	32.9
84	30.8	31.2	31.5	31.8	32.1	32.5	32.8	33.1	33.4
86	31.4	31.7	32.0	32.4	32.7	33.0	33.4	33.7	34.0
88	32.0	32.3	32.6	32.9	33.3	33.6	33.9	34.2	34.6
90	**32.5**	**32.8**	**33.2**	**33.5**	**33.8**	**34.1**	**34.5**	**34.8**	**35.1**
92	33.0	33.4	33.7	34.0	34.4	34.7	35.0	35.3	35.7
94	33.6	33.9	34.2	34.6	34.9	35.2	35.6	35.9	36.2
96	34.1	34.4	34.8	35.1	35.4	35.8	36.1	36.4	36.8
98	34.6	34.9	35.3	35.6	35.9	36.3	36.6	36.9	37.3
100	**35.1**	**35.5**	**35.8**	**36.1**	**36.5**	**36.8**	**37.1**	**37.5**	**37.8**
102	35.6	36.0	36.3	36.6	37.0	37.3	37.6	38.0	38.3
104	36.1	36.5	36.8	37.1	37.5	37.8	38.1	38.5	38.8
106	36.6	36.9	37.3	37.6	37.9	38.3	38.6	39.0	39.3
108	37.1	37.4	37.8	38.1	38.4	38.8	39.1	39.4	39.8
110	**37.6**	**37.9**	**38.2**	**38.6**	**38.9**	**39.2**	**39.6**	**39.9**	**40.3**
112	38.0	38.4	38.7	39.0	39.4	39.7	40.0	40.4	40.7
114	38.5	38.8	39.2	39.5	39.8	40.2	40.5	40.8	41.2
116	38.9	39.3	39.6	39.9	40.3	40.6	41.0	41.3	41.6
118	39.4	39.7	40.0	40.4	40.7	41.1	41.4	41.7	42.1
120	**39.8**	**40.1**	**40.5**	**40.8**	**41.2**	**41.5**	**41.8**	**42.2**	**42.5**
122	40.2	40.6	40.9	41.2	41.6	41.9	42.3	42.6	42.9
124	40.6	41.0	41.3	41.7	42.0	42.3	42.7	43.0	43.4
126	41.0	41.4	41.7	42.1	42.4	42.7	43.1	43.4	43.8

Example: If a woman's age is 39 years and the sum of three skinfolds equals 58 mm, then her percent fat is 24.1%.

Table was calculated from A. S. Jackson, M.L. Pollock, and A. Ward. Generalized equations for predicting body density of women. *Medicine and Science in Sports and Exercise* 12:175–182, 1980.

TABLE 4.7

Male Percent Bosy Fat Conversion from the Sum of Three Skinfolds

Sum of 3 Skinfolds (mm)	18–22	23–27	28–32	33–37	Age in Years 38–42	43–47	48–52	53–57	58–62
10	**1.6**	**2.2**	**2.7**	**3.2**	**3.8**	**4.3**	**4.8**	**5.4**	**5.9**
12	2.3	2.8	3.4	3.9	4.4	5.0	5.5	6.1	6.6
14	2.9	3.5	4.0	4.6	5.1	5.6	6.2	6.7	7.3
16	3.6	4.1	4.7	5.2	5.7	6.3	6.8	7.4	7.9
18	4.2	4.8	5.3	5.9	6.4	6.9	7.5	8.0	8.6
20	**4.9**	**5.4**	**6.0**	**6.5**	**7.0**	**7.6**	**8.1**	**8.7**	**9.2**
22	5.5	6.1	6.6	7.1	7.7	8.2	8.8	9.3	9.9
24	6.1	6.7	7.2	7.8	8.3	8.9	9.4	10.0	10.5
26	6.8	7.3	7.9	8.4	9.0	9.5	10.1	10.6	11.2
28	7.4	7.9	8.5	9.0	9.6	10.1	10.7	11.2	11.8
30	**8.0**	**8.6**	**9.1**	**9.7**	**10.2**	**10.8**	**11.3**	**11.9**	**12.4**
32	8.6	9.2	9.7	10.3	10.8	11.4	11.9	12.5	13.1
34	9.2	9.8	10.3	10.9	11.5	12.0	12.6	13.1	13.7
36	9.9	10.4	11.0	11.5	12.1	12.6	13.2	13.7	14.3
38	10.5	11.0	11.6	12.1	12.7	13.2	13.8	14.4	14.9
40	**11.1**	**11.6**	**12.2**	**12.7**	**13.3**	**13.8**	**14.4**	**15.0**	**15.5**
42	11.7	12.2	12.8	13.3	13.9	14.5	15.0	15.6	16.1
44	12.3	12.8	13.4	13.9	14.5	15.1	15.6	16.2	16.7
46	12.9	13.4	14.0	14.5	15.1	15.7	16.2	16.8	17.3
48	13.4	14.0	14.6	15.1	15.7	16.2	16.8	17.4	17.9
50	**14.0**	**14.6**	**15.1**	**15.7**	**16.3**	**16.8**	**17.4**	**18.0**	**18.5**
52	14.6	15.2	15.7	16.3	16.9	17.4	18.0	18.6	19.1
54	15.2	15.7	16.3	16.9	17.4	18.0	18.6	19.1	19.7
56	15.7	16.3	16.9	17.4	18.0	18.6	19.1	19.7	20.3
58	16.3	16.9	17.4	18.0	18.6	19.1	19.7	20.3	20.9
60	**16.9**	**17.4**	**18.0**	**18.6**	**19.1**	**19.7**	**20.3**	**20.9**	**21.4**
62	17.4	18.0	18.6	19.1	19.7	20.3	20.9	21.4	22.0
64	18.0	18.5	19.1	19.7	20.3	20.8	21.4	22.0	22.6
66	18.5	19.1	19.7	20.2	20.8	21.4	22.0	22.6	23.1
68	19.1	19.6	20.2	20.8	21.4	21.9	22.5	23.1	23.7
70	**19.6**	**20.2**	**20.8**	**21.3**	**21.9**	**22.5**	**23.1**	**23.7**	**24.2**
72	20.1	20.7	21.3	21.9	22.5	23.1	23.7	24.2	24.8
74	20.7	21.2	21.8	22.4	23.0	23.6	24.2	24.7	25.3
76	21.2	21.8	22.4	22.9	23.5	24.1	24.7	25.3	25.9
78	21.7	22.3	22.9	23.5	24.0	24.6	25.2	25.8	26.4
80	**22.2**	**22.8**	**23.4**	**24.0**	**24.6**	**25.2**	**25.7**	**26.3**	**26.9**
82	22.7	23.3	23.9	24.5	25.1	25.7	26.3	26.8	27.4
84	23.3	23.8	24.4	25.0	25.6	26.2	26.8	27.4	28.0
86	23.8	24.3	24.9	25.5	26.1	26.7	27.3	27.9	28.5
88	24.3	24.8	25.4	26.0	26.6	27.2	27.8	28.4	29.0
90	**24.7**	**25.3**	**25.9**	**26.5**	**27.1**	**27.7**	**28.3**	**28.9**	**29.5**
92	25.2	25.8	26.4	27.0	27.6	28.2	28.8	29.4	30.0
94	25.7	26.3	26.9	27.5	28.1	28.7	29.3	29.9	30.5
96	26.2	26.8	27.4	28.0	28.6	29.2	29.8	30.4	31.0
98	26.7	27.3	27.9	28.4	29.0	29.6	30.2	30.8	31.4
100	**27.1**	**27.7**	**28.3**	**28.9**	**29.5**	**30.1**	**30.7**	**31.3**	**31.9**
102	27.6	28.2	28.8	29.4	30.0	30.6	31.2	31.8	32.4
104	28.1	28.7	29.3	29.9	30.5	31.1	31.7	32.3	32.9
106	28.5	29.1	29.7	30.3	30.9	31.5	32.1	32.7	33.3
108	29.0	29.6	30.2	30.8	31.4	32.0	32.6	33.2	33.8
110	**29.4**	**30.0**	**30.6**	**31.2**	**31.8**	**32.4**	**33.0**	**33.6**	**34.2**
112	29.8	30.4	31.0	31.6	32.3	32.9	33.5	34.1	34.7
114	30.3	30.9	31.5	32.1	32.7	33.3	33.9	34.5	35.1
116	30.7	31.3	31.9	32.5	33.1	33.7	34.3	34.9	35.6

Example: If a man's age is 45 years and the sum of three skinfolds equals 50 mm, then his percent fat is 16.8%.

Table was calculated from A. S. Jackson and M. L. Pollock. Generalized equations for predicting body density of man. *British Journal of Nutrition* 40:497–504, 1978.

FIGURE 4.4

Female Skinfold Sites. All measurements are on the right side. (a) The triceps skinfold is a vertical fold midway between the top of the shoulder and the tip of the elbow. (b) The suprailium skinfold is a diagonal fold taken at the intersection of the top margin of the pelvic girdle and a vertical line dropped from the front margin of the shoulder. (c) The thigh skinfold is a vertical fold taken at the midpoint of a line down the center of the thigh from the crease at the hip joint to the tip of the knee cap.

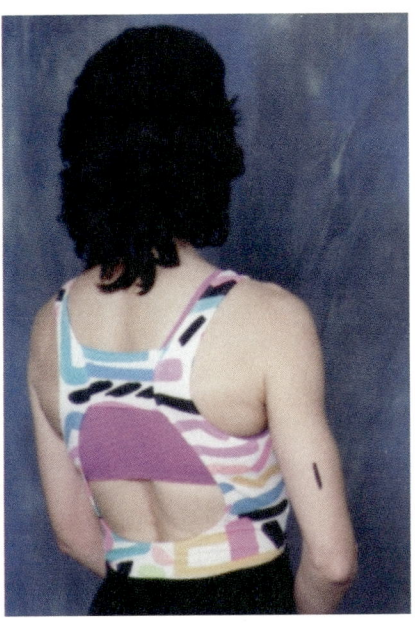 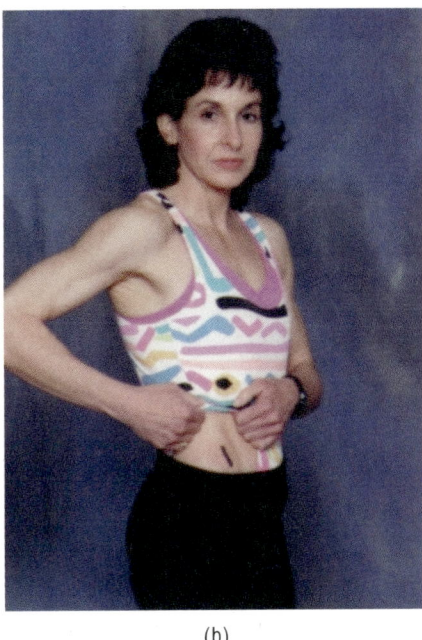 

(a)　　　　　　　　　　(b)　　　　　　　　　　(c)

FIGURE 4.5

Male Skinfold Sites. All measurements are on the right side. (a) The chest skinfold is a diagonal skinfold taken two-thirds of the way from the crease (between the pectoralis major muscle and the deltoid) to the nipple. (b) The abdominal skinfold is a vertical skinfold taken 1 inch from the navel. (c) The thigh skinfold (identical to female site) is a vertical fold taken at the midpoint of a line down the center of the thigh from the crease at the hip joint to the tip of the knee cap.

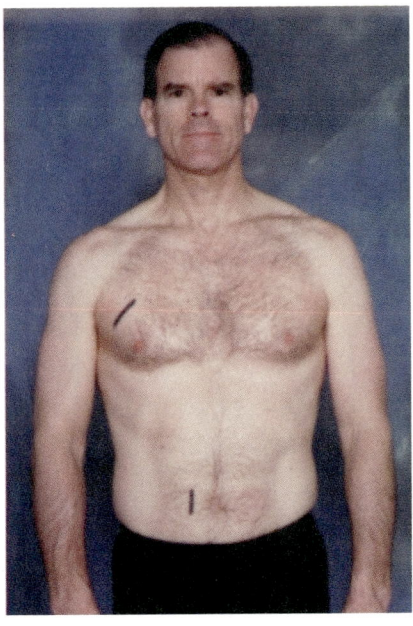 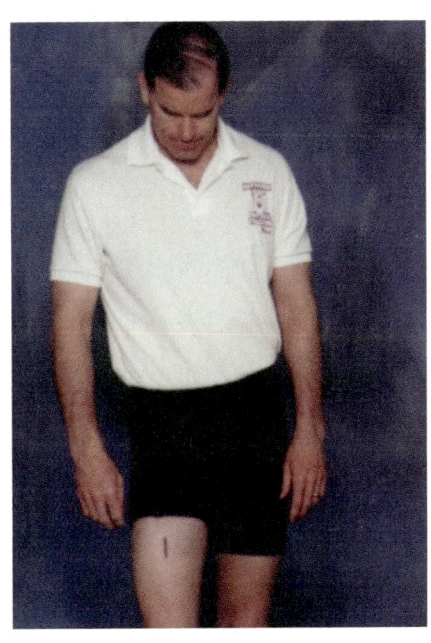

(a) (b)　　　　　　　　　　(c)

FIGURE 4.6

Bioelectric impedance analysis is simple, convenient, and painless.

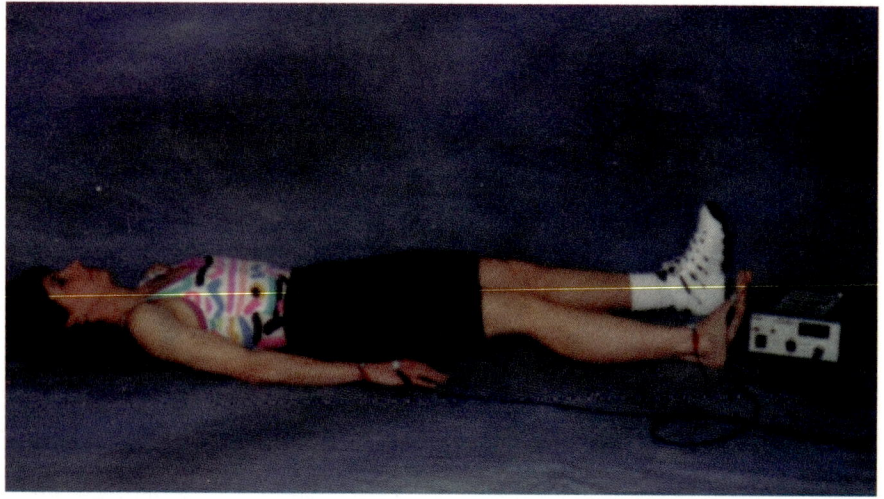

Bioelectrical Impedance Analysis

In the procedure for **bioelectrical impedance analysis (BIA),** an extremely low electrical current is passed through the body and the resistance of the body to the passage of the current is measured (Figure 4.6). The underlying principle of this method is that an electrical current passes more easily through muscle than fat because muscle contains more water and electrolytes than fat. The water and electrolytes are good conductors of electricity while the fat is a poor conductor. The procedure is simple to administer and little special training or skill is required.

A shortcoming with the BIA is that results are sensitive to the hydration level of the subject. If you are dehydrated at the time of measurement the results will be an over-estimation of body fat. Furthermore, this technique tends to overestimate body fat in lean and athletic subjects while underestimating body fat in the obese.

The BIA method holds promise for making accurate measurements both easily and quickly. Research on BIA is continuing with the objective of developing better equations to improve its accuracy. Because of its simplicity, BIA is a relatively good method for general assessment of body composition. The downside to using BIA is that the instrument costs about $3000.

Near-Infrared Interactance

A relatively new method for body composition assessment (available as the Futrex-5000) is becoming more common. In this method, a probe is placed directly on the biceps and a near-infrared light beam is emitted into the muscle (Figure 4.7). The light beam is scattered, absorbed, and reflected by the underlying tissue. Energy reflected back is measured by a detector in the probe and interpreted by the analyzer to predict body fat.

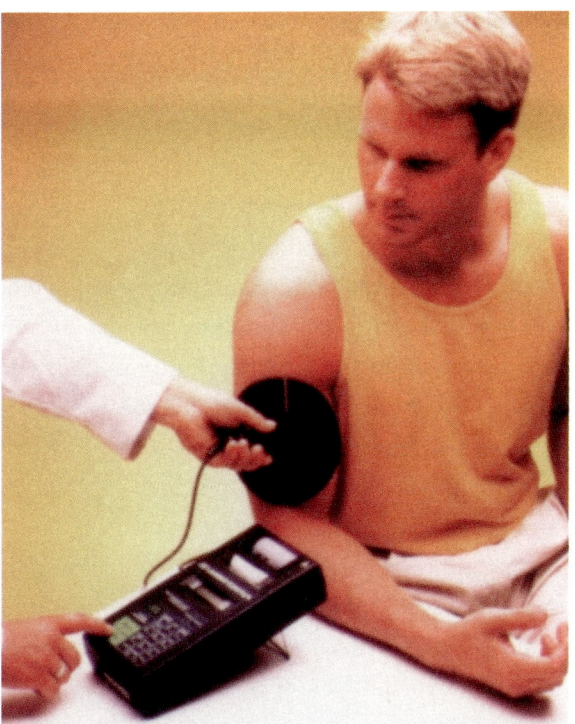

FIGURE 4.7

Near infrared reactance is a new and unproven method of determining body composition.

KEY CONCEPT

VALIDITY OF NEAR-INFRARED INTERACTANCE

The technology used in near-infrared interactance does a good job of measuring the amount of fat tissue immediately below the location of the probe. The problem with the method is trying to extrapolate from this single site measure to total body composition. It is like taking a single skinfold measure and then predicting total body fat. The best skinfold equations use multiple skinfolds because multiple skinfolds give a better picture of total body fatness.

Similar to the BIA in its ease of use, infrared interactance holds promise if some of the problems with it can be worked out. One of the major problems with this method is the assumption that measurement of a single adipose site can be used to predict body composition. Currently, the instrument used to make the necessary measurement can only be calibrated to measure one site. The near infrared interactance instrument costs about $3000, making it relatively expensive compared to skinfolds.

Undoubtedly more methods will be developed to measure body composition and the existing methods will continue to be refined. The most important thing you can do when you have your body composition measured is to appropriately interpret the results. **Remember that these body composition methods provide a range of probable values, not a single exact value!**

ACCURACY OF BODY COMPOSITION METHODS

There are two major sources of error in body composition measurements. The first source is the error inherent in the particular method chosen to be used. All the methods described make some general assumptions that are generally true in the majority of cases but they are not true in all cases. For example, the underwater weighing method makes the assumption that everyone's skeleton has the same amount of minerals in it. However, it is known that some people have more minerals and some have less than the average. Unfortunately, you do not know in any particular individual whether they are average or above or below average. This creates some inherent error in the methods which produces some inaccuracy in the results.

The second source of error in measuring body composition is in the way the procedure is carried out by whomever is doing the measuring. For example, the skinfold method is a common method of measuring body composition but in order for the method to be accurate, the person taking the measurements must know how to measure an accurate skinfold. Unless the skinfold measurement is correct, the determination of body composition will even have more error than what is inherent in the method. The methods vary in how much technical skill is necessary to accurately obtain the needed measurements.

The accuracy of body composition measures is expressed by the **standard error of estimate** or **SEE**. Assuming all measurements were correctly made, the SEE tells you how close the body composition measure is to the actual body composition. All methods of measuring body composition have an associated SEE that has been determined and verified in research studies. The correct interpretation of the SEE is critical to understanding what a body composition measure means.

The SEE is a number expressed in units of percent body fat and is interpreted in exactly the same way as the SEE for estimating maximal heart rate discussed in Chapter 2. For example, assume you measure your body composition using this method and you get a value for percent fat of 20%.

KEY CONCEPT

THE STANDARD ERROR OF ESTIMATE (SEE)

A further interpretation of the SEE can be made in the following way. Assume your obtained value for percent fat is 20%. There is a 68% probability that the actual percent fat is somewhere in the range of 20% plus or minus 3% (or 1 x SEE on either side of the measured value). There is also a 99.5% probability that the actual percent fat is somewhere in the range of 20% plus or minus 9% (or 3 x SEE on either side of the measured value).

If this body composition method has a SEE = 3%, then the SEE tells you that there is a 95% probability that your actual percent fat is somewhere in the range of 20% plus or minus 6% (the 6% is determined by 2 times the SEE or 2 x 3% = 6%). Rather than being able to say your body fat is 20%, you can only say that there is a 95% probability that your percent fat is between 14% and 26%. This range of probable values is called the **95% confidence interval** because it tells you how confident you can be that your actual percent fat is within this range.

It should be emphasized that the probable range of actual values based on the SEE is the best case scenario. It is assumed that the measurements were accurately determined. If there is inaccuracy in making the measurement necessary for determining the body composition, the SEE will be even greater.

All the methods of body composition assessment described have had their SEE values determined. As you might suspect, underwater weighing has the lowest error with the SEE = 2-3%. Skinfolds and BIA have approximately the same accuracy, with the SEE for both methods being 3-4%. The most inaccurate of the methods discussed in this chapter is near-infrared interactance, with a SEE = 4-6%. The range in the SEE for any method results from using the methods with different populations.

Table 4.8 compares the four methods relative to their accuracy, their cost, the time required to make the measurements, and the amount of technical training required to use the method. Selection of a method to measure your body composition may be out of your control, but with knowledge of the accuracy of each method, a valid interpretation of the value obtained can be made.

TABLE 4.8
Comparison of Body Composition Methods

Method	SEE	Equipment Cost	Time/Person	Technical Training
Underwater Weighing	2-3%	one time cost for tank, scales, and spirometer—$5000.	15 minutes	extensive training required
Skinfolds	3-4%	skinfold calipers from $20-250.	1-2 minutes	relative extensive training for locating and measuring skinfolds
Bioelectrical Impedance	3-4%	one time cost for instrument—$3000; electrodes per person—$0.50.	1-2 minutes	minimal training required
Near-Infrared Interactance	4-6%	one time cost for instrument—$3000.	1-2 minutes	minimal training required

WHAT IS A REASONABLE PERCENT FAT?

When the question is asked "What is a reasonable percent fat?" you have to ask "reasonable for what?" What is reasonable will be different for different people depending on several factors. Some factors are biological and, for the most part, cannot be changed. For example, gender has a tremendous influence on what would be a reasonable percent fat. On average, females will have a higher percent fat than males. Within each gender, genetics can substantially influence a particular individual's percent fat.

Other factors are related to environmental and cultural influences. In some cultures, having higher amounts of body fat is more acceptable than in other cultures. Environmental factors such as peer groups and family can exert tremendous influence on how a person views different levels of fatness. As previously indicated, whether or not a person is an athlete could affect what is considered a reasonable level of fatness.

However, in keeping with the emphasis of this text, the health impact of body composition should be the major criteria used to determine a reasonable level of fatness. If you stay within the "healthy range" of body composition, then the long-term impact will be a reduction in the incidence of diseases related to being either too thin or too fat.

Almost all the data that relates obesity to the incidence of disease and death has used either height-weight tables or BMI as the measure of obesity. Practically no epidemiological data is available using percent fat as the measure of obesity. Therefore, until data becomes available, it is difficult to make absolute recommendations regarding what is a healthy percent fat. However, based on several lines of evidence, general recommendations can be made.

Most experts agree that males should try to stay at or below 20% fat and females at or below 30% fat. The higher the percent fat above these cutpoints, the greater the incidence of disease is likely to be. When males exceed 30% and females exceed 40% fat, the incidence of disease should become a concern. Like other risky behaviors, the longer you are too fat, the more likely there are to be health consequences.

Likewise, there are healthy cutpoints on the lower end of the percent fat spectrum. The absolute minimal level of fatness is the level of essential fat, approximately 3% for males and 12 % for females. More reasonable and safe minimal values are 6% for males and 15% for females. However, genetics has such a strong influence on this end of the spectrum that it is hard to make individual recommendations. For some it would be impossible to achieve 10% and 15% for males and females, respectively. A reasonable recommendation is that if you have to chronically limit your calories so that it becomes a hour-by-hour and day-by-day struggle to maintain a low percent fat, you should adjust your goal percent fat to a higher level. After all, the "healthy" range goes all the way to 20% and 30% for males and females, respectively. Table 4.9 illustrates the method of computing the components of body composition including the ideal body weight and Table 4.10 identifies the risk levels associated with levels of percent fat.

TABLE 4.9

Computing the Components of Body Composition

In order to compute the components of body composition you have to know two of the following four components: **body weight (BW), %fat, fat weight (FW), or fat-free weight (FFW).** If you know two of the four components, you can compute the other two plus **ideal body weight (IBW).**

Example Computation:

Assume you know the following: **body weight = 200 lbs; %fat = 20%**

Compute the following: **fat weight and fat-free weight.**

Basic Formulas: **BW = FW + FFW**
FW = BW x %Fat (as a fraction)

Compute fat weight: **FW = 200 lbs x 0.20**
FW = 40 lbs

Compute fat-free weight: **FFW = BW − FW**
FFW = 200 lbs − 40 lbs
FFW = 160 lbs

In order to compute **ideal body weight**, you have to know your **ideal %fat**. The value for ideal %fat is somewhat arbitrary depending on your specific criteria but should be in the healthy range of %fat values. If you are an athlete, your ideal %fat might be lower than if you are not an athlete. Healthy values for males are between 6% and 20%. Healthy values for females are between 15% and 30%.

Assume that in our example, you decide that the ideal %fat is 10%. Once the ideal %fat has been identified, you can compute how much you would weigh if you lost enough fat weight to get down to your ideal %fat.

The ideal body weight is computed by dividing the fat-free weight by the ideal fat-free weight (expressed as a fraction). The ideal fat-free weight = 100 − ideal %fat. If, in the this example, the ideal %fat is 10% then the ideal fat-free weight is 90%. If the ideal %fat were 20%, then the ideal fat-free weight would be 80%. The ideal fat-free weight plus the ideal fat weight is always equal to 100.

Compute ideal body weight: **IBW = Current FFW / Ideal Fat-Free Weight.**
IBW = 160 lbs / 0.90
IBW = 177.8 lbs

In this example, you would have to loose from 200 lbs to 177.8 lbs in order to reduce %fat from 20% to 10%. This assumes that all weight loss is fat weight.

TABLE 4.10

Percentage Fat and Risk Levels

Risk Level	Percent Fat	
	Males	Females
Moderate	<6	<12
Very Low	6–12	12–20
Low	13–20	21–30
Moderate	21–25	31–35
High	26–40	36–50
Very High	≥ 41	≥ 51

The data for Americans clearly illustrate that, as a population, we get fatter as we get older. There is a popular belief that this is just a natural consequence of aging and is just part of getting older. In fact, there is no good biologic reason why we should get fatter as we get older. Our failure to maintain our activity level or to moderate our caloric consumption to match our expenditure results in a gradual increase in body fat over the years, a phenomena referred to as "creeping obesity." It kind of sneaks up on us and we suddenly realize that we weigh 15 or 20 pounds more than we did 5 years ago. Although this is the typical pattern, it is not the desirable pattern. If anything, we should lose weight as we get older due to loss of muscle mass that usually accompanies aging. The best solution is to remain active in order to maintain muscle mass and alter our eating behavior in order to avoid gaining fat weight. Maintaining a healthy percent fat throughout the lifespan will decrease disease and increase the quality of life.

REFERENCES

1. Behnke, A.R. (1965). Discussion. In: B.R. Menecky and S.M. Linde (Eds.), *Radioactivity in man* Springfield, IL: Charles C. Thomas.
2. Jackson, A.S., and Pollock, M.L. (1978). Generalized equations for predicting body density of men. *British Journal of Nutrition, 40,* 497-504.
3. Jackson, A.S., Pollock, M.L., and Ward, A. (1980). Generalized equations for predicting body density of women. *Medicine and Science in Sports and Exercise, 12,* 175-182.
4. Marwick, C. (1993). Obesity Experts Say Less Weight Still Best. *Journal of the American Medical Association*, 269:2617-2618.
5. National Institutes of Health. (1985). Consensus Development Conference Statement. Health Implications of Obesity. *Annuals of Internal Medicine*, 103:981-1077, 1985.

DEFINITION OF KEY TERMS

ideal body weight — body weight that falls within a weight range that is neither too low or high and minimizes chronic health risks. This weight is determined based on an ideal percent fat.

bioelectrical impedance analysis (BIA) — relatively new method for estimation of body composition that measures the resistance to a small current passed through the body. Body fat increases the resistance to the current.

body mass index — an index of the weight to height relationship used to evaluate how overweight or underweight a person is.

essential fat — amount of fat utilized by the body in such areas as the brain, cell membranes, and reproductive organs. Loss of these fats would result in physiological damage.

fat component — component of a body composition model that contains all of the body's fat. The fat component has a density less than water and makes a person weigh less underwater.

fat-free component — component of a body composition model that includes everything but the fat. The fat-free component has a density greater than water and makes a person weigh more underwater.

generalized equations — equations that use skinfold measurements to estimate body composition. These equations are most accurate in adolescent to middle-aged populations that are not extremely thin or obese.

near-infrared interactance — a method of body composition assessment based on the way a light beam is reflected and absorbed by tissue.

percent body fat — the percentage of the total body weight that is fat. This includes both the essential fat and the storage fat.

standard error of estimate (SEE) — a measure of the accuracy of prediction equations such as used with body composition assessments.

storage fat — fat on the body that is in excess of the essential fat. This is the type of fat that is intended to be lost through a weight reduction program.

underwater weighing — method of body composition assessment based on differences in density between the body's fat weight and fat-free weight. It is considered as one of the most accurate methods to estimate body composition.

LAB 4.1

ASSESSING BODY COMPOSITION WITH HEIGHT-WEIGHT RELATIONSHIPS

Name _____ ID _____ Sect _____ Time _____ Date _____

Date _____ Sex _____ Age _____ Height _____ in Weight _____ lbs

Purposes

1. To understand relationships between height and weight.

2. To determine health risk based on your current height and weight.

Directions

Recommended Weight Range

Determine your recommended weight range from Table 4.3.

Recommended Weight Range = _____lbs to _____lbs

Body Mass Index

Determine your Body Mass Index (BMI). Determine your risk level from Table 4.5.

$$BMI = (704.4 \times \text{weight in pounds}) \div (\text{height in inches})^2$$

$$BMI = 704.4 \times \text{_____} \ lbs \div (\text{_____} \ in \times \text{_____} \ in)$$

BMI = _____   Risk Level = _____

Waist to Hip Ratio

Determine your waist and hip circumferences using a cloth measuring tape. Your waist circumference is the smallest circumference between the top border of your hips and the bottom edge of your rib cage. Your hip circumference is the largest circumference around your buttocks (between your naval and lowest protruding portion of your rear end). Measure both circumferences by pulling the tape measure firmly but not so hard that in indents the underlying skin and adipose tissue. Make sure the tape measure is level when you make the measurement. Both measurements should be made while standing. (It is more difficult to make accurate measurements on yourself than for someone else to measure you).

Waist Circumference = _____ in   Hip Circumference = _____ in

(Continued)

LAB 4.1 (CONCLUDED)
ASSESSING BODY COMPOSITION WITH HEIGHT-WEIGHT RELATIONSHIPS

Determine the Waist to Hip Ratio (WHR) by dividing your waist circumference by your hip circumference. Determine your risk level based on low risk being < 0.9 for males and < 0.8 for females. Increased risk is ≥ 0.9 for males and ≥ 0.8 for females.

WHR = Waist Circumference ÷ Hip Circumference

WHR = _____ in ÷ _____ in

WHR = _____   Risk Level = _____

Answer the following questions regarding you body composition assessed with height-weight relations:

1. Were your risk levels determined from the BMI and the WHR consistent? Explain.

2. If your risk levels were not consistent, what accounted for the inconsistency? Was your height, weight, waist circumference, or hip circumference out of proportion? Explain.

3. If you could be any height and weight you wanted to be and could have any waist and hip circumference, what would the values be?

Height _____ in   Weight _____ in   Waist Circ. _____ in   Hip Circ. _____ in

What would your BMI and risk level and your WHR and risk level be at these new values?

BMI _____   Risk Level _____   WHR _____   Risk Level _____

LAB 4.2

ASSESSING BODY COMPOSITION WITH SKINFOLDS

Name _____ ID _____ Sect _____ Time _____ Date _____

Date _____ Sex _____ Age _____ Height _____ in Weight _____ lbs

Purposes

1. To determine %fat using the skinfold method.

2. To determine ideal body weight at your ideal %fat level.

Directions

Skinfold Measurements

Directions: Using information and instructions from Figure 4.3, measure the three skinfold sites illustrated for males and females. All skinfold measurements are in mm.

Females			**Males**		
Triceps	_____	mm	Chest	_____	mm
Suprailium	_____	mm	Abdominal	_____	mm
Thigh	_____	mm	Thigh	_____	mm
SUM	_____	mm	**SUM**	_____	mm

Convert the sum of the three skinfolds into %fat by using Table 4.9. Determine your risk level from Table 4.8.

%fat = _____ %   **Risk Level _____**

Compute the 95% Confidence Interval. The SEE for the Jackson and Pollock equations is 3%:

95% Confidence Interval = [%fat – 6%] to [%fat + 6%]
95% Confidence Interval = [_____% – 6%] to [_____ % + 6%]

95% Confidence Interval = _____ % to _____ %
You are 95% confident that your actual %fat is within this range.

(Continued)

LAB 4.2 (CONCLUDED)

ASSESSING BODY COMPOSITION WITH SKINFOLDS

Using your computed %fat, compute your fat weight, fat-free weight and ideal body weight.

Fat Weight = Body Weight x %Fat = _____ lb x _____ = _____ lb

Fat-Free Weight = Body Weight − Fat Weight = _____ lb − _____ lb = _____ lb

You must select a value for ideal %fat. What % fat would you like to be ?

Ideal %fat = _____ %

Compute your ideal body weight at the ideal %fat you selected:

Ideal Body Weight = Current Fat-Free Weight ÷ (Ideal Fat-Free Weight)

Ideal Body Weight = _____ lb ÷ _____

Ideal Body Weight = _____ lb

Sample calculation of Ideal Body Weight:

If Current Fat-Free Weight = 140 lb and Ideal %Fat = 15% then Ideal Fat-Free Weight is 100 − 15 or 85%

Ideal Body Weight = 140 lb ÷ (Ideal Fat-Free Weight)
= 140 ÷ 0.85
= 165 lb

ASSESSING BODY COMPOSITION WITH BIOELECTRICAL IMPEDANCE

Name _____ ID _____ Sect _____ Time _____ Date _____

Date _____   Sex _____   Age _____   Height _____ in   Weight _____ lbs

Purposes

1. To determine %fat using the bioelectrical impedance method.
2. To determine ideal body weight at your ideal %fat.

Directions

1. The bioelectrical impedance method uses a measure called **resistance** in a formula to compute % fat. If you are provided with a value for **%fat** from a computer print-out using bioelectric impedance, you can skip step #2 below. If you are provided only with a value for **resistance**, you need to compute %fat by following step #2 below.

2. The value for resistance is used in the following formula to estimate fat-free mass. Once fat-free mass is computed, %fat can be determined. Your height in inches must be converted to centimeters (cm) and your weight in pounds must be converted to kilograms (kg).

Record Your Resistance: _____ ohms

height in cm = inches × 2.54 = _____ inches × 2.54 = _____ cm

weight in kg = pounds ÷ 2.2 = _____ pounds ÷ 2.2 = _____ kg

For Males:

Fat-Free Mass in kg = [0.485 × (height in cm)^2 ÷ resistance] + (0.338 x weight in kg) + 5.32

Fat-Free Mass in kg = [0.485 × (_____ cm)^2 ÷ _____] + (0.338 x _____ kg) + 5.32

Fat Free Mass in kg = _____ kg

Fat-Free Mass in lb = _____ kg × 2.2 = _____ lb

(Continued)

For Females:

Fat-Free Mass in kg = [0.475 × (height in cm)² / resistance] + (0.295 x weight in kg) + 5.49

Fat-Free Mass in kg = [0.475 × (_____ cm)² ÷ _____] + (0.295 × _____ kg) + 5.49

Fat-Free Mass in kg = _____ kg

Fat-Free Mass in lb = _____ kg × 2.2 = _____ lb

Compute %Fat (Both Genders)

%Fat = [(Body Weight − Fat-Free Mass) ÷ Body Weight] × 100

%Fat = [(_____ lb − _____ lb) × _____ lb] × 100

%Fat = _____ %

%fat = _____ %   **Risk Level _____ (from Table 4.9)**

Compute the 95% Confidence Interval. The SEE for the impedance method is 3%:

95% Confidence Interval = [%fat − 6%] to [%fat + 6%]

95% Confidence Interval = [_____% − 6%] to [_____ % + 6%]

95% Confidence Interval = _____ % to _____ %
You are 95% confident that your actual %fat is within this range.

Using your computed %fat, compute your fat weight, fat-free weight and ideal body weight.

Fat Weight = Body Weight × %Fat = _____ lb × _____ = _____ lb

Fat-Free Weight = Body Weight − Fat Weight = _____ lb − _____ lb = _____ lb

(Continued)

ASSESSING BODY COMPOSITION WITH BIOELECTRICAL IMPEDANCE

Name _____ ID _____ Sect _____ Time _____ Date _____

Date _____ Sex _____ Age _____ Height _____ in Weight _____ lbs

You must select a value for ideal %fat. What % fat would you like to be ?

Ideal %Fat = _____%

Compute your ideal body weight at the ideal %fat you selected:

Ideal Body Weight = Current Fat-Free Weight ÷ (Ideal Fat-Free Weight)

Ideal Body Weight = _____ lb ÷ _____

Ideal Body Weight = _____ lb

Sample calculation of Ideal Body Weight:

If Current Fat-Free Weight = 140 lb and Ideal %Fat = 15% then Ideal Fat-Free Weight is 100 − 15 or 85%

Ideal Body Weight = 140 lb ÷ (Ideal Fat-Free Weight)

= 140 ÷ 0.85

= 165 lb

NOTES

NOTES

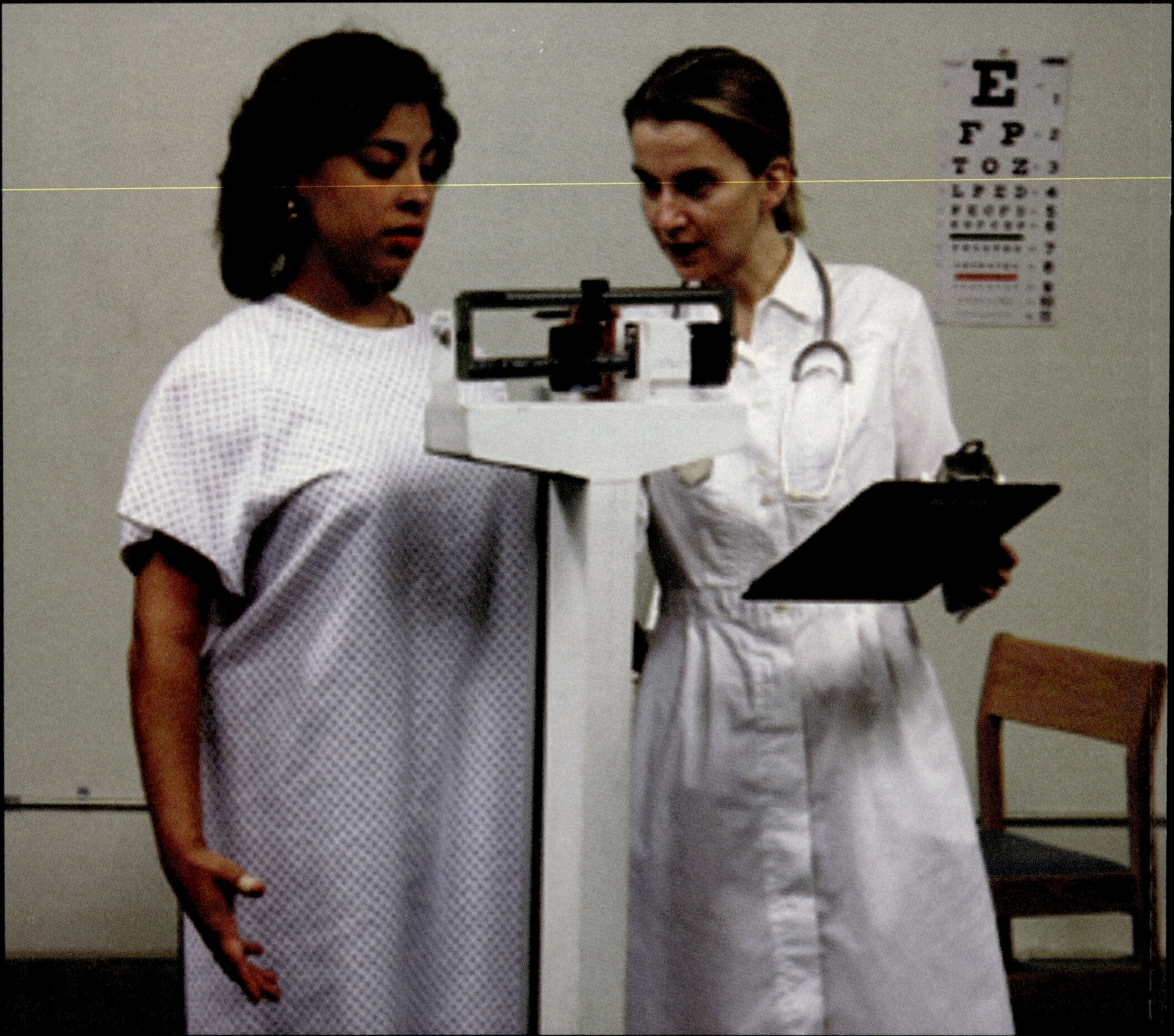

Weight Management

FRED KOLKHORST

INTRODUCTION

"Thin is in!" In the 1960s and 70s, as Americans began trying to achieve a leaner look, this statement became a truism. The lean look was glamorized during these times by a famous British model, appropriately named Twiggy, who personified the "ideal" image with her overly thin appearance. Although the look of today's models and movie stars are not as extreme as Twiggy's (and she is now at a healthier weight), society still values being thin. A look at any leading character in an advertisement, movie, or television show illustrates this concept; they almost always have a trim build. Even the famous American movie star and sex symbol of the 1950s and early 60s, Marilyn Monroe, would be judged as a little pudgy by today's standards.

We live in a culture in which leanness is desirable and have become preoccupied with trying to lose weight. Americans are estimated to spend over $30 billion dollars each year on items such as diet books and foods, health clubs and exercise equipment, and on various weight-loss organizations in an attempt to achieve a thinner appearance. Witness the numerous magazine headlines in a grocery market checkout lane that "reveal the secrets of weight loss that your doctor won't tell you" or "how to burn off

Today's society glamorizes being thin, particularly for females.

pounds of that unwanted fat in just days." Not only are adults conscious of their weight but surveys indicate 75% of high school girls are attempting to lose weight at any one time. Even in young children, personal appearance has become increasingly important, and dieting is not uncommon in as early as the fourth grade.

In spite of a society that glamorizes leanness, Americans continue to get fatter. American males average 7.3 pounds heavier than their counterparts 15 years ago. Moreover, it has been estimated that fully one third of all American adults are obese, and this figure rises each year. Even more alarming are studies indicating that obesity is becoming more prevalent in children and young people, and this is occurring when the publicizing of health problems related to obesity has never been greater.[16]

Research indicates that obesity is related to a wide variety of health problems and contributes to premature death. As body mass index, a general indicator of body fatness, increases above the healthly range, the death rate increases. Figure 5.1 shows the increase in prevalence of overweight adults in this country over the last four decades. It has been estimated that if overweight individuals were to normalize their weight, their life expectancy would be increased 3 years.[19]

FIGURE 5.1

Prevalence or Overweight in U.S. Adults, 1960–1991. Since 1960, there has been a steady increase in the percentage of the American population that is overweight.

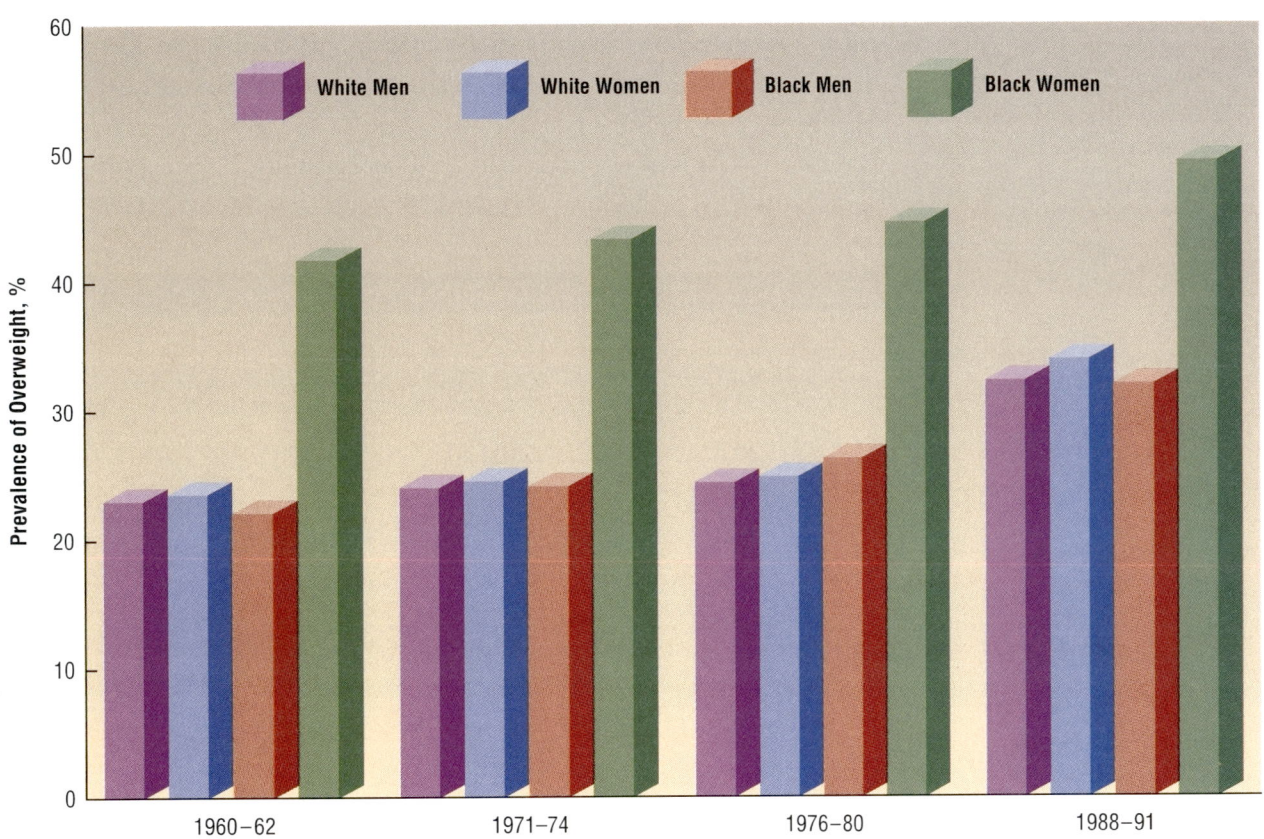

OBESITY

Obesity is a condition of excess body fat. Exactly how much body fat is considered excess is not agreed upon and is dependent on the measure of body composition used to quantify the body fat. Several measures of body fatness have been used to quantifiy obesity, among the most common being weight, body mass index, and percent body fat. Some of the problems with these measures of fatness are discussed in relation to body composition in Chapter 4.

Obesity and Health

In most westernized societies, and especially in the United States, the un-restricted access to high-caloric foods has created a climate conducive to obesity. As the American population gets older, we get fatter and as we get fatter, we have more health problems. Obesity is associated with a wide variety of health problems including premature death (Table 5.1). Especially prevalent in this country are cardiovascular disease, cancer, and adult-onset diabetes, all of which have a relationship to obesity.

By conservative estimates, one-third of American adults are obese. The percentage of adults classified as obese at any point in time will depend on the definition of obesity that is used. There is recent evidence that the definitions currently used may be too conservative and, in fact, more adults than have been previously recognized are at risk because of excess body fat. The current incidence of obesity far exceeds the government's *Healthy People 2000* goal of no more than 20% obese adults.

TABLE 5.1
Chronic Diseases and Health Concerns Related to Obesity

The risk of developing each of the following is significantly higher in the obese:
 • Cardiovascular diseases including high blood pressure and high cholesterol
 • Certain forms of cancer
    - Women—breast, uterus, ovaries, colon rectum
    - Men—prostate, colon, rectum
 • Adult-onset diabetes
 • Musculoskeletal problems due to excess weight on joints
 • Menstrual irregularities, infertility, problem pregnancies

Regional Body Fatness

Interestingly, differences in where our fat is stored affects the risks for many of our primary health concerns such as cardiovascular diseases, adult-onset diabetes, and hypertension.[11,12] It is not simply how much fat we have that is important but where the fat is located is also important. Regional body fatness is divided into two gender-related categories. Males tend to store excess fat in the abdominal region, a condition called **android obesity**. Females tend to store excess fat in the hips and thighs, a condition called **gynoid obesity**. Although not every male and female distributes fat in exactly these two ways, the majority do. The female distribution pattern is a more "healthy" type of fat distribution than is the male pattern in that individuals with gynoid obesity are at a lower risk of heart disease than those with adroid obesity.

One way to assess regional fat distribution is to measure the **waist-to-hip ratio (WHR)**. The WHR is determined by simply taking a cloth tape measure and measuring the smallest circumference between the naval and the bottom of the rib cage. Then measure the largest circumference of the hips while standing. The ratio is formed by dividing the waist circumference by the hip circumference. The risk of disease increases dramatically when the WHR is above 0.9 for males and 0.8 for females.

Obesity and Age

The trend in the U.S. is for adults to get fatter as they get older, at least until the age of 60. Figure 5.2 illustrates that the body mass index, a measure of fatness, continues to rise until about age 60. There are more obese adults

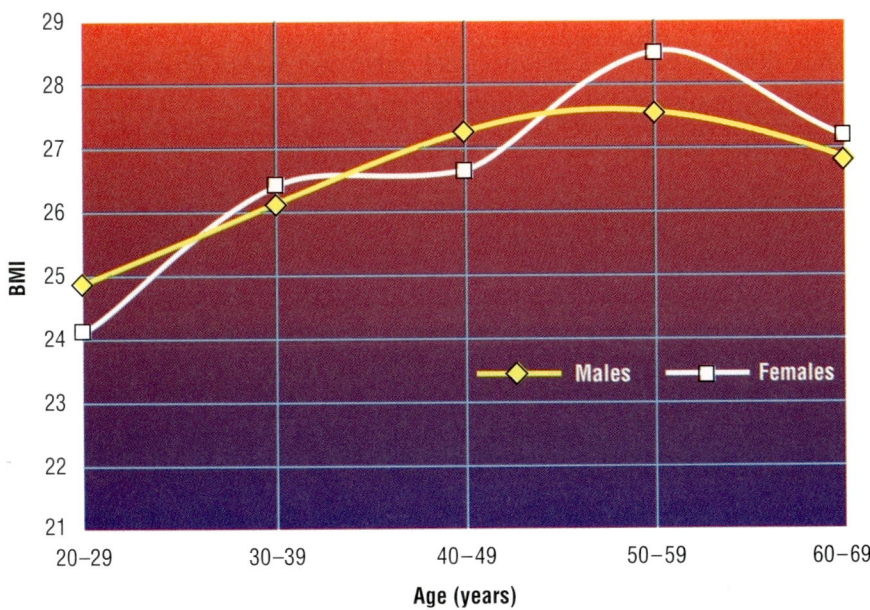

FIGURE 5.2

Increase in Fatness and Age in U.S. Adults. Americans increase body fatness from age 20 to the sixth decade of life.

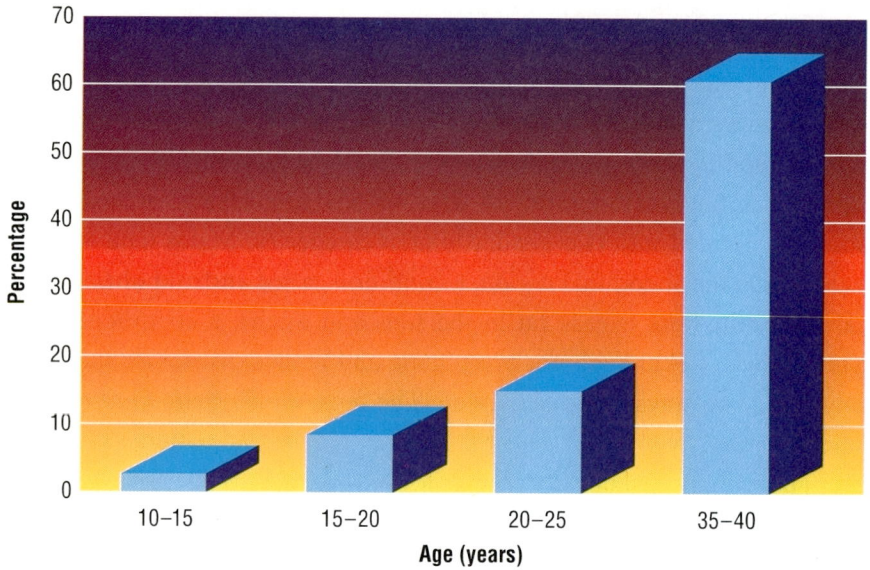

FIGURE 5.3

Prevalence of Blockage in Coronary Arteries and Age. By age 40, more than 60% of the population has blockage in the coronary arteries.

today than any other time in history. The average American is overweight by age 30 and the problem only gets worse.

Although a 20-year old overweight college student is still a low risk for a heart attack or stroke in the near future, this should not be misconstrued to mean that being overweight at a relatively early age carries little or no health risks. Many of the health-related problems associated with obesity actually began during early adulthood or sooner. Several studies have shown that over half of young adult men and women already have developed early stages of heart disease though symptoms do not appear for 20-30 years.[17,22] Figure 5.3 illustrates that the early beginnings of blockage in the arteries of the heart are found in 10-15 year olds. All of these chronic diseases are such that once they have become symptomatic, it is much more difficult to treat them. Unfortunately, the first symptom in many of these slowly developing chronic diseases can be a major catastrophe, like a fatal heart attack. The key to prevention is to begin a lifestyle now that will prevent the development of the disease.

Psychological and Social Implications of Obesity

Besides the implications on physical health, being overweight often has psychological and social consequences. Performing common activities becomes more trying. Clothes are more difficult to find. Car seats, plane seats, and restaurant seats are not usually built for larger bodies. Moreover, our society appears to subtly discriminate against overweight people as obese individuals are less likely to advance in social and professional opportunities. While weight usually has no bearing on the ability of one to perform her or his job, overweight people are more frequently passed over for acceptance into prestigious social organizations or job promotions.

While there does not seem to be any strong evidence to suggest that overweight people suffer more serious psychological problems than normal weight individuals, obese people may also have a poor perception of their own body image. Regardless of their accomplishments, some overweight people have not come to accept their body shape which leaves them discouraged and frustrated. One discouragement comes from a society that says part of being beautiful is being thin while another frustration comes from the difficulty in losing weight. If losing weight were simple to do, there would be a lot fewer obese people in the world.

WEIGHT LOSS

Trying to maintain or lose weight can be a very frustrating experience. Many young individuals who are at an ideal body weight, much to the exasperation of those who are not, have no problem with maintaining their present weight. However, the majority of individuals find that as they get older, maintaining an ideal weight becomes more difficult. Why is it so hard to lose those few extra pounds around our waist or thighs? This should be simple enough. After all, body weight decreases if the energy expended is greater than the energy consumed.

On the surface, this seems elementary. However, the fact that so many people have difficulty controlling their weight suggests the body's regulation for weight may be more complex than first appears. A discouraging statistic is that 95% of all people who begin a weight loss program end up regaining all their weight back in less than 5 years. Losing weight and keeping it off is more difficult for some than others because of genetics and differences in individual's physiologic and psychologic characteristics.

Obesity experts often classify the factors which contribute to obesity into three broad categories—genetics, cultural, and environmental (Figure 5.4). All of these factors can affect the way an individual consumes and expends energy, thus affecting weight gain and/or loss. Some factors are out of our control, at least for the time being. Genetics is one factor seemingly out of our control but there is currently intensive research being conducted to discover the gene or genes that promote obesity. However, many cultural and environmental factors can be positively altered to make it easier to loose weight.

FIGURE 5.4

Factors Accounting for Levels of Body Fat. Lifestyle, environment, and cultural factors account for the majority of body fatness.

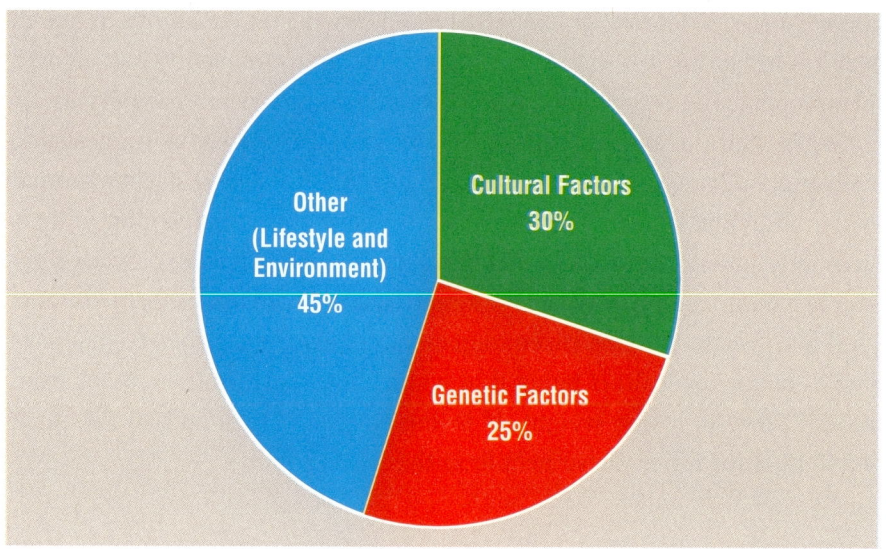

Fat Cells

Fat is stored in billions of tiny **fat cells**, called **adipose cells**. These fat cells are primarily located just beneath the skin and represent the majority of fat that is readily visable on a person. These storage depots can be compared to balloons that change in size as the amount of air in them changes. As we gain or lose body fat, the fat content inside these fat cells either increases or decreases, respectively. In an obese individual, more fat is stored in a fat cell so the diameter of the fat cells are larger than those from a non-obese person. Furthermore, an obese person tends to have a greater number of fat cells than a non-obese individual.[2] The combination of larger and more fat cells produces the typical appearance of obesity.

Adults with a larger number of fat cells have a more difficult time controlling their weight. Each fat cell is like a sponge that easily soaks up water. The more sponges there are, the more water that can be soaked up. A larger number of fat cells makes weight management more difficult because of the greater ease in fat uptake by the fat cells. One key to weight management may be the control of fat cell numbers.

However, the number of fat cells in our body is largely determined during our growing years and generally becomes fixed by the time we reach adulthood. Fat cells appear to rapidly increase in number primarily during two periods of our growth. The first period occurs during the first year of life. The second period begins around the age of 10 and continues through the adolescent growth.[10] After this time, the number of fat cells is thought to remain stable unless there is an extreme weight increase. Thus, weight changes during adulthood are largely due to changes in the size of the fat cells rather than the number of fat cells.

Some influence over the proliferation of fat cells during growth may be possible, but it is mostly under the control of our parents. Women who do not exceed recommended weight gains during pregnancy have babies with fat cells that are smaller in size and number as compared to babies of mothers who have large weight gains during pregnancy. The rate of increase in fat cell number may also be diminished by avoiding overfeeding during the adolescent years. Moreover, regular exercise during this period may slow down fat cell development. This is supported by several studies that observed fewer and smaller fat cells in young exercising animals than in a comparable sedentary group. If these results can be applied to humans, early prevention of obesity may be one of the most effective measures to avoid becoming too fat later in life.

Energy Balance

The amount of fat stored in our fat cells is influenced by the net sum of the energy intake and expenditure. If, over a period of time, the energy intake is greater than energy expenditure then body weight increases. This condition is referred to as a **positive energy balance**. The converse also is true, that is, body weight decreases when energy expended is greater than energy consumed. This is referred to as a **negative energy balance**. Energy intake is determined by the caloric intake from the consumption of food and is influenced by the body's satiety control center, the center for turning on and off the desire to eat. Energy expenditure is influenced primarily by the

TABLE 5.2
Factors Affecting Energy Balance

If **Energy Intake = Energy Expenditure**, then weight is **stable**
If **Energy Intake > Energy Expenditure**, then weight is **gained**
If **Energy Intake < Energy Expenditure**, then weight is **lost**

Factors Affecting Energy Intake:
- amount of fat calories consumed
- amount of fiber consumed
- body's satiety level

Factors Affecting Energy Expenditure:
- basal metabolic rate which is influenced by
  ⇒ total energy consumption
  ⇒ physical activity
  ⇒ muscle mass
- amount of physical activity

resting metabolic rate (RMR), the energy expended by the body for main-tenance of normal body functioning, as well as the level of physical activity. A more thorough understanding of the interactions of energy intake and expenditure can help to make better decisions and allow for greater control over body weight.

Energy Intake

Energy intake is the sum total of all the calories we eat. Energy in food is measured by a unit called a **kilocalorie (kcal)** which is equivalent to 1 Calorie (with a capital C) or 1,000 calories (with a lower case c). When the energy content of food is identified, it is almost invariably given in units of kcal. For example, when we say a slice of bread contains 90 Calories, that is the same as 90 kcals or 90,000 calories (with lower case c).

The energy content of various foods are determined experimentally in a device called a bomb calorimeter. In a bomb calorimeter, a food product is literally burned up and the amount of energy released is measued. How-ever, all the energy contained in food we consume is not necessarily made available to the body. There may be some variations in the number of calo-ries in food determined from bomb calorimetery and the number of calories that winds up as usable energy in the body.

Quantity of Calories

Some, but not all, individuals who have trouble controlling their weight simply are consuming too many calories for their level of energy expendi-ture. This illustrates the most fundamental principle of weight loss - **in order to lose weight, the energy consumed must be less than the energy ex-pended.** There does not have to be a caloric deficit at the end of each day, but over a period of time, the calories consumed must be less than the calories expended. For many people wishing to lose weight, cutting back on the number of calories consumed would be sufficient to manage their weight.

Diet Composition

Unfortunately, the total number of calories consumed compared to the number expended is not the only factor that influences weight gain or loss. A calorie from carbohydrate is not necessarily the same as a calorie from fat. Different types of calories seemed to be metabolized by the body in different ways.

In addition to the total caloric value of the food consumed, the compo-sition of the diet can affect the way the body handles the energy consumed.

Of the six macronutrients in foods–carbohydrates, proteins, fats, vitamins, minerals, and water–only carbohydrates, proteins, and fats contain energy. Both carbohydrates and proteins contain 4 kcal per gram of energy, while a gram of fat has 9 kcal of energy. Thus, fats are 2.25 times as dense in energy as either carbohydrates or proteins. Ethanol, the alcohol found in alcoholic beverages, also is energy-rich having 7 kcal per gram (Figure 5.5).

Recent studies suggest that the energy composition of the diet plays a significant role in weight management.[1] There appears to be differences in how the body metabolizes and stores energy from the macronutrients. In

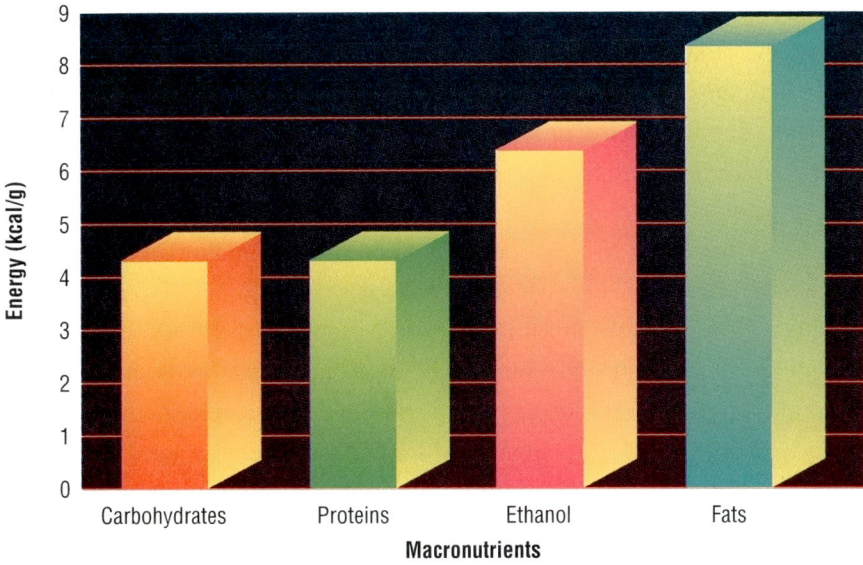

FIGURE 5.5

Caloric Density of Foods. Fat contains more than twice as many calories per gram than carbohydrates and protein.

The body is better able to metabolize excess calories in the form of carbohydrates.

short, not all energy is treated equally. The body has a hierarchy that it follows when metabolizing or storing the macronutrients of a meal.[7] If you consume fat, carbohydrate, or protein in the same proportions that they are used for fuel, the result will be a stable weight. If there is an imbalance in the proportion of fats, carbohydrates and protein consumed compared to what is used for fuel, the imbalance will result in storing the excesses as fat.

In this priority of calorie use, the first type of calorie to be metabolized is ethanol. Because the body has no capacity to store ethanol, it is completely metabolized and none of its energy is stored. However, during this time metabolism of fats and carbohydrates is suppressed. For example, if you go out and eat pizza and drink beer, over the succeeding several hours the body will readjust its use of the macronutrients used for energy. The beer will be the first thing to be metabolized. If large quantities of alcohol are consumed, the alcohol is metabolized over a substantial period of time, all the while depressing the amount of fat and carbohydrate metabolized.

Next to be metabolized are carbohydrates and proteins. Because the body can store only a relatively small quantity of carbohydrate and protein (without converting them to fat), the body attempts to metabolize most of the carbohydrate and protein consumed in excess of its capacity to store them. The body does this by increasing how much carbohydrate and protein it uses for energy. Amazingly, the body can increase its rate of metabolism to accommodate substantial excesses of carbohydrates and protein over short periods of time. However, substantial long-term excessive intakes are converted to fat and stored. This is why, over the long haul, it is important that total calories consumed equal total calories expended if weight is to be maintained.

Last to be metabolized are fats. Unlike the other macronutrients, the rate of fat metabolism is not so adaptable to excessive fat intakes, and fat intake in excess of the amount of fat used for energy is easily stored. Moreover,

---

KEY CONCEPT

THE ENERGY COST OF MAKING FAT

Excess calories from fat, carbohydrate, and protein can be converted to fat and stored in the body's adipose cells. But it is more difficult for the body to convert carbohydrate and protein to fat and store it as adipose fat than it is to store fat as adipose fat. When carbohydrate is converted to fat and stored, about 25% of the caloric value of the ingested excess carbohydrate is used as energy to convert the other 75% of the carbohydrate to fat.[1] When excess fat is stored, essentially all of the caloric value of the fat is stored. Simply put, if you are going to overconsume macronutrients, it is better to overconsume protein and carbohydrate.

the increased rate of metabolism from excesses of carbohydrates and proteins inhibit the rate of fat metabolism which further increases fat storage.

Because the body stores excess fat calories more easily than carbohydrate calories, individuals consuming a low-fat diet are better able to manage or lose weight compared with individuals consuming a diet equal in calories but higher in fat and lower in carbohydrates.[7] This also may be related to the satiating effects of the diet composition. Several studies have demonstrated that subjects, when allowed free access to only high-fat foods, actually consumed more calories than subjects with free access to only low-fat foods.[22] These results demonstrated a passive overconsumption of food intake with high-fat foods. Thus, the type of calories, not just the total calories consumed, influences weight loss.

Because of the close relation of dietary intake of fat and cholesterol with heart disease and certain cancers, health professionals advocate a reduction in fat consumption with an increase in the intake of complex carbohydrates. Approximately 36% of calories in the typical American diet come from fats while about 44% come from carbohydrates and 20% from proteins. The current recommendation by the American Heart Association is for dietary fat intake to be decreased to 30% or lower and carbohydrates increased to 55% or higher. Many health professionals and nutritionists think that the lower the fat intake the better as long as minimal needs for fat are met (Figure 5.6).

Reducing dietary fat intake makes weight loss easier and reduces risks of numerous health problems. Keep in mind, however, that there are nutritional needs for including some fat in the diet. Fats are used to transport fat-soluble vitamins, and two of the polyunsaturated fatty acids are essential to the body's metabolism (see Chapter 6 on Nutrition Principles).

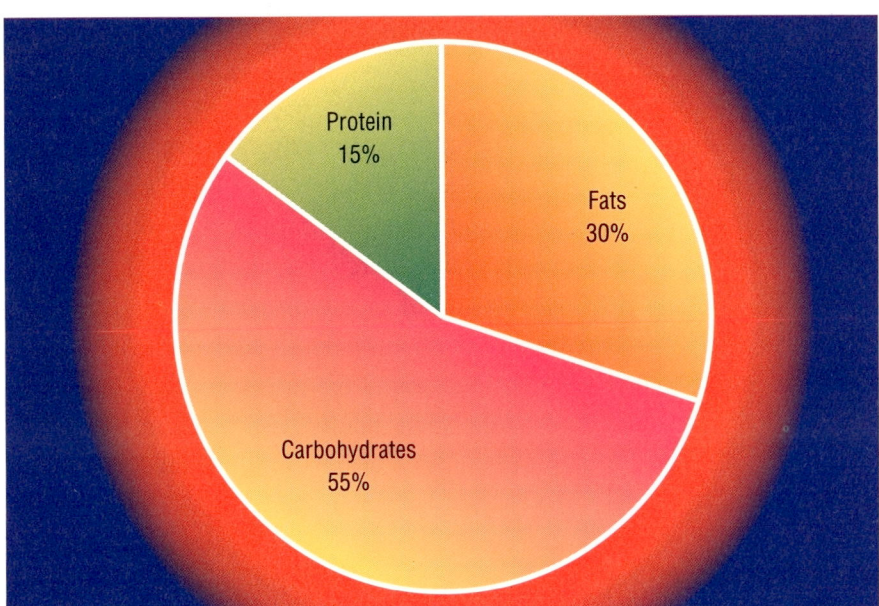

FIGURE 5.6

Recommended Intakes of Macronutrients as a Percentage of Daily Total Calories. A healthy diet consists of minimal fat, adequate protein, and lots of carbohydrates.

Fiber

Another important diet consideration is the consumption of fiber, a type of non-digestible complex carbohydrate. A high-fiber diet decreases the transit time of the food in the GI tract so that food is passed more quickly through the digestive system. The faster transit time appears to contribute to an effective weight control program. The physiological basis for this is not completely understood but it may be because there is less time available for the fat to be absorbed. Raw fruits, vegetables and whole grains are the types of foods highest in fiber. Generally speaking, the more processed a food is, the lower in fiber content.

Satiety

While weight loss can theoretically be achieved by reducing caloric and/or fat intake, psycho-physiological factors may intervene to make successful long-term weight loss difficult. Satiety is the feeling reached when we sense we have eaten just enough food to satisfy our hunger. Several areas in the central nervous system, including the hypothalamus, have been identified as influencing hunger and satiety. Signals from these centers create a strong desire to eat and can be strong enough to override our "will-power" to refrain from eating too much. This may explain, in part, the difficulty many people have in losing excess weight and/or permanently keeping it off.

Several of the drugs used to treat obesity act by reducing the appetite or increasing satiety and have been found to be useful adjuncts to weight loss programs. Additionally, fat consumption seems to have a greater effect on satiety than consuming carbohydrates or protein. Unfortunately, the effect of fat consumption on satiety is relatively slow and an individual often overconsumes fat before the appropriate signals to stop eating are generated.

Energy Expenditure

There are three components that comprise your daily caloric expenditure—the resting metabolic rate (RMR), the thermic effect of food, and the thermic effect of physical activity or exercise. The approximate contribution of each of these components to the daily energy expenditure is depicted in Figure 5.7. However, the contribution of these components can be highly variable in individuals depending on how physically active one is. For example, although physical activity accounts for less than 25% of energy expenditure for the average adult, some adults who work in physically demanding occupations may expend 50% or more of their energy through physical activity.

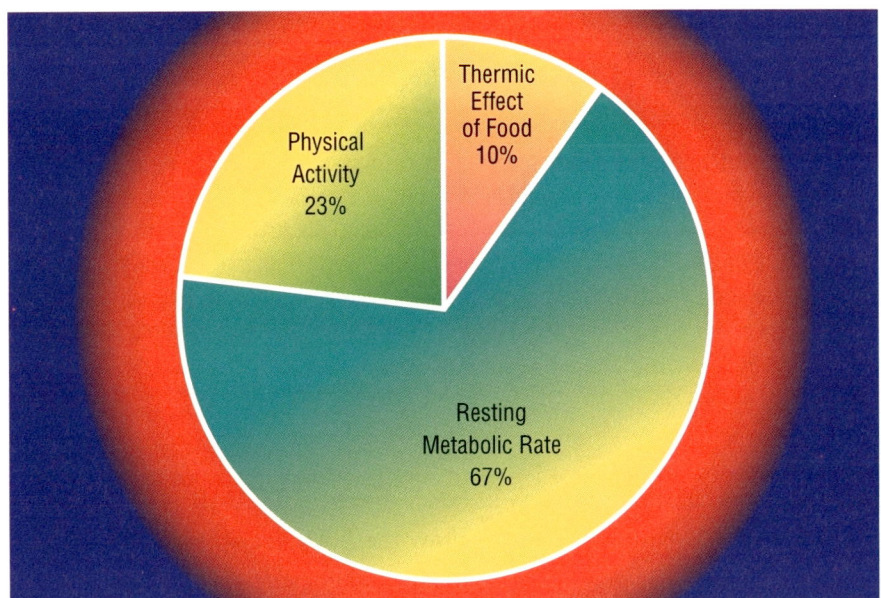

FIGURE 5.7

Components of Daily Energy Expenditure. The RMR accounts for "fixed" energy expenditure on a day-to-day basis while physical activity can be significantly increased or decreased to affect weight gain or loss.

Resting Metabolic Rate

The **resting metabolic rate (RMR)** represents the energy expended to simply maintain normal bodily functions such as the cardiovascular and respiratory systems. The RMR can be compared to the fuel (energy) required just to keep an automobile engine idling It is largely influenced by the amount of muscle mass an individual has, and as one gains or loses muscle, the RMR tends to increase or decrease, respectively. The RMR can be estimated from the height and weight relationships depicted in Table 5.3. Depending upon one's level of physical activity, the RMR has been estimated to account for 50 to 75% of the body's total daily energy expenditure and, thus, has significant influence on body weight.

Numerous investigations have studied the effect of diet and exercise on the metabolic rate. These studies demonstrate that when individuals greatly

TABLE 5.3
Estimating the Resting Metabolic Rate (RMR)

Females: RMR (kcal/day) = 447.593 + (7.869 × ht) + (4.203 × wt) − (4.330 × age)

Males: RMR (kcal/day) = 88.362 + (12.189 × ht) + (6.090 × wt) − (5.677 × age)

Where:

- ht = height in inches
- wt = weight in pounds
- age = years
- Equations are Revised Harris-Benedict Equations

KEY CONCEPT

PLATEAU IN WEIGHT LOSS

The phenomenon of a decreasing RMR in response to caloric restriction is illustrated by reports of individuals who consumed 800 kilocalories a day for several weeks. Initially, they lost weight but eventually reached a point at which they were unable to lose any further weight. Their RMR slowed down so much that these individuals were able to maintain weight on just 800 kilocalories a day. This is just slightly more calories than found in a McDonald's Quarter Pounder with Cheese and a small order of french fries.

decrease their caloric intake, as in crash dieting, the RMR also decreases by 20% to 25% or more.[4,15,18] Somehow the body recognizes the reduced energy intake from a very-low calorie diet and goes into an "energy conservation mode" by reducing the energy required to maintain the body's normal functioning. As a result, the body becomes more efficient with the reduced energy it receives by decreasing its energy expenditure. This increases the difficulty of further weight loss. However, numerous studies have suggested that exercise minimizes the decrease in RMR during periods of low-caloric consumption.[8,24] Most researchers agree, though, that exercise will not permanently increase an already normal RMR.

Set-Point

The phenomenon of a reduced energy intake decreasing the RMR illustrates the **set-point theory**. Basically, this theory states that the body has a particular level of body fat at which it wants to remain and will make metabolic adjustments in order to maintain its fat stores. The body's set-point also may be associated with the satiety control center. After rapid weight loss is attained, most people end up regaining the lost weight because of an over-stimulated appetite. In a recent well-publicized example, Oprah Winfrey, a popular television celebrity, used her talk show to display her rapid weight loss. Soon after nearing her goal, her weight quickly began increasing until she stabilized close to her original weight.

There is evidence that the set-point can be altered by diet and exercise. Low-fat diets and exercise may lower the set-point. Some time after Oprah Winfrey regained her weight, she embarked on a new program that included a low-fat diet and regular running. Although she doesn't talk much about her weight anymore, her new program has been quite successful as she has maintained her weight loss and even recently completed a 26.2-mile marathon race.

While weight loss may be quickly achieved on a very-low calorie diet, long-term adherence to such a diet is very difficult. Most people soon end up resuming their former ways and regain the lost weight. There is some concern about the effects on RMR from repeatedly losing and gaining weight, referred to as **weight cycling**. However, results of studies on weight cycling and its effect on the RMR have been inconsistent. Several investigators found that weight cycling decreased the RMR after subjects resumed their normal food consumption[3,13,14] while others have reported no effect on RMR.[20,25] As of this time, the evidence is unclear as to the long-term effects that weight cycling may have on the RMR.

Exercise

Regular exercise has been shown to be an effective part of successful weight control programs. Recent studies have concluded that weight gain is more correlated with decreased activity rather than increased caloric intake. Even though Americans actually eat 5-10% fewer calories than 20 years ago, body weight has continued to increase.

Unfortunately, some view energy expenditure during exercise as being relatively unimportant due to its seemingly small caloric expenditure. For example, an average size male uses only a little more than 100 kilocalories to run a mile. This is not even half the 280 kilocalories found in a Snickers candy bar. Because approximately 3,500 kilocalories are required to "burn up" a pound of fat, one would need to run about 35 miles in order to lose just 1 pound. Exercise might appear to be a poor way to lose weight because the energy expenditure required for exercise seems so modest. However, exercise should not be viewed as a means for rapid weight loss but rather as a long-term, effective method for weight management. The energy required to jog 2 miles every day results in the loss of 1 pound of fat in 18 days. Continuing the exercise for a month results in the loss of 1.7 pounds and almost 21 pounds after a year of jogging.

Some types of exercises burn more calories than others. Aerobic or cardiorespiratory exercises are the largest caloric burners. For any specific exercise, the higher the intensity of the exercise, the more calories you burn in any time period. Likewise, for any specific exercise, the longer you do the exercise, the more calories you burn.

Because high-intensity exercise cannot be maintained for very long except by well-conditioned individuals, its contribution to energy expenditure would be minimal. Sustained exercise at a moderate intensity is usually the most beneficial for expending energy. This would correspond to approximately 65-70% of the maximal heart rate or a perceived exertion of about 3 on the 0-10 point RPE scale. At this intensity, fat utilization by the body is maximized. Table 2.13 in Chapter 2 provides a list of various exercises and the equivalent energy expenditures.

Aerobic exercise is the type of exercise that can expend the greatest amount of energy.

KEY CONCEPT

IS WALKING BETTER THAN JOGGING?

Would it be better to walk or jog if the intent is to lose weight? It primarily depends on the total number of calories expended which is a function of the total distance covered. For example, if you have 30 minutes to exercise and you walk at a speed of 15 minutes per mile, you would cover 2 miles and expend approximately 200 kilocalories. If you jogged for the same 30 minutes at a speed of 10 minutes per mile, you would cover 3 miles and expend 300 kilocalories, 33% more than by walking. If, on the other hand, you really dislike to jog and would jog only 1 mile when you would be willing to walk 3 miles, then walking would be better. Over the long haul, the combination of intensity and duration which produces the greatest caloric expenditure is the best for weight reduction.

Walking can be a significant stimulus for weight loss if duration is extended.

Though studies generally show that the amount of fat loss from exercise alone is minimal in individuals of normal weight, exercise has considerably greater effects on the moderately overweight and obese. Exercise also results in a redistribution of body composition. Body fat is decreased while lean body mass is increased which reduces the body fat percentage. Furthermore, recent studies have shown that exercise tends to first reduce the abdominal fat, the most unhealthy location for fat.

Strength training is also of considerable value during a weight loss program. In weight loss programs using a moderate caloric restriction, the majority of weight loss is fat, but protein (muscle mass) loss accounts for some of the weight loss. In programs that use more severe caloric restriction, the amount of protein loss can be substantially more. Strength training diminishes the rate of protein loss which helps maintain lean body mass. Thus, an exercise program should include aerobic activities along with a strength training program. Occasional exercise isn't of much value to weight management, but, when included as a regular part of the lifestyle, can be an effective component of weight control.

In addition to the calories expended while exercising, exercise can indirectly benefit weight loss in other ways. During exercise, the metabolic rate and energy expenditure are increased, and after exercise remains elevated for a period of time resulting in further energy expenditure. The duration of the exercise recovery period varies depending upon the duration and intensity of the activity, but the additional energy used during this period may represent up to 15% of the exercise energy expenditure.

Thermic Effect of Foods

The thermic effect of foods (TEF), also known as diet-induced thermogenesis, is the caloric expenditure necessary to digest and absorb the three types of macronutrients. The caloric expenditure necessary is dependent on the quantity of food consumed and on the type of food consumed. Digestion and absorption of carbohydrates and fats requires an additional 5% of the total calories consumed. The TEF of protein is much higher, ranging from as much as 30% of the protein calories if protein is eaten alone, to about 10-15% in a typical mixed meal.

For unknown reasons, exercise performed within 30-60 minutes following a meal enhances the TEF of the meal. Mild to moderate exercise performed after a meal may double the TEF of the meal. The implications are that taking a walk following a meal rather than a nap may be the best thing you can do if you are interested in burning some calories.

COMPONENTS OF SUCCESSFUL WEIGHT LOSS PROGRAMS

The number one way people attempt to lose weight is by dieting. The term "diet" has connotations of consuming small quantities of food in order to lose weight rapidly. Unfortunately, after maintaining a diet for a short period of time, most people usually return to eating as before—too much fat and too many calories! Rather than using something short-term (i.e. dieting) to lose weight, one should attempt to make lifestyle changes to both diet and activity to maintain an ideal weight. The most effective types of weight control incorporate three aspects for modification of our lifestyle— diet, exercise, and behavior. There are no short cuts or tricks to losing weight, and no "magic" foods that "burn off" fat. Losing weight takes time, effort, and motivation in order to achieve and maintain the loss.

Diet Modification

A common attitude of those who attempt to lose weight is to lose it as quickly as possible. For two important reasons, a better approach is a slow weight loss of between 1-2 pounds per week.

The first reason a slow weight loss is desirable is that a slow rate of weight loss minimally affects the RMR. The second reason is that the loss of protein will also be minimal. Virtually all studies conducted on weight loss have shown that protein is lost as well as fat. The more rapid the rate of weight loss, the greater the protein loss. A slow rate of weight loss minimizes protein loss and maximizes fat loss.

For slow weight loss, daily energy intake should not be less than 500-1000 kcal per day less than the amount needed to maintain weight. For example, if you are able to maintain your weight on 2500 kcal per day, you should not reduce you caloric consumption to lower than 1500-2000 kcal per day. This amount of caloric reduction is appropriate as long as you maintain a minimal caloric intake of, on the average, 1,200 kcal for women or 1,500 kcal for men. These minimal caloric levels are necessary to maintain adequate intake of other necessary nutrients.

As discussed earlier, fats have a greater caloric density than carbohydrates or proteins. Thus, an important factor for effective weight management is modification of the type of food consumed. However, we may not always be fully aware of our fat intake because of the presence of "hidden fats" in many of the foods we eat, particularly processed foods. For example, peanut butter is made with peanuts, which by themselves are high in fat, but, additional fat is added so that about 75% of the calories in the final product are from fat. Potato chips, another favorite food, also are high in fat, with over 65% of calories in the form of various fats. While 2% milk is lower in fat content than whole milk, which is about 3.5% fat, the fat calories from 2% milk still constitutes around 25% of the total caloric value.

If you frequent fast-food restaurants, attempting to keep the fat calories less than 30% may take considerable readjustment of your diet. For example, the fat contribution to the total caloric value of a Bacon Double Cheeseburger from Burger King is 54%. An order of large fries from Dairy Queen is 45% and a Burrito Supreme from Taco Bell is 43%.

Increasing fiber and complex carbohydrate intake also has been shown to help weight management. Most of the fiber and complex carbohydrates in our diets come from fruits, vegetables, and grain products. Foods high in fiber and complex carbohydrates tend to fill you up more quickly because they are bulky foods and therefore are likely to reduce your total caloric consumption.

KEY CONCEPT

DETERMINING YOUR FAT CALORIES

To determine the percent of fat calories from a food, first, multiply the number of grams of fat in a serving by 9 kilocalories/gram which calculates the amount of fat calories in the food. Then, divide this number by the total number of kilocalories in the serving and multiply by 100. Reducing fat intake in the diet requires paying greater attention to food labels.

Example: Assume you eat two pieces of pizza that contain 500 kcal and 30 grams of fat in the two pieces. Your total fat calories are 30g x 9 kcal/g = 270 kcal. The percentage of total calories as fat is 270/500 = 54%.

Exercise Modifications

The major problem with any exercise program is continuing to exercise on a regular basis over a long period of time. Many people start out with good intentions but soon drop out. Exercise adherence is higher when one sets aside time to exercise and incorporates exercise into their daily routine. You have to put it in your schedule, just like you do any other important function.

For some, exercising with others may help as a motivational influence. Being accountable to someone else to show up for exercise can often make a difference. The positive camaraderie you get in a group setting will increase the likelihood that you will continue the exercise.

Selection of the appropriate exercise mode is also important to adherence. Your best chance of continuing an exercise program is if you enjoy doing the exercise. You may be able to do a type of exercise for a few weeks even though you literally hate doing it, but the chances are slim that you will maintain it for years. In this regards, variety can be a good tool to maintain adherence. Vary the type of exercise you do. You might run two days a week and bicycle two days. Any type of aerobic exercise is interchangeable relative to its potential benefit for weight reduction.

The most effective type of exercise for a weight control program is one that is of moderate intensity and is sustained over an extended period of time.[5] The benefits of exercise for weight management are more dependent upon total calories expended than on either duration or intensity independently. General recommendations for exercise in weight management call for performing an aerobic exercise continuously for 20-30 minutes at a moderate intensity and at least three times every week. Chapter 2 provides detailed information on designing an aerobic exercise program.

Exercise is more likely to be continued if the activity is enjoyable.

Behavior Modifications

While some people may need only minor changes in their diet and/or physical activity to achieve an ideal body weight, others may require further behavior modification. Most of our behaviors, particularly eating, involve acquired patterns of association. For example, when watching television in the evening, you may head to the kitchen during a commercial break or eat when feeling depressed or anxious. Behavior modification involves identifying these types of undesirable behaviors and then "unlearning" the associations. Table 5.4 lists common behavior modifications that can improve the chance of successful weight loss.

The first step is to identify those factors that lead to undesirable behaviors. A suggestion is to keep a diary of all the foods eaten as well as the reasons for eating. This activity may shed insight on those behavior patterns that contribute to overeating. One may find that eating occurs in response to certain situations such as boredom, studying for exams, or simply out of habit. Once the diary is completed, work to modify those negative behaviors. Don't buy fattening snacks to leave around the house or room. Carry low-fat snacks like fruit if you know that you may get hungry between meals. Don't leave food in sight; keep it away from where you might easily be able to reach for it. Self-discipline, or will power, is a key to breaking any well-established habit. You must take control of your life and be responsible for achieving your goals.

The above discussion pertains to self-treatment of mild to moderate overweight. Table 5.5 contains some recommendations from a world renowned expert in weight loss, Dr. Kelly Brownell. These are good recommendations to follow to get started on a healthful program for losing weight.

TABLE 5.4
Behavior Modifications For Successful Weight Control
• make a commitment to change
• set realistic goals
• incorporate exercise into your program
• develop healthy eating patterns
• avoid automatic eating
• stay busy
• plan meals ahead of time
• do not serve more food than you should eat
• avoid social binges
• avoid raids on the refrigerator
• practice stress management techniques

TABLE 5.5

Recommended Approach to Weight Loss

- **Set Reasonable Goals**. It is beneficial to determine where you currently are with respect to your weight. Using some method of body composition analysis that will be reliable will aid in this process. Remember that methods that determine your body fat give you more information than those that just determine weight to height relationships.

- **Do a Reality Check**. Have realistic expectations regarding weight loss. Don't expect to loose more than 1-2 pounds per week and realize that eventually weight loss will plateau. Be willing to be patient while the weight loss occurs.

- **Follow a Balanced, Low-Fat Diet**. When you reduce the number of calories you consume, it is even more important to eat a balanced diet in order to get all the nutrients you need. Reducing the fat sources in your diet will be the most effective way of reducing calories while preserving the nutrient content of your meals. If you are unsure of your nutrient intake, take a multiple vitamin to supplement your vitamins and minerals.

- **Reshape Bad Eating Habits**. Keeping a diary of when and what you eat will enable you to develop an overall view of your eating behaviors. You can then identify behaviors that contribute to overweight and devise lifestyle changes.

- **Exercise**. Exercise helps reduce weight by increasing energy expenditure, helping to control appetite, and by maintaining muscle mass. Find exercise modes you enjoy, incorporate both aerobic and strengthening into the program, and, above all, be consistent in performing your exercise.

- **Track Your Progress**. Don't weigh more than once per week. There will be some daily fluctuations so don't get too hung up if weight changes are not always in the desirable direction. Periodically determine your body composition using the same method each time. This will confirm fat weight loss is occurring.

- **Celebrate Your Success**. Periodic rewards as you progress through your program help to maintain motivation to continue. Pick rewards that you find personally satisfying.

Adapted from Brownell, K.D. (1989, June). When and How to Diet. *Psychology Today*, 40-46.

If you or someone you know is severely overweight, more intense treatment is necessary and competent professionals should be contacted to help insure a more probable likelihood of success.

WEIGHT LOSS FADS AND FALLACIES

In probably no other area has there been as much misinformation fed to the general public as in the area of weight loss. Unscrupulous individuals and companies have preyed upon the general public with enticing advertisements and unsupported claims of magical weight reduction. Many have been victims of such advertisements and ill-conceived programs in books and magazines. It is generally true in the area of weight loss that if it sounds too good to be true, it is probably not true.

Fad Diets

All diets that result in the loss of weight have one thing in common. They all reduce the energy consumption below the level of energy expenditure. Once the hype and novelty of the diet program is removed, the program must cause a caloric deficit in order to be effective. If a fad diet does result in weight loss, the bottom line is that it has produced a caloric deficit.

Unfortunately, the method by which a fad diet produces a caloric deficit is usually so restricting and distasteful that it cannot be continued for any extended period of time. Herein lies the major problem with fad diets. They can usually be maintained for only a short period of time. During the initial weeks of a fad diet, weight is usually lost due to caloric restriction and water loss but weight loss becomes more difficult with the passing of time. Pretty soon, you are tired of the diet and you discontinue it in favor of the resumption of old eating habits.

As discussed in the previous section, successful weight loss programs require a change in lifestyle. The change in lifestyle has to be tolerable enough that it will result in a permanent change in eating and exercise behaviors. Fad diets play no role in the long-term management of weight and should not be utilized.

Substantial weight loss can occur from exercise in a warm environment but the weight loss is primarily due to water loss, not fat loss.

Water Loss

During the first few days of a weight loss program, several pounds often are lost quickly, and, although this makes checking the scale exciting, the initial weight loss is mostly water loss. In the beginning of weight loss, the body's carbohydrate stores are first decreased along with the large amount of water used to store the carbohydrates. As the body readjusts to the stress of food restriction, the rate of weight loss decreases but the loss of fat increases. Just remember that to lose the equivalent of 1 pound of fat, you have to have a caloric deficit of 3500 kilocalories, the equivalent to walking or jogging approximately 35 miles.

Another gimmick for weight loss is using apparels that tightly cover either the whole body, like a nylon body suit, or certain parts of the body, such as the abdomen. Some of these devices advertise that you will to be able to "burn off fat while you sit or exercise." All these devices actually do is dehydrate the body cells beneath the suit. A quick check of the scales or waist line measurement after using one of these gimmicks might lead one to believe that they actually work, but after a short period of time during which the body has had a chance to rehydrate, the "lost" weight is returned. In addition to the fact that they don't work, exercising with these types of apparels covering major portions of the body during warm weather is potentially dangerous because they increase the heat load on the body.

Spot Reduction

Besides weight loss, many people also attempt to lose fat from specific areas of the body, particularly the abdomen, hips, and thighs. Various gimmicks or exercises have been tried in futile attempts to "spot reduce" specific body areas. Exercises, such as sit-ups for the stomach or leg lifts for the thighs, are useless endeavors to reduce regional fat deposits. There is an erroneous belief that fat near the exercising muscles will be used preferentially over fat from other areas of the body. While this may sound logical, in reality, it does not occur. An exercising muscle uses fats for energy which are taken from fat stores from all parts of the body, not just from the nearby area.

People will lose their fat from different body areas depending on gender and genetics, not on performing a specific exercise. This is particularly painful information for females because the number one area fat reduction is desired is in the hip and thighs. Unfortunately, these fat deposits are primarily related to gender and are part of the reproductive function of the female. In fact, many females will find it virtually impossible to lose weight in the thighs and hips.

Drugs and Herbs

Regardless of what you see advertised, there is no scientific support that fat burning can be increased by consuming certain drugs or herbs. There are drugs which will depress appetite and/or increase metabolism and produce a fat loss due to a caloric deficit, but most have potentially dangerous side effects and should not be taken without the advice of a physician.

The good news is that new drugs currently in the development stage could have significant impact on weight loss. These drugs act at the molecular level to alter our normal mechanisms that determine how fat we become. Gene research is producing hope of finding a specific gene or genes which control weight. Hopefully, in the not too distant future, new and safe methods of pharmacologic weight control will be available.

For many people, gaining weight is one of the last things they want to do. However, in some situations, weight gain may be desirable. For example, in athletics, becoming bigger and stronger will often enhance performance. For asthetic reasons, males often want to increase their muscle weight which should be the desire for most people wishing to add weight to their frame. In addition, it is sometimes advantageous for elderly individuals to add muscle because they have low body weights and minimal amounts of muscle.

Females have a lesser ability to increase muscle size than do males.

While many believe that increased protein intake is the most important nutritional factor for increasing muscle mass, increased carbohydrate intake is just as important if not more. Investigators generally conclude that an individual engaging in an intense weight training program will need a maximum of 2 times the RDA requirement for protein which is near the amount many Americans already consume. However, what has also been demonstrated is that a high carbohydrate intake is essential for increasing muscle mass. Studies have reported that protein breakdown is increased when carbohydrate intake is decreased. Conversely, more protein is retained than excreted by the body when carbohydrate intake is increased.

The health food stores are full of protein supplements in various forms from different manufacturers. While protein supplements can provide a source of protein, they are not better than normal food sources like meat. They are generally far more expensive that food sources, and the manufacturers often make outlandish claims that are totally unsupported.

In addition to protein, there are numerous other nutritional supplements available which are frequently used by those wishing to increase muscle mass, though their benefit to weight gain is questionable. Few of these products have been tested in controlled situations, and their use is often based on empirical and anecdotal evidence.

KEY CONCEPT

PROTEIN AND WEIGHT GAIN

In order to gain muscle mass, two ingredients are necessary. One is adequate amounts of protein. The other is the stimulus provided by resistance training. Either by itself will not promote muscle mass increase. The RDA for protein is approximately 0.4 grams of protein per pound of body weight. To illustrate this requirement, two McDonald's Quarter Pounders would meet the protein RDA for a 115-lb individual. The maximal requirement for protein to support intensive resistance training is 0.8 grams of protein per pound per day. Protein deficiencies are rare in the U.S. as we typically consume between 0.4-0.8 grams per day.

Chromium Picolinate

Chromium picolinate is a supplement purported to increase muscle mass. Chromium is a trace mineral that is involved in insulin dynamics. An early report suggested that its use increases lean body weight while decreasing fat weight. Subsequent reports have been inconclusive and many researchers presently do not consider it to influence lean body weight. However, more research needs to be conducted before a definitive statement one way or the other can be made regarding the benefits of chromium picolinate.

Creatine Monohydrate

One of the hottest supplements on the market today is **creatine monohydrate**, usually referred to as just creatine. Creatine is part of a high-energy molecule found in the body which is heavily involved in energy production for muscular contraction. It has been suggested that if creatine levels in body could be increased, more energy for muscular contraction would be available resulting in improvement in physical performance.[6] Because of the nature of the body's energy systems, creatine's effect should be primarily evident when performing high-intensity exercise like weight lifting. Also, muscle mass has been suggested to increase with supplementation, but, if it does, it is probably because the individual increased her/his intensity and duration of training. Creatine supplementation has not been studied long enough to determine if long-term use leads to any health problems, although It should be noted that the current cost of creatine is such that it makes supplementation an expensive endeavor. There is no evidence that short-term use of creatine will cause any problems.

Anabolic Steroids

Anabolic steroids are drugs that enhance muscle size and strength when used in combination with a resistance training program. They have been notoriously used by athletes for decades even though their use for producing muscle size and strength increases has always been illegal and unethical. Unfortunately, anabolic steroids do work and it is the increase in muscle size and strength that motivates individuals to use the illegal drugs.

Although anabolic steroids can produce substantial increases in muscle size and strength, they also produce many detrimental side effects, some of which are potentially life threatening. Table 5.6 lists the most common side effects of anabolic steroids in male and females. From a legal, medical, and ethical perspective, anabolic steroid use cannot be condoned.

TABLE 5.6
Potential Adverse Side Effects of Anabolic Steroids

Adverse Effects in Males	Adverse Effects in Females
Liver dysfunction including tumors	Liver dysfunction including tumors
Increased risk of cardiovascular disease	Increased risk of cardiovascular disease
Small number of sperm	Reduction in female sex hormones
Decreased testicular size	Menstrual cycle changes/ammenorrhea
Suppression of naturally occurring testosterone	Decreased sex drive
Decreased sex drive	Increased aggressive behavior and mood swings
Increased aggressive behavior and mood swings	Irreversible deepening of the voice
Hair loss	Increased body and facial hair
Acne	Acne
Disruption of bone growth in youths	

The Bottom Line Regarding Muscle Gain

Whether or not nutritional supplements actually aid gains in muscle weight is not clearly established. Certainly, some supplements may and some supplements need to be investigated further. It is known that hard work and enough carbohydrates to support the work effort are the most important factors. Muscle weight gain requires dedication to a strength training program while consuming sufficient carbohydrates, although the caloric intake should not be so much as to increase fat weight. An untrained individual may increase his/her muscle mass by up to 20% within the first year of regular heavy strength training, however the rate of increase tapers off and eventually plateaus. Genetics also plays a large role in the absolute capacity to increase muscle regardless of the amount of effort or the supplements used.

EATING DISORDERS

Problems with body weight are not limited to excess weight but can also afflict those on the low end of the weight spectrum. Eating disorders are characterized by severely abnormal eating and eating-related behaviors. The major eating disorders are **anorexia nervosa** and **bulimia nervosa**. Both of these eating disorders result in increased health problems and, in extreme cases of anorexia nervosa, increased risk of premature death.

The problem of eating disorders is afflicting an increasing number of people, especially adolescent girls and young women. The incidence rate for eating disorders is highest on college campuses where between 2-20% of women and up to 5% of men are afflicted. At the root of these psychological problems is an overconcern and often distorted view about one's weight and body shape which develops into eccentric compulsive behaviors. These concerns and distorted beliefs lead to dysfunctional attitudes about eating and result in the characteristic abnormal eating behaviors.

People who suffer from eating disorders are usually in denial about their condition and take great care to hide the disorder from close friends, roommates, and parents. Although individuals with an eating disorder do not believe their actions reflect any problems other than "being too fat", they offer many seemingly logical explanations and excuses in order to keep others from discovering their secret. Consequently, someone with an eating disorder is not overtly obvious to others, making it difficult to identify such an individual.

Anorexia Nervosa

Individuals suffering from anorexia nervosa are extremely thin and underweight because they don't eat enough. The incidence rate is somewhere between 1-2% of all women and about 95% of all cases of anorexia occur in females. The reason for this difference between the genders is not readily understood.

Anorexics have a deep-seated fear of body fat and are convinced of the need to lose still more weight even when they are already underweight. Further, they develop an incredible ability to suppress their appetite, and frequently couple their self-imposed starvation with excessive exercise in the continued attempt to lose additional weight. They may also use laxatives and diuretics to enhance weight loss.

Anorexics are often introverted, reserved, and insecure. In spite of these psycho-social characteristics, they tend to be highly achievement-oriented. They want to control all aspects of their lives and they fear loss of control.

Because anorexics are in denial about their problem, they often do not seek treatment. Appropriate therapy by trained professionals can be very beneficial for those who obtain it with about 70% of anorexics recovering or improving.[9] Restoring body weight is of prime importance as well as psychotherapy for their abnormal perceptions of their body. Anorexics have to learn to be more accepting of a less than perfect body. Unfortunately anorexia nervosa can be life-threatening for those who do not seek or respond to treatment.

Bulimia Nervosa

Bulimia nervosa is the most common eating disorder. Estimates of its incidence are 2-20% among college females and perhaps as high as 5% for college males.[21] As many as 14% of females may occasionally engage in bulimic behaviors, but don't fully develop the disorder. This condition is found mostly among women in their teens and twenties, but also occurs in older women as well as males.

Bulimia is characterized by episodes of binge eating alternating with purging (i.e. vomiting and use of laxatives or diuretics). During a binge, bulimics feel that they can't stop eating or control what or how much they eat. The primary symptoms of bulimia are consuming great quantities of food several times a week followed by vomiting, lack of control over eating behaviors, and an overly discontented view of their body shape and weight. They may also engage in excessive exercise as another means of controlling their weight. While the belief is that one with an eating disorder is extremely thin, bulimics may actually be overweight.

Bulimics tend to be more social than anorexics. In fact, they have a strong need for social approval. They may have large mood swings, including depression, accompanied by impulsive behaviors. Perhaps due to the increased likelihood of depression, bulimics may have a higher suicide risk. In addition to their psycho-social problems, bulimics tend to have more unhealthy behaviors such as smoking, drinking alcohol, and eating junk food.

Bulimics are less likely than anorexics to seek help, waiting an average of $5\frac{1}{2}$ years from the onset of symptomatic behaviors. The treatment for bulimia is similar to that for anorexia. Factual information about nutrition, weight control and the consequences of bulimic behavior are essential. Psychological therapy may be necessary as well as antidepressant drugs in cases of depression.

Some individuals exhibit most of the behaviors of the bulimic except purging. Some experts even categorize this as a separate eating disorder, called **binge eating disorder**.[21] These individuals are often overweight because they simply eat a lot of food. In additions to eating large quantities of food, they often exhibit other abnormal eating behaviors like eating rapidly, eating frequently, eating alone, and feeling disgusted or depressed for overeating. In some cases, binge eating disorder may lead to full-blown bulimia.

It is beyond the scope of this section to deal with all aspects of these serious eating disorders; the intent is simply to increase the awareness of the seriousness of eating disorders. Should you discover someone close to you has an eating disorder, that person will likely deny a problem exits, but he/she needs to be encouraged to seek professional help. Talk to a counselor

TABLE 5.7	
Symptoms of Eating Disorders	
Anorexia Nervosa	**Bulimia Nervosa**
• Refusal to maintain normal body weight either through a weight loss leading to a body weight 15% below expected weight or failure to make expected weight gain during growth such that weight is 15% below expected.	• Recurrent episodes of binge eating. Bulimics consume large amounts of food in short periods of time.
• Fear of fatness or weight gain even though being underweight.	• A feeling of lack of control over their abnormal eating behavior.
• Distorted body image to the extent of perceiving themselves as fat even though underweight.	• Frequent self-induced vomiting, use of laxatives, strict dieting or fasting, or vigorous exercise in order to loose weight or prevent weight gain.
• Absence of three consecutive menstrual cycles that would otherwise be expected to occur.	• Three months of two eating binges a week.
	• Overconcern with body shape and weight often resulting in depression.

in student support services or other appropriate health professionals to find out how to provide help. Also, many campuses and community agencies have support groups to assist those suffering with an eating disorder.

SUMMARY

There is no one best way to lose weight, no best exercise to do, or no best single diet to eat. Although there are literally hundreds of various weight loss programs available, many of them are based on misinformation and are useless for effective, long-term weight control. With a basic understanding of weight control principles, anyone can devise their own program. For those who want to lose only a few pounds, either a small change in eating habits or an increase in activity may be all that is needed. To lose more weight, both diet and exercise alterations are required. But, keep in mind that changes in lifestyle are the only effective method for long-term weight management.

When planning a weight control program, you should not establish rigid rules that make complete adherence highly improbable. Stringent rules, such as "never eating chocolate" or "running everyday," make 100% compliance unlikely. Eating one chocolate bar under such rules would then label the weight loss endeavor a failure. Rather, the rules should be to "allow an occasional chocolate bar" or "get in at least three workouts each week." Moderation and perseverance are the keys to successful weight management.

One final comment on weight control is appropriate. A major reason why many people attempt to lose weight is to improve appearance. Achieving the lean and trim look of many of today's models is probably not possible by most individuals. Some people, because of their genetic traits, may never be able to attain such a physique. Obsession with such a look can lead to anxiety and emotional distress or to psycho-physical illnesses such as anorexia or bulimia. Although, maintaining an ideal body weight is healthier than being overweight or underweight, the ultimate goal has to be practical. Often, acceptance of a less than perfect body turns out to be the most practical and healthy outcome.

EXPLORING WELLNESS ON THE WEB

Many resources are available on the World Wide Web. You can reinforce, expand and enhance the information presented in this chapter by accessing the following sites.

http://galaxy.einet.net — contains links to information about various types of diet therapy. Once at the site, click on the **Medicine** category, then click on **Therapeutics,** then click on **Diet Therapy.**

http://www.geocities.com/sunsetstrip/3761/ — provides links to much information on eating disorders including support groups.

http://www.CyberDiet.com — provides wide range of information on diet. This site has a fast foods analysis program, an daily food planner, as well as other helpful tools. It is maintained by a registered dietitian.

REFERENCES

1. Acheson, K.J., Schutz, Y., Bessard T., Anantharaman, K., Flatt, J., and Jequier, E. (1988). Glycogen Storage Capacity and de Novo Lipoenesis During Massive Carbohydrate Overfeeding in Man. *American Journal of Clinical Nutrition,* 48:240-247.

2. Bjorntorp, Per. (1983). The role of adipose tissue in human obesity. In: Greenwood, H. (Ed.). *Obesity*. New York: Churchill Livingstone.

3. Blackburn, G.L., Wilson, G.T., Kanders, B.S., et al. (1989). Weight cycling: the experience of human dieters. *American Journal of Clinical Nutrition,* 49:1105-1109.

4. Bray, G. (1969). Effect of caloric restriction on energy expenditure in obese patients. *Lancet,* 2:397-398.

5. Dusek, D. (1989). *Weight Management the Fitness Way: Exercise, Nutrition, Stress Control, Emotional Readiness,* Boston: Jones and Bartlett.

6. Earnest, C.P., Snell, P.G., Rodriquez, R., Almada, A.L., and Mithcell, T.L. (1995). The Effect of Creatine Monohydrate Ingestion on Anaerobic Indices, Muscular Strength and Body Composition. *Acta Phsiologica Scandinavica,* 153:207-209.

7. Flatt, J.P. (1987). Dietary Fat, Carbohydrate Balance, and Weight Maintenance: Effects of Exercise. *American Journal of Clinical Nutrition,* 45:296-306.

8. Hill, J.O., Sparling, P.B., Shields, T.W., Heller, P.A. (1987). Effects of exercise and food restriction on body composition and metabolic rate in obese women. *American Journal of Clinical Nutrition,* 46:622-630.

9. Hsu, L.K.G. (1988) The Outcome of Anorexia Nervosa: A Reappraisal. *Psychology & Medicine*, 18:807-812.

10. Kannel, W.B. (1983). Health and obesity. In: Conn, H. et al., (Eds.). *Health and Obesity*. New York: Raven Press.

11. Lapidus, L., Bengtsson, C., Larsson, B., Pennert, K., Rybo, E., & Sjostrom, L. (1984). Distribution of adipose tissue and risk of cardiovascular disease and death: 12-year follow-up of participants in the population study of women in Gothenburg, Sweden. *British Medical Journal*, 289:1257-1261.

12. Larsson, B., Svardsudd, K., Welin, L., Wilhelmsen, L., Bjorntorp, P., & Tibblin, G. (1984). Abdominal adipose tissue: distribution, obesity and risk of cardiovascular disease and death: 13-year follow-up of participants in the study of men born in 1913. *British Medical Journal*, 288:1401-1404.

13. Manore, M.M., Berry, T.E., Skinner, J.S., & Caroll, S.S. (1991). Energy expenditure at rest and during exercise in nonobese female cyclical dieters and in nondieting control subjects. *American Journal of Clinical Nutrition*, 54:41-46.

14. Melby, C.L., Schmidt, W.D., & Corrigan, D.L. (1990). Resting metabolic rate in weight cycling collegiate wrestlers compared to physically active non-cycling control subjects. *American Journal of Clinical Nutrition*, 52:409-414.

15. Melby, C.L., Sylliassen, S., & Rhodes, T. (1991). Diet-induced weight loss and metabolic changes in obese women with high verses low prior weight loss/regain. *Nutrition Research*, 11:971-978.

16. National Children's Youth Fitness Study (NCYFS). (1985). *Summary of findings from National Children and Youth Fitness Study*. Washington, D.C.: Department of Health and Human Services.

17. PDAY Research Group. (1990) Relationship of Atherosclerosis in Young Men to Serum Lipoproten Cholesterol Concentrations and Smoking. *Journal of the American Medical Association*, 264:3018-3024.

18. Ravussin, E., Burnand, B., Schutz, Y., & Jequier E. (1990). Energy expenditure before and during energy restriction on obese patients. *American Journal of Clinical Nutrition*, 41:753-759.

19. Rowe, J.W. (1985). Health Care of the Elderly. *New England Journal of Medicine*, 312:827-835.

20. Schmidt, W.D., Corrigan, D., & Melby C.L. (1993). Two seasons of weight cycling does not lower resting metabolic rate in college wrestlers. *Medicine and Science in Sports and Exercise*, 25:613-619.

21. Schotte, D. E. and Stunkard, a. J. (1987). Buimia vs. Bulimic Behaviors on a College Capmus. *Journal of the American Medical Association*, 258:1213-1215.

22. Stary, H.C. (1990). The Sequence of Cell and Matrix Changes in Atherosclerotic Lesions of Coronary Arteries in the First 40 Years of Life. *European Heart Jounral*, 11(suppl):3-19.

23. Stubbs, R.J., Harbron, C.G., Murgatroyd, P.R., Prentice A.M. (1995). Covert manipulation of dietary fat and energy density: effect on substrate flux and food intake in men feeding *ad libitum*. *American Journal of Clinical Nutrition*, 62:330-332.

24. Van Dale, D., Saris, W.H., Schoffelen, P.F. Ten Hoor, F. (1987). Does exercise give an additional effect in weight reduction regiments? (1987). *International Journal of Obesity*, 11:367-75.

25. van Dale, D., & Saris, W.H.M. (1989). Repetitive weight loss and weight regain: effect on weight reduction, resting metabolic rate, and lipolytic activity before and after exercise and/or diet treatment. *American Journal of Clinical Nutrition*, 49:409-416.

DEFINITIONS OF KEY TERMS

adipose cells or fat cells — cells in the body that contain the body's storage fat.

android-type obesity — the type of obesity most commonly seen in males. It is characterized by greater fat deposition in the abdominal area.

anabolic steroids — drugs used illegally to enhance muscle size and strength.

anorexia nervosa — an eating disorder characterized by an aversion to eating caused by a distorted self-image.

bulimia nervosa — an eating disorder characterized by binge eating following by purging the stomach contents by self-induced vomiting.

energy balance — difference between energy intake and energy expenditure. Any change in either of these will change the energy balance and, thus, body weight.

gynoid-type obesity — the type of obesity most commonly seen in females. It is characterized by greater fat deposition in the buttocks and thighs.

kilocalorie (kcal) — unit of energy which is used to quantify the amount of energy in food.

negative energy balance — when the calories consumed are less than the calories expended. This would result in a weight loss.

positive energy balance — when the calories consumed are greater than the calories expended. This would result in a weight gain.

resting metabolic rate (RMR) — rate of energy used by the body to maintain body functioning during resting conditions.

saiety — the feeling of fullness after consuming a meal.

set-point theory — theory which suggests that the body has a predetermined weight or amount of fat that it attempts to maintain in spite of small changes in energy intake or expenditure. However, prolonged changes in either intake or expenditure may readjust the set-point.

ESTIMATING DAILY ENERGY EXPENDITURE

Name _____ ID _____ Sect _____ Time _____ Date _____

Purpose

To estimate your average daily energy expenditure.

Directions

1. Determine your estimated resting metabolic rate using the equations below.

2. Determine your estimated energy expenditure from muscular activity using Table 2.13 and a daily log of your muscular activity.

Estimating Resting Metabolic Rate

Females

RMR (kcal/day) = 447.593 + (7.869 × ht) + (4.203 × wt) − (4.330 × age)

RMR (kcal/day) = 447.593 + (7.869 × _____ in) + (4.203 × _____ lb) − (4.330 × _____ yr)

RMR (kcal/day) = _____ kcal/day

Males

RMR (kcal/day) = 88.362 + (12.189 × ht) + (6.090 × wt) − (5.677 × age)

RMR (kcal/day) = 88.362 + (12.189 × _____ in) + 6.090 × _____ lb) − 5.677 × _____ yr)

RMR (kcal/day) = _____ kcal/day

(Continued)

Estimating Energy Expenditure from Muscular Activity

1. In the table below, record the different muscular activities that you do throughout the day. Group similar activities performed at similar intensities into the same activity category, i.e. estimate how much walking you do at the same pace during the day and list that as one activity. List any formal exercise you do as a separate activity category.

2. For each activity listed, use Table 2.13 to determine the $kcal \cdot lb^{-1} \cdot min^{-1}$, determine the total duration of the activity for the entire day, and record your weight.

3. Calculate the **Total kcal** column by multiplying $kcal \cdot lb^{-1} \cdot min^{-1} \times$ duration $\times$ weight.

4. Sum the total kcal for each activity to get the Total kcal/day.

Activity Category	$kcal \cdot lb^{-1} \cdot min^{-1}$	Duration (min)	Weight (lb)	Total kcal
_____	_____	_____	_____	_____
_____	_____	_____	_____	_____
_____	_____	_____	_____	_____
_____	_____	_____	_____	_____
_____	_____	_____	_____	_____

Total kcal/day from muscular activity: _____

Estimating Total Daily Energy Expenditure

Total Daily Energy Expenditure = (Resting Metabolic Rate $\times$ 1.1) + kcal from muscular activity

Total Daily Energy Expenditure = (_____ kcal $\times$ 1.1) + _____ kcal

Total Daily Energy Expenditure = _____ kcal/day

Note: The RMR is multiplied by 1.1 to account for energy expended by the digestive process following eating.

(Continued)

ESTIMATING DAILY ENERGY EXPENDITURE

Name _____ ID _____ Sect _____ Time _____ Date _____

Answer the following questions:

1. Considering your daily pattern of muscular activity, list ways you could increase your caloric expenditure other than doing formal exercise? For example, could you use stairs instead of an elevator?

2. Estimate how many additional kcals/day you could expend by making the changes in #1 above.

3. In addition to increasing your caloric expenditure by increasing muscular activity, how could you increase your total caloric deficit (produce a negative caloric balance) in order to loose weight?

NOTES

LAB 5.2

ASSESSING THE IMPORTANCE OF APPEARANCE

Name _____ ID _____ Sect _____ Time _____ Date _____

Purpose

To determine the importance you place on physical appearance.

Directions

1. Select one of the seven responses indicated below for each statement. Beside each statement, record the number of points corresponding to the response you selected. For example, for questions 1-6, an "agree" response would get 4 points. For questions 7-9, an "agree" response would get 2 points.

2. This instrument can be answered from two perspectives. The first is from your personal perspective. The second is from what you perceive to be the perspective of the opposite gender about your gender, i.e. if you are female, what to you perceive males think about females.

For questions 1-6, use the following responses and corresponding points.

Responses	Strongly Agree	Agree Somewhat	Agree	Neither Agree nor Disagree	Disagree	Disagree Somewhat	Strongly Disagree
Points	6	5	4	3	2	1	0

For questions 7-9, use the following responses and corresponding points.

Responses	Strongly Agree	Agree Somewhat	Agree	Neither Agree nor Disagree	Disagree	Disagree Somewhat	Strongly Disagree
Points	0	1	2	3	4	5	6

(Continued)

Statements   **Points**

1. Most people would prefer to go out with someone who is thin than someone who is overweight. _____

2. Clothes are made today so that only thin people can look good. _____

3. Fat people are often unhappy. _____

4. The thinner a person is, the more attractive they are. _____

5. A pretty or handsome face will not get you very far without a slim body. _____

6. Attractive people lead more fulfilling lives than unattractive people. _____

7. It is not true that attractive people are more interesting, poised, and socially outgoing than unattractive people. _____

8. It is more important that a person of your gender be attractive than a person of the opposite gender. _____

9. Attractiveness decreases the likelihood of professional success. _____

Total Points _____

Interpretation:

A **Total Points** of >45 means that you are significantly influenced by the great importance that current society places on appearance.

NOTES

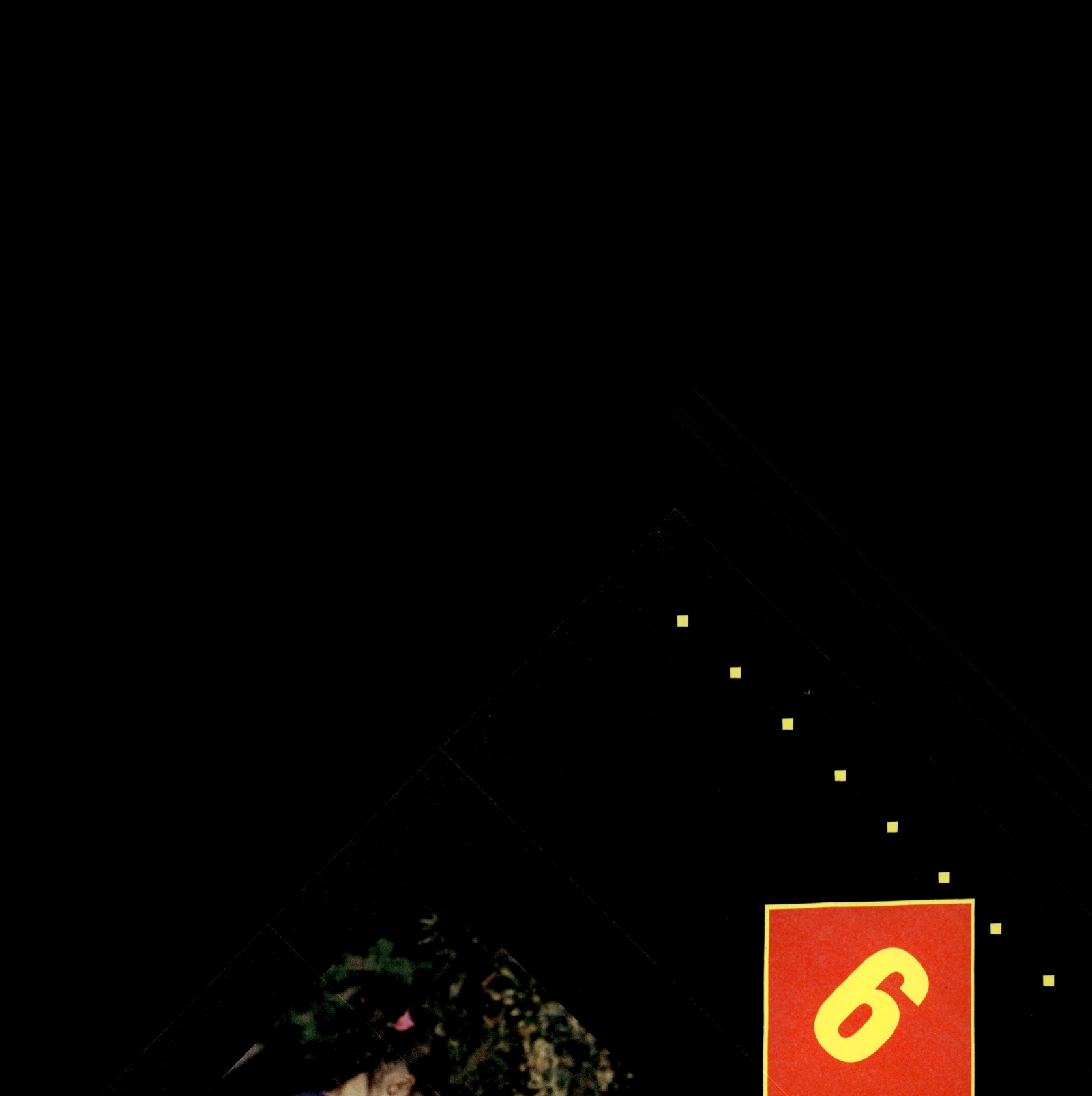

Nutrition Principles

Sue Joslyn

- Know the six major nutrients, their functions in the body, and their sources.

- Know effects of alcohol, aspartame, caffeine, and food additives.

- Apply dietary guidelines to your own diet.

- Be able to interpret food labels.

- Choose healthy groceries.

- Prepare foods nutritiously.

- Choose healthy foods when dining out.

- Understand benefits/risks of vegetarian diets.

- Understand nutritional needs for athletic performance.

- Understand nutritional needs of pregnant women.

- Identify the strengths and weaknesses of your own diet

KEY TERMS

amino acids
antioxidants
aspartame
bioavailability
blood glucose
caffeine
carbohydrates
complete proteins
complex carbohydrates
dietary fiber
disaccharides
ergogenic aids
fat-soluble vitamins
fats (lipids)
fatty acids
food additives
hydrogenated fat
hypoglycemia
incomplete proteins
insulin
lactovegetarian
minerals
monosaccharides
monounsaturated fats
ovolactovegetarian
polysaccharides
polyunsaturated fats
protein
saturated fat
simple carbohydrates
triglycerides
tropical oils
unsaturated fat
vegan
vitamins
water-soluble vitamins

INTRODUCTION

Research on the science of nutrition has uncovered monumental volumes of information on the complexity of the various nutrients in the body and their roles in overall health. Many of us may not be able to translate this overwhelming quantity of research into specific actions leading to healthy eating in real life.

The purpose of this chapter is to provide you with information on the nutritional needs of healthy individuals, so that you can plan and eat a healthier diet. Information on the major nutrients is provided in the first section of this chapter, which is essential to understanding the keys to dietary planning found in the second section. This chapter concludes with several assessment tools for you to evaluate your current dietary habits.

ESSENTIAL NUTRIENTS

Nutrients are the chemical compounds in foods which supply energy for metabolism, promote growth and repair of body tissues, and regulate body processes. There are six nutrient groups necessary for healthy human function—**carbohydrates**, **fats**, **protein**, **vitamins**, **minerals**, and **water**.

Carbohydrates, fats and protein are known as large or macronutrients because the body requires them in relatively large quantities. The macronutrients are also referred to as caloric nutrients because they provide energy for the body's needs. Water is also required in large quantities for normal body functions but it does not contain any calories. Conversely, vitamins and minerals are called small or micronutrients, because of their relatively small daily requirements. Vitamins and minerals, although extremely important for metabolism, provide no calories and are referred to as non-caloric nutrients. All these nutrients will be discussed individually in the next several sections of this chapter.

Carbohydrates

Carbohydrates, compounds found in plants, are made up of various combinations of the elements carbon, hydrogen and oxygen. They are the most efficient source of energy for the body, supplying 4 kcal (or Calories with a capital *C*) of energy per gram. Carbohydrates are also necessary for the complete oxidation of fat in the body, i.e. we need carbohydrates in our diet to burn fat.[5]

All carbohydrates are made up of one or more molecules of sugar (Table 6.1). There are two basic classifications of carbohydrates, based on the number of sugar molecules. Simple carbohydrates may be single molecules of sugar (**monosaccharides**) or double molecules (**disaccharides**). The monosaccharides include glucose (found in fruits, and is the end-product of all carbohydrate metabolism), fructose (in fruits and honey), and galactose (mainly found in milk sugar). The disaccharides are made up of combinations of monosaccharides, and include sucrose (table sugar), lactose (milk sugar), and maltose (found in some grains). Complex carbohydrates, or starches, contain chains of multiple sugar molecules (polysaccharides).[5]

When consumed, all carbohydrates are broken down into monosaccharides by enzymes in the digestive tract, and are absorbed as glucose molecules into the blood stream, where they are known as "blood sugar," or blood glucose. Blood glucose is used for energy, particularly by the brain, nervous system, and muscles. A low blood glucose level, known as **hypoglycemia**, can impair the normal function of the brain.

After entering the blood stream, glucose enters cells with the help of **insulin,** a hormone produced in the pancreas. Insulin acts to "open the gate" of the cell membrane, and allows the blood glucose molecules to enter the working cell to provide a source of energy. Insulin production and secretion is regulated by the amount of circulating glucose in the blood stream. Increased levels of blood glucose circulating throughout the body trigger increased amounts of insulin to be released into the blood stream.[21] Diabetes, a condition in which the secretion of insulin is not adequate, is characterized by high blood glucose levels because the glucose cannot get out of the blood and into the cells without insulin.

Cereal and grain products are excellent sources of complex carbohydrates.

TABLE 6.1		
Classes of Carbohydrates		
Chemical Name	**Type of Carbohydrate**	**Major Sources**
Monosaccharides	Glucose (dextrose)	Corn syrup
	Fructose	Fruits, honey
	Galactose	Milk
Disaccharides	Sucrose	Table sugar, sugar cane, sugar beets, molasses
	Lactose	Milk
	Maltose	Starch digestion, intermediate sweetener in food products
Polysaccharides	Starch	Grains and grain products, bread, crackers, pasta, rice, corn, bulgur, legumes, potatoes and other vegetables
	Glycogen	Animal meats, liver
	Dietary fiber	Whole grains, fruits, vegetables, seeds, nuts, skins of fruits

KEY CONCEPT

CARBOHYDRATES OR FAT FOR ENERGY?

What is more important for energy, carbohydrates or fat? Actually, they are both important, and both assume a predominant role in specific situations. For example, at rest, you derive about 70% of your energy needs from fat and about 30% from carbohydrates. However, as you become more physically active, the percentage contribution of fat decreases and carbohydrates increase. When you exercise vigorously, you are likely burning 70% carbohydrates and 30% fat, a complete reversal from the resting situation.

Complex and simple carbohydrates differ not only in their chemical composition, but also in their effects on the body. Ingesting large amounts of simple sugars causes rapid increases in the amount of circulating blood glucose. This phenomenon is commonly known as a "sugar high," referring to the initial increase in energy. You may eat a candy bar in the afternoon when your energy level begins to drag, hoping for a energy-boost from the sugar high. However, the result of large increases in blood glucose levels from simple sugars is that large amounts of insulin are released to handle the overload. This causes rapid depletion of circulating blood glucose, and a subsequent "crash" in energy levels. Ingesting complex carbohydrates does not produce this "high" or its related "crash." Glucose resulting from complex carbohydrate digestion is released into the blood stream at a more consistent and slower rate, maintaining relatively constant levels of insulin over a longer period of time, and thus preventing the crash in energy that follows the sugar high.

Sources of complex carbohydrates include whole grain breads and cereals, pasta and noodles, potatoes, rice, fruits, and vegetables. Simple carbohydrates are most commonly found in foods thought of as being "sweet" or "pastry-type" foods. An exception to this general rule is the simple carbohydrate fructose, commonly called fruit sugar because it is the predominant sugar in fruits.

Carbohydrates should make up approximately 55% or more of the total daily calories, with less than 10% coming from simple carbohydrates. A major problem with simple carbohydrates, except those in fruit, is that they are generally found in foods that contain very few other nutrients, especially vitamins and minerals. The current average American diet consists of approximately 22% complex and 25% simple carbohydrates, leaving quite a bit of room for improvement.[16]

Dietary deficiencies of carbohydrates are rare, although low carbohydrate diets are often the fad in weight loss schemes, such as high-protein powder drink plans. Without carbohydrates, your body is forced to use fat and protein as fuel. Fats burn inefficiently without the help of carbohydrates, and produce a by-product known as ketone bodies. These compounds are very acidic, and will build up in the body causing the body to become dangerously acidic. This situation is known as ketoacidosis, and is potentially fatal, leading to respiratory and cardiac arrest. Less serious cases of ketoacidosis can damage the brain and cause nausea, fatigue, and apathy.[14]

In addition to providing energy, carbohydrates are the only source of an important non-nutrient—**dietary fiber**. Dietary fiber is defined as those components of food that cannot be broken down by enzymes in the human digestive tract. Fiber passes through our digestive tract relatively intact.

Recent research indicates that fiber acts as a natural laxative, because of its increased water-holding capacity. Because of the faster movement of the intestinal contents through the colon, carcinogens (cancer-causing agents) and bacteria have less time in contact with the walls of the colon. This may lead to decreases in the incidence of colon cancer and several other diseases. The recommended quantity of fiber necessary for a healthy digestive system is between 25 and 35 grams every day.[16] Unfortunately, the average consumption of fiber is only about half the recommended level. Water is a necessary component for fiber to be effective, providing smooth transport of intestinal contents. If inadequate amounts of water and fluids are consumed along with fiber intake, constipation will result.

Fiber is highest in raw fruits, vegetables and unprocessed grain products. Table 6.2 lists the fiber content of several foods.

Fat

Fats (also known as lipids), are often considered the "bad guys" of nutrition, because they are linked with several disease processes as well as being primarily responsible for unsightly adipose tissue. However, some fat is a necessary component in a healthy diet because fat is used for several important body functions. Fat is a concentrated source of energy, providing 9 kcal of energy for every gram (compared to 4 kcal per gram for carbohydrates and proteins). Fats are a source of the essential fatty acids which the body requires but cannot make. Fat stored in the body act as insulation, preventing excessive heat loss, and protecting the body from extremes in environmental temperatures. Also, fat surrounds the vital organs of the body, protecting them from physical shock and trauma and is an essential component of cell membranes. As will be discussed in the section on vitamins, there are certain classes of vitamins that can only be transported through the body in combination with fats.[5]

TABLE 6.2
Fiber Content of Selected Foods

	Type of Food	Serving Size	Total Fiber (gm)	Calories
Cereals	Fiber One	1/2 cup	13.0	60
	Oatmeal	3/4 cup	1.6	108
	Shredded Wheat	2 biscuits	4.4	83
	Cap'n Crunch	3/4 cup	0.2	119
	Grape Nuts	1/4 cup	1.4	100
Breads	Whole Wheat	1 slice	2.4	61
	White	1 slice	trace	64
	Rye	1 slice	2.0	65
Crackers	Graham	2 squares	1.5	60
	Saltines	2 squares	trace	26
	Wheat Thins	8 crackers		72
	Triscuits	4 crackers		84
Fruits	Apple, with skin	1 medium	3.5	80
	Banana	1 medium	2.4	90
	Blueberries	1/2 cup	2.6	40
	Grapefruit	1/2 large	3.1	60
	Orange	1 medium	0.8	65
	Pear	1 medium	3.2	70
	Prunes	3 medium	3.0	60
	Strawberries	1/2 cup	1.5	22
Pasta/Rice/Legumes	Brown rice	1/2 cup cooked	1.0	97
	White rice	1/2 cup cooked	0.2	82
	Spaghetti	1 cup	1.1	155
	Spaghetti, whole wheat	1 cup	3.9	155
	Macaroni	1 cup	1.6	144
	Kidney beans	1/2 cup	7.3	110
	Lentils	1/2 cup	3.7	95
Vegetables	Peas	1/2 cup	3.6	55
	Potatoes	1 medium	2.5	105
	Corn on the cob	4" ear	4.2	100
	Broccoli	1/2 cup cooked	2.2	20
	Zucchini	1/2 cup cooked	1.8	10
	Lettuce	1 cup	0.9	10
	Mushrooms	1/2 cup raw	0.9	10
	Green pepper	1/2 cup raw	0.5	10

Source: Adapted from references 1, 11, and 14.

Most nutrition authorities recommend that the American population reduce their daily consumption of fat because fats make up approximately 42% of the total daily caloric intake in the typical American diet. Most authorities suggest that fat calories should be limited to no more than 30% of total daily calories with even lower intakes being more healthy.[13] The fat content in some foods such as butter and oil is fairly obvious. However, you may not be as aware of fat hiding in other foods. The percentage of calories from fat contained in some common foods is presented in Table 6.3.

One only has to look at the average American's waist-line to recognize that deficiencies of fat intake are extremely rare in the United States. The daily requirement of fat is equivalent to one tablespoon of oil, although many people ingest the equivalent of seven or eight tablespoons of oil. Excess fat in the diet is not necessary to produce storage fat in the body. If you consume too many calories from carbohydrates or protein, the unused amounts will be stored as body fat. You can quickly check the approximate amount of fat in your diet by answering the questions in Table 6.4.

Types of Fat

Fat is a general term that actually refers to a number of compounds, including triglycerides, sterols (such as cholesterol), and phospholipids. Triglycerides, composed of three fatty acids and a glycerol molecule, are the primary form in which fats are stored in humans and animals. When you eat animal fat, such as in meat, you are eating triglycerides. When you eat too many calories, the excess calories are stored as triglycerides in adipose tissue.

Fatty acids, the primary components of fats, are chains of carbon and hydrogen atoms combined in various arrangements. Classification of fats is based on the degree to which the hydrogen atoms fill the available positions along the fatty acid molecule. There are three types of fat based on this type of classification scheme- **saturated**, **monounsaturated**, and **polyunsaturated**.

Saturated fats have all available positions on the fatty acid molecule filled by hydrogen atoms. Saturated fats are found primarily in animal sources of fats, such as meats, milk, cheese, and butter. However, they are also found in coconut, palm, and palm kernel oils which are also known as "tropical oils." Health experts advise that no more than 10% of total daily calories come from saturated fats.[5]

Monounsaturated fats contain one empty position on the fatty acid molecule, and are found in products such as olive oil, peanut oil, and canola oil. Polyunsaturated fats contain more than one empty position on the fatty

Poly- and monounsaturated vegetable oils should be our primary source of fat.

TABLE 6.3
Percent Calories from Fat in Selected Foods

		Fat %	Total Calories
90 to 100% Fat	Lard (1 tbsp)	100	126
	Vegetable Oil (1 tbsp)	100	122
	Butter (1 tbsp)	100	108
	Margarine (1 tbsp)	100	108
	Mayonnaise (1 tbsp)	98	101
	Black olives (2 medium)	97	37
	Green olives (2 medium)	96	15
	Bleu cheese dressing (1 tbsp)	94	77
	Italian dressing (1 tbsp)	93	69
	Bacon (1 strip)	92	49
70 to 89% Fat	Cream Cheese (1 oz)	89	101
	Bologna (1 slice)	86	88
	French dressing (1 tbsp)	85	67
	Coleslaw w/mayo (1/4 cup)	84	172
	Hot dog (beef)	83	145
	Peanut butter (1 tbsp)	75	96
	Spareribs (3 medium)	74	122
	Cheddar cheese	72	112
50 to 69% Fat	Egg, boiled (1 medium)	69	78
	Cream of chicken soup	69	117
	Pork chop (3.5 oz)	66	354
	Tuna in oil (4 oz)	66	285
	Potato chips (3.5 oz)	62	580
	Hamburger (1 patty)	61	224
	Pound cake (1 slice)	58	141
	Chicken w/skin (3.5 oz)	56	243
	Tenderloin broiled (4 oz)	54	596
30 to 49% Fat	Whole milk	49	148
	Tortilla chips (3.5 oz)	48	507
	Ice cream (1 cup)	47	270
	Regular yogurt (1 cup)	45	139
	Lean ground beef (3.5 oz)	43	210
	Tuna in oil (4 oz drained)	41	197
	Cookies, commercial (1)	38	96
	Chicken w/o skin (3.5 oz)	35	129
	Chocolate fudge (1" sq)	33	137
	Ham, boiled (1 slice)	32	66
10 to 29% Fat	Crabmeat, steamed (3.5 oz)	20	92
	Lowfat yogurt (1 cup)	19	143
	Picante sauce (6 tbsp)	13	40
Less Than 10% Fat	Most fruits and vegetables		

Sources: References 11 and 14.

TABLE 6.4

Quick Fat Quiz

How often do you eat:	Seldom or never	1–2 times a week	3–5 times a week	Almost daily
1. Fried, deep-fat fried, or breaded foods?	_____	_____	_____	_____
2. Fatty meats (bacon, sausage, bologna, heavily marbled steaks or roasts)?	_____	_____	_____	_____
3. Whole milk, high-fat cheeses, ice cream?	_____	_____	_____	_____
4. High-fat desserts (pies, pastries, rich cakes)?	_____	_____	_____	_____
5. Rich sauces and gravies?	_____	_____	_____	_____
6. Oily salad dressings or mayo?	_____	_____	_____	_____
7. Whipped cream, table cream, sour cream, or cream cheese?	_____	_____	_____	_____
8. Butter or margarine on vegetables, rolls, or toast?	_____	_____	_____	_____

Take a look at your answers. Several responses in the last two columns means you may have a high fat intake. Is it time to cut back on foods high in fat?

Source: Reference 17.

KEY CONCEPT

LOW FAT BY WEIGHT

It is pretty common to see food products with advertising labels plastered on the front which say "95% fat-free" or some similar terminology. This is very deceptive to the unaware consumer because it is interpreted as meaning that only 5% of the calories in the product are from fat. However, this is often not the correct interpretation. The correct interpretation is usually that the product is only 5% fat by weight, or 95% of the product's weight is something other than fat. Usually, these products contain a lot of water as a percentage of their total weight which "dilutes" the non-fat calories. For example ground meat may be 90% lean, or 10% fat by weight, but the fat calories comprise 50% or more of the total calories. The water weight which makes up a large portion of the fat-free weight doesn't have any calories. So be aware at attempts to make you think you are getting a low-fat product when in fact it may have a high percentage of total calories as fat.

acid molecule, and are found primarily in vegetable sources of fats, such as sunflower oil, safflower oil, corn oil, and cottonseed oil. It is important to remember that although the tropical oils are made from plant sources similar to the polyunsaturated fats, they are quite different in their chemical compositions and their subsequent effects on the body.[7]

As you will read in Chapter 7, the best fats to consume are the monounsaturated and polyunsaturated fats because saturated fats increase the risk for disease, especially heart disease. Monounsaturated and polyunsaturated fat, in moderate amounts, may actually help prevent heart disease.

Consuming a lot of saturated fat increases your risk for heart disease because saturated fat stimulates the cells of the body to produce even more cholesterol than normal. Because of this effect, consuming saturated fat is probably an even greater health hazard than consuming cholesterol. Unfortunately, saturated fat and cholesterol are usually found in the same foods so a diet high in one is likely to be high in both, creating double trouble.

If you read food labels, you will frequently see that oils are often **"hydrogenated"** or **"partially hydrogenated."** The process of "hydrogenation" takes a "heart-healthly" fat like monounsaturated or polyunsaturated fat, and makes it "heart-unhealthy." The hydrogenation process takes the healthier unsaturated fats and "saturates" the molecules with hydrogen. The hydrogenated or partially hydrogenated fat then acts like a saturated fat in the body, leading to increased cholesterol production and increased risk for heart disease.

Why would food manufacturers purposefully use hydrogenation if it is so potentially unhealthy. Saturated fats have a longer shelf-life than unsaturated fats. Also, saturated fats are usually easier to bake and cook with because of the texture and a reduced tendency to separate. An example of these properties is seen in comparing "natural peanut butter" with a highly processed brand like Jiff. If you open a jar of natural peanut butter, you will find a layer of oil on top because the fat has separated from the solids. In processed peanut butter, the fat is hydrogenated and it stays emulsified and the product is very smooth and creamy. Processed peanut butter is visually appealing but natural peanut butter is much more healthy.

Hydrogenation also produces a type of hybrid fat referred to as "trans-fatty acids." Trans-fatty acids have recently been linked to heart disease and may turn out to be the worst type of fat you could eat.[22] A common source of trans-fatty acids in the diet is margarine and there is currently a debate regarding whether margarine or butter is worse for health. Even though butter contains more saturated fat and cholesterol, margarine contains more trans-fatty acids from the hydrogenation process. As this debate continues, it would probably be prudent to decrease your consumption of hydrogenated and partially hydrogenated oils as well as saturated fats.

TABLE 6.5

Fats and Oils—Differences in Fatty Acid Content

Vegetable Oils and Shortening	Polyunsaturated Fatty Acids	Monounsaturated Fatty Acids	Saturated Fatty Acids
Safflower oil	75%	12%	9%
Sunflower oil	66%	20%	10%
Corn oil	59%	24%	13%
Soybean Oil	58%	23%	14%
Cottonseed oil	52%	18%	26%
Canola oil	33%	55%	7%
Olive oil	8%	74%	13%
Peanut oil	32%	46%	17%
Soft tub margarine	31%	47%	18%
Stick margarine	18%	59%	19%
Palm oil	9%	37%	49%
Coconut oil	2%	6%	86%
Palm kernel oil	2%	11%	81%
Animal Fats			
Tuna fat	37%	26%	27%
Chicken fat	21%	45%	30%
Lard	11%	45%	40%
Beef fat	4%	42%	50%
Butter fat	4%	29%	62%

Table 6.5 indicates the relative amounts of different fatty acids in several fat-containing products. As you can see, most fats are a combination of all three types of fat. When we say a fat is a monounsaturated, polyunsaturated, or saturated fat, we are really saying that it is predominantly one or the other.

Cholesterol

Cholesterol is a white, powdery substance, made primarily in the liver, and sent through the blood to cells throughout the body. Cells (which can also produce cholesterol) use cholesterol for several important physiologic functions, including coating nerve fibers and producing several important hormones.

The cholesterol in the body comes from two sources, the food we eat and from cellular production. Even if we didn't eat any cholesterol in our diet, our bodies would produce enough cholesterol to meet the needs of the body. Unfortunately, not only do we eat too much cholesterol in our diet, but we also eat a lot of saturated fat and trans-fatty acids which stimulate the body to produce more cholesterol than the body needs for its normal purposes. This excess cholesterol is one factor causing an increased risk of coronary heart disease, so dietary reduction of saturated fats and cholesterol are strongly recommended for all people over two years of age.[4]

As indicated above, some cholesterol is very necessary to normal body function. The cholesterol in the body is actually comprised of several sub-types of cholesterol—**low density lipoprotein cholesterol (LDL-C)**, **high density lipoprotein cholesterol (HDL-C),** and **very low density lipoprotein cholesterol (VLDL-C)**. The "lipoprotein" term is used to designate the specific type of carrier protein used to carry the cholesterol around in the blood. Because cholesterol is like a fat and the blood is primarily water, cholesterol has to hook-up with proteins in order to be transported in the blood.

The HDL-C is known as the "good" cholesterol because of the way it is metabolized and handled by the body. It is not the cholesterol that causes clogged arteries. On the other hand, the LDL-C and VLDL-C are "bad" types of cholesterol because they do clog up arteries, causing coronary heart disease, stroke, and other vascular complications. The different sub-types of cholesterol are affected differently by factors such as diet and exercise. Consuming a diet high in saturated fat increases LDL-C and VLDL-C while regular exercise increases HDL-C.

Cholesterol is discussed in more detail in Chapter 7, but Table 6.6 lists values of cholesterol and relative risk levels. It is important for young adults to have their cholesterol measured periodically (about every 5 years) in order to determine if cholesterol is within an acceptable range. Middle-aged and older adults should have their cholesterol measured more often, probably every two years. The sooner a problem is detected, the easier it is to remedy the problem and reduce the chances of heart disease later in life.

TABLE 6.6		
Cholesterol Risk Classification		
Risk Classification	**Total Cholesterol (mg/dl)**	**LDL-Cholesterol (mg/dl)**
Low Risk	<200	<130
Moderate Risk	200–239	130–159
High Risk	>239	>159

Source: High Blood Cholesterol in Adults. National Cholesterol Education Program. U.S. Department of Health and Human Services

Protein

Protein is present in all cells of the body and is essential for life. It is necessary to build new tissue and repair muscle tissue. Enzymes, antibodies, and some hormones are made of protein. Collagen, which is a fibrous protein, gives support to skin and bones. Proteins help control water balance in the body, and act as pH buffers against extreme acidity or alkalinity. Protein can provide energy for the body, but only in unusual situations such as when total energy intake is low or engaging in prolonged, severe exercise.[10]

Protein is comprised of **amino acids**, referred to as the building blocks of protein. The digestive process breaks dietary protein into amino acids and the amino acids are transported in the blood throughout the body to wherever they are needed.

There are a total of 22 amino acids, of which 8 are considered essential because they can not be formed in the body. **Essential amino acids** must come from the food we eat. The other 14 **nonessential amino acids** need not come from the diet in their final form because they can be manufactured in the body by combining the basic elements of the foods we eat.[10]

Most protein from animal sources, including meat, fish, poultry, dairy products, and eggs, contain all of the essential amino acids, and are known as **complete proteins**. Plant sources of protein are often lacking in one or more of the essential amino acids and are classified as **incomplete protein**. However, adequate intake of all the essential amino acids is possible by combining sources of plant proteins, a technique used by vegetarians to get adequate essential amino acids. Eating plant protein is a good way to get adequate amounts of protein without taking in too much fat, since many animal sources of protein have high fat contents. Table 6.7 shows how to combine plant sources of incomplete proteins to provide all essential amino acids.[1, 7]

The recommended quantity of protein for adults is approximately 0.4 grams of protein per pound of bodyweight. Table 6.8 lists grams of protein and fat for several common foods.[10]

The RDA for protein is probably not adequate in all situations. Protein requirements increase in several situations, including pregnancy, injury, athletic training and competition, and stress. However, because most Americans' protein intake is well over the RDA for normal, healthy individuals, most people probably eat enough protein to cover an increased requirement in special situations.

Consuming more protein than is needed for normal body functions is not an advantage because excess protein will be converted to fat and stored in adipose tissues. Also, the digestion of protein requires the elimination of nitrogen from the protein, a task performed by the liver and kidneys. Diets with excess protein may increase the risk of damage to the liver and kidneys,

---

TABLE 6.7

Examples of Vegetarian Dishes with Complete Protein

Combine grains with legumes:

- Rice with lentils
- Peanut butter on whole wheat
- Beans on corn tortilla
- Wheat bread with baked beans
- Trail Mix with peanuts, soy nuts, and sunflower seeds

Combine grains with milk products:

- Oatmeal with milk
- Rice pudding
- Pizza
- Macaroni and cheese
- Quiche
- Spinach lasagne
- Cheese sandwich
- Cereal with milk

Combine grains with eggs:

- Rice pudding
- Oatmeal cookies
- Quiche
- Egg salad sandwich
- French toast

Adapted from references 1 and 7.

TABLE 6.8
Protein and Fat Content of Selected Foods

Food (cooked)	Calories	Protein in Grams	Percent Calories from Fat
Sirloin steak (3 oz)	170	26	36
Hamburger with bun	445	25	42
Bologna (3 oz)	260	10	83
Chicken, light meat, without skin (3 oz)	140	26	25
Chicken, dark meat, without skin (3 oz)	175	23	41
Tuna, in oil drained (3 oz)	158	23	40
Tuna, in water (3 oz)	116	23	16
Spareribs (3 oz)	338	25	77
American cheese (1 oz)	105	6	60
Cheddar cheese (1 oz)	144	7	56
Whole milk (1 cup)	150	8	43
Skim milk (1 cup)	85	8	5
Yogurt, plain (1 cup)	150	8	43
Yogurt, low fat (1 cup)	145	12	25
Egg, large	80	6	68
Pizza (1 slice)	290	15	28

Adapted from: *The Mount Sinai School of Medicine Complete Book of Nutrition* (14).

which have to work overtime trying to excrete the excess nitrogen. Osteoporosis is another potential consequence of excess protein intake, due to increased calcium excretion with high levels of protein intake.[10] Most individuals will get sufficient protein if they consume 12-15% of their total calories as protein, assuming total calories are adequate.

Vitamins

There are many vitamin and mineral supplements available.

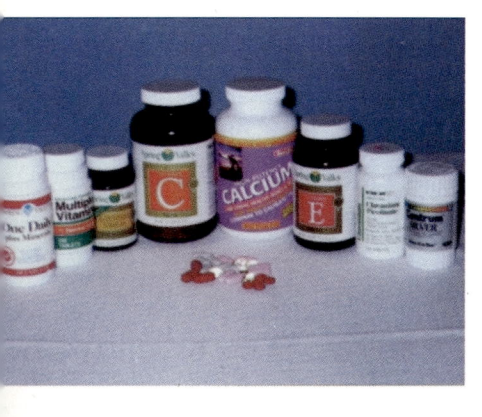

Vitamins are organic compounds derived from plants and animals. They are required in the diet in very small amounts, but are involved in almost every metabolic process in the body. Vitamins are necessary for utilization of all other nutrients, and regulate several body processes, including formation of blood cells and hormones. Most vitamins aid enzymes in biological reactions, and are necessary for normal reproduction.

Types of Vitamins

There are 13 specific vitamins, classified into two categories. **Fat-soluble vitamins** include vitamins A, D, E, and K. These vitamins are absorbed into the body with the help of fat in the diet. They are stored in the liver and fatty

KEY CONCEPT

THE REQUIREMENTS FOR VITAMINS AND MINERALS

Guidelines for the requirements for vitamins and minerals can be confusing because of the terminology used. There are actually three different standards used-the Recommended Dietary Allowances (RDA), the Estimated Safe and Adequate Daily Dietary Intakes (ESADDIs), and the Estimated Minimum Requirements (EMR). These standards are determined by the National Academy of Sciences, a government agency, and are periodically revised. The last revision occurred in 1989.

The RDAs are defined as the levels of intake of essential nutrients judged to be adequate to meet the known needs of virtually all healthy persons. The RDAs provide a built-in safety factor specific to each nutrient and therefore exceed the actual requirement for most individuals. The RDAs should also be viewed as time-averaged goals. It is not necessary to consume the RDA each day for each nutrient, but over time, the average consumption should meet the RDAs. RDAs are provided for all vitamins except biotin and pantothenic acid, and for the minerals calcium, phosphorus, magnesium, iron zinc, iodine and selenium.

Because less information is known about the requirements for some vitamins and minerals, ESADDIs are provided for these vitamins and minerals instead of RDAs. ESADDIs provide a range of intakes thought to meet the requirements for those nutrients. ESADDIs are provided for biotin, pantothenic acid, copper, manganeese, fluoride, chromium, and molybdenum.

The requirement for the electrolytes (and minerals) sodium, potassium, and chloride are stated as EMRs. This is because the average intake of these electrolytes usually far exceeds their requirement so that deficiencies would be rare.

tissues, and are not easily excreted from the body. Therefore, deficiencies are rare, even if intake is not at the recommended level every day. The fat-soluble vitamins can reach toxic levels relatively quickly in the body, especially with mega-dose supplementation.[5, 21]

The eight B-complex vitamins and vitamin C are classified **as water-soluble vitamins**. These are transported in the body in water, and are excreted in urine, especially with excess intake. The water-soluble vitamins are not stored in the body, therefore, deficiencies can develop relatively quickly (4-6 weeks) with inadequate daily intake. However, even water-soluble vitamins can be toxic in large amounts.[5, 21]

There are several other substances that are thought to be vitamins by some health enthusiasts, but are not considered as such by the scientists who determine our daily nutrient requirements. The health claims of these substances are often based on anecdotal evidence, and are not proven scientifically. Table 6.9 contains the recognized vitamins with their functions and best food sources. Table 6.10 shows the RDA for all the vitamins and minerals.

TABLE 6.9

Vitamins: Function, Source, and Deficiency Signs

Vitamin	Function	Source	Deficiency Signs
Fat-Soluble			
A (retinol)	maintenance of eyes, vision, skin, linings of nose and mouth, immune function	dairy products, liver, orange and deep green vegetables	night blindness, poor immune response, dry and scaling skin
D (calciferol)	Calcium metabolism, development of bones and teeth	dairy products, egg yolk *sunlight*	Rickets (bone deformities) in children, osteomalacia (bone softening) in adults
E (tocopherol)	protection and maintenance of cellular membranes	vegetable oils and their products, nuts, seeds	anemias
K (phylloquinone)	aids in blood clotting	green vegetables, tea, meats, fruits	bleeding and hemorrhage
Water-Soluble			
Thiamin (B_1)	energy metabolism	dairy products, meat, eggs, enriched grain products, green leafy vegetables	skin lesions
Riboflavin (B_2)	energy metabolism	pork, legumes, peanuts, whole grain, poultry, leafy vegetables	nerve dysfunction
Niacin	energy metabolism	nuts, meats, grains, legumes	skin disorders, diarrhea
Pyridoxine (B_6)	amino acid metabolism	meats, whole grains, vegetables	nervous and muscular disorders
Folacin	DNA and RNA metabolism	green vegetables, orange juice, nuts, whole-grain	GI disturbance
B_{12}	DNA and RNA metabolism	liver, meat, eggs, milk	nervous system damage, some kinds of anemia
Pantothenic acid	energy metabolism	most foods	fatigue, sleep disturbance, nausea, poor coordination
Biotin	energy metabolism	meats, vegetables, legumes	dermatitis, depression, muscular pain
C (ascorbic acid)	maintenance and repair of connective tissue, promotes wound healing, antioxidant	fruits and vegetables, especially broccoli, cabbage, cantaloupe, citrus fruits, red and green peppers	skin spots, bleeding gums, weakness, delayed wound healing, impaired immune system

Vitamin Supplementation

Who needs vitamin supplements? A common belief held by much of the population is that if some vitamins are beneficial, more, in the form of vitamin supplements, must be better. This belief helps to support the multi-million dollar vitamin industry, but is it legitimate? For the most part, vitamin supplementation is unnecessary if a well-balanced diet is consumed. With a well-balanced diet that contains the appropriate quantity of calories, the RDA for vitamins and minerals is probably obtained. However, if a well-balanced diet is not eaten, supplementation with a one-a-day type vitamin may be warranted. A one-a-day type vitamin usually provides 100% of the RDA for vitamins, enough to be helpful if a poor diet is consumed, but not enough to cause any problems. It is always better to try to change your dietary habits and eat a well-balanced diet that provides sufficient vitamins than to rely on vitamin supplementation. However, in the real world, eating a well-balanced diet may be difficult (especially in college) and vitamin supplementation can provide a temporary bridge to a time when you can change your diet for the better.

In addition to those consuming a nutritionally poor diet, there are several other groups of individuals who may truly benefit from vitamin supplementation, especially with the advice of a physician. Infants and women who are pregnant or lactating (nursing) are commonly given vitamin supplements to ensure proper development of the child. It is especially important that these individuals do not take mega-doses of vitamins, which have been linked with birth defects and developmental problems.[5, 21]

Another group who may benefit from vitamin supplementation is cigarette smokers. Recent studies have indicated an association between beta-carotene (a form of vitamin A) and reduced risk of lung cancer. This is certainly not considered as an alternative to quitting smoking, but may be of benefit to individuals who have inadequate dietary intake of vitamins.[5, 21]

Women who take oral contraceptives, people who use several other types of medications, and heavy drinkers (no associations implied) may have deficiencies of several of the B vitamins and vitamin C. Individuals who have diseases which affect their immune system (including cancer patients) or diseases of the digestive tract may have vitamin deficiencies, along with surgical patients and elderly persons. A diet that contains fewer than 1200 calories per day is likely to be deficient in several vitamins.

If you fall into some of these special categories, seek the advice of a physician or knowledgeable health professional regarding the need to supplement. Since symptoms of vitamin deficiencies may take years to manifest, taking some precautionary measures may be the best route to follow.

TABLE 6.10

Recommended Dietary Allowances (RDA)[a]

Age and sex	Weight[b] (pounds)	Height[b] (inches)	Protein	Fat-soluble vitamins				Water-soluble vitamins		
				Vitamin A	Vitamin D	Vitamin E	Vitamin K	Vitamin C	Thiamin	Riboflavin
			gm	µg RE[c]	µg[d]	mg αTE[e]	µg	mg	mg	mg
Infants										
0.0-0.5	13	24	13	375	7.5	3	5	30	0.3	0.4
0.5-1.0	20	28	14	375	10	4	10	35	0.4	0.5
Children										
1-3	29	35	16	400	10	6	15	40	0.7	0.8
4-6	44	44	24	500	10	7	20	45	0.9	1.1
7-10	62	52	28	700	10	7	30	45	1.0	1.2
Males										
11-14	99	62	45	1,000	10	10	45	50	1.3	1.5
15-18	145	69	59	1,000	10	10	65	60	1.5	1.8
19-24	160	70	58	1,000	10	10	70	60	1.5	1.7
25-50	174	70	63	1,000	5	10	80	60	1.5	1.7
≥51	170	68	63	1,000	5	10	80	60	1.2	1.4
Females										
11-14	101	62	46	800	10	8	45	50	1.1	1.3
15-18	120	64	44	800	10	8	55	60	1.1	1.3
19-24	128	65	46	800	10	8	60	60	1.1	1.3
25-50	138	64	50	800	5	8	65	60	1.1	1.3
≥51	143	63	50	800	5	8	65	60	1.0	1.2
pregnant			60	800	10	10	65	70	1.5	1.6
lactating										
1st 6 months			65	1,300	10	12	65	95	1.6	1.8
2nd 6 months			62	1,200	10	11	65	90	1.6	1.7

[a]The RDAs are intended to provide for individual variations among most normal persons under usual environmental stresses.

[b]Weights and heights are medians for the U.S. population of the designated age. The use of these figures does not imply that the height-to-weight ratios are ideal.

[c]retinol equivalents. 1 retinol equivalent = 1 µg β-carotene.

Adapted from reference 9.

Water-soluble vitamins (continued)				Minerals						
Niacin	Vitamin B₆	Folate	Vitamin B₁₂	Cal-cium	Phos-phorus	Mag-nesium	Iron	Zinc	Iodine	Sele-nium
mg NE^f	mg	µg	µg	mg	mg	mg	mg	mg	µg	µg
5	0.3	25	0.3	400	300	40	6	5	40	10
6	0.6	35	0.5	600	500	60	10	5	50	15
9	1.0	50	0.7	800	800	80	10	10	70	20
12	1.1	75	1.0	800	800	120	10	10	90	20
13	1.4	100	1.4	800	800	170	10	10	120	30
17	1.7	150	2.0	1,200	1,200	270	12	15	150	40
20	2.0	200	2.0	1,200	1,200	400	12	15	150	50
19	2.0	200	2.0	1,200	1,200	350	10	15	150	70
19	2.0	200	2.0	800	800	350	10	15	150	70
15	2.0	200	2.0	800	800	350	10	15	150	70
15	1.4	150	2.0	1,200	1,200	280	15	12	150	45
15	1.5	180	2.0	1,200	1,200	300	15	12	150	50
15	1.6	180	2.0	1,200	1,200	280	15	12	150	55
15	1.6	180	2.0	800	800	280	15	12	150	55
13	1.6	180	2.0	800	800	280	10	12	150	55
17	2.2	400	2.2	1,200	1,200	320	30	15	175	65
20	2.1	280	2.6	1,200	1,200	355	15	19	200	75
20	2.1	260	2.6	1,200	1,200	340	15	16	200	75

^d As cholecalciferol. 10 mg cholecalciferol = 400 IU of vitamin D

^e α-Tocopherol equivalents. 1 mg dα tocopherol = 1 α-TE.

^f 1 NE (niacin equivalent) is equal to 1 mg of niacin or 60 mg of dietary trytophan.

Nature vs. Man

Are "natural" vitamins better than man-made synthetic vitamins? Research indicates that natural vitamins are not better for the body than synthetic vitamins, since your body can not tell the difference between them. The chemical structure of natural and synthetic vitamins are exactly the same. However, those that argue in favor of natural vitamins contend that there may be other unknown chemicals or compounds in the natural-source of vitamins that enhances the natural vitamin. There is no evidence to date that this is the case.

One thing that is known is that supplements containing natural vitamins are usually more expensive, as are vitamin pills containing mega-doses of specific compounds. It appears that this may be a situation in which you really do not get what you pay for since synthetic vitamins appear just a beneficial as the more expensive natural vitamins.

Minerals

Minerals are solid inorganic (contain no carbon molecules) substances that are catalysts of several vital physiologic functions in the body. Minerals regulate muscle contraction and relaxation, and transmit nerve impulses. Some minerals make up the structural framework of the body (calcium), while others form components of essential body compounds such as hormones, enzymes, pigment, and hemoglobin. Minerals help to maintain proper water balance and acid-base balance in the body.[5, 21]

Other minerals are found in body tissues, and may be important to human nutrition, but their roles have not been defined. Several other minerals found in the body, such as mercury, cadmium, and lead, may be extremely toxic if their levels are too high.

An important consideration regarding mineral requirements is the **bioavailability** of minerals, which represents the efficiency of the body to absorb the mineral. For example, the recommended daily intake of iron is ten times greater than our bodies' actual physiologic needs, because we can only absorb about 10% of the iron from foods we eat.

The six major minerals in the body are calcium, phosphorus, magnesium, potassium, sodium, and chloride. They are known as the macrominerals, since the daily requirement of these minerals is greater than 100 mg. The 14 remaining minerals are called trace minerals, since they are needed in quantities less than 100 mg per day. Although all of the minerals are vitally important for our health, nutritional aspects of calcium, iron, and sodium are described here.[5, 21] Table 6.11 contains a listing of all the minerals and related information.

TABLE 6.11

Minerals: Function, Source, and Dificiency Signs

Mineral	Function	Source	Deficiency Signs
Major Minerals			
Calcium (Ca^{2+})	bone and tooth formation, blood clotting, nerve and muscle function	dairy products, green vegetables	bone loss in adults
Phosphorus (PO^{3-})	bone and tooth formation, acid-base balance, chemical energy	dairy products, poultry, whole grains	weakness, bone demineralization
Magnesium (Mg^{2+})	enzyme function	whole grains, green leafy vegetables	neurological disturbances
Potassium (K^+)	water balance, nerve function	meats, milk, fruits and vegetables, whole grains	muscular weakness
Sulfur (S)	Acid-base balance, liver function	protein, dried food	poor growth, liver damage
Sodium (Na^+)	action potentials in all cells, water balance	processed foods of all types, table salt, small amounts if fruits and vegetables	high blood pressure, muscle cramping
Chloride (Cl^-)	acid-base balance, membrane potentials	table salt, processed foods	muscle cramping, decreased appetite
Trace Minerals			
Iron (Fe)	part of hemoglobin, myoglobin, and enzymes	meats, eggs, whole grains, green leafy vegetables	iron deficiency anemia, weakness, poor immune function
Copper (Cu)	enzyme formation	seafood, nuts, beans, meat, water	anemia, bone and cardiovascular changes
Zinc (Zn)	enzyme formation	meats, seafood, whole grains	poor growth, poor immune function
Iodine (I)	component of thyroid hormone	marine fish and shellfish, dairy products, iodized salt	goiter (enlarged thyroid)
Fluoride (F)	teeth and bone formation and maintenance	water, tea, seafood	tooth decay
Selenium (Se)	enzyme formation, functions with Vitamin E, antioxidant	seafood, meat, whole grains	muscle pain, poor immune function
Cobalt (Co)	part of vitamin B_{12}	animal products	unknown
Chromium (Cr)	glucose metabolism, insulin function	brewer's yeast, liver, seafood, meat	poor glucose metabolism, impaired insulin function
Manganese (Mn)	enzyme formation	nuts, whole grains, fruits, vegetables	abnormal bone and cartilage
Molybdenum (Mo)	enzyme function	fats, vegetable oils, meats, whole grains	disorder in nitrogen excretion

Calcium

Calcium is the body's most abundant mineral, and it's the macromineral most likely to be in short supply in the diets of many Americans. Deficiencies of calcium have been linked with several degenerative diseases, such as osteoporosis, hypertension, and colon cancer. Ninety-eight percent of calcium in the body is found in the skeleton, where it gives strength by the formation of salts. One percent of body calcium is used for tooth formation, and the remaining one percent is present in soft tissues throughout the body, where it plays a major part in muscular contraction and relaxation.[8]

The recommended daily requirement of calcium is 1200 mg per day for college-aged females and 1200 mg per day for college-aged males. There are increased requirements for pregnant and lactating women. Calcium content is highest in dairy products, as shown in Table 6.12. Some nutrients in foods, such as vitamin D and lactose, help our bodies to absorb more calcium from the foods we eat. On the other hand, excess dietary intake of protein, fat, caffeine, and fiber may reduce the amount of calcium our bodies absorb.[5, 21]

Sodium

Sodium is one of the principal positive ions, or **electrolytes**, in body fluid. It helps maintain normal body-fluid balance and acid-base balance. Sodium

---

KEY CONCEPT

SODIUM AND HIGH BLOOD PRESSURE

For decades scientist have been studying the link between sodium intake and high blood pressure. It has been recognized for many decades that in some individuals, high sodium intake was related to high blood pressure. But, fortunately, this appears to be the exception rather than the rule.

A small percentage (probably less than 15%) of the population are "salt sensitive," meaning that they are likely to have an increase in blood pressure if sodium intake is too high. For these individuals, reducing sodium intake may normalize high blood pressure and may prevent getting high blood pressure in those with normal blood pressure. Unfortunately, it is a trial-and-error situation to determine who is and who is not salt sensitive. A general recommendation is made to individuals with high blood pressure to reduce their sodium intake to less than 3,000 mg per day but it does not always result in a reduction of blood pressure.

If you are not salt sensitive, you can consume 5,000-10,000 mg of sodium per day (the average intake of Americans) without any apparent effect on blood pressure. However, some believe that salt sensitivity can be acquired by consuming high amounts of sodium over years. Therefore, it may be prudent to begin to limit sodium intake now in order to potentially prevent salt sensitivity and perhaps high blood pressure from occurring several decades down the road. There is no known benefit to consuming the large quantities that Americans typically consume.

TABLE 6.12

Calcium Content of Selected Foods

Food	Calcium (mg)	Calories
Dairy Products		
Whole milk (1 cup)	290	150
Skim milk (1 cup)	302	85
2% milk (1 cup)	297	121
Buttermilk (1 cup)	285	99
Chocolate milk (2%, 1 cup)	284	179
Hot cocoa (whole milk, 1 cup)	298	218
Milkshake (vanilla, 1 cup)	457	350
Plain yogurt (1 cup)		
Whole milk	274	150
Lowfat	415	145
Skim milk	452	127
Fruits and Vegetables		
Orange, 1 medium	56	65
Papaya, 1 medium	72	117
Dried prunes (10)	43	200
Baked beans (8 oz)	175	250
Beet greens, raw (3.5 oz)	119	24
Broccoli, raw (1 stalk)	103	32
Broccoli, cooked (2/3 cup)	88	26
Cabbage, shredded (1 cup)	49	24
Chard, raw (3.5 oz)	88	25
Collard greens, cooked (1/2 cup)	152	29
Dandelion greens, cooked (1/2 cup)	140	33
Endive, raw (20 leaves)	81	20
Garbanzo beans (chick-peas) (3.5 oz)	71	179
Green beans, frozen, cooked (2/3 cup)	38	26
Kale, raw (3.5 oz)	179	38
Lettuce, romaine (3.5 oz)	68	18
Lettuce, iceberg (3.5 oz)	20	13
Mustard greens, raw (3.5 oz)	183	31
Rhubarb, raw (1 cup)	266	29
Soybean curd (Tofu) (3.5 oz)	128	72
Spinach, raw (3.5 oz)	93	26
Spinach, cooked (1/2 cup)	83	21
Squash, cooked, Butternut (1 cup)	82	139
Sweet potato, baked (1 large)	72	254
Watercress, raw (3.5 oz)	151	19

Adapted from reference 11.

is critical for transmission of nerve impulses and muscular contraction and relaxation. On the other hand, high sodium intake has been associated with hypertension and fluid retention. There is no RDA established for sodium, but the estimated minimum requirement (EMR) is 500 mg per day. Since the average American consumes 5,000-10,000 mg per day, getting enough sodium is not a problem.[5, 21] The problem is getting too much sodium since high sodium intakes have been related to high blood pressure.

Sodium is found widely in nature, but only small quantities are in foods. Often, however, significant amounts of table salt, which is made of sodium chloride, are added to foods, either by the consumer or by the manufacturer. In general, fresh or frozen foods are often low in sodium, while processed foods often have high amounts of sodium added. For example, one serving of corn on the cob prepared without additional salt has only a trace (less than 1 mg) of sodium, while one serving of canned corn has 236 mg of sodium. Notice the difference in Table 6.13 in the sodium content between

TABLE 6.13

Comparing Sodium Content Between Fresh and Canned/Processed Foods

Food	Canned/Processed Sodium (mg)	Fresh/Frozen Sodium (mg)
Baked beans (1/2 cup)	650	7
Corn (1/2 cup)	251	4
Green beans (1/2 cup)	295	2
Kidney beans (2/5 cup)	300	3
Lima beans (3/5 cup)	317	1
Mixed vegetables (2/3 cup)	279	41
Mushrooms (1/3 cup)	400	15
Peas (2/3 cup)	291	1
Tomatos (1/2 cup)	249	3
Beans & franks (1 cup)	1092	228
Chicken noodle soup (1 cup)	1107	
Cream of mushroom soup (1 cup)	1031	
Tomato soup (1 cup)	932	
French dressing (1 tbsp)	214	
Breakfast links (5)	600	
Bologna (1 slice)	270	
Hot dog (1)	504	
Ham lean only, cooked, fresh		54
Cured (3.5 oz)	1020	
Sausage (1 oz)	740	
Bacon (1 slice)	342	20
Sloppy Joe (5 oz meat & sauce)	1120	
Hamburger (1 patty)		40
V-8 vegetable juice (8 oz)	715	
Low sodium V-8	47	
Whole wheat bread (1 slice)	159	
Whole wheat bread crumbs (1 cup)	648	
Tuna (6.5 oz)	745	40

Adapted from reference 11.

fresh and processed foods. Sodium may also be a hidden ingredient in processed foods, as you will see in the section describing food labels.

Iron

Iron is one of the trace minerals, with a recommended daily intake of 10 mg for men and 18 mg for women. The major function of iron in the body is in the formation of **hemoglobin**, the compound in blood that transports oxygen from the lungs to the tissues. Iron deficiencies cause anemia, or low levels of iron in the blood. Symptoms of anemia include paleness, feeling tired, and low energy.[14, 16]

Dietary iron comes in two forms: heme iron, which is from animal sources (associated with hemoglobin); and non-heme iron, found in plant foods. Heme iron has greater bioavailability, with approximately 10 to 30 percent absorbed by the body, compared to 2 to 10 percent absorbed from non-heme iron. Bioavailability of non-heme iron is affected to some extent by certain dietary factors. Consuming sources of vitamin C at the same meal with non-heme iron sources increases the amount of iron absorbed by the body. For example, drinking orange juice (a significant source of vitamin C) at the same meal with enriched bread (a source of non-heme iron) will increase the amount of iron absorbed by the body. Conversely, consuming excess fiber, coffee, or tea at the same meal with non-heme iron will decrease the bioavailability of iron. The iron content of several heme and non-heme foods is listed in Table 6.14.[11, 16]

While supplemental iron in the form of pills will alleviate anemia, the amount of supplementation should be closely monitored by a physician. Too much iron will lead to constipation or diarrhea in most people, along with nausea. Excessive iron intake inhibits the absorption of zinc, a mineral that aids healing and the immune system. Recent studies have found that people who store high amounts of iron have a greater risk of developing certain types of cancer. Therefore, it is best not to take iron supplements unless you need to. Pregnant women and people who have been diagnosed as iron-deficient will certainly benefit from iron supplementation, but only with the advice of their physician. By choosing the right foods, most people can easily meet their daily requirements.

Antioxidants

As part of the normal process of making ATP aerobically, potentially damaging substances called free radicals are produced. Free radicals can potentially damage cells and have been postulated to be involved in heart disease and cancer. Normally, our bodies have natural defenses against free radical

TABLE 6.14
Iron Content of Heme and Non-Heme Foods

Heme Sources		Non-Heme Sources	
Food	**Iron (mg)**	**Food**	**Iron (mg)**
Hamburger (1 patty)		Dried fruit	
		Prunes (10)	2.08
Ribeye steak (3.5 oz)	2.6	Raisins (2/3 cup)	2.08
		Strawberries (1 cup)	1.12
		Watermelon (2 cups)	.56
Sloppy Joe (5 oz meat & sauce)	1.8	Cornbread (1 piece)	1.00
		Whole wheat bread (1 slice)	.86
Bacon	.1	Bran muffin (1)	1.26
		Baked beans (1 cup)	3.63
Ham (2 slices)	3.0	Black eyed peas (1/2 cup, frozen)	2.80
		Broccoli, raw (1 stalk)	1.10
		frozen (1/2 cup)	.84
Liver (beef, 3.5 oz)	8.8	Cauliflower, raw (1 cup pieces)	1.10
		frozen (1/2 cup)	.40
Bologna (1 slice)	.2	Chard, raw (3.5 oz)	3.20
		Garbanzo beans (3.5 oz)	3.00
Chicken, w/o skin, roasted (3.5 oz)	1.2	Blackstrap molasses (1 tbsp)	2.30
		Cap'n Crunch (1 serving)	13.90
		Total (1 serving)	18.00
Turkey, w/o skin, roasted (3.5 oz)	1.8	Product 19 (1 serving)	18.00
		Life Cereal (1 serving)	7.47
Egg yolks	1.0	Grape Nuts (1 serving)	1.22

Adapted from references 8 and 11.

damage. Several vitamins and minerals—Vitamins A, C, and E, and the mineral selenium—are involved in the natural defenses that help protect against free radicals and are therefor called **antioxidants**.

Recent studies have questioned the adequacy of our natural defenses, especially when oxygen metabolism is increased, as with exercise. It has been hypothesized that inadequate vitamin and mineral intakes may lead to increased free radical damage, especially if free radical production is elevated in exercise. It has been suggested that individuals involved in moderate to heavy exercise may need increased intakes of antioxidant vitamins and minerals to bolster their natural defenses. It has also been suggested that increased intakes of antioxidants may reduce the risk of heart disease and cancer.[23]

Studies that have investigated the efficacy of anitoxidants in protecting against free radicals have neither confirmed nor denied their efficacy.[23] This area is receiving a lot of attention and more definitive answers may be available in the near future. In the meantime, what is a person to do? The prudent thing is to recommend for antioxidants the same recommendations made for vitamins in general. If you are concerned about your antioxidant intake, increase your consumption of fresh fruits, vegetables, and grain products to increase your intake of antioxidants. It would not be harmful to supplement the antioxidant vitamins and minerals at 1-2 times the RDA until more definitive information becomes available regarding their role in health.

Water

Water is the most critical "nutrient" required by the body. Individuals can live for weeks without food or even years without some essential nutrients, but will survive only a few days without water. This critical dependency on water is due to the fact that the body is about 60% water and all the cells function in a watery environment.

Water has a multitude of functions in the body. It acts as a medium for thousands of biochemical reactions. Water carries nutrients to cells through the blood and lymphatic system, and carries waste from cells for excretion in urine and sweat. The distribution of heat throughout the body and the regulation of body temperature is modulated by water. Extra heat is dissipated through water evaporation from the body surface (sweat) and from the lungs. Also, water helps distribute heat throughout the body and maintain body temperature at 98.6°F even when ambient temperature is much colder. Water is a lubricant in joints, between organs, and around the eyeballs, and is one of the major components in digestive juices.[8, 21]

To insure adequate water intake, a minimum of 6 to 8 cups of water or other fluids should be consumed in a normal day. If the weather is hot or if you participate in physical activity, the water requirement will be greater. In general, pure water is best for fluid replacement. However, an exception to this general rule is when exercising in warm weather for longer than 45-60 minutes. In this type of situation, a sport drink containing some carbohydrate and sodium is probably better than just plain water.[8]

Juices and milk provide, in addition to fluid, vitamins, minerals, and calories, while pop, flavored drinks, alcohol, and sugared punches supply empty calories with little or no nutrients. It is OK to periodically drink some of the less desirable sources of fluid, but it is not good to make them your predominant source. Remember that alcohol and drinks containing caffeine act as diuretics contributing to water loss rather than water gain.

In addition to exercise, other conditions may increase the need for fluid intake. Hot weather, fever, and infection increases the need for fluid. It is also important to recognize that thirst is not a very reliable indicator of the need for water. The simplest method of detecting the need for fluid is the color of your urine. When body water is adequate, the urine is a pale yellow in color. As dehydration occurs, the urine becomes more concentrated and turns a darker yellow in color.

The body can tolerate fairly significant levels of dehydration for short periods of time, but chronic dehydration causes problems. Symptoms of mild dehydration include fatigue, headache, and sullenness. More serious complications can occur with inadequate fluid, including heat cramps, heat exhaustion, and heat stroke. Heat cramps are painful muscle spasms caused by depletion of water in working muscles. Heat exhaustion is characterized by extreme weakness, exhaustion, headache, dizziness, and profuse sweating. Heat stroke is a critical medical emergency with symptoms of dry, hot skin, and a flushed appearance, with fever running from 106-109°F. Heat stroke will progress to unconsciousness, coma, and death unless treated immediately.[8]

Additional Food Components

Alcohol

Alcohol is not classified as a food, but is a depressant drug. Pure alcohol contains no vitamins, minerals, or proteins, but has seven kcal per gram. However, an alcoholic beverage like beer does contain some nutrients due to the content of other food products in the beverage. The caloric content of several common alcoholic drinks is listed in Table 6.15.

Alcohol is not stored in the body, but is absorbed immediately from the stomach into the bloodstream and is metabolized by the liver. Alcohol is preferentially metabolized before carbohydrates and fats and the consumption of alcohol depresses the normal use of these other caloric nutrients. This immediate energy source from ingested alcohol causes food normally used for energy to be stored as fat.

Consuming alcohol usually results in an immediate increase in appetite, followed in approximately 40 minutes with suppression of appetite. Once the effects of alcohol begin to wear off, extreme physiologic hunger ("the munchies") may cause individuals to consume large quantities of food. Continued heavy drinking leads to nutritional deficiencies.[14]

Alcoholic beverages, taken in moderation, appear to have no detrimental effects on normal, healthy, non-pregnant adults. In fact, studies have found that moderate alcohol consumption (1 or 2 drinks) is associated with decreased risk for heart disease. The dietary guidelines for Americans recommend if you drink alcoholic beverages, do so in moderation.

If alcohol is consumed, it should be consumed in moderation.

TABLE 6.15
Caloric Content of Alcoholic and Non-Alcoholic Drinks

Beverage	Calories
Club soda or seltzer (8 oz)	0
Diet soda (8 oz)	2
Tomato juice (8 oz)	42
White table wine (4 oz)	80
Tonic water (8 oz)	80
Red table wine (4 oz)	84
Ice tea (sweetened) (8 oz)	99
Soda pop (8 oz)	100
Orange juice (8 oz)	109
Whiskey sour (3 oz)	123
Beer (12 oz)	146
Martini (2.5 oz)	156
Gin and Tonic (7.5 oz)	171
Screwdriver (7 oz)	174
Piña Colada (4.5 oz)	262

Adapted from reference 14.

The only exception for alcohol use in healthy adults is during pregnancy. Pregnant women who use alcohol, especially around the time of conception, are at greatly increased risk of having a baby born with Fetal Alcohol Syndrome (FAS). A child with FAS has very similar characteristics to a child with Down's Syndrome, including mental retardation. It is not known how much alcohol causes FAS, so it is recommended that pregnant women avoid drinking alcohol entirely.

Alcohol becomes a problem when it is consumed excessively. How do you make the choice not to drink? How will you fit in at a party where everyone is drinking but you? These issues and others are discussed in more detail in Chapter 8. Suffice it to say that alcohol is like most other foods that potentially can be bad for our health—when consumed in moderation, there is no harm. It is when overconsumption becomes the norm that problems develop.

Aspartame

Aspartame, commonly known by its brand name **Nutrasweet**, is a sugar substitute found in many processed foods. Aspartame has as many calories as sugar by weight (4 calories per gram), but is 180 times sweeter tasting, so much less aspartame is required in foods to provide the same sweet taste. There is a lot of controversy surrounding the safety and use of aspartame, but no significant evidence exists which would indicate the product is harmful at reasonable levels of consumption. The established safe level of consumption is 22 mg per pound of body-weight per day (equivalent to eighteen cans of diet soda for a 150 pound individual).[14]

Warnings are printed on food packages containing aspartame for individuals with an inherited metabolic disorder known as phenylketonuria (PKU). When a person with PKU ingests any food containing amino acids (proteins), there is an incomplete breakdown of the molecules. This leads to a buildup of toxins in the brain causing permanent mental retardation. Aspartame contains amino acids, and therefore manufacturers must label foods containing aspartame (Nutrasweet) as a warning to individuals with PKU. Currently, all infants born in the United States are tested at birth for PKU. If an infant has this rare disorder, he or she is placed on a special protein-free diet, avoiding the serious neurological consequences.

Caffeine

Caffeine, a stimulant to the central nervous system, is one of the world's most widely-used drugs. Table 6.16 lists the caffeine content of several foods.

In small amounts, caffeine enhances alertness and postpones drowsiness. However, with continued use, caffeine consumption can lead to insomnia, anxiety, irritability, depression, stomach irritation and heartburn. Caffeine is also a diuretic, stimulating water loss. Heavy caffeine users may experience psychological withdrawal symptoms (headache, nausea, vomiting, fatigue) when discontinuing use.

In some individuals, caffeine may cause heart rhythm irregularities. These irregularities are more common in females and can often be controlled by reducing caffeine intake. There have also been studies showing a link between caffeine intake and heart disease. However, these conclusions have not been consistent and the United States Surgeon General's report concluded that no definitive evidence for the effects of caffeine on heart disease could be drawn from most investigations to date, and that

TABLE 6.16
Caffeine Content of Beverages

Beverage	Caffeine (mg)	Beverage	Caffeine (mg)
Coffee (5 oz)		Soda pop (12 oz)	
Drip	60–180	Jolt	72
Percolated	40–175	Mountain Dew	54
Instant	30–120	Mellow Yellow	52
Decaffeinated	1–5	Coca-Cola (cherry or classic)	46
Tea (5 oz)		Sunkist Orange	40
1-min steep	933	Dr Pepper	40
5-min steep	20–50	Pepsi	38
Ice tea (12 oz)	22–36	Diet Pepsi	36
Hot cocoa (6 oz)	2–20	7-Up	0
Chocolate milk (8 oz)	2–7	A&W Root Beer	0

CAFFEINE AND ENDURANCE EXERCISE

One of the effects of consuming caffeine is that there is an acute increase in the amount of fatty acids in the blood. The increase in fatty acids in the blood increases the use of fats by muscles. For individuals engaged in endurance activities lasting longer than 60-90 minutes (like a marathon), increasing the use of fat by the muscle can be an advantage because it postpones the use of carbohydrate (glycogen) in the muscle and may prevent the depletion of carbohydrate. Carbohydrate depletion is a primary concern to the endurance athlete because performance suffers significantly when carbohydrates are depleted.

Consuming caffeine about 1 hour before endurance exercise has been effective in some in increasing fat utilization by muscle and potentially sparing carbohydrates. Individuals most susceptible to this effect are those not used to drinking caffeine. Chronic caffeine drinkers do not show the same effect. So, if you want to potentially boost your performance in an endurance competition, you might try consuming the caffeine equivalent to 1-2 cups of coffee about an hour before the competition.

further studies were required. As with alcohol, caffeine appears to have no significant detrimental effects when consumed in moderation.

Fat Substitutes

As the emphasis on consuming lower fat foods continues to be voiced by government agencies as well as practically all consumer health groups, the food technology industry has been trying to produce acceptable fat substitutes. The goal is to produce a fat substitute that has all the positive qualities of fat related to food processing and preparation while reducing or eliminating the negative aspects of high calories and other health consequences.

Usually, reduced- and low-fat foods have a combination of ingredients to replace fat since no one single, totally acceptable substitute has been developed. Common ingredients used as fat substitutes are protein, carbohydrate, and fat-based agents.

The most recent fat substitute to get FDA approval is **olestra,** a carbohydrate-based agent (sucrose polyester). Although very similar to fat in most of its qualities, olestra is not able to be digested by humans and therefore does not have any caloric value. The down side is that olestra produces GI tract upset in some individuals, especially when consumed in large quantities.

Olestra is currently approved for use in snacks such as flavored and unflavored chips, crisps, and crackers. These uses include the substitution of fat for frying as well as sources of fat in dough conditioners, oil sprays, and flavors. Major brands of chips are starting to use olestra for frying their chips.

Food Additives

Food additives include all materials deliberately added to food to help manufacture and preserve food, improve palatability and eye-appeal. There are several positive implications of additives, including increased shelf life of food which allows for transport of foods around the world at any time of year. Additives lower the cost of food, because the food can be produced and sold in large amounts. This is of benefit to people with low incomes, who are most at risk of nutritional deficiencies. Food additives result in less food being wasted. Artificial sweeteners are considered food additives, and result in individuals consuming fewer calories. Some additives are actually components of other foods that have been added as preservatives, such as thiamin, and citric, ascorbic, and benzoic acids.[14]

Unfortunately there are several drawbacks to food additives. Sugar and salt, two of the most common additives, can lead to, or exacerbate, chronic disorders. Sugar can affect tooth decay, obesity, and diabetes, and salt can affect hypertension and congestive heart failure. Some additives have been implicated as carcinogens (cancer-causing agents), including the sweeteners cyclamates and saccharin, and nitrite used to preserve bacon and ham.

The list of additives "generally recognized as safe" (GRAS) contains over 700 food additives considered safe. However, processed foods containing food additives are most often lower in nutritional value than fresh and frozen foods, so the key to health with additives is moderation. So, when you have the choice, select your foods in this priority order—fresh foods first, frozen foods second, and canned or highly processed foods last.

DIETARY PLANNING

Dietary Guidelines for Americans

"Eating a well-balanced diet is the key to good nutrition." What exactly does this mean? The diet must contain adequate amounts of the essential nutrients to sustain growth and repair body tissues, and it must be balanced in caloric intake for control of body weight. Figures 6.1 and 6.2 compare the current average intake of macronutrients for Americans and the recommended dietary goals.

As can be seen from Figure 6.1, average Americans eat too much fat and not enough carbohydrates. Too much of the fat eaten is saturated fat and too much of the carbohydrates are simple carbohydrates. Fat consumption should be reduced to less than 30% with two-thirds of the fat coming for unsaturated sources. Carbohydrate consumption should be increased to 55% or greater of total calories with most coming from complex carbohydrates. Protein intake should be 12-15% of total calories with attention paid to getting adequate essential amino acids.

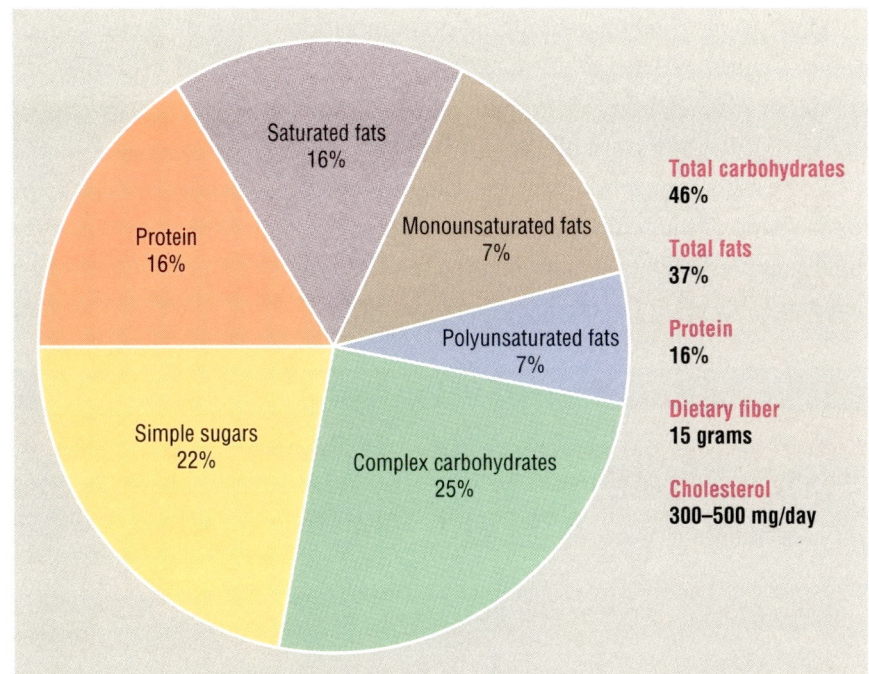

FIGURE 6.1

The current average intake of nutrients.

Saturated fats
16%

Protein
16%

Monounsaturated fats
7%

Polyunsaturated fats
7%

Simple sugars
22%

Complex carbohydrates
25%

Total carbohydrates
46%

Total fats
37%

Protein
16%

Dietary fiber
15 grams

Cholesterol
300–500 mg/day

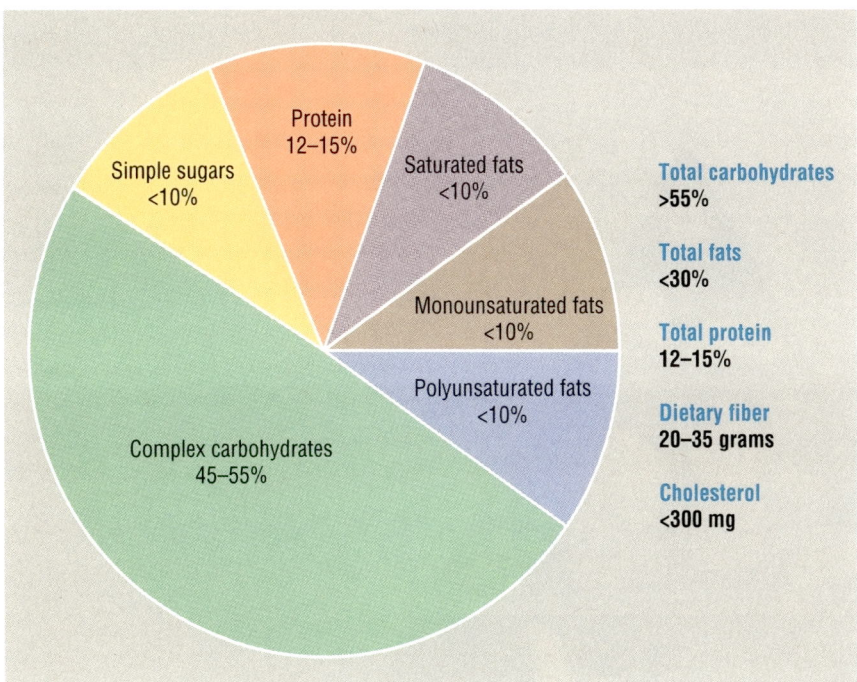

FIGURE 6.2

The recommended intake of nutrients.

Simple sugars
<10%

Protein
12–15%

Saturated fats
<10%

Monounsaturated fats
<10%

Polyunsaturated fats
<10%

Complex carbohydrates
45–55%

Total carbohydrates
>55%

Total fats
<30%

Total protein
12–15%

Dietary fiber
20–35 grams

Cholesterol
<300 mg

Food alone can not make you healthy. Good health also depends on your heredity, your environment, and your lifestyle—exercise, cigarette smoking, drug and alcohol use. However, a balanced diet can help keep you healthy, and may improve your health. The United States Department of Agriculture (USDA) has examined the majority of research on nutrition, and has recommended general dietary guidelines for choosing and preparing foods, and for meeting the dietary goals. A summary of these recommendations is in Table 6.17.

Many of us grew up associating good nutrition with the "Basic 4" food group—fruits and vegetables, dairy products, meats and proteins, and grains. In 1992, the USDA expanded on this basic 4 concept and developed an "Eating Right Pyramid", as shown in Figure 6.3.

The concept of good nutrition using the pyramid includes eating more foods found at the bottom of the pyramid, and less of those found near the top. Examples of common amounts of food servings used in the pyramid are listed in Table 6.19. Granted, these dietary principles are broad in scope and

TABLE 6.17
USDA Recommended Dietary Guidelines
• Eat a variety of foods
• Maintain a healthy weight
• Choose a diet low in fat, saturated fat, and cholesterol
• Choose a diet with plenty of vegetables, fruits, and grain products
• Use sugars in moderation
• Use salt and sodium in moderation
• If you drink alcohol, drink in moderation

FIGURE 6.3

The Food Pyramid depicting the recommended servings of different foods. As you go from the base of the pyramid to the top, the recommended servings decrease.

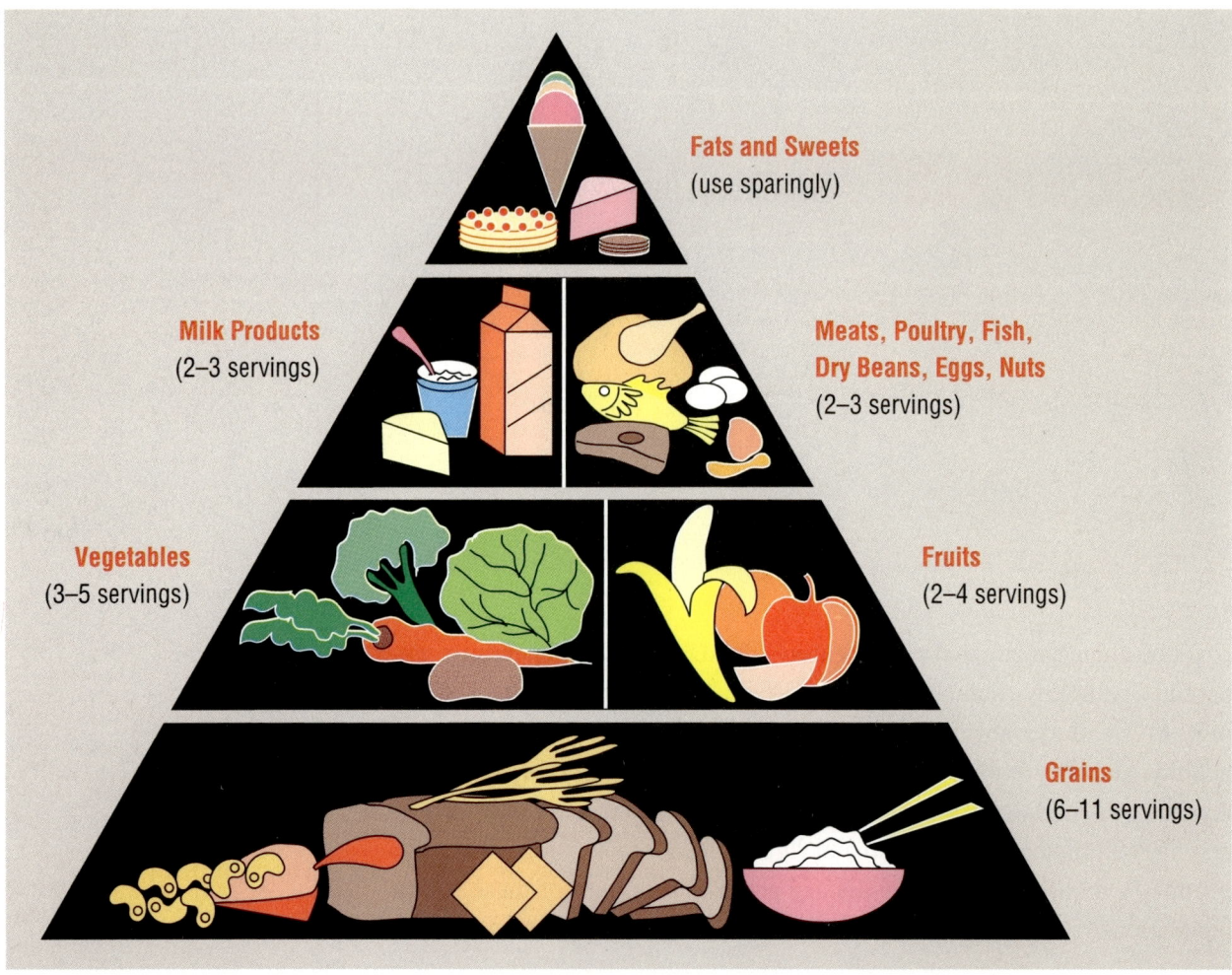

Fats and Sweets (use sparingly)

Milk Products (2–3 servings)

Meats, Poultry, Fish, Dry Beans, Eggs, Nuts (2–3 servings)

Vegetables (3–5 servings)

Fruits (2–4 servings)

Grains (6–11 servings)

the best methods for putting them into practice will be discussed in this section.

When To Eat

With busy schedules and not enough time in the day, it becomes difficult to eat on a regular schedule. However, regularly scheduled feeding times will help ensure a greater level of mental alertness and physical stamina to get you through the busy day. Eating at scheduled intervals also helps prevent uncontrolled eating between meals or gorging during a meal.

As mentioned previously, our bodies use a combination of fat and carbohydrates for energy. However, the brain and nervous system can only use carbohyrates for energy so there needs to be a constant supply of carbohyrates to nourish the nervous system. This constant supply comes from two places—the carbohydrates consumed throughout the day, and from carbohydrates stored in the liver (liver glycogen). One of the important functions of the liver is to maintain an adequate level of blood glucose at all times so the nervous system will always have a carbohydrate source.

The liver can only store enough carbohydrate to last for approximately 4-6 hours or even less time if a lot of energy is being expended (as in exercise). If you do not regularly eat carbohydrates throughout the day, the liver can become depleted of carbohydrates and blood glucose drops, a condition known as **hypoglycemia** or **low blood glucose**. Hypoglycemia produces typical nervous system dysfunction symptoms of lethargy, irritability, nervouness, headache, and light-headedness. You just don't feel energetic and mental and physical abilities begin to diminish.

Breakfast is often said to be the most important meal of the day and there are good physiologic reasons why it is. Breakfast is important because it provides carbohydrates following the typical 8-12 hour overnight fast during which time the liver has been significantly depleted of carbohydrates. Liver depletion will vary depending on what and how much was eaten in the last 24-48 hours. If you do not eat breakfast containing some carbohydrates, by the time lunch rolls around, you could be hypoglycemic.

By consuming carbohyrates at each meal at regular intervals throughout the day, the liver is kept supplied with carbohydrates and your nervous system remains happy. If you also exercise during the day, liver carbodhyrate will further be depleted, increasing the need to consume carbohyrate. Some will find it important to eat a snack in the mid-morning and mid-afternoon in order to supplement the carbohydrates coming from the primary meals.

In additiion to providing a regular carbohydrate souce, eating at regular intervals also affects hungar sensations. One of the primary factors causing the hungar sensation is an empty stomach. Putting something in the stomach at regular intervals will delay or reduce the sensation of hungar and perhaps prevent the likelihood of overeating because of a powerful hungar drive.

A breakfast which includes carbohydrates will help maintain blood glucose throughout the morning.

Higher bulk foods, like complex carbohydrates seem to do the best job because they simply fill-up the stomach more.

Food Labels

In May 1994, the Food and Drug Administration and the U.S. Department of Health and Human Services mandated new federal regulations regarding food labels. An example of the new food label compared to the old label is in Figure 6.4. The new title "Nutrition Facts" lets the consumer know the label meets new federal regulation. On the old food labels, only the name of the product, net weight, and manufacturer were required by law. Many manufacturers included other information for consumers' use. New labels must include total calories, fat calories, total fat, saturated fat, cholesterol, sodium, total carbohydrates, dietary fiber, sugars, protein, vitamins A and C, calcium, and iron. The voluntary elements allowed include calories from saturated fat, polyunsaturated fat, monounsaturated fat, potassium, soluble fiber, insoluble fiber, sugar alcohol, other carbohydrates, and other essential vitamins and minerals. These mandatory and voluntary elements are the only things allowed on the new label.

The new labels are an improvement over the old labels, but there are still components displayed that may be misleading to consumers. Although serving size may be more representative of actual amounts eaten, some serving sizes may still be unrepresentative. For example, a serving of graham crackers is "8 crackers." To the manufacturer, 8 crackers equals 2 large crackers with lines imprinted on the top of the cracker indicating 4 sections per cracker. Some bags of snack chips may indicate a small two-ounce bag from a vending machine contains 2 servings. Although the new labels are better than the old ones with regard to serving size, you must still be cognizant of what constitutes a serving.

Another misleading element of the new label is the "% Daily Value" column. This percentage is based on a 2,000 kcal/day diet. Many women, people trying to lose weight, and inactive individuals may consume less than 2,000 kcal/day, or may want to consume less than the 65g fat/day recommended.

So with the new labels as misleading as the old regarding percent daily value, how do you select healthy foods? One simple trick is to look at the "Total Fat" grams. Multiply that number by 30, and if the resulting number is greater than the total calories, the food is more than 30% fat. If the resulting number is less than the total calories, the food would be a healthy choice, less than 30% fat.

For example, if you look at the new nutrition label in Figure 6.4, the total fat grams are 13g. Multiply 13 by 30, which equals 390. This is more than the listed calories of 260, which means more than 30% of the calories in this food product are from fat. This is a high-fat product. Some individuals may

FIGURE 6.4

The new food labels.

The New Nutrition Label

(A) The new title signifies the label meets the new requirements. **(B)** Serving sizes must be expressed both in common household measures and metric units and are uniform across product lines. **(C)** Calories from fat are now required to assist consumers in limiting their fat intake. **(D)** The new list of nutrients includes those most important to the health of consumers. **(E)** Percent of daily value is now required and interprets how a food fits into a total diet. **(F)** DVs are set at two caloric levels so that consumers can adjust their values to their own caloric needs. **(G)** Calories from 1 gram of the macronutrients is required. This label is only a sample. Exact specifications are in the final rules.

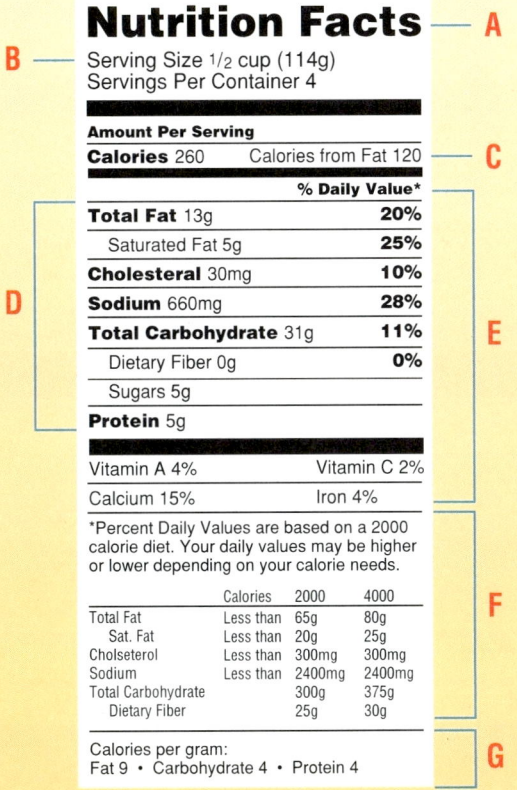

The Old Nutrition Label

(A) The old title, Nutrition Information per Serving, signifies the label does not meet the new requirements. **(B)** Serving sizes are determined by the manufacturer. **(C)** Nutrients reflect previous concern of preventing nutrient deficiencies. **(D)** Vitamins and minerals are expressed as a percentage of the U.S. Recommended Daily Allowance (U.S. RDA).
This label is only a sample. Exact specifications are in the Code of Federal Regulations.

INFORMATION PANEL

NUTRITION INFORMATION	PER SERVING	NUTRITION INFORMATION	PER SERVING
SERVING SIZE	11 1/4 OZ.	CARBOHYDRATE	36g
SERVINGS PER CONTAINER	1	FAT	5g
CALORIES	250	CHOLESTEROL	35mg
PROTEIN	14g	SODIUM	980mg

PERCENTAGE OF U.S. RECOMMENDED DAILY ALLOWANCE (U.S. RDA)

PROTEIN	30	RIBOFLAVIN	10
VITAMIN A	2	NIACIN	20
VITAMIN C	15	CALCIUM	4
THIAMINE	10	IRON	4

want to have fewer than 30% of their total daily calories from fat, and would therefore limit the number of products they consume where the fat grams multiplied times 30 is close to the total calorie value.

In the early 1990's, the director of the United States Food and Drug Administration (FDA), Dr. David A. Kessler, was on a campaign to end label hype. Previously, food labels exaggerated benefits of foods, and were purposefully misleading. Dr. Kessler claimed that new labeling would "clear up confusion; help us make healthy choices; and encourage product innovation, so that companies are more interested in tinkering with the food in the package, not the words on the label."

New FDA proposals that went into effect in May of 1994, required nutrition labeling (stating values of nutrients) on nearly all packaged foods. Furthermore, specific terms were now defined by the FDA, and not left up to the whims of manufacturers. The FDA's definitions for terms found on labels are listed in Table 6.18.

TABLE 6.18
FDA Label Terms

Label Term	Meaning
low fat	three grams of fat or less per serving or per 100 grams (to make sure high fat foods aren't disguised in small portions)
xx% fat-free	truly low fat foods—not hot dogs or cold cuts
light, lite	one-third fewer calories than a comparable product
low cholesterol	one serving has less than 2 mg of cholesterol and 2 g free saturated fat: foods that have never had cholesterol must highlight that information: foods that are cholesterol free but high fat (oils, potato chips) may not use this claim
low calorie	fewer than 40 calories per serving and per 100 grams
reduced calorie	must contain at least one-third fewer calories than the product for which it substitutes and must compare standard and reduced calorie versions on the label.
fresh	raw: not processed, reconstituted, frozen, or preserved
high in . . .	one serving must provide 20% or more of the RDA
a source of . . .	one serving must provide 10-19% of the RDA
low sodium	less than 140 mg per serving or per 100 grams
reduced sodium	must have the usualy level of sodium reduced by at least 75% from the regular version
sodium-free	less than 5 mg per serving
sugar-free/sugarless	no table sugar (sucrose) was added to the food. However, there may be other sweeteners, such as fructose, corn syrup, honey, or molasses, which are as caloric as sugar

Grocery Shopping

Food shopping is an important part of following the dietary guidelines. Our good nutritional intentions may be foiled if we dash madly down the supermarket aisles, tossing whatever looks tastiest into our carts. At first, shopping for foods that fit within our nutritional guidelines may take a little more effort, but with a little practice, shopping nutritiously will come naturally. Nutritious foods that fit within the guidelines can be found in every aisle at the grocery store.

Before you shop, prepare yourself. Eat before you go grocery shopping, to prevent "impulse" buying (grabbing everything at eye-level). Also, remember the goal for fat consumption is no more than 30% of total caloric intake. Read nutrition labels and aim for foods that have 3 grams or fewer of fat per 100 calories of food product. Since each gram of fat has approximately 9 kcal, this rule will keep your total fat intake at or below the recommended level.

The Produce Section

Nearly every item in the produce section is a nutritious choice. Vegetables and fruits are good sources of vitamins A and C and fiber. Select at least three cruciferous vegetables a week (broccoli, cabbage, brussel sprouts, cauliflower) to reduce your risk of cancer. Grab a sack of potatoes—they make great microwave meals topped with steamed vegetables and low-fat cheeses. Three to five servings of vegetables and two to four servings of fruit each day are recommended. In order to retain as much nutrition as

The produce sections in the supermarket is a good source of highly nutritious foods.

possible in fruits and vegetables, eat them raw or with minimal preparation, such as in steaming. Resist the temptation to soak vegetables in rich, calorie-laden sauces.

The Dairy Case

In the dairy case, you'll find products with a variety of fat, calories, and sodium content. Skim milk, low-fat milk, and plain low-fat yogurt provide the most calcium for the amount of calories and fat in the product. Regular yogurts, cottage cheese, and cheese come in a variety of styles that vary widely in fat content. Choose those made with lowfat milk rather than with whole milk or cream. Low-fat cheeses include part-skim mozzarella, or reduced-fat cheddar or Monterey Jack. When buying margarine, look for tubs (rather than sticks) that list liquid vegetable oil as the first ingredient because tub margarine contains less saturated fat (the softer the margarine, the less saturated fat). Although diet margarine's are still 100% fat, they contain water, which reduces the total calorie and fat amount per serving.

Processed American cheese and cheese spreads are lower in calcium and much higher in sodium than most natural cheeses, and are less desirable dairy choices. Dairy products are good sources of calcium and protein. At least two servings each day are recommended, with children, teens, and pregnant and breastfeeding women requiring three or more servings.

Skim milk is a great source of protein and calcium without any fat.

The Meat Counter

At the meat counter, the fat content varies widely. Fat is often "marbled" throughout meat, which may be difficult to spot.

Leaner choices include:

- beef—round, loin, sirloin, and chuck steaks or roasts (select grade contains less fat than choice, which contains less than prime)

- pork—tenderloin, center loin roasts and chops, ham (high salt content)

- lamb—leg, loin roasts and chops, foreshank

- chicken and turkey, especially light meat

- most fish and shellfish

Ground beef is available containing different amounts of fat. Greater than 90% lean, ground round, or ground sirloin are the lowest in fat. Remember, although a meat product might say 90% lean or 97% lean, that does not mean the product contains only 10% or 3% of calories as fat. The percentage listed indicates the percent fat or lean by total product weight, not

Selectively choosing meats low in fat will help control fat intake.

KEY CONCEPT

FISH AND FISH OIL

Several decades ago, it was discovered that Eskimos in Greenland ate a very high fat diet but had a low incidence of heart disease. This was completely contrary to what was seen in westernized countries like the U.S. Upon further investigation, it was determined that most of the fat the Eskimos ate was from fish. Since then, science has found that fish fat contains special polyunsaturated fatty acids, called omega-3 fatty acids, which have a different effect on the body than fat from animal products. Fish oils appear to reduce the incidence of heart disease but the exact mechanism is not understood but it probably involves lowering of cholesterol and making platelets slick so they will not clump together to form blood clots.

Fish oil supplements have become a staple in the vitamin isle of the drug store or health-food store. Although fish oil can be consumed in the form of supplements, the recommendation that makes more sense is to just eat more fish in your diet.

---

by total calories. A product may contain a large amount of water, which would increase its weight but not decrease its total fat content. Check for the total grams of fat per serving to determine how "lean" a product is.

Try ground turkey or chicken as a low-fat substitute for ground beef, but check the label or ask to make sure the poultry skin is not included. Processed meats, like hotdogs, bacon, sausage, and luncheon meats are high in fat and sodium but reduced fat and sodium versions are often available.

Foods in the meat, poultry, and fish groups are good sources of protein, iron, zinc, and vitamin B6. No more than three to five ounces per day are recommended. Dry beans, peas, nuts, seeds, peanut butter, or eggs may be substituted for animal protein but attention should be paid to getting adequate essential amino acids if they constitute a major protein source.

Canned and Packaged Food Aisle

For convenience, easy storage, and long shelf life, the canned and packaged foods aisle provides many nutritious choices. There are several things to keep in mind for nutritious shopping. Most canned foods (vegetables, prepared meals) are higher in sodium than homemade or fresh. Look for "reduced sodium" or "no-salt-added" on the label. Choose canned fruits without added sugar or packed in fruit juice, and bottled fruit juices instead of fruit drinks, which are typically only 10% fruit juice. Water-packed tuna is much lower in calories and fat than oil-packed tuna, and is an excellent low-fat source of protein. Mayonnaise and salad dressings are typically high fat, and can sabotage an otherwise healthy meal. New versions of mayonnaise and bottled salad dressings are made without fat, and add flavor to low-fat meals.

The Frozen Food Aisle

Low-fat ice cream and yogurt are good sources of calcium.

Thanks to the popularity and convenience of microwaves, the frozen food section overflows with nutritious choices for complete meals, snacks, desserts, and side dishes. Select frozen dinners that contain fewer than 300 calories, 10 grams of fat, and 1,000 mg sodium. Nutritious, high-carbohydrate side dishes, such as fruit or vegetable salad, can be added to complete the meal. Choose plain frozen vegetables, rather than those in cheese or cream sauce. Many frozen waffles and pancakes are low in fat, and high in carbohydrates and fiber. Frozen deserts such as sherbets, sorbets, and frozen yogurt are lower in fat than most ice creams, and high in calcium. Most brands produce low-fat varieties of frozen yogurt and ice cream.

The Bread and Cereal Aisles

Grain products are important sources of starch, protein, iron, fiber, magnesium, folate, and several B vitamins. However, not all grain products are wise nutritious choices. Total sugars in cereal can range from less than 1 percent to more than 55% by weight. Choose cereals with at least 3 to 5 grams of dietary fiber, less than 2 grams of fat, and sugar (and other sweeteners) near the end of the ingredient list. Beware of granolas and "natural" cereals, which can provide considerable amounts of calories, fat, and sugar. Select whole-grain muffins, breads, bagels, pasta, and rolls for added fiber and low-fat calories. Six to eleven servings of grain products per day are recommended.

The Snack Aisle

Most snack foods contain a lot of fat and sugars. To satisfy a sweet tooth, angel food cake (without icing), ginger snaps, fig bars or molasses cookies are best. Check the labels for types of fat used. Remember the tropical oils and lard are high in saturated fats, so look for products made with vegetable oils. Read labels carefully in the snack aisle. Most chips, crackers, cookies and some flavored brands of popcorn contain more than 40% of calories as fat, even though their labels may say they contain "no tropical oils" or are "cholesterol-free." Crackers vary quite a bit in fat and sodium content so you should select crackers with no more than 2 grams fat per serving.

A great deal of damage can be done to an otherwise healthy diet by overconsuming snack foods. Sitting in front of the TV and eating several ounces of chips two or three times a week can be a disaster. The calories and fat can add up real quick if you are not selective and moderate in eating snack items. Fortunately, several national manufactures of snack foods are making virtually fat-free varieties which still maintain most of the taste of the traditional varieties. Like everything else that is new and different, you need to allow some time for your taste to adjust but before you know it, you will be just as satisfied with the low-fat snacks.

Preparing Foods Nutritiously

Nutritious cooking? Yuck. Low-fat means low-flavor. No-salt means no taste. These are common beliefs, but are not true. There are a wide variety of dried and fresh herbs and spices available to take the place of adding salt to food. Each teaspoon of table salt added to food provides 2,000 mg of sodium, which is in addition to sodium naturally occurring in many foods.[19, 20]

There are many easy low-fat cooking methods that do not rob the foods of flavor, but enhance the true flavor of food. Broiling, baking, microwaving, and steaming are methods of cooking that do not require added fats such as oils or margarine. For each teaspoon of fat you do not use, you'll save 5 grams and 45 kcal of fat . Many cookbooks are available describing healthy recipes and food preparation and can be found in most bookstores.

The method of food preparation can dramatically alter the calories and fat.

Eating Out

Restaurants usually provide a variety in types of foods and preparation methods. Items are often prepared to order, so you can ask that foods be prepared differently than the menu specifies. Terms used in describing menu items often provide clues as to fat and sodium content of the foods.[6, 18, 19]

Dorm food is notorious for contributing to the phenomenon known as the "freshmen 15"—the fifteen pounds gained by many new college students. This weight increase in college freshmen is triggered by many factors, including increased stress, homesickness, and boredom, but is primarily caused by poor nutritional choices—eating too much of the wrong kinds of foods. When a student is away from home for the first time, he or she makes choices regarding many lifestyle decisions, including nutrition.

An example of poor nutritional choices in the dorm were revealed by a survey on health behavior of students at the University of Northern Iowa, conducted in the early 1990's. The results of the survey, known sarcastically as "the Cap'n Crunch Report," indicated that 56,000 servings of Cap'n Crunch were consumed by UNI students during one semester, more servings than the next nine most popular cereals put together. That amount is equivalent to one and three-quarters tons of Cap'n Crunch. Even though most students know that this brand of cereal is high in simple sugars and low in fiber (not a nutritious decision), it was still the most popular choice for breakfast.

More nutritious choices for breakfast include selections that are low in fat and sugar, but high in complex carbohydrates and fiber. A substantial breakfast will curb your appetite for hours and stabilize your blood sugar and mood. In addition, a good breakfast will help you avoid mid-morning snacks, which are often high in fat.

Most students know how difficult it is to stay awake during afternoon classes, right after consuming a big lunch. Carbohydrates, which fill your muscles with energy, may put you to sleep when consumed at noon. A light lunch high in protein, on the other hand, may enhance your mental performance. Recent research from the Massachusettes Institute of Technology recommends a low-fat, low-calorie, high-protein lunch for maximum afternoon alertness. Examples of lunches that fit this formula include tuna or turkey on wheat bread with a piece of fruit, salad topped with cottage cheese or yogurt, and a few whole-grain rolls, or two slices of veggie pizza with low-fat cheese. The study also found the mood-altering effects (sluggishness) of carbohydrates eaten at noon appear in approximately one hour and lasts around three hours.

Fast foods are not necessarily "junk" foods. Most fast foods provide essential nutrients, including protein, vitamins, and minerals, but are often low in calcium, vitamins A and C, and fiber, and high in fat and sodium. However, many fast food restaurants are changing their menus to meet consumer demand for healthier foods. Remember that a lot of the fat calories in burgers and sandwiches are from the sauces, so opt for a burger without mayonnaise or a fish sandwich without tarter sauce. It is up to the individual consumer to make wise choices when grabbing a quick meal at McDonalds or Burger King. High-fat and high-calorie foods will always be available, but no one is forcing you to purchase them.

Special Diets

Vegetarian Diets

There are three basic types of vegetarian diets as follows:[1, 3, 7]

1. Vegans, or strict vegetarians. No animal products of any kind are consumed.

2. Lactovegetarians. Dairy products such as milk, cheese, and butter are included; no eggs, meat, fish, or poultry.

3. Ovolactovegetarians. Eggs and dairy products are included; no meat, fish, or poultry.

Less strict followers of vegetarianism may rely mainly on plant foods, but occasionally eat meat, fish, or poultry. Individuals make the choice to become vegetarian for several possible reasons, including religious convictions, ecologic considerations, or health and hygienic reasons. Whatever the motivation, a vegetarian diet can be protective of several health problems, such as heart disease, obesity, and cancer. Vegetarian diets are low in fat, cholesterol, and calories, and are high in fiber.

However, the vegetarian diet is not a magic cure-all. Non-vegetarians who choose their foods carefully and follow the nutritional guidelines may attain the same health benefits as the vegetarian. Despite the evidence that adults can live healthfully on a vegetarian diet, infants and very young children need animal sources of protein to grow properly.

Vegetarians need to be even more conscious of their food choices than non-vegetarians. As mentioned earlier in this chapter, plant sources of protein are considered "incomplete," since they do not provide all of the essential amino acids. Also, some vitamins and minerals, especially iron, are found mainly in meat products. Individuals who choose to follow vegetarian diets can easily compensate for these deficiencies. Carefully combining incomplete sources of protein, listed earlier in Table 6.7, will provide all of the essential amino acids. Strict vegetarians may develop deficiencies in vitamin B_{12} (thiamin) and B_2 (riboflavin), since amounts are low in plant

The fat in a burger can be reduced by eliminating mayonnaise or using a low-fat variety.

food. Vitamin B_{12} deficiency leads to severe forms of anemia (megaloblastic anemia). Vitamin B_{12} is found in dairy products, fish, eggs, and meat, and vitamin B_2 is found in some vegetables such as beet greens, broccoli, and collards, and in dairy products. The addition of any of these foods to the diet will prevent deficiencies, but strict vegans need a vitamin B_{12} supplement. Mineral deficiencies of iron, calcium, and zinc may occur with strict vegans. Iron-rich plant foods include nuts, beans, peanuts, spinach, dates, prune juice, and iron-enriched grain products. Calcium-rich plant foods include broccoli, cabbage, mustard greens, and spinach. When dairy products are added to the vegetarian diet, very significant amounts of calcium are supplied. Plant foods high in zinc content include whole wheat bread products, peas, corn, and carrots.[1, 3, 7]

Sports Nutrition

Nutritional recommendations for sport performance, whether it be for recreational or highly competitive purposes, are similar to recommendations for a general healthy diet—high in carbohydrates and low in fat for a healthy heart diet.[2, 12] Beyond that general advice, athletes may need to consume more total calories, preferably by increasing carbohydrate-rich foods. Much of the energy used in vigorous activity comes from carbohydrates and carbohydrate energy is essential for high-level performance.

Several nutrients have been considered as **ergogenic aids**, defined as substances or procedures used to improve athletic performance. Some athletes believe that consuming alcoholic beverages is equivalent to "carbo-loading" or creating stores of fuel for athletic performance. As mentioned

Proper nutrition is critical to optimal sport performance.

earlier, alcohol does not get stored as muscle glycogen. Also, alcohol has a dehydrating effect, which is detrimental to performance.

Caffeine was once thought to cause the body to burn proportionately more fat, which would conserve the limited carbohydrate stores in the body. Recent research indicates that individuals who have adequately trained themselves, are ready to compete, and have consumed high-carbohydrate meals will not get a boost in performance from ingesting caffeine.

The current recommended daily intake of protein is approximately 0.4 grams per pound of body weight for sedentary individuals. Results of studies indicate that for physically active people, 0.80 grams protein per pound may be more appropriate. This recommended intake is for endurance athletes as well as power athletes, such as weightlifters. However, most Americans eat more protein than they need, and the higher recommended intake for athletes means there is less excess in what they already consume. Protein consumed in excess of the body's requirement for protein does not increase muscle mass, but is stored as fat.

High doses of vitamins and minerals do not affect athletic performance unless there were preexisting deficiencies, and, as with non-athletes, high doses should not be consumed without the guidance of a physician. Most athletes get more than enough vitamins and minerals from the increased quantity of food they consume as long as they eat a balanced diet. Foods that are "nutrient dense" (those that have lots of vitamins and minerals per calorie) are excellent choices for healthy diets. Examples of nutrient dense foods are low-fat milk and yogurt, broccoli, tomatoes, strawberries, oranges, lean beef, chicken, turkey, fish, bran cereals, whole wheat and fortified grain products.

Traditionally, excercise scientists used to advise drinking only water during exercise. Now, research indicates that drinks with simple carbohydrates and sodium consumed during endurance exercise can enhance performance. Sports drinks that contain combinations of glucose polymers (chains of sugar molecules) and natural sugars (glucose and fructose) provide the best source of energy for the muscle during exercise. However, specialty drinks are not a must because consuming any type of carbohydrate can aid endurance performance that lasts longer than 60-90 minutes. You could easily make your own brew with water and sugar with the only catch being that the carbohydrate content should be less than 10%. Each athlete must experiment to find what works best without causing stomach upset.

Although consuming sport drinks can be advantageous during exercise, drinking fluids that claim to replenish electrolytes (sodium and potassium) lost through sweating is not necessary following workouts. During exercise, proportionately more water than electrolytes are lost in sweat, which actually increases the concentration of electrolytes in the body. Initially, fluid replacement is the important consideration. The small amount of electrolytes lost during exercise can easily be replaced through eating foods such as orange juice and bananas.

Pregnancy

Nutrition and pregnancy is an important consideration for many young adults, who are not only taking care of their own health, but the health of their unborn children. Often, normally health-conscious women may lose all control of nutritious eating habits, claiming to be "eating for two." However, these women must remember they are not eating for two adults. Meeting the nutritional needs in pregnancy is important to the normal development of the child and the health of the mother.[9, 15]

Hopefully, pregnant women will realize they are responsible for the nutritional well-being of a completely dependent, unborn child, and use pregnancy as a time for making permanent healthy changes in the way they eat. Although making changes after becoming pregnant is important, many experts say that by the time a woman is pregnant, it may be too late to make the kinds of changes that will most benefit the fetus. Optimal maternal nutrition should begin long before conception.

It is generally accepted that weight gain during pregnancy should be between 25 and 35 pounds. If a woman is overweight prior to pregnancy, she should aim towards a weight gain in the lower end of the range. However,

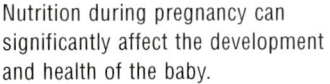

Nutrition during pregnancy can significantly affect the development and health of the baby.

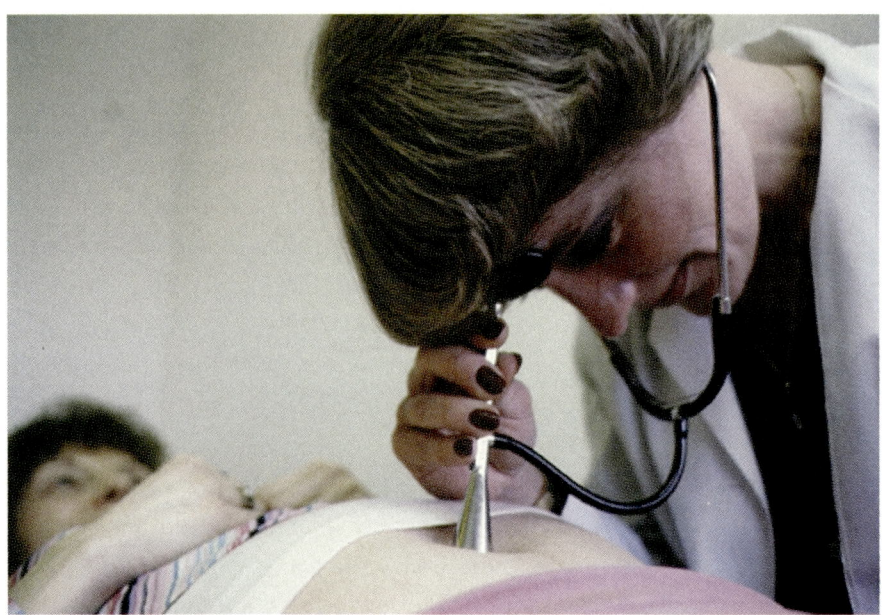

pregnancy is not the time to try to get rid of fat that was present before getting pregnant. This may prevent the unborn child from receiving nutrients critical for normal development.

Nutritional requirements change during pregnancy. The amount of protein—critical for building new tissue—increases by two-thirds. As stated earlier, most Americans are already eating this amount of protein. However, women who are limiting their caloric intake may be shortchanging their protein intake. Protein deficiencies may cause growth retardation and/or mental deficiency. Adequate protein is also important to prevent the development of toxemia (life-threatening metabolic disturbance) late in pregnancy.

Calcium is needed in large quantities to build bones and for other vital body functions. A 25% increase in calcium is recommended, for a total of 1200–1500 mg per day. If a woman does not get adequate amounts of calcium, the developing baby will take much of the calcium it needs from the mother anyway. Calcium will be forced out of the mother's bones, weakening them, and bone growth may be abnormal in the developing baby.

Iron is essential to the formation of healthy red blood cells, and a woman's blood volume doubles during pregnancy. As with calcium, the developing baby will take all the iron it needs from the mother whether or not she has enough for herself. Iron deficiencies may lead to anemia and exhaustion, and, since most women of childbearing age do not have iron stores in their bodies, iron supplements are routinely prescribed for pregnant women.

Folacin (one of the B vitamins) is especially critical for the development of a normal central nervous system (CNS). Several recent studies have shown that women with folacin deficiencies are at increased risk of having babies born with severe life-threatening birth defects such as anencephaly and spina bifida. Folacin is needed in the development of the CNS in the first two to four weeks after pregnancy. This is often before a woman knows she is pregnant, which supports the argument for good nutritional practices for at least three months prior to conception. The need for other B vitamins also increased during pregnancy.

Recommended amounts of other vitamins and minerals increase proportionately during pregnancy. Vitamin/mineral supplements are often prescribed by a physician, but a woman can not make up for poor nutritional habits with supplements. Proper nutrition is critical during pregnancy to insure normal development of the child and good health of the mother. These necessary changes in nutrition reinforce the need for healthy nutrition and lifestyle beginning prior to conception, and early prenatal medical care.

Planning Your Daily Diet

Using the food pyramid (Figure 6.3) and nutrition facts for selected foods (Figure 6.5), along with the Daily Diet Planner (Table 6.19), you can plan your own daily diet very easily. In the left columns of Table 6.19 are three calorie plans, and the total numbers of servings per day for each plan. If you are an inactive woman, you may be eating 1,600 kcal per day. If you are an active woman or an inactive man, you may be eating approximately 2,200

TABLES 6.19
Daily Diet Planner

	Calories/day			Type of food No. of servings
	1,600	2,200	2,800	**Breakfast**
	Number of servings			
Oils	0	0	0	**Snack**
Meat group	2 5 oz.	2 6 oz.	2 7 oz.	**Lunch**
Milk products	2–3	2–3	2–3	**Snack**
Fruit	2	3	4	
Vegetables	3	4	5	**Dinner**
Bread	6	9	11	**Snack**

What counts as one serving?

Bread group:

1 slice bread
1/2 cup cooked rice
1/2 cup cooked cereal
1 ounce ready-to-eat cereal

Fruit group:

1 piece fruit or melon
3/4 cup juice
1/2 cup canned fruit
1/4 cup dried fruit

Meat group:

2 1/2 to 3 ounces cooked lean, meat, poultry, fish
(1 ounce meat = 1/2 cup cooked beans, 1 egg, or 2 tbsp. peanut butter)

Vegetable group:

1/2 cup chopped raw or cooked
1 cup leafy raw

Milk group:

1 cup milk or yogurt
1 1/2 ounce natural cheese
2 ounces processed cheese

Fats and sweets:

Limit calories from these especially if you need to lose weight kcal per day. For active men, approximately 2,800 kcal per day may be your plan. Fill in the daily meal plans on the right for each meal and snack, using up all the required food servings. For example, it may be easy for you to include a milk serving at breakfast and late snack. You also may include a serving from the meat and meat products at lunch and dinner. Add in servings as appropriate, and as convenient for your own lifestyle.

Nutritional Assessments

This chapter has presented information necessary for making healthy decisions regarding nutrition. This section will provide opportunities to examine your eating habits. The assessment tool presents you with an in-depth method for assessing the quantity and quality of nutrients in your diet, and recommendations for changes you may need to make for a healthy diet.

Diet Diary

One of the best methods to accurately determine if you are eating foods within recommended nutrient guidelines is to actually record everything you eat during the day for several consecutive days, and calculate totals for the large and small nutrients. The key to accurate analyses is to be specific in recording the quantity and specific type of foods consumed. For example, instead of writing "ham sandwich," enter each component of the sandwich, such as "2 slices of whole wheat bread, 2 ounces sliced lean ham, 1 tsp mustard, 1 slice tomato." If you eat at MacDonald's, don't write down a burger and fries, but indicate whether it was a Big Mac or a cheeseburger.

Once you have entered your daily food intake for at least three to five consecutive days (including weekend days), you can analyze your diet in one of two ways. You can look up food values in tables, such as those presented by the U. S. Department of Agriculture, and compare your values to the US RDA. An alternative and much easier method is to use a computer software package designed to analyze nutrients in your diet. There are many such programs available, ranging in cost from fifty to several hundred dollars. These programs provide excellent data bases of foods including almost every food you could imagine. The computer makes all the calculations and provides a breakdown of total calories, fat calories, carbohydrate calories, protein calories, vitamins and minerals.

Figure 6.5 is a sample printout from one nutrition analysis program called the DINE System.[4] This program gives you an overall nutritional score, the DINE score (ranges from 0-10), based on comparisons between "Your Diet" and an "Ideal Diet." Messages are provided on your printout, indicating areas of nutritional concern. They emphasize and alert you to potentially significant problems in your food choices.

FIGURE 6.5

This typical printout from a nutritional analysis program can provide important information about your diet.

Food Record — Wed, Jun 7, 1995

Meal Code	Amount	Description
Brk 1342	1.71 CUP	CEREAL, Life, Quaker
Brk 3675	0.75 CUP	MILK, Skim
Brk 970	2.00 SLC	BREAD, Whole wheat (16 slices per loaf)
Brk 3573	1.00 TBS	MARGARINE, Spread, tub, corn oil, reduced calorie, Shedd's Spread
Brk 5565	1.00 TAB	VITAMINS, High potency multivitamin w/ minerals, tablet, Theragran
Lun 3981	0.80 CUP	PEACHES, Raw, sliced
Lun 404	1.50 FRT	BANANAS, Raw (8-3/4 in long x 1-13/32 in dia)
Lun 3675	1.00 CUP	MILK, Skim
Lun 5642	1.00 CNT	YOGURT, Vanilla, lowfat
Sn4 5314	3.75 CUP	TEA, Brewed, 1 bag brewed 3 minutes
Sn4 1166	1.00 BAR	CANDY BAR, Butterfinger (2 oz bar)
Sn4 5314	6.00 CUP	TEA, Brewed, 1 bag brewed 3 minutes
Sn4 3322	0.75 CUP	JUICE, Tomato, canned, Campbell's
Sn4 5624	1.00 CNT	YOGURT, Fruit varieties, lowfat, Fresh Flavors, Dannon
Sn4 2348	1.00 SVG	FAST FOODS, McDONALD's, Soft serve cone

Food Analysis — Jun 6, 1 day — US, BLDS

		Your Diet	Ideal Diet	DINE Score
	Total Calories	1802	2128 – 2352	0.00
Large Nutrients	Protein (Cal)	407	224 – 336	0.00
	Saturated Fat (Cal)	249	224 or less	0.00
	Monounsat Fat (Cal)	249	224 or less	0.00
	Polyunsat Fat (Cal)	65	224 or less	+ 0.50
	Complex Carb (Cal)	617	1008 – 1792	0.00
	Dietary Fiber (g)	13	20 – 35	0.00
	Sugar (Cal)	202	224 or less	+ 1.00
Small Nutrients	Cholesterol (mg)	229	300 or less	+ 1.00
	Sodium (mg)	4484	500 – 3300	0.00
	Potassium (mg)	3145	2000 – 5625	+ 0.50
	Vitamin A (RE)	563	1000 or more	0.00
	Vitamin C (mg)	36	60 or more	0.00
	Iron (mg)	14	10 or more	+ 0.50
	Calcium (mg)	1123	800 or more	+ 0.25
	Phosphorus (mg)	1690	800 or more	+ 0.25

* Patent Pending #07/671,196

DINE Score*: 4.00 Fair

Additional Values

		Your Diet	Recommended
			% of Total Calories
Calories	Protein	23%	10% to 15%
	Total Fat	31%	30% or less
	Saturated Fat	14%	10% or less
	Monounsat Fat	14%	10% or less
	Polyunsat Fat	4%	10% or less
	Complex Carb	34%	45% to 80%
	Added Sugar	11%	10% or less
	Alcohol	0%	8% or less
			% of Protein Calories
Protein	Plant Protein	22%	50% or more
	Animal Protein	78%	50% or less
			% of Fat Calories
Fat	Plant Fat	29%	50% or more
	Animal Fat	71%	30% or less
	Fish Fat	0%	20% or less
			% Calories by Meal
Meals	Breakfast	7%	25% – 35%
	Lunch	28%	25% – 35%
	Dinner	65%	25% – 35%
	Snack	0%	8% – 12%
Other Nutrients	Aspartame	0 mg	3250 mg or less
	Caffeine	162 mg	400 mg or less
Ratios	Pol/Sat ratio	0.26	1.00 or less
	Sodm/Potm ratio	1.43	1.00 or less
	Calc/Phos ratio	0.66	1.00 or less

SUMMARY

There is an old saying—it is hard to teach an old dog new tricks. There is probably no area that this is more true than in nutrition. So often, an attempt is made to totally change a diet that has been eaten for years or even decades. After a few days or weeks, the effort becomes fruitless and the old diet becomes the status quo once again.

A better approach is to take smaller steps in hopes of eventually reaching the goal. Don't try to change everything at once. Start with one or two focal points and get those under control before you move on to others. For example, if you drink a lot of sugar pop, begin by cutting down on the amount you drink. You might try substituting sugar-free as opposed to eliminating it altogether. Next, tackle snack foods. Begin to substitute fruit or lower fat and calorie snacks. Your next focus might be reducing the amount of red meat eaten by replacing it with fish or poultry. Taking these types of smaller steps on a regular and progressive basis will get you to where you want to go but the journey will be far less painful and far more successful.

Remember that the goal does not have to be a "perfect" diet. Eating a "reasonable" diet will be very beneficial. Everyone will not be able to reduce fat calories to less than 25% of total calories, but reducing to 30% is far better than staying at 40%. Also, what you eat on any single day will not have a significant impact on your overall diet. But, if you excessively consume on a particular day, you should adjust your intake on another day or days to adjust for the day you overcomsumed. What is important in the long term is the way you eat "on average," not on any single day.

EXPLORING WELLNESS ON THE WEB

Many resources are available on the World Wide Web. You can reinforce, expand and enhance the information presented in this chapter by accessing the following sites.

http://www.cspinet.org/ — Center for Science in the Public Interest site. They publish the Nutrition Action health letter, nutrition quizzes, and a long list of web sites on nutrition and related topics.

http://vm.cfsan.fda.gov/label.html — FDA's Center for Food Safety and Applied Nutrition food label page which describes the food labels in detail as well as other nutrition information.

http://www.veg.org/veg/ — the Vegetarian Resource Group's Vegetarianism in a Nutshell page provides extensive information about vegetarian diets.

http://www.olen.com/food/ — provides fast food facts and a search function to find the calorie, fat, sodium, and cholesterol values of menu items from fast food chains. From the Minnesota Attorney General's Office.

REFERENCES

1. Brody, J. (1981). *Jane Brody's Nutrition Book*. New York: WW Norton & Company.
2. Center for Science in the Public Interest. (1988). Eat to swim, bike, run. *Nutrition Action Health Letter*, 15(5), 4-6.
3. Center for Science in the Public Interest. (1988). Is vegetarianism kid's stuff? *Nutrition Action Health Letter*, 15(10), 13.
4. Dennison, D., Dennison, K. (1990). *The DINE System: How to Improve Your Nutrition and Health*. Buffalo, NY; DINE Systems, Inc.
5. Hegarty, V. (1988). *Decisions in Nutrition*. St. Louis: Mosby College Publishing.
6. Kleckner, C., Kostas, G., & Rojohn, K. (1986). *Nutrition Tips: Eating Out*. Dallas, TX: The Cooper Clinic, The Aerobics Center.
7. Lappé, F.M. (1982). *Diet for a Small Planet*. New York: Ballantine Books.
8. McArdle, W.D., Katch, F.I., Katch, V.L. (1991), *Exercise Physiology: Energy, Nutrition, and Human Performance*, 3rd edition. Philadelphia: Lea & Febiger.
9. Monsen, E.R. (1989).The 10th edition of the Recommended Dietary Allowances: What's new in the 1989 RDA's? *Journal of the American Dietetic Association*, 89(12), 1748-1752.
10. Paul, G.L. (1989). Dietary protein requirements of physically active individuals. *Sports Medicine*, 8(3), 154-176.
11. Pennington, J.A.T., Church, H.N. (1985). *Food Values of Portions Commonly Used*. New York: Harper & Row, Publishers.
12. Rosato, F.D. (1990). *Fitness and Wellness: The Physical Connection* (2nd edition). New York: West Publishing Co.
13. Steering Committee of the American Heart Association (1986). Dietary guidelines for healthy American adults: A statement for physicians and health professionals by the Nutrition Committee, American Heart Association. *Circulation*, 74(6); 1465A-1468A.

14. Herbert, V. (ed). (1990). The Mount Sinai School of Medicine Complete Book of Nutrition. New York: St. Martin's Press.

15. The Nutrition Foundation, Inc. (1984). Present Knowledge in Nutrition, Washington, DC: The Nutrition Foundation.

16. United States Department of Agriculture (1986). Dietary Guidelines for Americans. Hyattsville, MD: United States Department of Agriculture.

17. United States Department of Agriculture (1990). Dietary Guidelines for Americans. Hyattsville, MD: United States Department of Agriculture.

18. United States Department of Agriculture (1990). Eating Better when Eating Out. Washington, DC: United States Government Printing Office.

19. United States Department of Agriculture (1990). Preparing Foods and Planning Menus. Washington, DC: US Government Printing Office.

20. United States Department of Agriculture (1990). Shopping for Food and Making Meals in Minutes. Washington, DC: United States Government Printing Office.

21. Williams, M.H. (1983). *Nutrition for Fitness and Sport. Dubuque*, IA: Wm.C. Brown Publishers.

22. Willett, W.C. and Ascherio, A. (1994). Trans fatty acids: are the effects only marginal? *Journal of Public Health*, 84, 722.

23. Witt, E.H., Reznick, A.Z., Viguie, C.A., Starke-Reed, P., and Packer, L. (1992). Exercise, oxidative damage, and effects of antioxidant manipulation. *Journal of Nutrition*, 122, 766-773.

DEFINITIONS OF KEY TERMS

amino acids — building blocks of proteins; categorized by source—from the diet or manufactured in the body (non-essential), or diet only (essential).

antioxidants — substances, mostly vitamins and minerals, that help to defend the body against cellular damage produced by free radicals.

aspartame — (Nutrasweet™) sugar substitute.

bioavailability — the measure of how efficiencently the body is able to absorb minerals.

blood glucose — ingested carbohydrates broken down in the digestive tract and absorbed into the bloodstream.

caffeine — central nervous system stimulant.

carbohydrates — most efficient energy source for the body (4 kcal/g).

complete proteins — dietary proteins that contain all essential amino acids; animal sources.

complex carbohydrates — multiple sugar molecules (polysaccharides).

dietary fiber — carbohydrate that does not provide nutrient value, but acts as a natural laxative.

disaccharides — a simple carbohydrate compose of two sugars.

ergogenic aids — substances or procedures used to improve athletic performance.

fat-soluble vitamins — Vitamins A, D, E, and K; absorbed in the body with the help of fat; stored in the liver and fatty tissues.

fats (lipids) — concentrated energy source for the body (9 kcal/g).

fatty acids — chains of carbon and hydrogen atoms; one component of fats; categorized by saturation level of molecule.

food additives — materials deliberately added to food to help manufacture and preserve food.

hydrogenated fat — an unsaturated fat that has been changed into a saturated fat by chemical means.

hypoglycemia — low blood glucose.

incomplete proteins — dietary proteins that do not contain all essential amino acids; plant sources.

insulin — hormone that allows blood glucose to enter working cells.

lactovegetarian — dairy products such as milk, cheese and butter are included in vegetarian diet.

minerals — inorganic compounds that are catalysts of several vital physiologic functions in the body.

monosaccharides — the simplest form of sugar molecules. Glucose and fructose are the primary monosaccharides in foods.

monounsaturated fats — one of the "healthy" types of fatty acids in which there is one double bond between carbon atoms.

ovolactovegetarian — eggs and dairy products are included in vegetarian diet.

polysaccharides — molecules containing more than two sugars. The primary polysaccharides in foods are starch, dextrin, cellulose, and glycogen.

polyunsaturated fats — one of the "healthy" types of fatty acids in which there are more than one double bond between carbon atoms.

protein — primarily used to build new tissue and repair muscle tissue.

simple carbohydrates — single sugar molecules (monosaccharides) or double sugar molecules (disaccharides).

triglycerides — primary form of fat stored in the body.

tropical oils — plant sources of saturated fats.

unsaturated fats — the "unhealthy" type of fatty acids in which there are no double bonds between carbon atoms.

vegan — strict vegetarian; no animal products of any kind are consumed.

vitamins — organic compounds involved in almost every metabolic process in the body.

water-soluble vitamins — Vitamins C and the B complex; transported in the body in water.

LAB 6.1
ASSESSING YOUR FAT INTAKE

Name _____ ID _____ Sect _____ Time _____ Date _____

Purpose

To estimate the grams of fat eaten in a typical day.

Directions

1. For each of the food categories listed below, indicate the number of times per week, on the average, you eat items from that category. None of the food items in the categories are low fat or reduced fat items. They are all "regular fat content" items.

2. Multiply the number of servings per week times the risk multiplier to get the Fat Points. Sum all the fat points to get Total Fat Points.

3. Evaluate your Total Fat Points using the risk table below.

	Risk Multiplier	Number of servings/week	Fat Points
How often do you eat:			
Fried, deep-fat fried, or breaded foods?	1.0	× _____ =	_____
Meats such as bacon, sausage, luncheon meats, and heavily marbled steaks and roasts?	2.0	× _____ =	_____
Whole milk, cheese, and ice cream?	1.5	× _____ =	_____
Desserts such as pies, pastries, and cakes?	1.0	× _____ =	_____
Cream sauces and gravies?	1.5	× _____ =	_____
Oily salad dressings or mayonnaise?	1.0	× _____ =	_____
Whipped cream, table cream, sour cream and cream cheese?	1.75	× _____ =	_____
Butter or margarine on vegetables, bread, rolls, or toast?	1.5	× _____ =	_____

Total Fat Points _____

Interpretation:

Total Fat Points	Risk Category	Comments
<10	Low Risk	Your fat intake is probably less than 30% of total calories per day. This is an acceptable level.
10-30	Moderate Risk	Your fat intake is probably >30% of total calories per day. You should attempt to reduce you fat intake.
>30	High Risk	Your fat intake is too great. The risk of heart disease and cancer are significantly elevated. You need to reduce your fat intake.

(Continued)

LAB 6.1 (CONCLUDED)

ASSESSING YOUR FAT INTAKE

Answer the following:

1. If you are consuming too much fat, indicate specific items consumed that you would be willing to reduce in your diet.

2. Pick three items you consume on a regular basis that are high fat foods and identify why you eat these items on a regular basis.

LAB 6.2
PLANNING YOUR DAILY DIET

Name _____ ID _____ Sect _____ Time _____ Date _____

Purposes

1. To plan a 3-day diet that provides recommended servings from the food pyramid.

2. To track your diet for 3 days to determine if you followed your diet plan.

Directions

1. In Table A below, record the number of servings from the food groups from the food pyramid that will meet your daily caloric requirement. Refer to the listing of foods in each group in order to put foods into the appropriate groups.

Food Groups	Foods in Group
Meat	meat, poultry, fish, dry beans, eggs, and nuts
Dairy	milk, yogurt, and cheese
Fruit	all fruits
Vegetables	all vegetables
Bread	bread, cereal, rice, and pasta
Fats	fats, oils, and sweets

Table A.

Food Groups ⇒	Meat	Dairy	Fruit	Vegetables	Bread	Fats
Recommended Daily Servings	2-3	2-3	2-4	3-5	6-11	Sparingly
Your Daily Servings	_____	_____	_____	_____	_____	_____

(Continued)

2. Using the servings you recorded in Table A, indicate where you would place the servings in a daily menu in Table B. The total number of servings in each food category in Table B should be the same as the number you recorded for your daily servings in Table A.

Table B.

Meals	Meat	Dairy	Fruit	Vegetables	Bread	Fats
Breakfast						
Snack						
Lunch						
Snack						
Dinner						
Snack						
Total ⇒						

3. Using Table B as a guide, attempt to eat foods for 3 days that follows your daily plan. Record your food groups and servings in the tables below. (Do not record your actual foods eaten here, just the servings of the food groups. Use a separate sheet to keep a record of your actual foods eaten for reference.

Meals: Day 1	Meat	Dairy	Fruit	Vegetables	Bread	Fats
Breakfast						
Snack						
Lunch						
Snack						
Dinner						
Snack						
Total ⇒						

(Continued)

LAB 6.2 (CONCLUDED)

PLANNING YOUR DAILY DIET

Name _____ ID _____ Sect _____ Time _____ Date _____

Meals: Day 2	Meat	Dairy	Fruit	Vegetables	Bread	Fats
Breakfast	_____	_____	_____	_____	_____	_____
Snack	_____	_____	_____	_____	_____	_____
Lunch	_____	_____	_____	_____	_____	_____
Snack	_____	_____	_____	_____	_____	_____
Dinner	_____	_____	_____	_____	_____	_____
Snack	_____	_____	_____	_____	_____	_____
Total ⇒	_____	_____	_____	_____	_____	_____

Meals: Day 3	Meat	Dairy	Fruit	Vegetables	Bread	Fats
Breakfast	_____	_____	_____	_____	_____	_____
Snack	_____	_____	_____	_____	_____	_____
Lunch	_____	_____	_____	_____	_____	_____
Snack	_____	_____	_____	_____	_____	_____
Dinner	_____	_____	_____	_____	_____	_____
Snack	_____	_____	_____	_____	_____	_____
Total ⇒	_____	_____	_____	_____	_____	_____

How close were you able to follow your plan?

List specific barriers that prevented you from following your plan.

NOTES

LAB 6.3

ASSESSING YOUR DIET

Name _____ ID _____ Sect _____ Time _____ Date _____

Purpose

1. To determine your typical average intake of all essential nutrients.

2. To identify foods you consume which are high in fat and simple sugars.

3. To identify foods you consume which have a high nutrient content.

Directions

1. Using the record sheet, record everything you eat and drink for a period of at least **two weekdays** and **one weekend day**. A three-day intake will provide a good assessment of you diet if the days you record represent "typical" days. Photocopy as many copies of the food record sheet as you need. It is best to use one food record sheet for each day.

2. This analysis is only as accurate as your record of the type and amount of food eaten. Be as specific as you can and record the specific type of food eaten (including brand name if known), how it was prepared, and the amount of food eaten in units of ounces, cups, tablespoons, etc.

3. Using a computer program than analyzes the diet (such as DineHealthy), enter all the foods recorded and perform the functions necessary to generate a printout of your diet.

Answer the following questions:

1. Using the recommended guidelines regarding percentages of fats, carbohydrates, and protein, how did your diet compare to the recommended quantities? Explain.

(Continued)

ASSESSING YOUR DIET

2. What specific nutrients are you consuming below the RDA? How could you change your diet to improve the intake of these nutrients?

3. If your fat intake is above the recommended guidelines, what foods in your diet could you consume less of in order to reduce your fat intake?

4. Before you did this diet analysis, what was your subjective opinion of your diet? What is your opinion now that you have more objective information?

(Continued)

LAB 6.3 (CONCLUDED)

ASSESSING YOUR DIET

Name _____ ID _____ Sect _____ Time _____ Date _____

Food Record Sheet

Date of Food Record: Date _____ Day _____

Food Item and Preparation Method	Quantity	Food Item and Preparation Method	Quantity

Breakfast: _____ _____   **Snack 2:** _____ _____

_____ _____   _____ _____

_____ _____   _____ _____

_____ _____   _____ _____

_____ _____   **Dinner:** _____ _____

_____ _____   _____ _____

_____ _____   _____ _____

_____ _____   _____ _____

Snack 1: _____ _____   _____ _____

_____ _____   _____ _____

_____ _____   _____ _____

_____ _____   _____ _____

Lunch: _____ _____   _____ _____

_____ _____   _____ _____

_____ _____   _____ _____

_____ _____   _____ _____

_____ _____   _____ _____

_____ _____   _____ _____

_____ _____   **Snack 3:** _____ _____

_____ _____   _____ _____

_____ _____   _____ _____

_____ _____   _____ _____

NOTES

NOTES

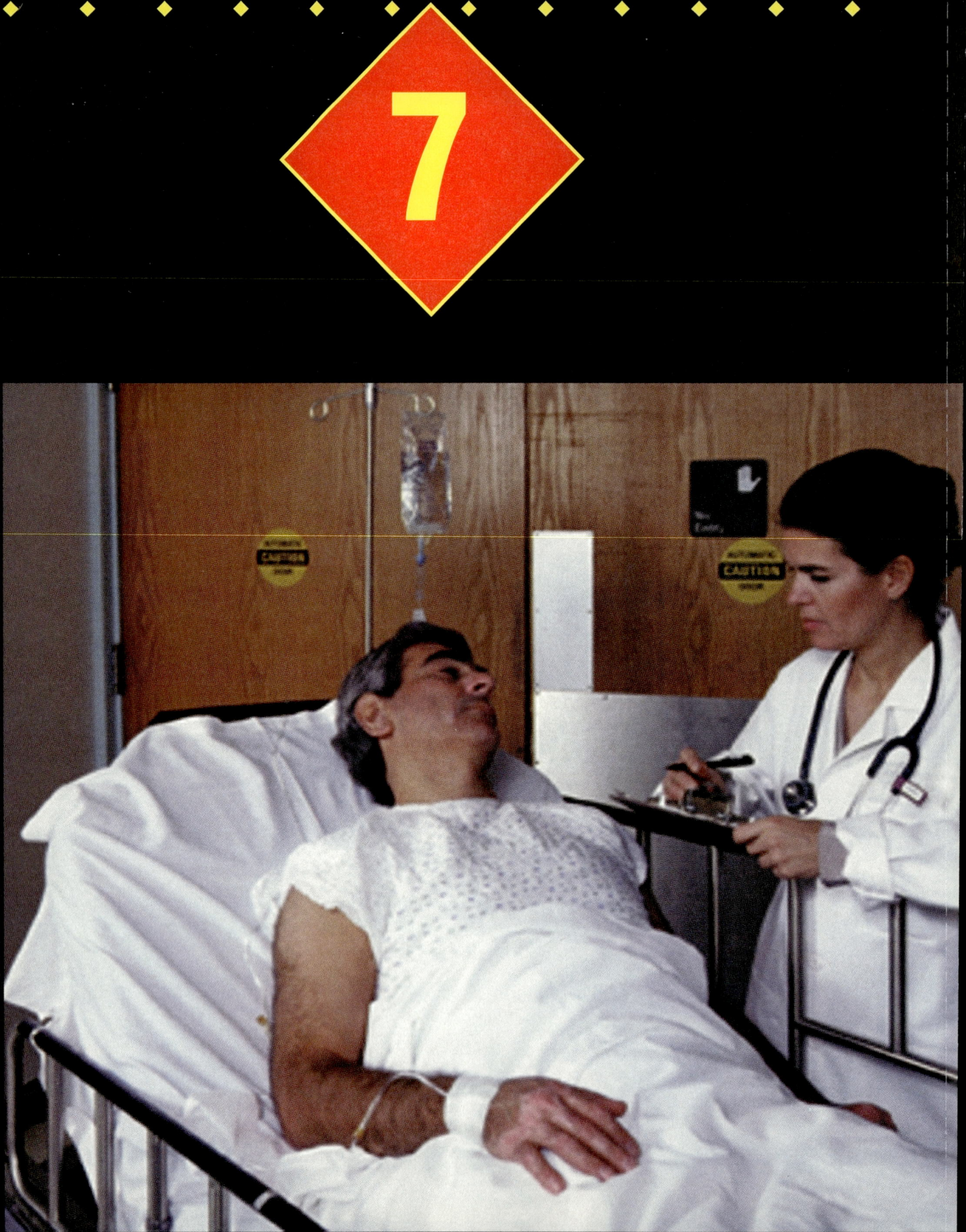

Lifestyle Diseases

FORREST DOLGENER

INTRODUCTION

Early in this century, many Americans died from infectious diseases caused by viruses and bacteria. As vaccines and antibiotics were developed and became widely available, the major causes of death changed. Today, the diseases that cause the greatest numbers of deaths and general medical disability are related to the way we live. We can think of them as being **lifestyle diseases**.

Lifestyle diseases usually develop over decades, not weeks as with infectious diseases, and they are the consequences of the way we live. They are so slow to develop that we may have no idea that anything is wrong until it is too late to do much about it. Diseases like heart disease, cancer, osteoporosis, and diabetes are excellent examples of lifestyle diseases. Their cost to this country is enormous in terms of both death and disability, but also in terms of lost productivity and economic drain.

There is some good news to this story. The good news is that many of theses diseases can be either prevented or significantly reduced merely by changing some of our daily habits. Being more selective in what we eat, exercising on a regular basis, maintaining a normal weight, not smoking, and not drinking alcohol excessively are major lifestyle behaviors that can have a significant impact on our health.

In this chapter, four of the major lifestyle diseases are discussed- heart disease, cancer, diabetes, and osteoporosis (obesity was discussed in Chapter 5). By understanding how these diseases develop, their risk factors, and how to prevent them, you can significantly impact for the good your quality and length of life. No one wants to be incapacitated early in life or die prematurely. The nature of your lifestyle over the next several decades will have a major impact on your chances of suffering from lifestyle diseases.

Coronary Heart Disease

Cardiovascular disease (CVD) is a generic term used to identify a large number of diseases that involve the heart and blood vessels. The three most common cardiovascular diseases are coronary heart disease, high blood pressure, and stroke. Over 60 million Americans, one in four, has one or more types of CVD. Every 33 seconds an American dies of CVD, almost 1 million annually.[3] Although the death rate from CVD has declined some over the recent years, especially for males, it is still the biggest killer in this country. Figure 7.1 depicts the death rate for CVD from 1979-1992.

The specific type of CVD that accounts for over half of deaths from CVD per year is **coronary heart disease (CHD)** (also referred to as coronary artery disease and ischemic heart disease). In 1993, almost 500,000

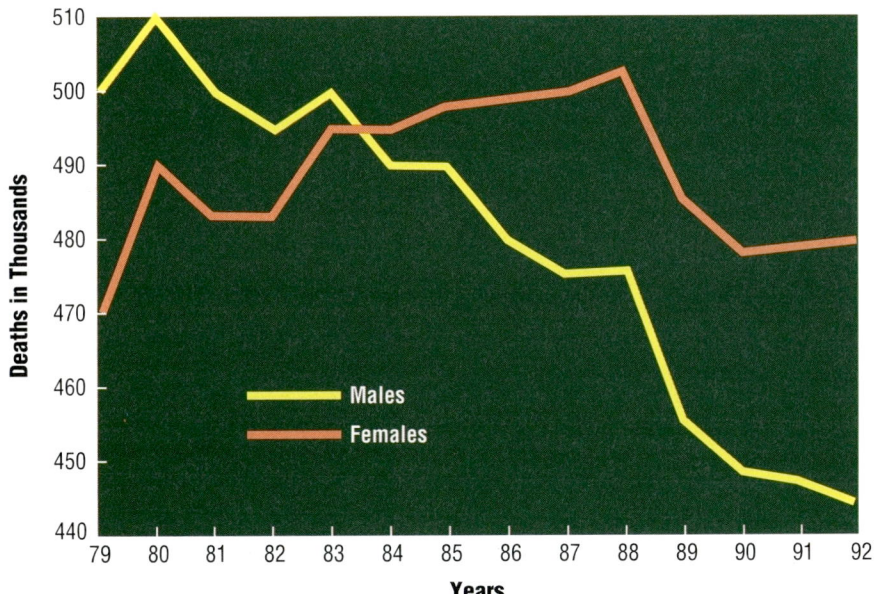

FIGURE 7.1

Deaths Due to Cardiovascular Disease in the U.S. There has been some decrease in the death rate from heart disease over the last 10 years.

Americans died from CHD, 1 of every 4.6 deaths in this country. Heart attack caused by CHD is the single largest killer of American males and females. Each year about 1.5 million Americans will have an heart attack and about one-third of them will die, many before they reach a hospital.

The Development of CHD

CHD is a disease process in which the arteries that supply the heart muscle with blood (coronary arteries) become clogged (Figure 7.2) with a plaque-type material composed of cellular debris and cholesterol. This process of clogging of arteries is called **atherosclerosis** and it is similar to scale build-up on the inside of a drain pipe (Figure 7.3). If the coronary arteries become sufficiently clogged, blood flow is reduced to a level that cannot supply enough oxygen to the heart muscle.

The development of clogged coronary arteries probably begins in late childhood or adolescence in most individuals. Over several decades, the arteries become progressively more clogged until symptoms are produced. It is interesting to note that the coronary arteries have to have 50-75% of their opening clogged before symptoms are produced. This is why there are no symptoms during the first several decades while the arteries are becoming progressively more clogged-up.

Insufficient oxygen supply to the heart muscle can produce a **heart attack (myocardial infarction),** a condition in which a part of the heart muscle dies and becomes non-functional. If enough of the heart muscle is damaged, the heart may not be able to pump enough blood to the rest of the body's tissues, causing a general collapse of the circulation and death of

FIGURE 7.2

There are two primary coronary arteries that supply the entire heart muscle with blood.

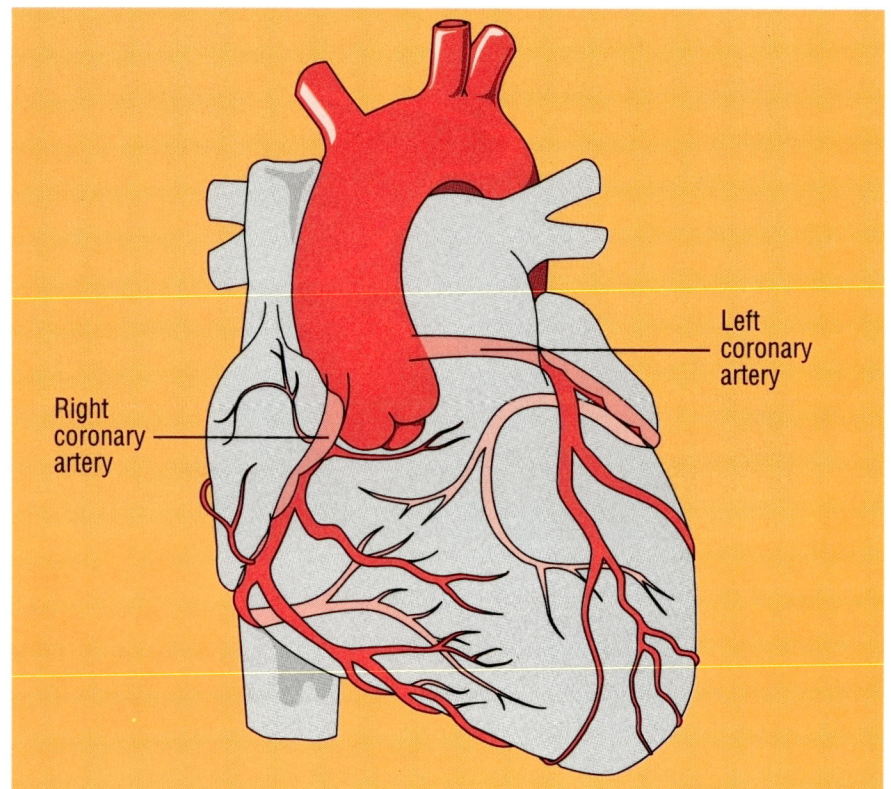

Right coronary artery

Left coronary artery

FIGURE 7.3

The inside of a normal artery (top view) is clean and smooth. Beginning in childhood, fatty deposits begin to form (center view). After decades, the artery may become so clogged that blood flow to the heart is decreased (bottom view).

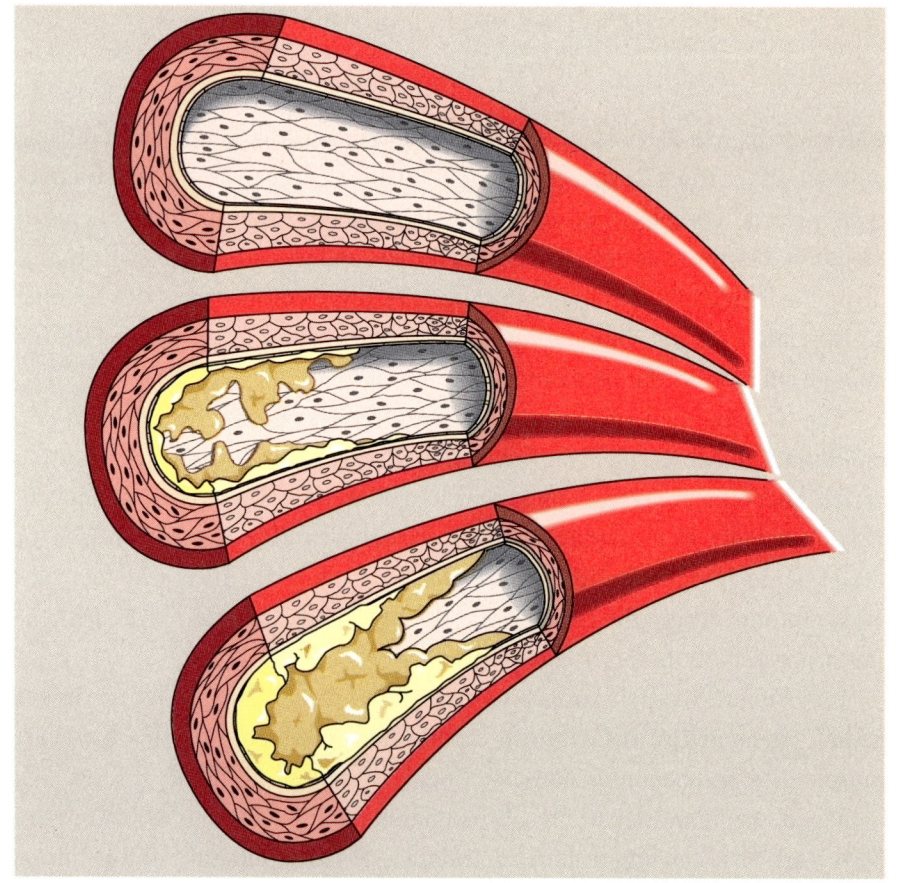

CAN EXERCISE CAUSE A HEART ATTACK?

Exercise of any type increases the amount of oxygen the heart needs in order to pump blood. In situations where the coronary arteries are partially clogged with plaque, the amount of oxygen than can be supplied to the heart is limited. If the pumping demand placed on the heart by the exercise exceeds the ability of the coronary arteries to supply oxygen, a heart attack could result. However, most individuals would have some type of warning, usually angina, that tells them they need to reduce the amount of exercise they are doing. Because it usually takes 4-5 decades before the coronary arteries are clogged enough to cause symptoms, it would be highly unusual for college-aged individuals to have advanced heart disease.

other tissues in the body. If you suspect that yourself or someone else is having a heart attack, it is extremely critical to seek medical attention quickly so the amount of damage to the heart can be minimized.

Often times, a heart attack damages only a small portion of the heart resulting in minimal damage to the pumping ability of the heart. Some individuals can live a fairly normal life in spite of having had a heart attack. However, when CHD is diagnosed, it is important the progression of the disease be stopped in order to prevent future and perhaps more serious heart attacks.

Symptoms of CHD

There are several characteristic symptoms that occur when the heart muscle does not receive adequate oxygen. The most consistent symptom is chest pain called **angina pectoris**. Most often, angina is a pain or discomfort that is felt in the center of the chest directly under the sternum or breastbone. Sometimes, rather than being a distinct pain, angina feels like pressure on the chest as if something heavy was standing on the chest or like a constriction around the chest. In some individuals, angina may not be located in the center of the chest but may be located in the neck and jaw area, in the back, or radiating down the arms.

Most of the time, the angina occurs in response to some kind of physical effort, such as exercise. As the physical effort increases, the angina increases. If the physical effort is reduced, the angina is reduced. In cases of severe disease, angina may occur at rest when there is no associated physical effort.

Other symptoms that are warning signs of insufficient oxygenation of the heart are unusual shortness of breath and lightheadedness. Should any of these symptoms occur, you should stop whatever you are doing and seek

TABLE 7.1

Heart Attack Warning Signals and Actions

Know the warning signals of a heart attack:

- uncomfortable pressure, fullness, squeezing or pain in the center of the chest that lasts more than a few minutes, or goes away and comes back.
- Pain that spreads to the shoulders, neck or arms
- Chest discomfort with lightheadedness, fainting, sweating, nausea or shortness of breath.

Not all these warning signs occur in every heart attack. But if some start to occur, don't wait. Get help immediately. Delay can be deadly! If you are with someone experiencing the signs of a heart attack and the warning signs last more than a few minutes, act immediately.

- Expect denial from someone with chest discomfort. But don't take "no" for an answer. Insist on taking prompt action.
- Call the emergency service, or
- Get to the nearest hospital emergency room that offers 24-hour emergency cardiac care.
- Give CPR if necessary and you are properly trained.

KEY CONCEPT

CORONARY HEART DISEASE AND STROKE: UNFRIENDLY BEDFELLOWS

Stroke is a form of cardiovascular disease that affects the arteries of the brain. The same process that causes CHD is primarily responsible for causing stroke—a lack of oxygen delivery to the brain caused by a clogged artery. Strokes account for approximately 16% of deaths from CVD. Many of the same risk factors for CHD are risk factors for stroke, in particular high blood pressure, smoking, and co-existing CHD.

medical attention. Too often, symptoms of CHD are ignored until a catastrophe like a heart attack occurs. Recognition of these warning signs of CHD can mean the difference between life and death.

Risk Factors for CHD

The major risk factors for CHD can be classified as alterable and unalterable. Alterable risk factors are those you can do something about and include sedentary lifestyle, smoking, high blood cholesterol, diabetes mellitus, and high blood pressure. Unalterable risk factors are those you cannot do anything about and include gender, age and heredity.[4] Lab 7.1 at the end of this chapter is an activity that develops a profile of the accumulated risk from all the risk factors.

Sedentary Lifestyle

The medical community has finally officially recognized something that many have suspected for a long time—that physical inactivity is a major risk factor for CHD. Several recent studies have removed all doubt as to the role that inactivity plays in the risk for heart disease. In one of these studies, inactivity was a greater risk factor than the other traditional risk factors of high blood pressure, high cholesterol, and smoking.[5] As discussed in Chapter 2, the type of exercise that significantly reduces the risk for CHD doesn't have to be high intensity and long duration. It needs to be regular and 1,000-2,000 kcal per week need to be expended. More exercise may be better, but not in proportion to the time and effort spent. Although aerobic exercise is the best type of exercise, other types of exercise can be beneficial and should not be discounted (see Chapter 2 for a complete discussion of exercise).

High Blood Cholesterol

The blockage that forms in the coronary arteries is a mixture of cellular debris and cholesterol. Cholesterol is a soft, fat-like substance found in the body's cells and is used to form cell membranes, hormones and other important substances. Cholesterol is a necessary component of the body but we normally have too much of it.

People get cholesterol in two ways. The body produces it (about 1,000 mg/day) and we consume it in our diets (about 400-500 mg/day). The combination of the two sources produces so much cholesterol that the body has difficulty handling it.

Although other factors are necessary, high blood cholesterol is a key component in the formation of the blockage in the arteries. After several decades of research on atherosclerosis, it is now recognized that the process is highly complex and still not completely understood. As was discussed in Chapter 6, there are three major types of cholesterol in the blood called HDL-cholesterol (HDL-C), LDL-cholesterol (LDL-C), and VLDL-cholesterol (VLDL-C). The LDL- and HDL-cholesterol are partly responsible for clogging the arteries and the HDL-cholesterol reduces the risk of CHD.[4]

It is recommended that every adult have their cholesterol measured to determine the need for follow-up. The earlier you can do this, the more likely you can alter the normal progression of the clogging of the coronary arteries.[7]

Different methods of evaluating levels of cholesterol have been proposed. The one most frequently used is to measure the total cholesterol. Measuring total cholesterol is relatively inexpensive and does not require a fast beforehand. Depending on the value of the total cholesterol, further evaluation may be necessary. Table 7.2 shows the recommended follow-up depending on the initial total cholesterol value and co-existing risk factors.[7]

An active lifestyle can decrease risk for coronary heart disease.

TABLE 7.2

Initial Classification and Follow-Up Based on Total Cholesterol Value

If This	And This	Then Do This
Total Cholesterol <200 mg/dl		1. Repeat cholesterol measurement within 5 years or with physical examination. 2. Provide general dietary and risk factor education
Total Cholesterol is 200–239 mg/dl	One or no additional risk factor is present.	1. Start low-fat diet. 2. Measure cholesterol annually.
Total Cholesterol is 200–239 mg/dl	Coronary heart disease is present or two or more additional risk factors are present.	1. Get LDL cholesterol measured.
Total Cholesterol is >239 mg/dl		1. Get LDL cholesterol measured.

FIGURE 7.4

Total Cholesterol Values for U.S. Adults, 1988–1991. Total cholesterol for males and females are similar if the entire population is averaged but there are age group differences.

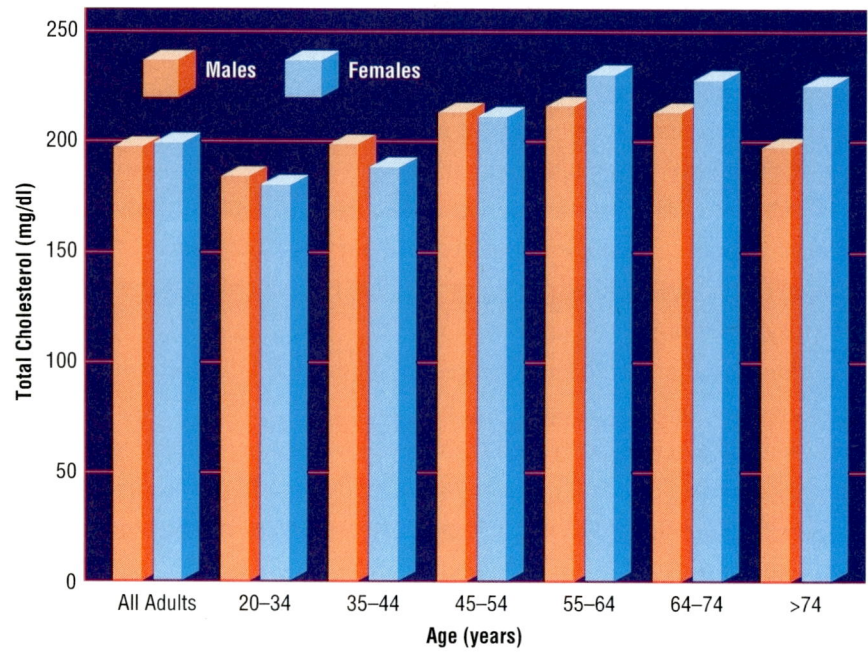

Figure 7.4 compares the mean total cholesterol values for males and females across age groups. Notice that beginning with the ages 55-64, females increase their total cholesterol, the consequence of menopause.

Another method of assessing risk due to cholesterol is to use the **TC/HDL Ratio**, commonly referred to as the **risk ratio**. The risk ratio is formed by dividing the total cholesterol value by the HDL-C value. The ratio indirectly tells how much LDL-C cholesterol is present without having to measure LDL-C. The reason this is advantageous is because measuring

LDL-C is more difficult and expensive than measuring HDL-C. Since HDL-C is the good cholesterol, you would like to have as much of your total cholesterol to be HDL-C as possible. Therefore, you would like the TC/HDL ratio to be as close to 1 as possible. Table 7.3 shows risk categories for various values of the risk ratio. Figure 7.5 shows the relationhip between risk ratio values and risk of a heart attack. As can be seen, as the risk ratio increases from 3 to approximately 6 or 7, the risk of heart attack almost quadruples.

As a rule, females have higher HDL-C levels than men, partially accounting for the lower risk in females prior to menopaus. This relationship is illustrated in Figure 7.6 and is consistent across all ages.

The initial approach for managing high cholesterol is to alter the diet. Many people with high cholesterol will have a significant reduction in

TABLE 7.3
The TC/HDL Risk Ratio and CHD Risk

Risk Ratio	Risk Category
<3.5	very low risk
3.5 – 5.9	low risk
6.0 – 7.9	moderate risk
7.9 – 10.0	high risk
>10.0	very high risk

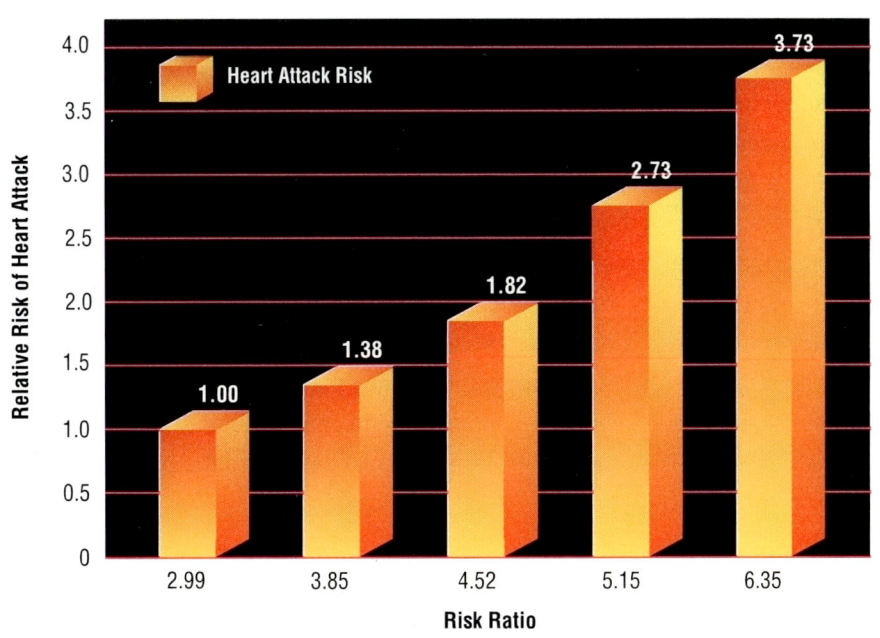

FIGURE 7.5

Risk Ratio and Heart Attack Risk. The risk of heart attack increases as the risk ratio increases. Source: Stampfer, M.J., et al. (1991). A prospective study of cholesterol, apolipoproteins, and the risk of myocardial infarction. *New England Journal of Medicine.* 325:373–381.

FIGURE 7.6

HDL-C Levels in U.S. Adults, 1988–1991. Females have higher HDL-C levels than males at every age. Source: Johnson, C.L., et al. (1993). Declining serum total cholesterol levels among U.S. adults. The National Health and Nutrition Examination Surveys. *Journal of the American Medical Association,* 269:3002–3008.

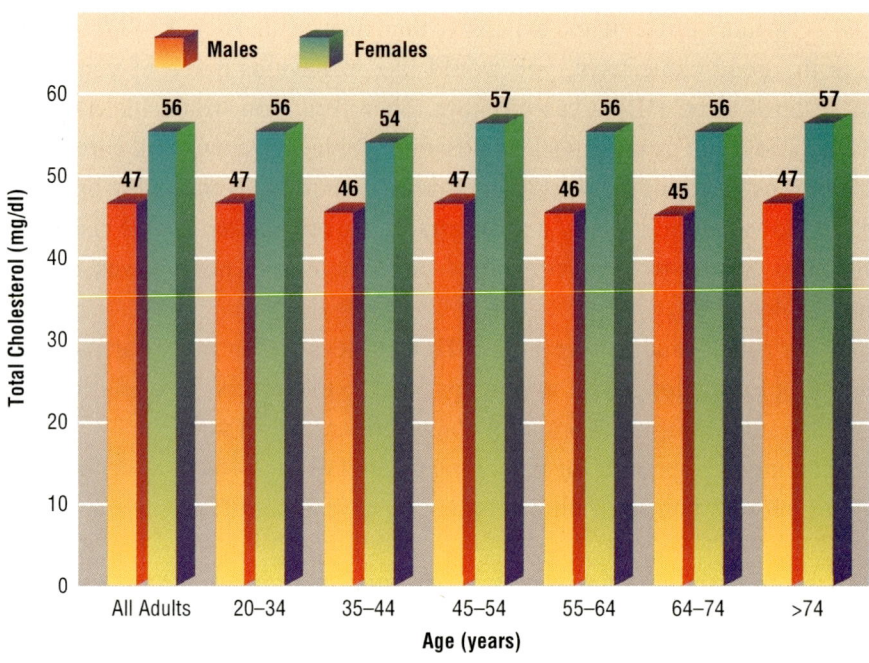

cholesterol after reducing their intake of saturated fat and cholesterol as discussed in Chapter 6. Additionally, aerobic exercise can lower LDL-C and raise HDL-C. However, in some individuals with high cholesterol, medication may be necessary to fully manage the condition.

High Blood Pressure

The blood pressure is the pressure in the large arteries close to the heart. It is caused by the force of the blood pushing on the walls of the arteries as the blood flows through the arteries. There are two phases of blood pressure—**systolic pressure** and **diastolic pressure**—and two numbers are necessary to quantify the blood pressure. The systolic pressure is the highest pressure developed in the arteries when the heart is contracting and pumping blood into the arteries. The diastolic pressure is the lowest pressure in the arteries when the heart is relaxing and no blood is being pumped. Both pressures have significance and are used to interpret the overall blood pressure response.

Blood pressure is measured with a sphygmomanometer and stethoscope. Both the systolic and diastolic pressures are measured resulting in a high number and a low number. The pressure is normally measured in the upper arm because this is where the pressure is most similar to the pressure in the aorta, the large artery coming out of the left ventricle.

High blood pressure (hypertension) has been long recognized as a major risk factor for CHD. Over 50 million Americans currently have high blood pressure. The link between high blood pressure and CHD is thought to be related to the "injury hypothesis" of how blockage in the arteries occurs.

The injury hypothesis says that deposits form in the coronary arteries following some type of initial damage to the lining of the arteries. It is thought that a chronically elevated blood pressure damages the arterial wall and sets up the environment in which CHD can develop. Table 7.4 provides the values of the systolic and diastolic pressures and their risk levels and recommended follow-up.

It has been extremely difficult to determine the exact cause of high blood pressure. In 95% of cases, there is no identifiable cause and the high blood pressure is called **essential hypertension**. Two lifestyle risk factors—high sodium intake and being overweight—seem to be important in some individuals but not in everyone. For those individuals who are sensitive to sodium intake, keeping the intake low has a beneficial effect on high blood pressure. If you already have high blood pressure, cutting down on your sodium intake may lower your blood pressure.

Not everyone that has high blood pressure is overweight and not everyone that is overweight has high blood pressure. However, maintaining a normal body weight can be critical for some because reducing body weight may be all that is necessary to control blood pressure.

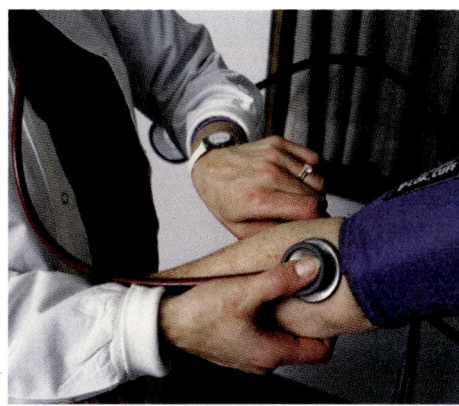

Blood pressure is easy to measure with a blood pressure cuff and stethoscope.

TABLE 7.4		
Blood Pressure Classification and Risk		
Blood Pressure (mmHg)	**Blood Pressure Classification Risk Level**	**Recommended Follow-up**
DIASTOLIC		
< 85	Normal Blood Pressure Low Risk	Recheck within 2 years
85 – 89	High Normal Blood Pressure Mild Risk	Recheck within 1 year
90 – 104	Mild Hypertension Moderate Risk	Confirm within 2 months
105 – 114	Moderate Hypertension High Risk	Seek medical evaluation within 2 weeks
> 114	Severe Hypertension Very High Risk	Seek medical evaluation immediately
SYSTOLIC		
< 140	Normal Blood Pressure Low Risk	Recheck within 2 years
140 – 159	Borderline Isolated Systolic Hypertension Mild Risk	Confirm within 2 months
> 159	Isolated Systolic Hypertension Moderate Risk	Seek medical evaluation within 2 weeks

If lifestyle management doesn't normalize blood pressure, medication is normally required. There are many effective blood pressure medications available and even though there may be some side-effects, the normalizing of blood pressure is very important. Untreated high blood pressure is a major risk factor for heart disease, kidney disease, and stroke. Since high blood pressure has no obvious symptoms, it is important to have your blood pressure checked periodically. If you know you have high blood pressure, check it at regular intervals.

Smoking

A smokers' risk of heart attack is more than twice that of nonsmokers. Cigarette smoking is the greatest risk factor for sudden cardiac death with smokers having two to four times the risk of nonsmokers. Smokers who have a heart attack are more likely to die and die suddenly (within 1 hour) than nonsmokers.[4]

Like high blood pressure, smoking appears to damage the arterial lining providing the environment for the development of heart disease. Other by-products of smoking, such as nicotine and carbon monoxide, make the heart work harder than it needs to and makes it more susceptible to irregular heart beats. Because smoking increases the risk of abnormal heart beats it is a major risk factor for "sudden cardiac death," a condition in which an apparently healthy individual suddenly dies from an abnormal heart rhythm which results in heart fibrillation and loss of pump function of the heart.

Evidence also indicates that chronic exposure to second-hand smoke increases the risk of heart disease. The risk of death is increased by 30% for people exposed the second-hand smoke at home or in the workplace.[4]

It is encouraging for those that smoke that once you stop smoking, the risk for CHD and sudden cardiac death syndrome is dramatically lowered. After quitting smoking for two years, the risk for a former smoker is the same as for someone who has never smoked. It is important to stop smoking before the signs of heart disease appear.

Diabetes Mellitus

In addition to being a devastating disease in and of itself, diabetes is also a major risk factor for CHD. Coronary heart disease is the most common cause of death in diabetic adults. Even asymptomatic diabetic individuals over the age of 35 are likely to have significant CHD. Of particular concern in diabetic individuals is that diabetes can reduce the effectiveness of the normal warning mechanisms that non-diabetics with CHD have, especially angina. Because diabetes damages the nervous system, diabetics have reduced or totally absent anginal responses, i.e. they may not get chest pain even when there is insufficient blood flow to the heart.

High blood glucose levels can damage the lining of the arteries and the inability of glucose to be normally metabolized causes an abnormal use of fat by cells. Specifics on the risk factors and consequences of diabetes are discussed in a later section of this chapter.

Age

Age is a risk factor for CHD because the development of CHD takes decades. There is good evidence that in many individuals, the process that clogs the coronary arteries begins in adolescence or late childhood. The insidious process continues for decades until the arteries become so clogged that symptoms are produced. The longer the process develops, the more likely the disease will become symptomatic and potentially catastrophic.

It is a rare situation that a college-aged individual would have symptomatic CHD, especially a heart attack. Most heart attacks occur in middle-aged and older individuals. However, it is important to recognize that the process that leads to a heart attack is developing throughout the college years and will continue to progress unless risk factors are controlled. The earlier the risk factors are controlled, the more likely the disease will not ever get to the point of causing problems.

Gender

For decades, heart disease has been thought of as a disease that strikes primarily males even though CHD causes more deaths in females than any other disease. Within the last decade, more attention and research has been focused on females. It is now recognized that CHD is a disease that afflicts both males and females, just at different times in their lives.

Heart disease becomes symptomatic in males about 10-15 years earlier than in females. This is probably because of the protective effect of the female sex hormones prior to menopause. After menopause, the rate of CHD in females accelerates to about the same rate as in males.

Coronary heart disease has the same consequence in males and females. It is important that both genders attempt to modify risk factors as early in their lives as possible in order to prevent CHD from developing into a severe debilitating disease.

Heredity

There is definitely a genetic component to heart disease. If your family has a history of heart attack or other manifestations of CHD, you are more likely to develop the disease. Although you can't do anything about who your parents are, you can be more vigorous at controlling the alterable risk factors if you know you have a genetic propensity for the disease.

Preventing and Reversing Coronary Heart Disease

You have two basic choices to make regarding CHD. Do you want to try to prevent the development of the disease or do you want to have to manage the disease once it becomes advanced and symptomatic? The best choice, by far, is to prevent the disease from developing to the point that it causes a problem. As has been emphasized throughout this section, knowing the risk factors and modifying them when necessary is the approach to use. You should quit smoking, check your blood pressure periodically to make sure it is within the normal range, check your cholesterol level in early adulthood, exercise on a regular basis, and maintain a normal body weight. Maintaining an optimal risk factor profile will make a big impact on your risk for developing CHD. You can't do anything about age, gender, and heredity, but you can sure do a lot with the other risk factors.

Remember that your risk for developing CHD is dependent on an accumulation of the effects of all the risk factors. You may not be able to control all of them optimally, but controlling one or two is better than not controlling any. Don't give up if all your risk factors are not perfect but try to work on those that you are able to manage.

Once CHD has developed all hope is not lost even though it becomes more difficult to manage. There is recent evidence that CHD can be partially reversed, i.e. the arteries can be unclogged, by adhering to a strict dietary and exercise regime. Even for those with advanced CHD, exercise and diet can play a central role in maintaining a quality of life that will make life worth living.

CANCER

Cancer is a disease characterized by abnormal growth of abnormal cells. Rather than these abnormal cells following the normal pattern of growth, they multiply in an unregulated and uncontrolled manner. Cancer cells usually become very numerous and can spread to all parts of the body, eventually causing death if left unchecked.

A concentrated mass of cells, sometimes enclosed by a membrane, is called a **tumor.** A tumor can be composed of normal cells, in which chase is a **benign tumor**, or it can be composed of cancer cells, in which case it is a **malignant tumor**. Malignant tumors grow and infiltrate surrounding tissue and can **metastasize** or spread to other parts of the body through the circulatory or lymphatic system, where they start other colonies of abnormal cells. Because cancer cells have the ability to metastasize, it is imperative that cancer be detected early while it is localized to a small area. As the cancer spreads throughout the body, it becomes more difficult to treat.

Malignant tumors are classified according to the types of cells that give rise to the cancer. There are four general categories of cancers- **carcinomas, sarcomas, lymphomas, and leukemias.**

Carcinomas are tumors that develop in the outside layers (epithelial layer) of cells including skin, glands (breast, uterus, prostate), cells lining the respiratory tract (lungs, bronchi), and gastrointestinal tract (mouth, stomach, colon, rectum). Carcinomas account for approximately 85% of malignant tumors.

Sarcomas are tumors that arise from connective and fibrous tissue like muscle, bone, cartilage, and the membranes covering muscles and fat. Only about 2% of tumors are sarcomas.

Lymphomas are tumors of the lymph glands, part of the body's infection-fighting mechanisms. Lymphomas arise from changes in the white blood cells. Leukemias are tumors of the blood cells and blood-forming tissues such as bone marrow.

More than 1.2 million new cases of cancer are diagnosed each year, excluding curable types of skin cancers. Although survival rates vary significantly for different types of cancers, approximately 4 of 10 patients who get cancer this year are expected to be alive 5 years after diagnosis.[1] Cancer is second only to heart disease as a cause of death in the U.S. Table 7.5 shows the expected death rates for different types of cancers for 1997. Figure 7.7 shows the cancer rates in the U.S. according to gender and ethnicity.[1]

FIGURE 7.7

Cancer Incidence Rates. Cancer rates differ in the United States across different ethnic groups. Source: American Cancer Society. www.cancer.org.

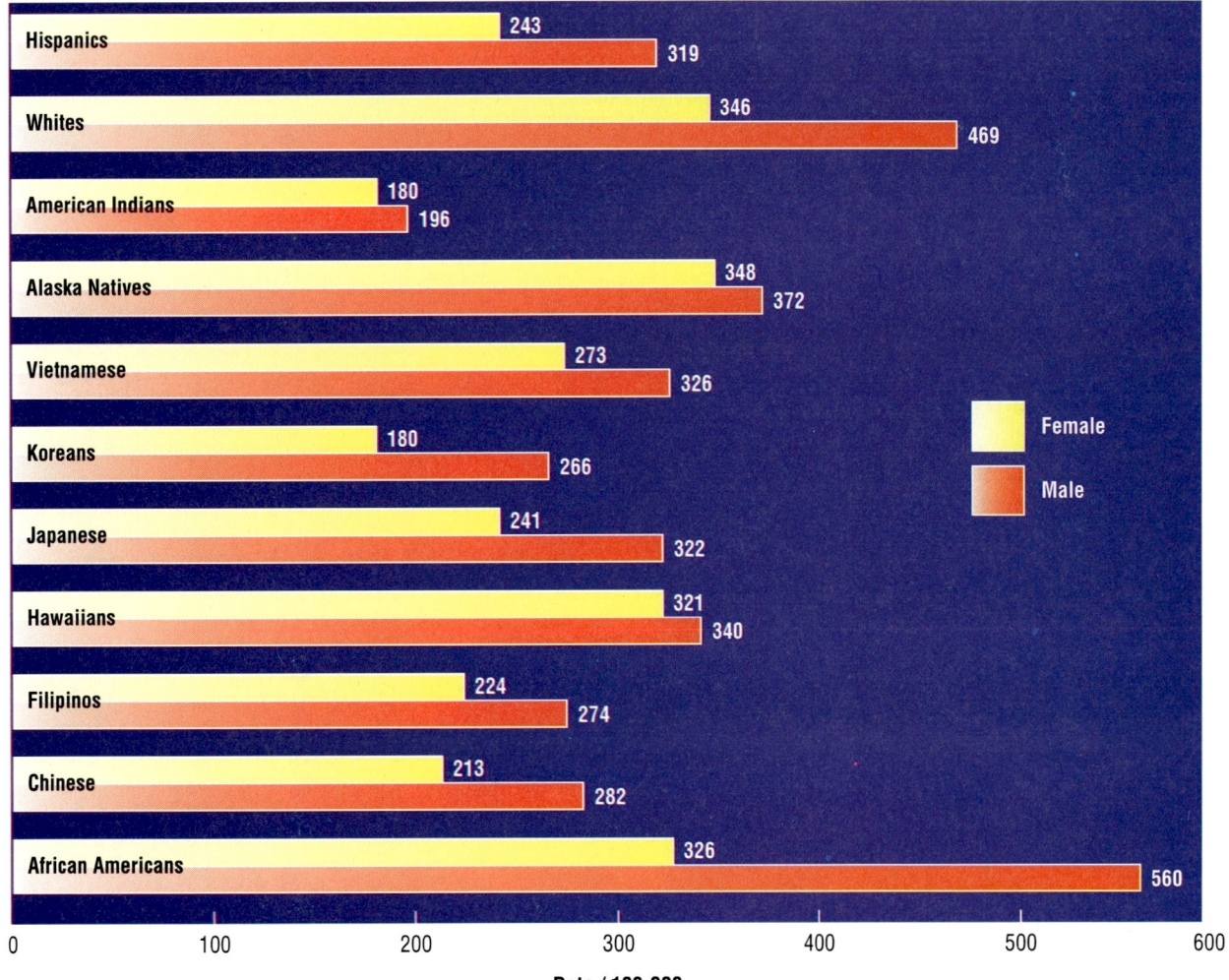

Ethnic Group	Female	Male
Hispanics	243	319
Whites	346	469
American Indians	180	196
Alaska Natives	348	372
Vietnamese	273	326
Koreans	180	266
Japanese	241	322
Hawaiians	321	340
Filipinos	224	274
Chinese	213	282
African Americans	326	560

Rate / 100,000

TABLE 7.5

Incidence, Deaths, Risk Factors, and Warning Signs of Selected Cancers, 1997

Site	Estimated New Cases 1997	Estimated Deaths 1997	5-Year Survival Rate	Risk Factors	Warning Signs
Breast	180,200	44,190	97%	age; personal or family history of breast cancer; some forms of benign breast disease; early menarche; late menopause; lengthy exposure to postmenopausal estrogens; recent use of oral contraceptives; never having children; first live birth at a late age	abnormality on mammogram; lump, thickening, swelling, dimpling, skin irritation, distortion, retraction, pain in breast,; tenderness of nipple; nipple discharge
Cervix	14,500	4,800	69%	human papillomavirus; first intercourse at an early age; multiple sexual partners; cigarette smoking	abnormal vaginal bleeding or spotting; abnormal vaginal discharge
Endometrium	34,900	6,000	95% if detected early	estrogen-related exposures; tamoxifen; early menarche; late menopause; never having children; history of failure to ovulate	abnormal uterine bleeding or spotting
Ovary	26,000	14,200	46%	age; never had children; history of breast cancer	enlargement of abdomen; stomach discomfort, gas, or distention that cannot be explained by other cause
Testicular	7,200	350	91%	age (20-34)	small, painless lump on testicle; change in shape; dull ache or heaviness in groin or scrotum
Lung	178,000	160,400	14%	cigarette smoking; exposure to arsenic, radon, asbestos; radiation exposure; side-stream smoke	persistent cough; sputum streaked with blood; chest pain; recurring pneumonia or bronchitis

Site	Estimated New Cases 1997	Estimated Deaths 1997	5-Year Survival Rate	Risk Factors	Warning Signs
Colon and Rectum	131,200	54,900	61%	personal or family history of colorectal cancer or polyps and inflammatory bowel disease; physical inactivity; high-fat/low-fiber diet	rectal bleeding; blood in the stool; change in bowel habits
Pancreas	27,600	28,100	4%	age; smoking; high fat diet	none
Prostate	334,500	41,800	99% if detected early	age; African American	weak or interrupted urine flow; inability to urinate or difficulty starting or stopping; frequent urination; blood in urine; pain or burning on urination
Bladder	54,500	11,700	93%	smoking	blood in urine; increased frequency of urination
Oral Cavity and Pharynx	30,750	8,440	53%	cigarette, cigar or pipe smoking; smokeless tobacco; alcohol	sore that does not heal; lump or thickening; difficulty in swallowing & chewing
Skin (melanoma)	40,300	7,300	87% if detected early	ultraviolet radiation; fair complexion; family history	Any change on skin especially change in size or color of mole or other darkly pigmented growth.
Leukemia	28,300	21,310	42%	radiation and chemical exposure; retrovirus	fatigue; paleness; weight loss; repeated infections; bruising easily; nosebleeds or other hemorrhages
Lymphoma	61,100	25,280	81% for Hodgkin; 51% for non-Hodgkins's	reduced immune function; exposure to certain infectious agents	enlarged lymph nodes; itching; fever; night sweats; anemia; weight loss

Source: American Cancer Society

TABLE 7.6
Early Warning Signs of Cancer: CAUTION

C	Change in bowel or bladder habits
A	A sore that does not heal
U	Unusual bleeding or discharge
T	Thickening or lump in breast or elsewhere
I	Indigestion or difficulty in swallowing
O	Obvious change in a wart or mole
N	Nagging cough or hoarseness

General Warning Signs

Warning signs for specific types of cancers vary. However, there are some general warning signs that are useful for general awareness and should be observed closely by all. The American Cancer Society emphasizes these early warning signs using the acronym **CAUTION** (Table 7.6). The earlier cancer is diagnosed, the better the chances are for effective treatment and survival. More specific warning signs for different types of cancers are found in Table 7.5.

Risk Factors for Cancer

General risk factors for cancer include **heredity, nutritional factors, smoking, and environmental hazards**.[1] These general risk factors affect specific cancers in different ways but reducing the number of risk factors will produce substantial reduction of cancer risk. As is the case with most risk factors, some are alterable and some are not. While you cannot change the unalterable risk factors, you can pay special attention to those that are manageable.

Heredity

Certain cancers are more likely to occur in individuals that have inherited a damaged or activated oncogene, a gene that normally helps to control cell growth. Cancers that have an inherited component are colon, breast, and perhaps prostate. Individuals that have a family history of these types of cancers should be vigilant about the other risk factors, especially those specific for these types of cancers.

Nutritional Factors

Existing scientific evidence suggests that about one-third of the cancer deaths in the U.S. each year is due to nutritional factors.[1] Many nutritional factors can affect cancer risk: types of foods, food preparation methods, food variety, portion sizes, and total calories consumed. Cancer risk can be reduced by an overall dietary pattern that includes a high proportion of plant foods (fruits, vegetables, grains, and beans), limited amounts of meat, dairy, and other high-fat foods, and a balance of caloric intake and caloric expenditure.

Eating fruits and vegetables (green and dark yellow vegetables and those in the cabbage family, soy products, and legumes) protect for cancers at many sites, particularly cancers of the gastrointestinal and respiratory tracts. Grains are an important source of folate, calcium and selenium, all of which have been associated with a lower risk of colon cancer.

Other vitamins and minerals have been associated with reduced cancer rates. Generally, these are the so-called antioxidants vitamin C, beta-carotene, vitamin E and selenium (see the section on antioxidants in Chapter 6). The association of a diet high in fruits, vegetables, and grain products with reduced cancer rates may be due to a high intake of antioxidants.

Another factor found in fruits, vegetables, and grain products is fiber and a high fiber intake has been associated with reduced risk of colon cancer. There may be other unknown agents in fruits, vegetables, and grain products which account for part of their positive affect on cancers.

Diets high in saturated fats have been associated with an increase in the risk of cancers of the colon, rectum, prostate, endometrium, and to a lesser extent, the breast. Consumption of red meat has been associated with increased colon and prostate cancers. The exact mechanism of how fat increases the risk are not understood and the best advice is to try to reduce the consumption of fat in general and saturated fat in particular.

Eating fruits and vegetables reduces the risk of certain types of cancer.

Being overweight increases the risk for colon, rectum, prostate, endometrium, breast, and kidney cancers. The exact mechanism accounting for this relationship is not known but it could be related to excess caloric consumption, an increase in fat consumption, or a inactive lifestyle, all of which can lead to obesity. Since a balance of caloric intake and caloric expenditure is necessary to maintain a healthy body weight, physical activity should play a significant role. In fact, studies have shown physical inactivity to be an independent risk factor for cancer.[5]

Alcohol consumption as been associated with cancers of the oral cavity, esophagus, and larynx. The effect of alcohol on these cancers is augmented by smoking. Alcohol consumption has also been associated with an increase in breast cancer. An average of three drinks per day is associated with a doubling in the risk of breast cancer.

Smoking

One-third of cancer deaths each year are due to cigarette smoking. Smoking tobacco and sidestream smoke both have their greatest impact on lung cancer which accounts for 13% of the cancers diagnosed. The incidence rate of lung cancer is declining in men but increasing in women. Smoking tobacco and using smokeless tobacco also are associated with cancer of the oral cavity, esophagus, and larynx and the risk increases when tobacco is combined with alcohol.

Additional Environmental Hazards

According to the American Cancer Society, environmental causes probably account for well over half of all cancers. These environmental hazards include lifestyle factors such as diet and smoking, but they also include exposure to elements of the environment that we may not be able to control. The degree of cancer risk from environmental hazards depends on the concentration or intensity of the carcinogen and the amount of exposure a person receives. Many environmental hazards are due to various chemicals (asbestos, benzene, vinyl chloride, arsenic) and radiation (including UV radiation or sunlight, x-rays, radon).

Some of our concern about environmental cancer risks often focuses on risks which have not been proven or on situations where exposure to contaminants is negligible. Although many pesticides are widely used in food production and marketing, they are found in concentrations that are generally well within established safety levels. Electromagnetic radiation at frequencies below ionizing and ultraviolet levels (radiowaves, radar, microwaves, and electrical and magnetic fields) has not been associated with cancer. Toxic wastes in dump sites can threaten health through air, water, and soil pollution but community exposure appears to involve very low or negligible levels.

Always wear sunblock when exposed to prolonged UV rays.

Prevention, Early Detection and Treatment

Like with other diseases, if given the choice, most would want to avoid cancer if at all possible. Fortunately, many types of cancers are caused by factors you can do something about if you choose to do so. In fact, many of the same types of lifestyle behaviors that reduce the risk of heart disease and diabetes reduce the risk of cancer. Among the most important are not smoking, eating a healthy diet and exercising regularly, avoiding overexposure to the sun, and avoiding other environmental hazards. Table 7.7 lists the recommendations from the American Cancer Society regarding prevention of cancer.

TABLE 7.7
How To Prevent Cancer

The American Cancer Society recommends the following methods to prevent cancer:

- Stop smoking and heavy use of alcohol. All cancers caused by cigarette smoking and heavy use of alcohol could be prevented completely.
- Choose most of the foods you eat from plant sources. Eat five or more servings of fruits and vegetables each day. Eat other foods from plant sources, such as breads, cereals, grain products, rice, pasta, or beans several times each day.
- Limit your intake of high-fat foods, particularly from animal sources.
- Protect yourself from overexposure to the sun and tanning beds.
- Take advantage of screening examinations by health care professionals which can result in the detection of cancers of the breast, tongue, mouth, colon, rectum, cervix, prostate, testis, and melanoma at earlier stages.
- Use self-examination for cancers of the breast, testis, and skin.
- Be physically active and achieve and maintain a healthy body weight. Physical activity can help protect against some cancers, either by balancing caloric intake with energy expenditure or by other mechanism.

HOW TO DO BREAST SELF-EXAMINATION

Why Do the Breast Self-Exam?

There are many good reasons for doing a breast self-exam each month. One reason is that it is easy to do and the more you do it, the better you will get at it. When you get to know how your breasts normally feel, you will quickly be able to feel any change, and early detection is the key to successful treatment and cure.

Remember: A breast self-exam could save your breast—and save your life. Most breast lumps are found by women themselves, but, in fact, most lumps in the breast are not cancer. Be safe, be sure.

When to Do Breast Self-Exam

The best time to do breast self-exam is right after your period, when the breasts are not tender or swollen. If you do not have regular periods or sometimes skip a month, do it on the same day every month.

Now, How to Do Breast Self-Exam

1. Lie down and put a pillow under your right shoulder. Place your right arm behind your head.

2. Use the finger pads of your three middle fingers on your left hand to feel for lumps or thickening. Your finger pads are the top third of each finger.

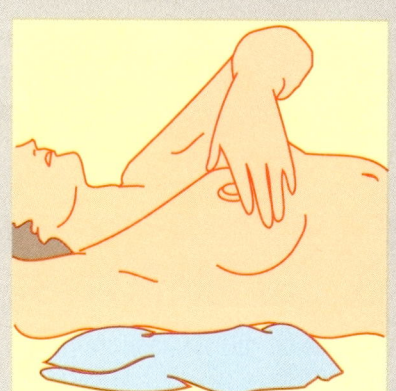 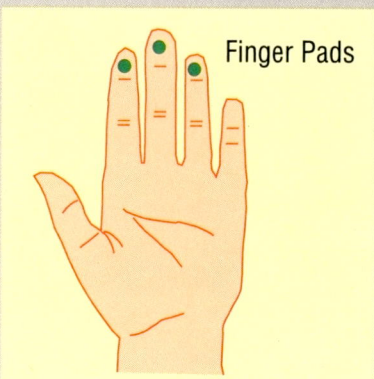

Finger Pads

3. Press firmly enough to know how your breast feels. If you're not sure how hard to press, ask your health care provider. Or try to copy the way your health care provider uses the finger pads during a breast exam. Learn what your breast feels like most of the time. A firm ridge in the lower curve of each breast is normal.

(Continued)

KEY CONCEPT (CONCLUDED)

HOW TO DO BREAST SELF-EXAMINATION

4. Move around the breast in a set way. You can choose either the circle (A), the up and down line (B), or the wedge (C). Do it the same way every time. It will help you to make sure that you've gone over the entire breast area, and to remember how your breast feels.

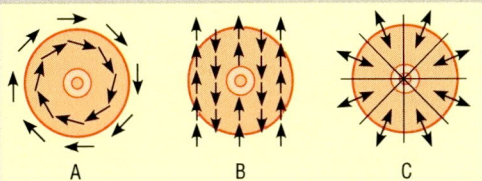

5. Now examine your left breast using right hand finger pads.

6. If you find any changes, see your doctor right away.

For Added Safety:

You should also check your breasts while standing in front of a mirror right after you do your breast self each month. See if there are any changes in the way your breasts look: dimpling of the skin, changes in the nipple, or redness or swelling.

You might also want to do a breast self-exam while you're in the shower. Your soapy hands will glide over the wet skin making it easy to check how your breasts feel.

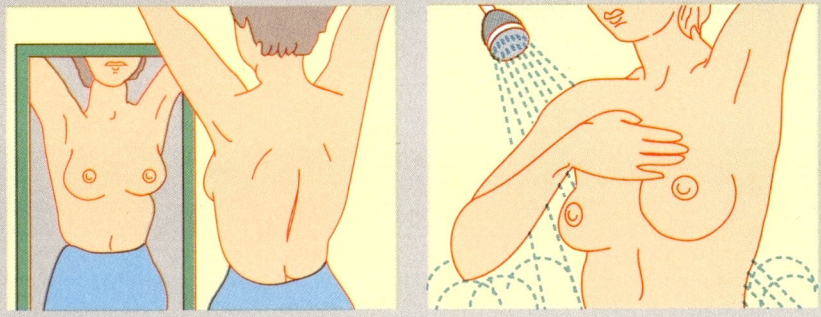

Source: American Cancer Society.

TESTICULAR SELF-EXAMINATION

Testicular Self-Examination

Testicular cancer is the most common type of cancer in men ages 20 to 35. Yet, because it accounts for only about 1 percent of all cancers in men, many people have never heard of this type of cancer.

Testicular cancer is of special concern to young men. It can occur anytime after age 15. It is less common in middle-aged and older men. White men are four times more likely to develop testicular cancer than black men. The rate among Hispanic men lies between those of blacks and whites.

Two groups of men have a greater risk of developing testicular cancer—those whose testicles have not descended into the scrotum and those whose testicles descended after age 6. Testicular cancer is 3 to 17 times more likely to develop in these men.

Testicles are male reproductive organs. They produce and store sperm. They also produce testosterone, a hormone that causes such male traits as facial hair and lower voice pitch. Testicles are smooth, oval-shaped, and somewhat firm to the touch. They are below the penis in a sac of skin called the scrotum.

The testicles normally descend into the scrotum before birth. Parents should have their infant sons examined by a doctor to be sure that the testicles have properly descended. If they have not, this can be easily corrected with surgery.

Fifteen years ago, testicular cancer was often fatal because it spread quickly to vital organs such as the lungs. Today, due to advances in treatment, testicular cancer is one of the most curable cancers, especially if detected and treated properly.

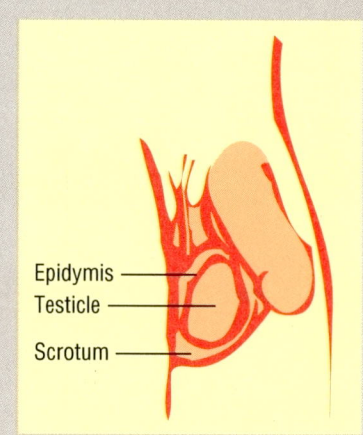

Symptoms

The most common symptom of testicular cancer is a small, painless lump in a testicle or a slightly enlarged testicle. It is important for men to become familiar with the size and feeling of their normal testicles, so that they can detect changes if they occur.

Other possible symptoms include a feeling of heaviness in the scrotum, a dull ache in the lower stomach or groin, a change in the way a testicle feels, or a sudden accumulation of blood or fluid in the scrotum. These symptoms can also be caused by infections or other conditions that are not cancer. A doctor can tell you if you have cancer and what the proper treatment should be.

(Continued)

TESTICULAR SELF-EXAMINATION

How to Do TSE

A simple procedure called testicular self-exam (TSE) can increase the chances of finding a tumor early.

Men should perform TSE once a month—after a warm bath or shower. The heat causes the scrotal skin to relax, making it easier to find anything unusual. TSE is simple and only takes a few minutes:

- Examine each testicle gently with both hands. The index and middle fingers should be placed underneath the testicle while the thumbs are placed on the top. Roll the testicle gently between the thumbs and fingers. One testicle may be larger than the other. This is normal.

- The epididymis is a cord-like structure on the top and back of the testicle that stores and transports the sperm. Do not confuse the epididymis with an abnormal lump.

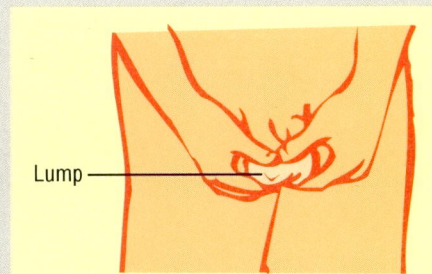

Lump

- Feel for any abnormal lumps—on the front or the side of the testicle. These lumps are usually painless.

If you do find a lump, you should contact your doctor right away. The lump may be due to an infection, and a doctor can decide the proper treatment. If the lump is not an infection, it is likely to be cancer. Remember that testicular cancer is highly curable, especially when detected and treated early. Testicular cancer almost always occurs in only one testicle, and the other testicle is all that is needed for full sexual function.

Routine testicular self-exams are important, but they cannot substitute for a doctor's examination. Your doctor should examine your testicles when you have a physical exam. You also can ask your doctor to check the way you do TSE.

Source: National Institutes of Health, National Cancer Institute.

TABLE 7.8			
Screening Recommendations for the Early Detection of Cancer			
Test	**Population**		**Frequency**
	Gender	**Age**	
Sigmoidoscopy, preferably flexible	M & F	≥50	Every 3-5 years
Fecal Occult Blood	M & F	≥50	Every year
Digital Rectal Exam	M & F	≥40	Every year
Prostate Exam including PSA	M	≥50	Every year
Breast Self-exam	F	≥20	Every month
Breast Clinical Exam	F	20-40	Every 3 years
		>40	Every year
Mammography	F	40-49	Every 1-2 years
		≥50	Every year
Pap Test	F	All women ≥ age 18 or who are or have been sexually active, should have an annual Pap test and pelvic exam. After a woman has had three or more consecutive satisfactory normal annual exams, the Pap test may be performed less frequently.	

The key to surviving most forms of cancers is early detection and treatment. Most cancers, when detected early, have good survival rates. Unfortunately, some cancers are difficult to detect and others have poor survival rates even when detected early. Table 7.5 lists the 5-year survival rates for common forms of cancer along with early warning signs. In addition to these early warning signs, there are some screening methods that will provide early detection for some forms of cancers. The screening recommendations of the American Cancer Society for the early detection of cancer are in Table 7.8.

DIABETES MELLITUS

Diabetes mellitus, usually called **diabetes**, is a disease in which the body is unable to properly metabolize carbohydrates, fats, and proteins. Although the primary problem is carbohydrate metabolism, abnormal carbohydrate metabolism causes abnormal fat and protein metabolism. The abnormal metabolism of carbohydrates produces an abnormally high blood glucose concentration, the characteristic sign of diabetes.

Diabetes affects 3-5% of the population, with at least 5 million Americans having known disease and about an equal number undiagnosed. Females are 50% more likely to develop diabetes and the prevalence is higher

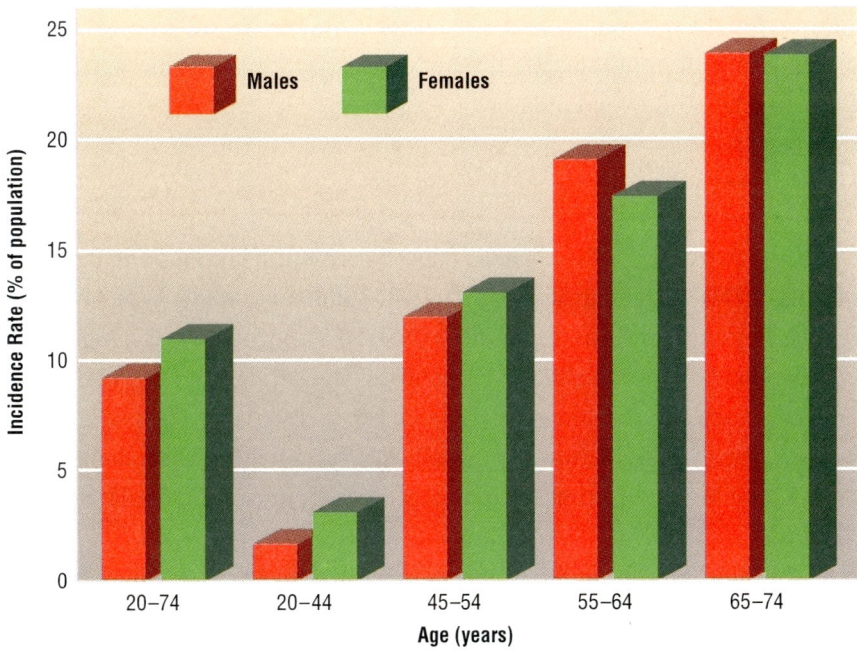

FIGURE 7.8

Incidence of Diabetes in the U.S.
The incidence rate of diabetes increases as age increases in both males and females. Source: Harris, M.I. (1989). Impaired glucose tolerance in the U.S. population. *Diabetes Care,* 12:464–474.

in blacks than whites. Figure 7.8 shows the incidence rate for diabetes for gender and age. Note that the incidence of diabetes increases as the population gets older.

The Development of Diabetes

When carbohydrates are consumed in the diet, they are broken down in digestion to glucose. From the digestive process, glucose is dumped into the blood and is known as blood glucose. Once in the blood, the glucose is circulated around the body and delivered to all the tissues. But in order for many tissues to be able use the glucose to produce ATP, the glucose has to enter the cells from the blood, a process requiring the help of **insulin**. Without insulin, the glucose has a very difficult time entering many types of cells.

Insulin is secreted by the **pancreas**, a long, thin organ located behind the stomach. Normally, whenever glucose is absorbed into the blood, just the right amount of insulin is secreted. If not enough insulin is secreted or if the insulin doesn't have the effect it should, the glucose accumulates in the blood until it reaches abnormally high levels.

The normal amount of fasting blood glucose is about 80-90 mg/dl. This is what your blood glucose would be in the morning following an overnight fast. Following a typical meal containing carbohydrate, the blood glucose concentration increases for about two hours but falls back to normal levels as the blood glucose goes into the cells with the help of insulin. It is important that some glucose is always in the blood because the nervous system depends on blood glucose for its energy. If blood glucose gets too low, a condition called **hypoglycemia**, the nervous system begins to dysfunction, resulting in symptoms such as fatigue, lethargy, lightheadedness, irritability, headache, and even coma.

Types of Diabetes

There are two types of diabetes- **Type I** or **insulin-dependent diabetes mellitus (IDDM)** accounting for about 10% of diabetics and **Type II** or **non insulin-dependent diabetes mellitus (NIDDM),** accounting for about 90% of diabetics. In Type I diabetes, the pancreas doesn't secrete any insulin. In Type II diabetes, either the pancreas doesn't secrete enough insulin or the insulin doesn't work the way it normally should. In either case, the glucose in the blood has a hard time getting into the cells and it accumulates in the blood.

Even though high levels of blood glucose caused by diabetes may go undetected for some time, there are certain symptoms of diabetes that can alert an individual to a potential problem. The most common symptoms are listed in Table 7.9. The one that is most likely to be noticed first is a chronic thirst. If you are experiencing some or all of these symptoms, it is important to get an evaluation by a physician.

Chronically high blood glucose levels can produce serious consequences, including death. Many of the chronic effects of diabetes result from the increased dependency on fats as energy. Diabetes increases the risk for heart disease, stroke, kidney failure, and blindness and is currently the seventh leading cause of death in the U.S.[3]

Although diabetes cannot be cured, it can be treated/managed. The goal of treatment/management is to produce normal carbohydrate, fat, and protein metabolism and thereby decrease the risk of disabling disease and premature death. Type I diabetics usually have to take insulin, either by injections or by constant infusion pumps. Type II diabetics often can manage their diabetes with diet and weight reduction with some needing medication.

TABLE 7.9
Symptoms of Diabetes
• Thirst
• Fatigue
• Weakness
• Weight loss
• Hunger
• Overeating
• Blurred Vision

Risk Factors

Risk factors for diabetes include heredity, age (for Type II), obesity (especially android obesity), and physical inactivity. As is the case for many of the chronic diseases that afflict adults, some of the risk factors are alterable and some are not. Trying to modify the alterable risk factors is an important tool in the battle against diabetes.

Heredity

Genetic factors undoubtedly contribute to the development of diabetes. First-degree relatives are 3 to 6 times more likely to develop diabetes during their lifetime than individuals without a family history of diabetes.[10] If you have a family history of diabetes and since you cannot change who your parents and relatives are, you need to be particularly aware of the other risk factors.

Age

Age is a risk factor in Type II diabetes because the decrease in sensitivity of tissues to insulin appears to develop over time in response to factors such as obesity and activity levels. In fact, Type II diabetes is commonly referred to as adult-onset diabetes because in usually develops in adults as opposed to children. The longer a person is obese or inactive, the more likely they will develop Type II diabetes.

Obesity

Approximately 70 - 90% of adults with Type II diabetes are obese. Although obesity is a risk factor for diabetes it is not a simple matter of just being obese or not obese. The type of obesity is a much better predictor of diabetes than is the level of body fatness. Android obesity (male-pattern obesity), in which much of the fat is in the abdominal region, is a greater risk factor than is gynoid obesity (female-pattern obesity). Obesity is a risk factor because insulin resistance is increased with obesity. Over time, insulin resistance can cause the pancreas to progressively lose its ability to secrete insulin. Figure 7.9 shows the risk of Type II diabetes according to body mass index, a measure of obesity. The risk of Type II diabetes increases about three times in the obese compared to normal-weighted individuals.

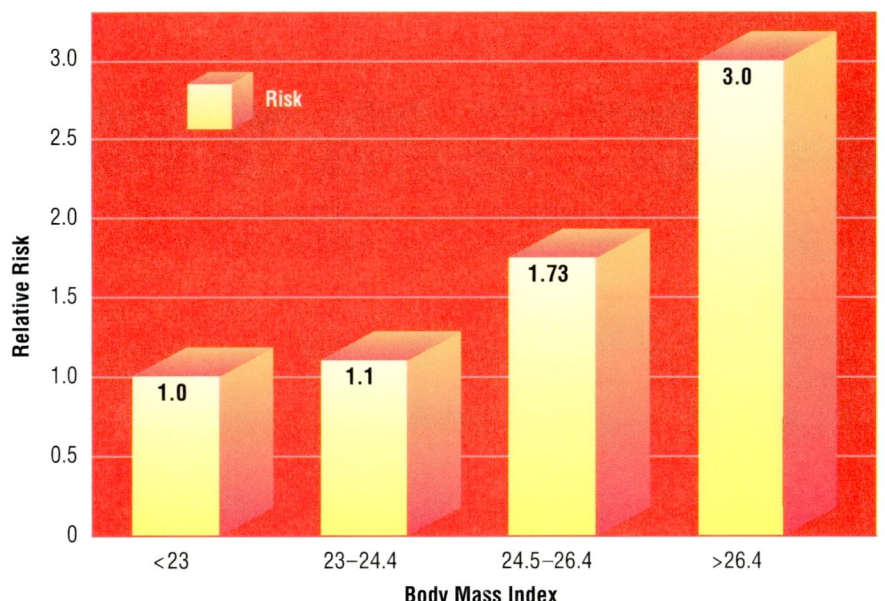

FIGURE 7.9

Diabetes Risk and Obesity. There is a 300% increase in the risk of Type II diabetes in the obese. Source: Manson, J.E., et al. (1992). A prospective study of exercise and incidence of diabetes among U.S. male physicians. *Journal of the American Medical Association,* 268:63–67.

Physical Inactivity

Physical inactivity is a risk factor for diabetes in two ways. First, physical inactivity increases the risk of obesity. Secondly, physical inactivity causes a decrease in the sensitivity of skeletal muscle to insulin. In other words, in the inactive individual, it takes more insulin to do the job. Exercise, improves the ability of muscle to take up glucose so that not as much insulin is required.

Because there is a genetic link, diabetes cannot be totally prevented, especially Type I diabetes. However, because risk factors can be modified through diet and lifestyle, several things can be done to reduce the risk of developing diabetes. Maintaining an active lifestyle and a normal body weight are probably the two most important things that can be done. Regular exercise helps maintain both the normal action of insulin and normal weight.

Diabetes and Diet

Nutrition plays a significant role in diabetes, especially in Type II diabetics. Obesity is a major risk factor for Type II diabetes and weight reduction can be an effective treatment for Type II diabetes. About 80% of Type II diabetics are overweight when they are diagnosed. A primary goal of an overweight diabetic should be to normalize body weight because this may be sufficient to control the diabetes. Therefore, adhering to the same type of advice presented in Chapter 5 on weight management is important.

Although eating specific types of foods probably does not cause a person to develop diabetes, once diabetes is present, eating certain foods can aggravate the disease. The diabetics diet should be similar to the heart-healthy diet recommended in Chapter 6. It should consist primarily of complex carbohydrates with minimal amounts of simple sugars, fat, and alcohol.

KEY CONCEPT

MEASURING BLOOD GLUCOSE

The recent availability of relatively inexpensive blood glucose monitors has make it much easier for diabetics to measure their blood glucose on a regular basis. A small sample of blood is obtained, usually from a finger prick, and blood glucose is obtained in a matter of minutes. Type I diabetics should check their blood glucose several times throughout the day to ensure good glucose control. When a Type I diabetic exercises, glucose should be checked before, during, and after exercise whenever possible.

Diabetes and Exercise

Exercise can be highly beneficial for both types of diabetics. The benefits of exercise are listed in Table 7.10. In particular, exercise can help maintain a more normal weight which is often all that is necessary to manage Type II diabetes.

The type of exercise that is most beneficial for diabetics is aerobic exercise. Not only does aerobic exercise burn the greatest number of calories, but it is easily quantifiable, an important consideration for the diabetic. Because exercise affects the requirement for carbohydrates and fats, doing the same amount of exercise each day is important for Type I diabetics because the regulation of insulin is easier. If the amount of exercise is constantly varied, more or less insulin will be necessary.

If you are diabetic on medication and if you want to start an exercise program, you should consult your physician since it may require an alteration of the amount of medication taken. Table 7.11 lists some important recommendations for the exercising diabetic. By following these recommendations, exercise can be safe and effective.

TABLE 7.10
Health Benefits of Physical Activity in Diabetics

- Improved physical fitness
- Prevention or reduction of obesity
- Improved metabolic control
- Reduced risk of coronary heart disease
- Improved blood lipid profile
- Psychosocial benefits

TABLE 7.11
Recommendations for Diabetic Exercisers

- Make sure your physician is aware you are initiating an exercise program
- Monitor blood glucose frequently when initiating an exercise program
- Do not exercise if glucose concentration is >400 mg/dl
- Inject insulin in an area such as the abdomen that is not active during exercise
- Avoid exercise during periods of peak insulin activity
- Eat carbohydrate snacks before and during prolonged exercise bouts
- Be knowledgeable of the signs and symptoms of hypo- and hyperglycemia
- Exercise with a partner
- Wear a medic alert bracelet
- Make sure to wear good shoes and check feet regularly for sores

Regular exercise can help manage diabetes.

Just because a person is diabetic, does not mean they cannot be a vigorous exerciser or a competitive athlete. Many successful athletes have been diabetic. However, diabetes does make it necessary to follow strategies that ensure a constant control of blood glucose.

OSTEOPOROSIS

Osteoporosis is a disease characterized by low bone mass and deterioration of bone tissue leading to increased incidence of bone fractures, particularly those of the vertebrae, wrist, and hip. By the time bones begin to fracture, up to 30% of the bone mass may have been lost.[8]

Osteoporosis is a silent disease that progresses without any outward sign, sometimes for decades, until a fracture occurs. The disease progresses from about the second and third decades of life until the symptoms of bone fractures and structural deformities become evident in the elderly. However, it is critical to understand that the process which eventually results in osteoporosis begins developing in the twenties and thirties and only becomes evident in the later stages of life.

During the first two or three decades of life, the skeletal system continues to mature and bone mass increases. The greatest increase in bone mass occurs during puberty in both males and females but the absolute amount of bone mass is greater in males. Prior to puberty, there is no difference in bone mass between genders. Peak bone mass, defined as the amount of bony tissue present at the end of the skeletal maturation occurs sometimes between the age of 20 -35 years in most individuals. As we continue to age, bone mass decreases. The likelihood of developing osteoporosis is dependent on how much bone mass is present when bone mass loss begins, and the rate at which bone mass loss occurs. The goal is to arrive at skeletal maturity with as much bone mass as possible and to slow the rate of bone mass loss as much as possible.

Factors Affecting Peak Bone Mass

Several factors influence bone mass accumulation during growth - heredity, gender, nutrition, endocrine factors, mechanical forces, and exposure to risk factors. In order to prevent or postpone osteoporosis, these factors must be considered as early in life as possible in order to develop as much bone mass as possible and to loose the least amount of bone mass possible as aging occurs.

Heredity

Genetic factors are estimated to contribute 70%-80% to the biological potential for peak bone mass.[9] Having a family history of osteoporosis increases the chances of developing the disease. Since you can not choose your parents, it is important to pay close attention to the factors you can influence.

Mechanical Forces (Exercise)

There are numerous studies showing that active men and women have a higher bone mass than sedentary individuals but it has been more difficult to show that exercise substantially increases bone mass.[6] This apparent contradiction can be explained in one of two ways. It may be that active individuals have a genetic predisposition for being active and it is the genetic factors that accounts for the majority of the increased bone mass in active individuals. Alternatively, it may be that in order for exercise to be effective in increasing bone mass, the exercise must occur over decades as opposed to the relatively short periods used in many of the studies on exercise and bone mass. This emphasizes the importance of a lifetime of physical activity, and not just periodic, inconsistent exercise.

There is evidence that the type of exercise is an important consideration. The best type of exercise appears to be exercise that produces mechanical forces on the bones, i.e. weight-bearing exercise. Figure 7.10 shows the difference in bone mass among different types of athletes compared to inactive individuals. Notice that athletes participating in non weight-bearing exercise (swimming) have lower bone masses than those participating in weight-bearing exercise. It is important to emphasize that the impact of exercise is influenced by other factors such as hormonal levels and nutrition. In fact, some athletes participating in weight-bearing exercise (running) may show low bone mass because they strive to have low body weights and therefore their nutrition is poor.

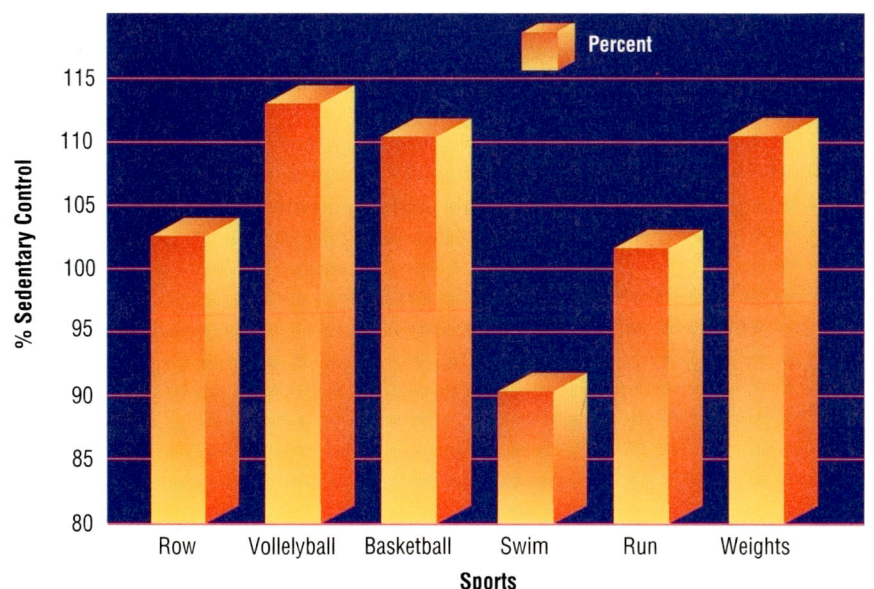

FIGURE 7.10

Bone Mass in Athletes as a Percentage of Bone Mass in Sedentary Individuals. Weight-bearing exercise increases bone mass. Source: Drinkwater, B.L. (1994). Does physical activity play a role in preventing osteoporosis? *Research Quarterly for Exercise and Sport,* 65:197–206.

Gender

Osteoporosis afflicts four times as many women as men. The primary reason women have more of a problem is that they develop less bone mass during their first two or three decades so that when they begin to loose bone, they are more likely to lose enough to cause a problem.

There is also an interaction between bone mass and sex hormones in females. During the years immediately following the cessation of menses, there is a rapid loss of bone associated with the decrease in endogenous estrogen levels. This is why early menopause or surgical removal of the ovaries increases the likelihood of osteoporosis, necessitating hormone replacement therapy at the time of menopause.

Nutrition

Adequate calcium intake is essential to forming and maintaining adequate bone mass. During the first two or three decades of bone development, adequate calcium intake is critical to achieving peak adult bone mass. Following the time of peak bone mass, adequate calcium intake will reduce the rate of bone loss that occurs with aging.

The RDA for calcium is 1200 mg for males and females ages 11-24. After age 24, it is 800 mg. Many think the RDA is too low, especially for females at risk for osteoporosis. Most individuals get much of their calcium from dairy foods but other sources can be used. People who don't consume dairy foods can meet their calcium needs with foods that are fortified with calcium, such as orange juice, or with calcium supplements. Other good sources of calcium are broccoli and dark-green leafy vegetables like kale, tofu, canned fish (eaten with bones), and fortified bread and cereal products. In addition to an adequate source of calcium, vitamin D is also necessary in order for the calcium to be absorbed and used.

Endocrine Factors

Normal levels of female sex hormones are essential for normal bone development in the female. Young females who stop menstruating because of conditions such as anorexia, or because of excessive physical exercise, are at increased risk of developing low peak bone mass. The National Osteoporosis Foundation in conjunction with the National Institutes of Health recommends estrogen replacement therapy for women whose ovaries are removed before age 50.[8]

Risk Factors for Osteoporosis

The development of osteoporosis is dependent on the peak bone mass achieved and on how rapidly bone is lost following the achievement of peak bone mass. The risk factors for osteoporosis can have their impact on either phase of the bone mass development or loss. It is also important that risk factors be identified early in life before peak bone mass is achieved or it becomes difficult to have much impact on peak bone mass. Table 7.12 lists the major risk factors for osteoporosis from the National Osteoporosis Foundation.

TABLE 7.12
Risk Factors for Osteoporosis

- **Age**. The older you are, the greater your risk of osteoporosis. Your bones become less dense and weaker after the age where peak bone mass is achieved.

- **Gender**. Your chances of developing osteoporosis are greater if you are a woman. Women have less bone tissue and lose bone more rapidly than men because of the changes involved in menopause.

- **Race**. Caucasian and Asian women are more likely to develop osteoporosis. However, African American and Hispanic women are also at significant risk.

- **Bone Structure and Body Weight**. Small-boned and thin women are at greater risk.

- **Menopause/Menstrual History**. Normal or early menopause (brought about naturally or because of surgery) increases your risk of developing osteoporosis. In addition, women who stop menstruating before menopause because of conditions such as anorexia or bulimia, or because of excessive physical exercise, may also lose bone tissue and develop osteoporosis.

- **Lifestyle**. Smoking, drinking too much alcohol, consuming inadequate calcium and getting little or no weight bearing exercise increases the risk of osteoporosis.

- **Medications and Disease**. Osteoporosis is associated with certain medications (cortisone-like drugs) and is a recognized complication of a number of medical conditions, including endocrine disorders (having an overactive thyroid), rheumatoid arthritis, and immobilization.

- **Family History**. Susceptibility to fractures may be, in part, hereditary. Young women whose mothers have a history of vertebral fractures also seem to have reduced bone mass.

Source: National Osteoporosis Foundation

Preventing Osteoporosis

Building strong bones, especially before the age of 35, can be the best defense against developing osteoporosis, and a healthy lifestyle can be critically important for developing and keeping bones strong. The factors listed in the previous section on developing peak bone mass are critical for combating osteoporosis. Waiting until after peak bone mass is already determined can be too late for optimal prevention of osteoporosis.

IT'S YOUR CHOICE

One of the nice things about living in our country is that you have a lot of choice about what you can do. Most of the things you choose to do, you do so willingly. No one is holding a gun to your head and forcing you to smoke, drink excessively, or be a couch potato. Unfortunately, many of the choices you make hurt you in the long run.

It is difficult to internalize the concept that what you do today may significantly impact your life for the worse 20 or 30 years in the future. Today you may feel great. Two or three years of nutritional abuse, being a couch potato, or drinking excessively may not produce any noticeable symptoms of permanent damage. Unfortunately, if this type of behavior is continued for 20 years, the symptoms may appear only after the damage has been done. The old cliché "you can't teach an old dog new tricks" is particularly applicable. The longer you practice a habit, the harder it is to change it. The best time to change lifestyle behaviors is before they become so ingrained they become impossible to change. The choice is yours. You can make appropriate behavioral changes now or suffer the potential consequences down the road.

On the bright side, appropriate lifestyle behaviors such as eating right and exercising regularly, allow you to enjoy life more. You feel more energetic, get more accomplished, and generally have a great attitude towards life. Isn't this the better choice?

EXPLORING WELLNESS ON THE WEB

Many resources are available on the World Wide Web. You can reinforce, expand and enhance the information presented in this chapter by accessing the following sites.

Heart Disease

American Heart Association: **www.amhrt.org**

National Heart, Lung, and Blood Institute: **www.nhlbi.nih.gov**

Cancer

American Cancer Society: **www.cancer.org**

National Cancer Institute: **www.nci.nih.gov**

Diabetes Mellitus

International Diabetes Foundation: **www.idf.org**

National Institute of Diabetes and Digestive and Kidney Disease: **www.niddk.nih.gov**

Osteoporosis

National Osteoprorosis Foundation: **www.nof.org**

Osteoporosis and Related Bone Diseases: **www.osteo.org**

REFERENCES

1. American Cancer Society. (1997). *Cancer Facts & Figures*. Available at www.cancer.org.
2. American College of Sports Medicine. (1995). *ACSM's Guidelines for Exercise Testing and Prescription*. 5th edition. Baltimore: Williams & Wilkins.
3. American Heart Association. (1997). *Statistics*. Available at www.amhrt.org.
4. American Heart Association. (1994). *Heart and Stroke Facts*. Dallas: The American Heart Association.
5. Blair, S.N., Kohl, H.W., Paffenbarger, R.S., Clark, D.G., Cooper, K.H., & Gibbons, L.W. (1989). Physical fitness and all-cause mortality. *Journal of the American Medical Association*, 262, 2395-2401.
6. Drinkwater, B. L. (1993). Exercise in the prevention of osteoporosis. *Osteoporosis International*, 3(suppl. 1), 167-171.
7. National Cholesterol Education Program. (1989). Report of the Expert Panel on Detection, Evaluation, and Treatment of High Blood Cholesterol in Adults. U.S. Department of Health and Human Services, National Institutes of Health.
8. National Osteoporosis Foundation. How Can I Prevent Osteoporosis. Available at www.nof.org.
9. Pollitzer, W. S., & Anderson, J. B. (1989). Ethnic and genetic differences in bone mass: A review with a hereditary vs environmental perspective. *American Journal of Clinical Nutrition*, 50, 1244-1259.
10. Yki-Jarvinen, Hannele. (1994). Pathogenesis of non-insulin-dependent diabetes mellitus. *Lancet*, 343, January 8.

DEFINITIONS OF KEY TERMS

angina pectoris — chest pains resulting from insufficient oxygen supply to the heart muscle.

atherosclerosis — the process whereby the inner layers of artery walls become blocked due to deposits of fat, cholesterol and other substances, collectively referred to as "plaque."

benign — non-cancerous.

blood glucose — glucose in the blood that is being circulated and delivered to tissues of the body. Also called blood sugar.

cholesterol — a type of lipid found in animal tissues. High cholesterol is related to formation of plaque in the arteries.

coronary arteries — two arteries arising from the aorta that provide blood to the heart muscle. When these arteries become clogged with plaque, it is called coronary heart disease.

coronary heart disease (CHD) — a disease process whereby the arteries that supply the heart with blood, the coronary arteries, get narrowed by a build-up of a fatty material called plaque. This narrowing of the arteries reduces blood flow and oxygen delivery to the heart muscle.

diabetes mellitus — a disease of abnormal glucose metabolism. As a result of the inability of glucose to enter cells, glucose levels in the blood rise to high values.

diastolic blood pressure — the low reading for blood pressure. It is the pressure of the blood in the arteries when the heart is resting between pumps.

HDL-Cholesterol — high density lipoprotein cholesterol, the so called "good" cholesterol. HDL-cholesterol is being delivered to be metabolized and gotten rid of so it doesn't cause a problem.

heart attack — the result of insufficient oxygen supply to the heart muscle. The heart muscle cells die as a result.

insulin — a hormone secreted by the pancreas that helps glucose enter cells of the body.

LDL-Cholesterol — low density lipoprotein cholesterol, the so called "bad" cholesterol which is found in the plaque blocking the arteries.

malignant — cancerous.

melanoma — a deadly and virulent form of skin cancer.

metastasized — spreading cancer.

osteoporosis — a disease causing thinning and weakening of bone.

plaque- a fatty material that forms on the inside lining of arteries. Cholesterol is a major component of the fatty material.

risk ratio — a ratio of total cholesterol to HDL-cholesterol (TC/HDL-C). It is a measure of how much of the total cholesterol is HDL-C or good cholesterol. The lower the ratio the better. Ratios less than 3.5 are considered low risk.

saturated fat — animal fat. Saturated fat consumption causes the body to produce more cholesterol than the body needs resulting in high cholesterol values.

systolic blood pressure — the high reading for blood pressure. It is the pressure of the blood in the arteries when the heart is pumping.

LAB 7.1

ASSESSING CORONARY HEART DISEASE RISK*

Name _____ ID _____ Sect _____ Time _____ Date _____

Purpose

To determine your risk of developing coronary heart disease.

Directions

Assess your current status with respect to each of the risk factors in the table below. Put the appropriate point value for each risk factor in the blank in the column labeled **Score**. Total all the scores for a final **Total Score**.

Risk Factors	Criteria	Risk Value	Your Score
Age	Age 56 or over	1	_____
Gender	Male	1	_____

Family History	If you have:
	Blood relatives who have had a heart attack
	    or stroke at or before age 60
	Blood relatives who have had a heart attack
	    or stroke after age 60
		
		12
		
		6
			
			_____

Personal History	If you are 50 or under and have had a heart attack,
	    stroke, or surgery to reduce blockage in arteries
	    anywhere in the body
	If you are 51 or over and have had a heart attack,
	    stroke, or surgery to reduce blockage in arteries
	    anywhere in the body
		
		20
		
		10
			
			_____

Diabetes	If you are age 40 or less and have diabetes If you are age 41-55 and have diabetes Any age with diabetes that is controlled with diet or diabetes developing after age 55	10 5 3	 _____

Smoking	Two packs per day or more
	One to two packs per day or quit smoking less than
	    one year ago or smoke 6 or more cigars a day or
	    inhale a pipe regularly
	Less than one pack per day or quit smoking
	    more than one year ago
		10
		
		6
		
		3
			
			_____

(Continued)

LAB 7.1 (CONCLUDED)

ASSESSING CORONARY HEART DISEASE RISK*

Cholesterol (If cholesterol level is not known, answer #8)	If your total cholesterol is: >275 mg/dl 225-275 mg/dl	10 5 _____
Diet (if you answered #7, do not answer #8)	If your normal eating pattern includes: One serving of red meat daily, more than seven eggs a week, and daily consumption of butter, whole milk, and cheese. Red meat 4-6 times a week, 4-7 eggs a week, margarine, low fat dairy products and some cheese.	8 4 _____
High Blood Pressure	If either number is: 160/100 or higher 140/90 to 159/99	10 5 _____
Weight	Compute your ideal weight using: Males = 110 lb plus 5 lb for each inch over 60" Females = 100 lb plus 5 lb for each inch over 60" If you are the following lb overweight: 25 pounds overweight 10-24 pounds overweight	4 2 _____
Exercise	If you engage in any aerobic exercise for more than 15 minutes each session for: less than once a week 1 to 2 times a week	4 2 _____
Stress	If you are: Frustrated when waiting in line, often in a hurry to complete work or keep appointments, easily angered, irritable Impatient when waiting, occasionally hurried, or occasionally moody	4 2 _____

Total Score _____

Risk Classification:

If you were able to answer question #9:

High Risk	≥ 40
Medium Risk	20-39
Low Risk	≤ 19

If you were not able to answer question #9:

High Risk	≥ 36
Medium Risk	19-35
Low Risk	≤ 18

*Adapted from the Arizona Heart Institute Cardiovascular Risk Factor Analysis.

LAB 7.2

ASSESSING CANCER RISK

Name _____ ID _____ Sect _____ Time _____ Date _____

Purpose

To determine your risk of developing various types of cancers.

Directions

1. Circle the response that best describes your characteristics and behaviors. Select one best response to each characteristic/behavior even though one of the responses may not exactly apply to you.

2. Males should answer only the first three sections. Females should answer all sections unless you have had a complete hysterectomy, in which case females skip the sections on cervical and endometrial cancers.

3. Sum all the points circled for each section and record in the **Total Points** blank at the end of the section. Use the chart at the end of this lab to assess your risk based on the total points for each type of cancer.

LUNG CANCER

1. Gender

    (2) - Male (1) - Female

2. Age

    (1) - 39 or less   (2) - 40 to 45

    (5) - 50 to 59   (7) - >59

3. Smoking behavior

    (1) - nonsmoker   (8) - smoker

4. Type of smoking

    (1) - cigarettes or little cigars

    (3) - pipe and/or cigar, but no cigarettes

    (2) - ex-smoker

    (1) - nonsmoker

5. Amount of cigarettes smoked per day

    (1) - zero

    (5) - Less than 1/2 pack

    (9) - 1/2 - 1 pack

    (15) - 1-2 packs

    (20) - 2 or more packs

6. Type of cigarette

    (10) - High tar/nicotine

    (9) - medium tar/nicotine

    (7) - low tar/nicotine

    (1) - Nonsmoker

7. Duration of smoking

    (1) - never smoked

    (3) - Ex-smoker

    (5) - Up to 15 years

    (10) - 15-25 years

    (20) - 25 or more years

8. Type of industrial work

    (3) - Mining

    (5) - Uranium and radioactive products

    (7) - Asbestos

    Total Points - Lung Cancer _____

(Continued)

SKIN CANCER

1. Frequent work or play in the sun

   (10) - Yes   (1) - No

2. Work in mines, around coal tars, or around radioactivity

   (10) - Yes   (1) - No

3. Complexion - fair skin and/or light skin

   (10) - Yes   (1) - No

   Total Points - Skin Cancer _____

COLON AND RECTAL CANCER

1. Age

   (10) - <40

   (20) - 40 to 59

   (50) - 60 and over

2. Has anyone in you immediate family ever had

   (20) - Colon cancer

   (10) - One or more colon polyps

   (1) - Neither

3. Have you ever had

   (100) - Colon cancer

   (40) - One or more colon polyps

   (20) - Ulcerative colitis

   (10) - Cancer of the breasts or uterus

   (1) - None

4. Bleeding from the rectum (other than obvious hemorrhoids or piles)

   (75) - Yes   (1) - No

   Total Points - Colon and Rectal Cancer _____

BREAST CANCER (WOMEN ONLY)

1. Age group

   (10) - 20 to 34

   (40) - 35 to 49

   (90) - 50 and over

2. Racial group

   (5) - Asian

   (20) - African American

   (25) - Non-Hispanic White

   (10) - Hispanic

3. Family history

   (30) - Mother, sister, aunt, or grandmother with breast cancer

   (10) - none

4. Your history

   (10) - No breast disease

   (25) - Previous lumps or cysts

   (100) - Previous breast cancer

5. Maternity

   (10) - 1st pregnancy before 25

   (15) - 1st pregnancy after 25

   (20) - no pregnancies

   Total Points - Breast Cancer _____

CERVICAL CANCER (WOMEN ONLY)

1. Age Group

   (10) - Less than 25

   (20) - 25 to 39

   (30) - 40 and over

2. Racial group

   (10) - Asian

   (20) - African American

   (10) - Non-Hispanic

   (20) - Hispanic

(Continued)

Name _____ ID _____ Sect _____ Time _____ Date _____

3. Number of pregnancies

   (10) - zero

   (20) - 1 to 3

   (30) - 4 and over

4. Viral infections

   (10) - Herpes and other viral infections or ulcer formations on the vagina

   (1) - Never

5. Age at first intercourse

   (40) - Before 15

   (30) - 15 to 19

   (20) - 20 to 24

   (10) - 25 and over

   (5)- Never

6. Bleeding between periods or after intercourse

   (40) - Yes   (1) - No

   Total Points - Cervical Cancer _____

ENDOMETRIAL CANCER

1. Age

   (5) - 39 years and under

   (20) - 40 - 49 years

   (60) - 50 years and over

2. Race

   (10) - black   (10) - Hispanic

   (10) - oriental   (20) - white

3. Births

   (15) - none

   (7) - 1 to 4

   (5) - 5 or more

4. Weight

   (50) - 50 or more pounds overweight

   (15) - 20 to 49 pounds overweight

   (10) - underweight for height

   (10) - normal weight

5. Diabetes

   (3) - Yes   (1) - No

6. Estrogen hormone intake

   (15) - Yes, regularly

   (12) - Yes, occasionally

   (10) - None

7. Abnormal uterine bleeding

   (40) - Yes   (1) - No

8. High blood pressure

   (3) - Yes   (1) - No

   Total Points - Endometrial Cancer _____

(Continued)

Risk Level Interpretation

Type of Cancer	Very Low Risk	Low Risk	Moderate Risk	High Risk	Very High Risk
Lung/Colon	6-24	25-40	41-54	55-74	≥75
Rectum		13-29	30-69	≥70	
Skin		3	10-20	20-30	
Breast		45-100	100-199	≥200	
Cervical		40-69	70-99	≥100	
Endometrial		45-69	60-99	≥100	

Adapted from American Cancer Society material.

NOTES

Health Concerns of Psychoactive Drugs, Tobacco and Alcohol

Scott W. Roberts

INTRODUCTION

The use of drugs in America seriously threatens our health, productivity and quality of life. Approximately 30 percent of all Americans die prematurely due to the use of drugs, alcohol, and tobacco. From an economic standpoint, drug use costs the nation's economy over 100 billion dollars a year. Much of this cost is attributed to lost productivity. However, the problem of drug use involves a wide range of issues. This chapter focuses on the long- and short-term effects of drugs on the body's health, the process of addiction, drug education, and personal awareness.

THE PROCESS OF DRUG ADDICTION

The World Health Organization defines addiction as a pathological relationship to any mood-altering experience that has life-damaging results. Simply stated, addiction is any behavior that is triggered by a compulsion. The well known book titled, *The Addictive Personality: Roots, Rituals and Recovery,* by Craig Nakken describes three characteristics of individuals with addictive personalities. An addictive individual usually exhibits at least one of the following traits:

- Individuals who never have bonded with other people

- Individuals who have been taught not to trust others

- Individuals who do not have healthy relationships with friends, family and lovers

Chemical or drug addiction produces the most profound addiction because drugs can cause mood changes. Initially the drug provides a sense of pleasure and /or stability that seems to be obtainable only through the drug. Chemical or drug addiction in itself is progressive because individuals seek drugs as a relief from unpleasant feelings or situations. Drugs also cause cellular changes so that the body requires the chemicals to function comfortably.

It is often difficult to tell when a habit has become an addiction. Table 8.1 may help to clarify the fragile line between habit and addiction.

Health professionals recognize the process of chemical or drug addiction using four main criteria. They are:

- Continual involvement in addictive behavior despite negative health, legal, financial, or social consequence

- Loss of control when engaging in the addictive behavior

TABLE 8.1
Drug Addiction and Drug Habituation

Drug Addiction	Drug Habituation
Drug addiction is a state of periodic or chronic intoxication produced by the repeated consumption of a drug (natural or synthetic). Its characteristics include:	Drug habituation (habit) is a condition resulting from the repeated consumption of a drug. Its characteristics include:
An overpowering desire or need (compulsion) to continue taking the drug and to obtain it by any means.	A desire (but not a compulsion) to continue taking the drug for the sense of improved well-being which it engenders.
A tendency to increase the dose.	Little or no tendency to increase the dose.
A psychic (psychological) and generally a physical dependence on the effects of the drug.	Some degree of psychic dependency on the effect of the drug, but absence of physical dependence.
Detrimental effect on the individual and on society.	Detrimental effects, if any, primarily on the individual.

- Denial—the inability to perceive that there is a problem

- Relapse—a strong tendency or pattern of relapse when the substance is taken away from the individual.

Howard Schaffer, a Harvard psychologist states, "addiction is a two edged sword, it serves as it destroys." Individuals lose control and continue addictive behavior despite the negative consequences. Table 8.2 highlights the dynamics of addiction. Table 8.3 gives the general warning signs of chemical addiction.

ADDICTION AND THE FAMILY

The effects of drug or chemical addiction are not limited to the addict. Unfortunately, children suffer for their parents' mistakes, as the basic emotional needs of children in addictive homes are rarely or inconsistently met. In addition, many young children face sexual or other forms of abuse. Furthermore, children from addictive homes are at a high risk for developing their own addiction.

There are unmeasurable social costs for children raised in addictive homes. Many times they are deprived of a proper education and their ability to foster relationships with others is impaired. Basically, they lack the stability that is needed for proper social and intellectual development.

The family dynamics in addictive homes are dysfunctional. Many times the non-addictive family members experience feelings that their family is different than other families. They may also experience feelings of shame.

TABLE 8.2
Dynamics of Addiction

- Distorted balance between pleasure, work and pain.
- Individual is either miserable or high causing a constant state of denial.
- Eventually, a substance is not used for pleasure, but for relief of pain.

TABLE 8.3
Warning Signs of Chemical or Drug Addiction

- Antisocial behavior
- Chronic dishonesty (lying, stealing, cheating)
- Possession of large amounts of money
- Inappropriate anger or hostility
- Reduced motivation
- Reduced self-esteem
- Diminished interest in extracurricular activities and hobbies
- Unhealthy appearance

Normal family relationships can be torn apart if a member becomes dependent on drugs, alcohol or other addictive behaviors.

KEY CONCEPT

COST OF CHEMICAL ADDICTION IN LIVES

In 1997 there were approximately ten thousand deaths in the U.S. directly attributed to chemical addiction. When one considers the impact of drug-related infant deaths, motor-vehicle deaths and drug-related diseases, such as hepatitis and HIV, the true death rate is twenty thousand deaths per year. Most statistical figures do not reflect the estimated 200,000 that die each year from alcohol use or the 500,000 that die each year from tobacco-related illness.

Eventually the non-addictive family members begin displaying addictive behaviors (i.e. lying, denial), but they do not view themselves as needing help.

Many children from dysfunctional homes suffer from what psychologists call post-traumatic stress disorder (PTSD). This condition was first recognized in combat soldiers. Individuals who suffer from PTSD may experience the following symptoms:

- Psychic numbing-ability to suspend feeling
- Survivor guilt—irrational, but painful sense of guilt (i.e. children believe it is their fault that dad or mom drink)
- Hypervigilance—a radar that helps individuals monitor their surroundings
- Re-experience of trauma—a flashback or sudden re-emergence of feelings, thoughts and behaviors that were present during trauma

Concept of Codependency

Codependency is defined as an unconscious addiction to another person's dysfunctional behavior. The concept of codependency was first applied to the wives of alcoholics who were said to be "co-alcoholics."[8] Now codependency is also seen as a major outcome of the dysfunctional family system. A codependent's environment is highly unstable, stressful, unpredictable, and, in general, disorderly. Codependents often exhibit compulsive behaviors but they never view themselves as needing help. They actually become unaware of their own feelings, needs, and, in some cases, their own drug abuse.[2]

The codependent transcends through three distinct stages that lead to the loss of control and denial. In the first stage, **experimental codependency,** the codependent will attempt to control the addict's use of drugs. Often this is done by " joining the party" and using drugs themselves. In this stage, the codependent is likely to mimic the compulsive behaviors of the addict in an effort to show the addict how they appear to others. This can be dangerous because the codependent runs the risk of becoming addicted also.

The next stage is termed **situational codependency**. In this stage the codependent attempts to minimize the addict's behavior when speaking to others or tries to cover up the outward display of drug addiction during social events. During this stage, the codependent is actually enabling (see concept of enabling below) the behavior to continue.

The next stage is **complete codependency**. This occurs when life focuses entirely on the addict's drug problem or dysfunctional behavior. During this stage, one crisis turns into another and the codependent allows the behavior to continue. An example would be a wife allowing her husband to drive while intoxicated. Figure 8.1 illustrates the three stages described.

FIGURE 8.1

Three Stages of Codependency.
Illustration by Meegan Hamilton

Experimental Codependency   Situational Codependency   Complete Codependency

Concept of Enabling

Enabling individuals are people who knowingly or unknowingly protect addicts from the natural consequences of their behavior. Thus, the addict is never held responsible for his/her own actions. Codependents are primary enablers of their addicted loved ones. An example would be the wife of an alcoholic who calls her husband's boss to explain that her husband will not be in today because he has a bad cold, when he is really drunk or hung over.

Enabling is rarely conscious or intentional and most people are really just trying to help. This help is misguided, however, and just perpetuates the addictive behavior. In order to end enabling behavior one must learn new techniques for interacting with the addicted individual. One technique to stop enabling behaviors is the "Tuff Love" philosophy which says that the addictive individual is accountable and responsible for the consequences of his/her own behavior.

ALCOHOL AND SOCIETY

According to the U.S. Department of Education, sixty percent of all American adults are regular drinkers, and alcohol use is involved in 240,000 deaths per year. Heavy consumption of alcohol or "binge drinking" is defined in the *Journal of the American Medical Association* as consumption of five or more drinks in a row for men and four or more drinks in a row for women.[13] Binge drinking has been associated with unplanned and unsafe sexual activities, physical and sexual assault, unintentional injuries, and various other criminal violations. In addition, poor academic performance among high school and college students, as well as interpersonal problems are attributed to alcohol usage.[13]

Drinking can adversely affect your health long-term or, when combined with driving, can injure and kill instantly.

Alcohol Perspectives

Alcohol is integrated into every aspect of the American lifestyle. This fact alone causes many parents, educators, clergy, law enforcement personnel, and justice system officials to deny and ignore the impact of alcohol on our society. To date, the war on drugs excludes alcohol as an enemy.

Drinking is socially approved by our society for relaxation purposes. Some psychologists propose that alcohol helps individuals transcend into an altered state of consciousness. Alcohol releases individuals from their inhibitions as well as their concerns.

Cultural Patterns for Drinking

Drinking behavior patterns are often influenced by cultural and environmental up-bringing. For example, Germans often have beer during celebrations such as their Oktoberfest. In France and Italy, children and adults drink wine at the dinner table. In America it is standard to drink most of our alcohol away from main meals. Chinese families generally don't drink in the home because the Asiatic biochemistry doesn't process alcohol very well. Orientals posses a gene that inhibits the effectiveness of aldehyde dehyrogenase, therefore a toxic accumulation of acetaldehyde forms which leads to reactions such as the "flushing response" (red face) along with nausea and sweating.

Impact of Alcohol on Women

Physiologically women appear to produce lower levels of the enzyme aldehyde dehydrogenase which is responsible for the metabolism of alcohol. The result is that women absorb about 30 percent more alcohol than men into the bloodstream before the liver metabolizes it. This enables alcohol to reach the brain and other vital organs very quickly, producing rapid intoxication as well as high toxicity levels in vital organs.

The penalties for excessive use of alcohol are more severe for women than men. A commonly understood fact among alcohol treatment specialists is that women may drink less and for shorter periods of time than men yet they experience greater physiological consequences. Alcoholic women have a higher mortality rate than alcoholic men.[4] Premature deaths from accidents, violence and digestive disorders such as pancreatitis and cirrhosis, are higher among women.[6]

Alcohol consumption has also been associated with breast cancer. Recent studies have warned women about drinking alcohol at moderate levels. In two separate studies reported in *The John Hopkins Medical Letter*[7] women who drank moderately were 50 percent more likely to develop breast cancer than non-drinkers. Finally, alcohol consumption has been linked with osteoporosis. Alcohol not only blocks the absorption of nutrients, including calcium, but its diuretic effect flushes important nutrients out of the body.

Alcohol on Campus

The December 7, 1994 issue of the *Journal of the American Medical Association* (JAMA)[12] contained a national survey of college student's drinking behavior. The survey, conducted at 140 campuses across the country, also reported on health and alcohol related problems among the students. In summary, 44 percent of college students that responded to the *JAMA* survey

Drinking patterns differ among different cultures.

Binge drinking is common behavior on campus.

Illustration by Meegan Hamilton

Raising the drinking age has saved an increasing number of lives each year since 1975.

Source: National Highway Traffic Safety Administration.

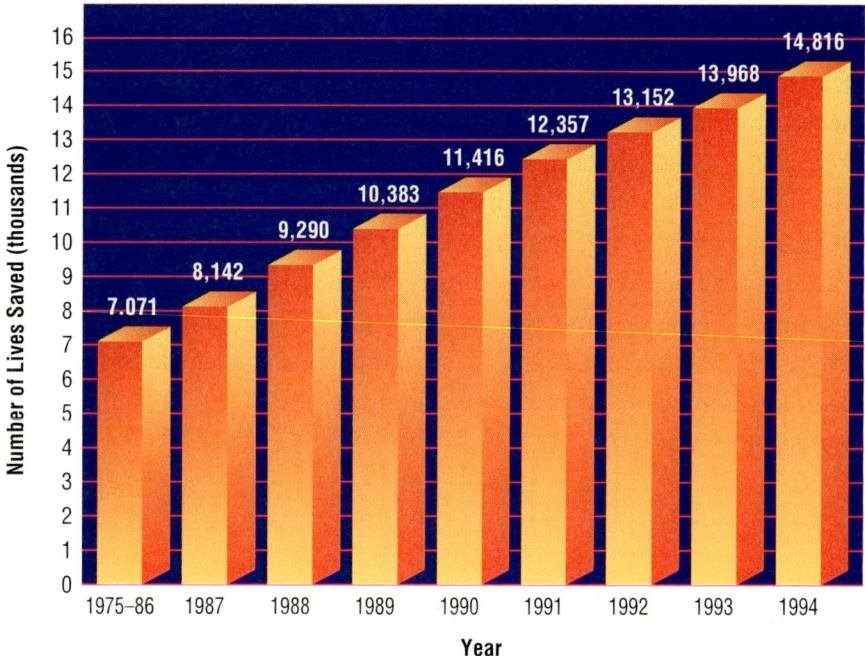

were binge drinkers. Close to half, 47 percent of the frequent binge drinkers, experienced five or more different drinking-related problems which included physical injuries, engaging in unplanned sex, and verbal or physical assault. The Commission on Substance Abuse at Colleges and Universities found that alcohol was involved in two-thirds of college student's suicides, in 90 percent of campus rapes, and in 95 percent of violent crime on campus. Many college and universities have banned the sale of alcohol on campus to anyone under the age of twenty-one. The National Highway Traffic Safety Administration (NHTSA) has estimated that the 21 year-old minimum drinking age laws have reduced traffic fatalities among 18- to 20-year olds by 13 percent and saved an estimated 14,816 lives since 1975 (see Figure 8.2).

Drinking and Driving

Alcohol is believed to be the cause of more than half of all fatal automobile accidents in the United States. Every thirty-two minutes someone dies from an alcohol-related traffic accident.[10] Problem drinkers are a small fraction of the total drinking population and cause more than their share of traffic accidents but the majority of alcohol-related traffic accidents are caused by individuals who have never been identified as problem drinkers or alcoholics. For instance, younger drivers have more than their share of alcohol-related accidents. Table 8.4 summarizes the Objectives for Alcohol Use from *Healthy People 2000* which targets young adults.[9] Table 8.5 summarizes current strategies that are helping reduce the usage of alcohol by young adults.

TABLE 8.4

Healthy People 2000 Objectives for Alcohol Use

The U.S. Department of Health and Human Services has the following goals for the year 2000:

- Establish effective driver's license suspension or revocation laws in all 50 states for people caught driving under the influence of alcohol or drugs.

- Establish laws in all 50 states that reduce legal blood alcohol concentration to 0.04% in adults and 0.00% in those younger than 21.

- Have less than 28% of high school seniors and less than 32% of college students engage in episodes of heavy drinking.

- Establish laws that more effectively limit access to alcohol by minors in all 50 states.

- Reduce deaths from alcohol-related motor vehicle accidents to 8.5 per 100,000 people.

TABLE 8.5

Summation of Current Strategies to Reduce Alcohol Use In Young Adults

- Identify repeat offenders through computer technology.

- Publicize, in the mass media, the danger of drinking and driving especially targeting young adults.

- Evoke pressure on high school and college campuses to enforce strict alcohol and drug policies.

- Establish non-alcoholic recreational activities on or near campus to provide students with an alternative to alcohol-related activities.

- Set up peer education programs, support groups and other non-judgmental opportunities for students to seek help and information.

Short-Term Physiological Effects

Alcohol affects the brain by depressing the highest brain functions first, primarily those in the frontal lobes which involve values and self-aware-ness. Next, the drinker's decision making, judgment, and reaction time are all adversely affected. Alcohol affects sensation and perception by decreasing both visual and hearing acuity. It also alters sensitivity to odor and taste. The consumption of alcohol impairs emotions by reducing inhibitions and fears. This usually leads to an increase in risk-taking behaviors.

Regular users of alcohol experience symptoms of anxiety, tiredness, and impaired concentration after sleep. This occurs because REM (rapid eye movement) or dream sleep patterns are impaired by alcohol. Acute doses of alcohol increase heart rate and blood pressure by constricting arteries supplying the heart. If a large enough quantity of alcohol is consumed, brain

TABLE 8.6

Sensible Practices for Serving and Drinking Alcohol

Drinking Alcohol	Serving Alcohol
Restrict your drinking, even on special occasions.	Plan a party so that guests can move around and won't be tempted to just stand in a corner and drink.
Avoid drinking daily or regularly.	
Know your limit and make sure you don't exceed it. Keep track of your drinks.	
Avoid mixed drinks that use two kinds of liquor. They are stronger and will get you drunk faster.	Pace the drinks. Serve drinks at reasonable intervals, but don't push them.
Drink slowly. The faster you drink, the drunker you'll get.	Make sure people get what they expect in their drinks. Don't serve doubles.
Never drink on an empty stomach. Food slows down the absorption of alcohol.	
Break the habit of thinking that you need to drink alcohol to have a good time at parties.	Serve plenty of non-salty snacks.
Make conversation while you're drinking, to get your attention away from the alcohol.	Serve some non-alcoholic beverages.
Avoid bars and lounges when you are just killing time in an airport or train station.	Don't end the party with drinks. Stop serving liquor and offer coffee, tea, and a good-sized snack.
At parties or dinners, delay having your first drink as long as possible, to cut down on the amount of time you spend drinking.	
Accept a drink only if you really want one.	DON'T LET ANYONE WHO SEEMS EVEN SLIGHTLY TIPSY GET BEHIND THE WHEEL OF A CAR.
When you eat out, have your drinks with dinner, not afterward.	
If a friend suggests that you have a drinking problem, take the comment seriously and get help.	

functions are severely depressed and breathing could cease altogether. The practice of binge (large quantities in a short time span) drinking mentioned earlier in this chapter has been responsible for a few deaths in recent years. In most cases, the user vomits before this occurs, thus saving themselves from death by alcohol overdose.

Alcohol can be used sensibly, thus reducing the risk of adverse side effects. Table 8.6 gives some recommendations for serving and drinking alcohol.

Chronic Physiologic Effects

Long-term effects of prolonged alcohol consumption can produce a combination of physiologically and psychologically chronic conditions. The most common affliction associated with heavy consumption of alcohol is liver disease. When one consumes alcohol, the role of the liver is to metabolize alcohol. Chronic consumption forces the liver to metabolize excessive amounts. When the liver overworks, it produces fat which begins to accumulate in the liver. This eventually leads to scarring and destruction of healthy, functional liver cells. The end result is a small, rock-hard liver with very little functioning cells remaining. This deterioration, called **cirrhosis of the liver**, is often a fatal condition.

Chronic alcohol consumption is also associated with damage to the cardiovascular system. Heavy drinking increases the work load on the heart and reduces the coronary blood flow to the heart muscle. This naturally decreases cardiac output and the heart beat becomes erratic (**arrhythmia**). In addition to causing arrhythmia, heavy alcohol consumption can cause a condition called **cardiomyopathy.** This condition often leads to damage of the valves and musculature of the heart.

Chronic heavy drinking is also linked with an increased risk of cancer of the mouth, esophagus, stomach, liver and bladder. The risk of these cancers is often greater if the person smokes cigarettes or uses tobacco products and is a heavy user of alcohol. Cancer in the oral cavity and pharynx was responsible for 8,260 deaths in 1996.[1] The majority of individuals who fall prey to this type of cancer are males who have abused both alcohol and tobacco. Alcohol also acts as a catalyst of cancer in the lungs, pancreas, prostate, and intestines. Figure 8.3 summarizes long-term risks associated with chronic alcohol use.

FIGURE 8.3

Long-term effects of chronic alcohol use.

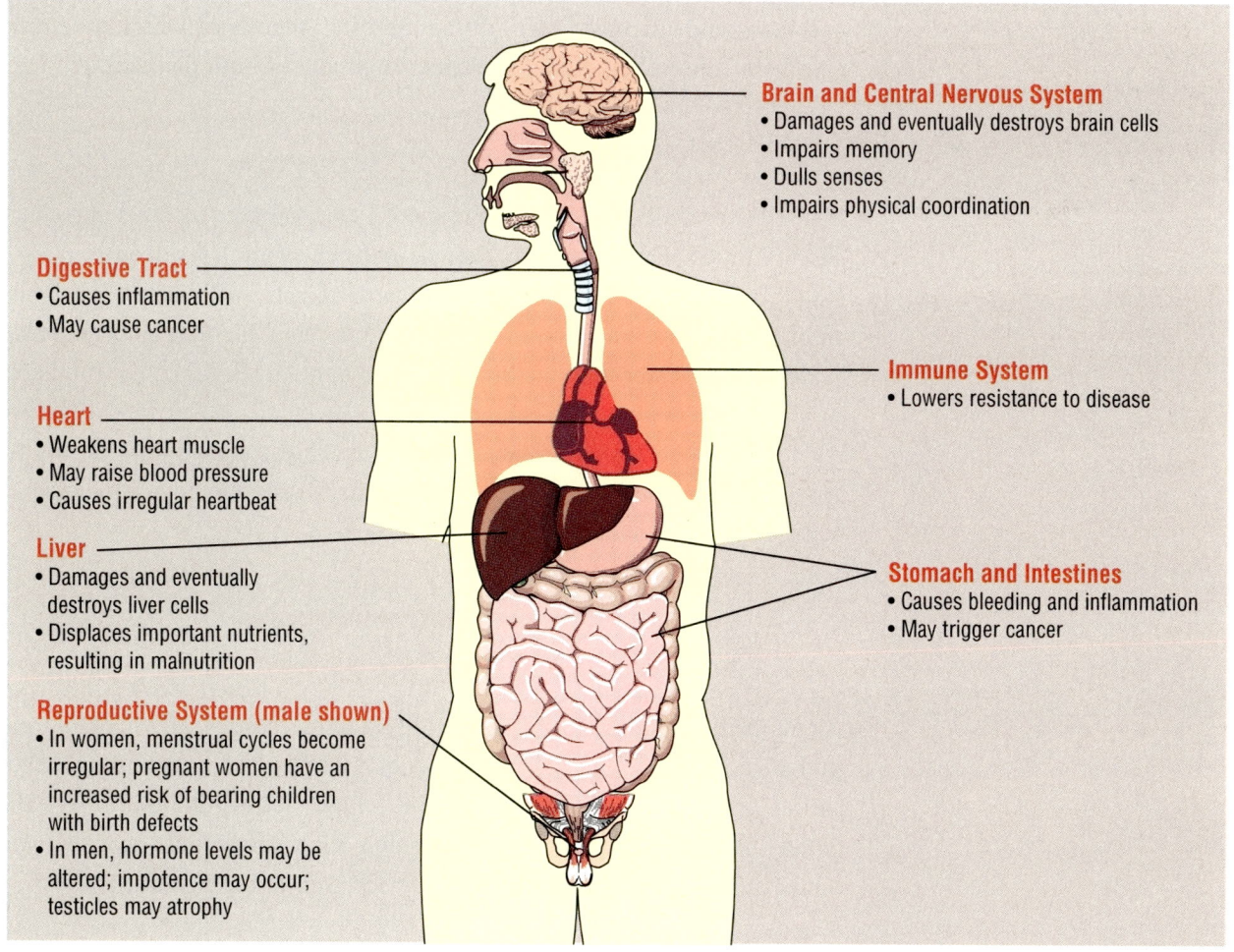

Brain and Central Nervous System
• Damages and eventually destroys brain cells
• Impairs memory
• Dulls senses
• Impairs physical coordination

Digestive Tract
• Causes inflammation
• May cause cancer

Immune System
• Lowers resistance to disease

Heart
• Weakens heart muscle
• May raise blood pressure
• Causes irregular heartbeat

Liver
• Damages and eventually destroys liver cells
• Displaces important nutrients, resulting in malnutrition

Stomach and Intestines
• Causes bleeding and inflammation
• May trigger cancer

Reproductive System (male shown)
• In women, menstrual cycles become irregular; pregnant women have an increased risk of bearing children with birth defects
• In men, hormone levels may be altered; impotence may occur; testicles may atrophy

Nervous System and Nutritional Problems

Alcohol has virtually no nutritional value (empty calories). Since heavy drinkers substitute alcohol for healthy foods, they usually experience nutritional deficiencies. Chronic consumption of alcohol also disrupts normal digestion processes. This usually results in inflammation of the stomach lining (gastritis), stomach ulcers, and intestinal lesions or sores which interfere with proper metabolism of vitamins and minerals. This malnourished state may predispose the chronic alcoholic to certain diseases of the nervous system.

Two of the most common nervous system diseases associated with malnutrition and alcoholism are **Wernicke's syndrome** and **Korsakoff's psychosis**. Wernicke's syndrome is associated with thiamine deficiency. It is characterized by double vision, involuntary and rapid movements of the eyes, lack of muscular coordination, and decreased mental function, which may be mild or severe.

The cause of Korsakoff's psychosis can be traced to degenerative changes in the thalamus as a result of a deficiency in B complex vitamins, especially thiamine and B_{12}. The condition is a form of amnesia, characterized by a loss of short term memory and the inability to learn new skills. Korsakoff's psychosis and Wernicke's syndrome are often manifested simultaneously and the alcoholic individual exhibits symptoms of both diseases.

Fetal Alcohol Syndrome

Ingestion of alcohol by a pregnant woman can damage the fetus and cause abnormalities. This condition, known as **fetal alcohol syndrome**, is estimated to be the third leading cause of birth defects and mental retardation among newborns. The alcohol content in the fetus' blood may be as much as ten times greater than the blood alcohol content (BAC) of the mother's, so even a small amount of alcohol could endanger normal fetal development. It is especially important to curtail alcohol consumption during the first weeks or months of prenatal development since the nervous system is being formed at that time.

THEORIES OF ALCOHOLISM

Alcoholism is multifactorial. There are as many reasons why people drink as there are alcoholics. Alcoholism is not specific to social standing, occupation, intelligence, education, national origin, race or religion. In fact, the typical alcoholics are not skid row bums. They are middle management executives in their middle thirties, married, and living in suburbia.

Type I and Type II Alcoholics

There are two basic types of alcoholic behavior patterns. A Type I alcoholic is an individual whose symptoms are fairly mild. For example, a Type I alcoholic is rarely involved in criminal activity and seldom demonstrates violent behavior. Type I drinkers usually have at least one parent of either sex that is an alcoholic. Females as well as males show Type I alcoholic behavior and their drinking patterns often begin later in life (late twenties). Finally, the environment is believed to be the "releaser" for Type I alcoholic drinking behaviors.

Type II behavior is only found in males and is believed to pass from father to son. The behavior pattern is independent of environmental influences. This male limited pattern has been associated with extremely violent behavior and criminal activity. Type II behavior usually shows up in the teens or early twenties. Some experts believe that Type II individuals are addicted as soon as they take their first drink of alcohol.

Genetic Theory

Recent research has uncovered evidence linking a specific gene to alcohol addiction. The gene is a receptor gene for dopamine, a biochemical substance found in certain areas of the brain that plays a vital role in one's pleasure responses. The theory is that alcoholics are deficient in dopamine so they seek pleasurable feelings through alcohol.

There is some evidence that heredity plays a role in alcoholism, particularly among males. Studies of adopted children have shown that sons of alcoholics are three to four times more likely to become alcoholics than sons of non-alcoholics, regardless of whether they were raised by the alcoholic parents or by non-alcoholic adoptive parents.[11]

Sociocultural Theory

The perception of drunken behavior as deviant depends on the culture in which it occurs. Many behaviorists point out that society has ambivalent attitudes and conflicting values regarding alcohol. For example, on the one hand our culture subliminally encourages alcoholism by accepting "relief drinking" and promoting the perception that intoxication is funny and "manly." On the other hand, our values tell us that alcoholism is deviant behavior and it causes many problems in our country.

Society sends mixed messages, therefore there are a mixture of reasons for drinking. Some people drink to be "social", others drink to express their defiance against society.

Psychological Theory

The psychological theory states that alcoholics drink in an attempt to decrease their stress levels. Since alcohol induces pleasure and helps one avoid discomfort or pain, the act of drinking reinforces drinking behavior and the cycle of abuse begins.

Alcoholic or addictive individuals seem to share some general personality characteristics including:

- Immaturity
- Impulsiveness
- Low self-esteem
- Self-destructive behavior
- Compulsiveness

It is not clear whether these personality characteristics predispose one to alcoholism or whether they are the result of years of abuse.

TOBACCO AND SOCIETY

Nicotine, the main psychoactive component of tobacco, is the primary reason people continue to use tobacco products. According to the Centers for Disease Control, tobacco kills 434,000 U.S. citizens each year. Tobacco related deaths exceed those related to alcohol, cocaine, heroin, homicide, suicide, fires, car accidents, and AIDS combined (see Figure 8.4). Once an

FIGURE 8.4

Comparison of tobacco-related deaths versus alcohol, cocaine, crack, heroin, homicide, suicide, car accidents, fires, and AIDS.

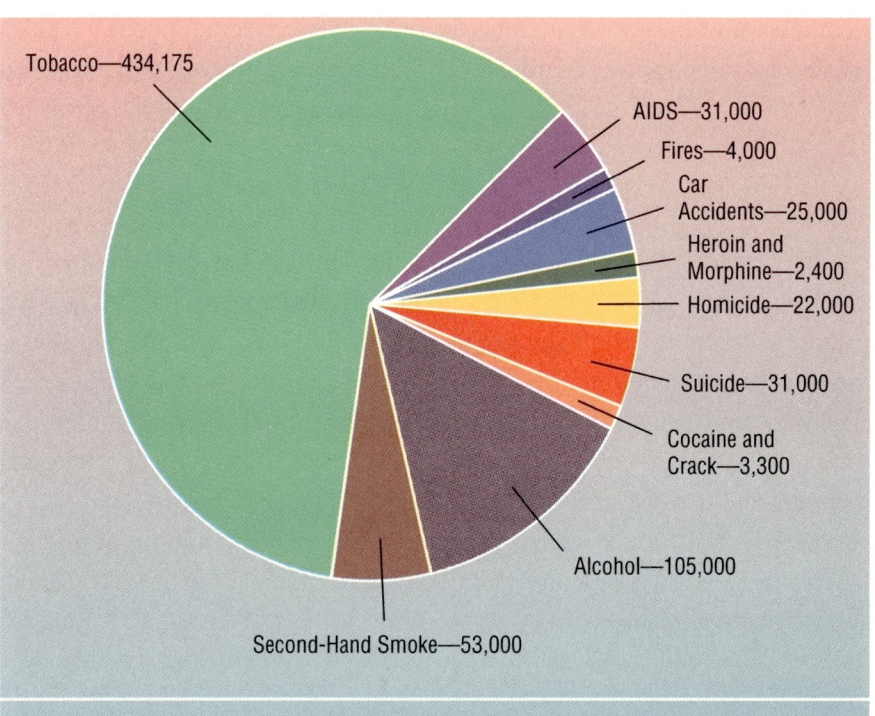

Source of Statistics: U.S. Centers for Disease Control, National Safety Council, National Center For Health Statistics, and the Environmental Protection Agency.

individual is addicted to nicotine they lose the ability to quit smoking or control the frequency of tobacco use. Nicotine's primary attraction is that it is a legal drug that provides both relaxation and stimulation. This section will focus on the physiological effects of tobacco and related health and educational concerns.

Tobacco (Nicotine) and Health

Tobacco addiction has long been considered a psychological dependence. However, in recent years, researchers have shown that tobacco (nicotine) can be a physiological addiction. Addicts who are allowed to inject nicotine intravenously often compare the experience to heroin use. The physiological effects of smoking and smoking cessation are shown in Tables 8.7 and 8.8.

KEY CONCEPT

HARMFUL EFFECTS OF TOBACCO

Cigarette smoking is one of the leading preventable causes of disability and death in the United States. More Americans have died from smoking than have died from fighting in World War II and Vietnam together.

TABLE 8.7

Physiological Effects of Tobacco Smoking

- Speeds up heart rate, thus increasing the heart's need for oxygen.
- Raises blood pressure.
- Reduces the oxygen-carrying capacity of the blood due to carbon monoxide intake.
- Increases the likelihood of clot formation which could cause heart attack and stroke.
- Loss of functional cilia in the lung, thus impairing the cleaning function of the lungs.
- Reduces circulation in the capillaries causing cold hands and feet.
- Decreases lung capacity.
- Thickens mucus, thus increasing the risk of chronic sinusitis (sinus infection).
- Increases risk of lung cancer, laryngeal cancer, oral cancer, esophageal cancer, bladder cancer, pancreatic cancer, kidney cancer, coronary heart disease, emphysema, chronic bronchitis, and peptic ulcers.
- Interferes with estrogen production in women leading to early menopause and osteoporosis.
- Increases drug tolerance so larger doses are needed for illness and pain. Also vaccinations may not be effective.
- Suppresses immunity, thus increasing the likelihood of colds, flu and other diseases.
- Interferes with normal sleep patterns.
- Causes progressive hearing loss for low sound frequencies.
- Increases plaque formation on teeth.
- Increases likelihood of abnormal sperm production.
- Women who smoke and take oral contraceptives increase their risk of heart attack and stroke.
- Pregnant women who smoke deprive the developing fetus of oxygen and may cause premature birth, smaller birth weight, spontaneous abortion, and impaired fetal development.

TABLE 8.8
Physiological Effects of Smoking Cessation

Within 20 Minutes:	• Blood pressure drops to normal. • Pulse rate drops to normal. • Body temperature of hands and feet increases to normal
Within 8 Hours:	• Carbon monoxide level in the blood drops to normal. • Oxygen level in the blood increases to normal.
Within 24 Hours:	• Chances of heart attack decreases.
Within 48 Hours:	• Nerve endings start to regrow. • Sense of smell and taste is enhanced.
Within 72 Hours:	• Bronchial tubes relax, making breathing easier. • Lung capacity increases.
Within Two Weeks to Three Months:	• Circulation improves. • Walking becomes easier. • Lung function increases up to 30 percent.
Within One to Nine Months:	• Coughing, sinus congestion, fatigue, shortness of breath decrease. • Cilia regrow in lungs increasing ability to clean lungs and reduce infection. • Body's overall energy level increases.
At Five Years:	• Lung cancer death rate for average smoker (1 pack a day) decreases from 137 per 100,000 people to 72 per 100,000. After 10 years, rate drops to 12 deaths per 100,000 or almost the rate of nonsmokers.
At Ten Years:	• Precancerous cells are replaced. • Other cancers (mouth, larynx, esophagus, bladder, kidney and pancreas) decrease (there are 30 chemicals in tobacco smoke that cause cancer).

Source: American Cancer Society.

The health concerns of tobacco use are many, but the most common ailment resulting from tobacco smoking is lung cancer. It is responsible for one-fourth of all male cancer deaths. In 1984, lung cancer in women surpassed breast cancer as the leading cause of death. Lung cancer risk increases with an increase in the number of cigarettes smoked per day, duration of smoking, and degree of inhalation. The age at which a person starts smoking and the tar and nicotine content of the cigarettes are also factors.

Laryngeal cancer is significantly higher in smokers than non-smokers and is related to the amount smoked. There is also a causal relationship between smoking and cancers of the kidney, urinary bladder, pancreas, oral cavity, and esophagus.

Two other health afflictions associated with tobacco smoke are **bronchitis and emphysema**, both of which are classified as **chronic obstructive pulmonary diseases (COPD)**. Bronchitis, an inflammatory condition of the upper part of the respiratory tract, is isolated in the larger bronchial airway of the trachea. The symptoms are excessive mucus production and a large amount of sputum which cause a continual cough. Shortness of breath is experienced, especially during exercise. The long term health concern is the vulnerability to develop other respiratory illnesses in the compromised or weakened area.

Emphysema is the result of the destruction of elasticity in the tiny air sacs of the lungs (alveoli). The purpose of the alveoli are to aid in the gaseous exchange of oxygen and carbon dioxide in the lungs. As emphysema progresses, the ability of the lungs to exchange gases is so seriously impaired that the bloodstream becomes low in oxygen and retains carbon dioxide. The end result is an overworked heart, causing in most cases, heart failure, or the need to lead a sedentary lifestyle.

Smoking tobacco during pregnancy can have serious health consequences for the fetus. Nicotine causes reduced blood flow to the placenta, and tissue development and growth are greatly reduced. Other adverse effects range from spontaneous abortion, low birth weight, still birth, premature birth, and neonatal death.

A link between cigarette smoking and breast cancer was discovered in a survey of 3,240 Danish women. All the women in the study had a mammography because of a suspicious clinical finding. It was discovered that the prevalence of breast cancer was 7 percent in non-smokers, and 15 percent in those who had smoked for thirty or more years.[7]

Many individuals want to quit smoking but aren't sure how to begin. Table 8.9 on the following page gives some guidelines for breaking the smoking habit. In addition to smoking cessation programs, research has made available four main types of nicotine replacement systems. They are nicotine patches, nicotine sprays, nicotine inhalers and nicotine gum. The main advantage of nicotine replacement systems is that users no longer damage lung tissue. Unfortunately, if smokers continue to smoke or the product is abused, toxic levels of nicotine can be absorbed into the blood system.

Smokeless Tobacco

A popular form of tobacco use today is smokeless tobacco. It is estimated that 22 million people engage in tobacco chewing. Smokeless tobacco can lead to periodontal gum disease, erosion of teeth, tooth decay, and oral cancer. Another health risk associated with chewing tobacco is the danger of becoming habituated to nicotine, which could ultimately lead to tobacco smoking. Oral cancer occurs several times more frequently among smokeless tobacco users compared with non-tobacco users. The risk of cancer of the cheek and gum is nearly fifty-fold greater among long-term smokeless tobacco users.[1]

Smoking is not cool.
Illustration by Meegan Hamilton

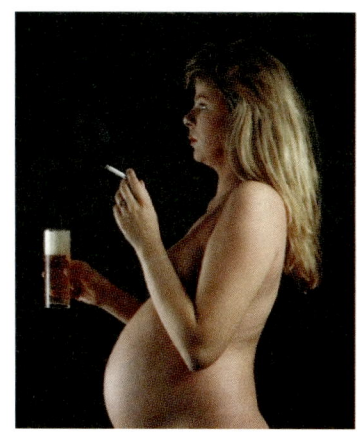

Drinking and smoking during pregnancy can be detrimental to the fetus.

TABLE 8.9

Guidelines for Breaking the Smoking Habit

How to Begin

- List all the reasons why you want to stop smoking.
- Keep a diary recording times of day and the circumstances of your smoking behavior. Be particularly mindful of the feelings that lead you to light up.
- Tell your family and friends you are going to quit and ask for their support.
- Switch to a brand of cigarettes you dislike. Try not to smoke two packs of the same brand in a row.

Next Step—Cut Down

- Smoke only one half of each cigarette.
- Don't smoke when you first experience a craving, but wait several minutes. During this time change your activity or talk to someone.
- Do not buy cigarettes by the carton. Wait until one pack is empty before buying another.
- Make cigarettes difficult to get. Don't carry them with you.
- Don't smoke automatically. Smoke only when you really want to.
- Reward yourself in some way other than smoking.
- Reach for a glass of juice instead of a cigarette for a pick-me-up.

Behavioral Changes After Quitting

- Whenever you feel uncomfortable sensations from having stopped smoking, remind yourself that they are signs of your body's return to health and that they will soon pass.
- If you miss the sensation of having a cigarette in your hand, play with something—a pencil, a paper clip, a marble.
- Instead of smoking after meals, get up from the table and brush your teeth or go for a walk.
- Temporarily avoid situations you strongly associate with the pleasurable acts of smoking.
- Develop a clean, fresh non-smoking environment around yourself—at work and at home.
- Until you are confident of your ability to stay off cigarettes, limit your socializing to healthful, outdoor activities or to situations in which smoking is prohibited.
- Look at cigarette ads more critically. Remind yourself that cigarette companies are making money at the expense of your health and well-being.
- Substitute relaxation and deep breathing for smoking in stressful situations.
- Absorb yourself in activities that are meaningful to you.
- Never allow yourself to think that "one won't hurt"—it will!

Source: U.S. Department of Health, Education and Welfare.

Secondhand Smoke (Passive Smoking)

Secondhand smoke (passive smoking) is the third leading cause of preventable deaths in this country, exceeded only by active smoking and alcohol use. It is estimated that 46,000 to 54,500 non-smoking Americans die each year from the effects of passive smoking. Passive smoking increases the risk of both lung cancer and heart disease with the majority of deaths due to heart disease. A non-smoker living with a smoker has a 20 to 30 percent increased risk of death from heart disease, and the heavier the smoker, the greater the risk.[8]

Sidestream smoke accounts for 85 percent of the smoke in a room. Sidestream smoke drifts up from the hot end of a cigarette so it has not been drawn through the cigarette filter. It contains high amounts of tar and nicotine. Many people experience allergic reactions to cigarette smoke such as eye, nose, and throat irritation, headaches, respiratory irritation and coughing. Carbon monoxide from exhaled smoke could reach unsafe levels in an enclosed area and cause angina attacks among individuals with coronary heart disease. The harmful effects of passive smoking are especially critical for children. Table 8.10 highlights some adverse health effects of secondhand smoke.

DRUGS AND SOCIETY

There are legitimate health reasons for using legal drugs such as to relieve pain or disease symptoms. However, the same drugs may also be taken to increase pleasurable sensations and/or to escape from the stresses of life. These psychoactive drugs, once referred to as recreational drugs, alter the thoughts, feelings, perceptions, and mood of individuals. The classifications of psychoactive drugs are summarized in Table 8.11.

Drugs taken for pleasure are dangerous and not essential to health and wellbeing. Drugs impair memory, alertness and achievement. Their use can lead to disintegration of social relationships and economic security. Most important of all, the consequences of using drugs can last a lifetime.

General Health Concerns

Certain drugs, such as barbiturates and opiates, create what is termed **physical dependence**. This dependence is one of the major health concerns of drug use. With repeated administration, these drugs actually become part of the body's chemistry. If regular use of the drug halts, the body experiences a physiological trauma known as **withdrawal syndrome**.

When the body is exposed to continued regular use of a drug, it develops a **tolerance** to the drug. This means that larger doses are needed to receive

---

TABLE 8.10

Adverse Health Effects of Secondhand Smoke

- Secondhand smoke causes disease in healthy non-smokers (i.e. lung cancer).

- Children of parents who smoke have an increased frequency of respiratory infections, increased respiratory symptoms during illness and allergies compared to children of non-smoking parents.

- Children of parents who smoke show smaller increases in lung function as the lung matures compared to children of non-smoking parents.

- Separating smokers and non-smokers in the same air space reduces, but does not eliminate, the exposure of non-smokers to environmental tobacco smoke.

Adapted from the Public Health Service, 1986. The health consequences of involuntary smoking, 7. A report of the Surgeon General, Washington, D.C.: U.S. Government Printing Office. DHHS Publication No. (CDC) 87–8398

TABLE 8.11

Classifications of Psychoactive Drugs

Drug Classification	Common and Trade Names	Physical Dependence	Tolerance Develops	Effects of Average Dose
Alcohol	Beer Wine Whiskey	Yes	Yes	Loss of inhibitions, decreased alertness and coordination
Nicotine	(in tobacco)	Yes	Yes	Increased heart rate, excitation
Cannabia	Marijuana Hashish	None	Yes	Altered perceptions, euphoria; may cause panic, confusion or hallucinations
Cocaine	Cocaine Hydrochloride	None	No	Mood elevation, increased alertness, increased heart rate and blood pressure
Stimulants	Benzedrine Dexedrine Methedrine Preludin Ritalin	Mild to none	Yes	Increased alertness and mood elevation, suppression of appetite, decreased fatigue; may cause anxiety, headache, insomnia, chills, rise in blood pressure
Major Tranquilizers (phenothiazines)	Mellaris Thorazine	None	No	Heavy sedation; may cause confusion and muscle rigidity
Minor Tranquilizers	Equanil/Miltown Librium Valium	Yes	No	Mild sedation, slight euphoria; may cause dizziness or drowsiness
Sedatives	Amytal Nembutal Phenobarbital Seconal Doriden Quaalude	Yes	Yes	Relaxation; may induce sleep, reduces muscle coordination
Hallucinogens	LSD PCP Mescaline Peyote Psilocybin	None	Yes	Visual and sensory distortion, changes perception and mood
Narcotics	Codeine Demerol Heroin/Methadone Morphine Opium/Percodan	Yes	Yes	Causes euphoria and drowsiness, reduces pain
Analgesics	Darvon Talwin	Yes	Yes	Pain relief; may cause anxiety and hallucinations
Inhalants	Amyl Nitrite Butyl Nitrite Nitrous Oxide	None	?	Loss of inhibition, confusion, euphoria, headache and dizziness

the same initial effect. The frequency of use increases and a practice of combining drugs to receive an effect is a common ritual.

Psychological dependence occurs when drug use becomes the center of one's life. Psychological dependence can lead to an erosion of family relationships, friendships, values, and goals. Over a period of time, drug use heightens negative feelings and can leave the user suicidal. Statistics have shown that more than half of all adolescent suicides are drug-related.

Drugs and their harmful side effects can be present long after use has stopped. Fat-soluble drugs such as marijuana, phencyclidine hydrochloride (PCP), and lysergic acid diethylamide (LSD) are stored in the fatty tissues of the body. The metabolism of drug accumulations in the fatty tissues causes delayed effects known as **flashbacks**. This phenomenon has been reported to occur weeks and even months after drug use has terminated. The accumulation of drugs in the fatty tissues can also be detrimental to the fetus of a pregnant woman. If the drug is metabolized and passes through the placenta barrier, it could impair fetal development.

Finally, the consequences of drug use can impair memory, sensation, and perception. Psychoactive drugs interfere with the brain's ability to synthesize and sort out new information. This "altered state" of functioning can lead to accident situations (i.e. falls or driving accidents).

Health Concerns of Specific Drugs

This last section deals with health concerns related to specific drugs. Hallucinogens, stimulants, depressants, inhalants, narcotics and designer drugs are discussed first. The chapter concludes with the concept of "Gateway" drugs and the health concerns of marijuana and cocaine.

Hallucinogens

This group of drugs is also known generally as psychedelics and refers to a group of drugs whose primary effect is to alter perceptions of reality, thoughts and feelings. Most of these drugs are either ingested or smoked and their effects can be variable depending on how much is taken.

LSD (lysergic acid diethylamide) is one of the most powerful hallucinogens. An average dose of LSD produces several hours of hallucinations and the particular drug episode is highly influenced, for better or worse, by the environmental setting and the user's expectations and attitudes. Common effects induced by LSD include changes in mood, sensation, perception, and feelings of depersonalization. LSD also activates the sympathetic nervous system causing body temperature and blood pressure to rise, sweating, and dilation of the pupils of the eyes. All hallucinogenic drugs are powerful mediators of brain functions. They are unreliable because of their potential to provoke psychotic behavior.

KEY CONCEPT

USE OF STIMULANTS

In the United States approximately four million Americans use amphetamines for non-medical reasons. Of the four million, three million use cocaine, 47 million smoke cigarettes, and 100 million drink coffee and cola drinks. The use of stimulants becomes a daily routine for most American citizens.

Phencyclidine (PCP), also known as "angel dust," was first developed as an animal tranquilizer. The adverse health effects are unpredictable and often include violent episodes. Depending on the dosage, PCP can act as a stimulant, depressant, or hallucinogen. The drug usually produces feelings of paranoia, confusion, restlessness, disorientation, and depersonalization. High doses can cause coma, psychosis, and cessation of breathing. PCP is sometimes laced in marijuana or sold falsely as LSD. This is dangerous as the user is unaware of what they are being exposed to.

Other hallucinogens include mescaline (peyote), psilocybin, STP (dimethoxy methyl amphetamine), and many others. Most of these hallucinogens have effects similar to LSD, although their effects can vary.

Stimulants

Amphetamines are classified as stimulants. They are usually taken orally but can also be injected. Amphetamines are commonly abused because they suppress appetite and counteract fatigue. These drugs produce feelings of euphoria, increased energy, and self-confidence. Excessive use of amphetamines can cause headaches, irritability, insomnia, panic, confusion, and delirium. Chronic use can evoke an amphetamine psychosis which involves an auditory and/or visual hallucination, delusions, and mood swings.

Caffeine is categorized as a mild stimulant and is found in a variety of products including coffee, tea, chocolate, and cola drinks. Caffeine stimulates the central nervous system and acts on the kidneys as a diuretic. Low doses offset fatigue and increase rapidity and clarity of thought. High doses produce nervousness, restlessness, tremors, and insomnia.

Street and prescription amphetamines often look the same. The danger of street amphetamines (speed) is that often they are more potent and laced with other toxic substances.

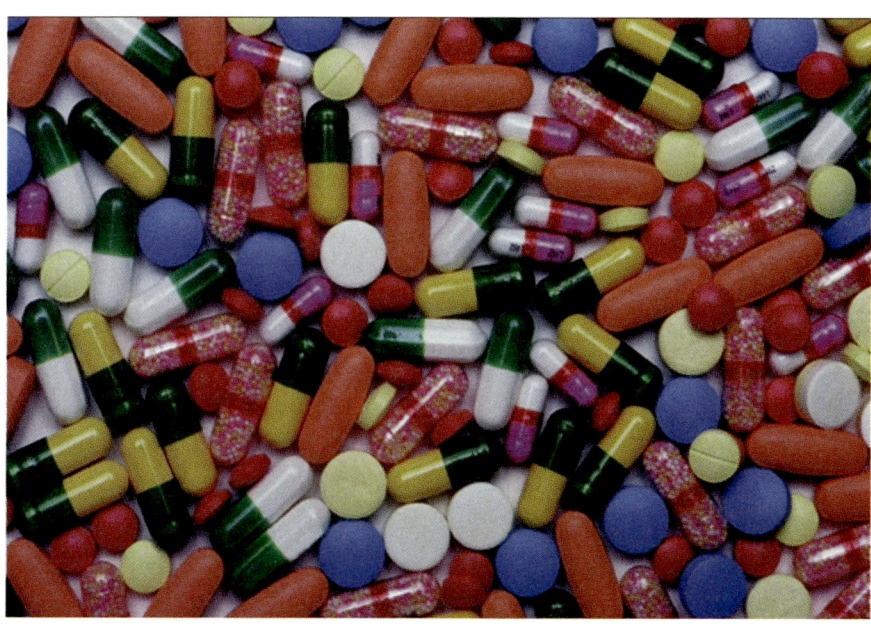

Depressants

Depressants include sedatives, tranquilizers, hypnotics, and alcohol (which was discussed in the beginning of this chapter). In low doses, depressants produce a mild state of euphoria, reduce inhibitions, and lessen tension. In higher doses they may impair mood, speech, and motor coordination. The danger of all depressants is the potential for the user to become physically and psychologically dependent upon them. Over time, one may develop a tolerance to the drug and increase the dose. Cessation of use results in withdrawal symptoms that range from restlessness, insomnia, and anxiety, to convulsions and death.

Inhalants

Aerosols, solvents, and anesthetics are considered inhalants. These commonly abused substances are used by inhaling vapors which depress the central nervous system. Side effects that are produced include a sense of euphoria, loss of inhibitions, and a sense of excitement. Chronic use impairs the health of the individual by damaging the kidneys, liver, and lungs. Serious damage can also occur to the heart because normal rhythmic beating is often interrupted.

Narcotics

Narcotics are a group of chemically similar drugs that depress the central nervous system. They include heroin, methadone, codeine, morphine, and opium. Capsules and tablets such as Percodan and Darvon are also considered narcotics. Intially, narcotics produce a feeling of euphoria that is often followed by nausea, vomiting, and drowsiness. Constricted pupils, watery eyes and itching may also occur. Narcotic tolerance develops rapidly and physical dependence is likely. Overdose symptoms range from slow and shallow breathing with clammy skin, to convulsions and coma ending in death. Many narcotics are administered by syringes. Contaminated needles can transmit diseases such as AIDS, endocarditis, and hepatitis.

Designer Drugs

All illegal drugs are defined in terms of their chemical formulas. To avoid legal restrictions, underground chemists modify the molecular structure of certain illegal drugs to produce analogs known as **designer drugs**. These so called designer drugs can be several hundred times stronger than the drug they are designed to imitate. Often, irreversible brain damage is caused with as little as one dose. Two of the most popular designer drugs used today are Fentanyl, an analog of heroin known as China White, and Ecstasy, an analog of amphetamines and hallucinogens.

Some legal prescription drugs, when abused, can lead to addiction and the same consequences as illegal drugs.

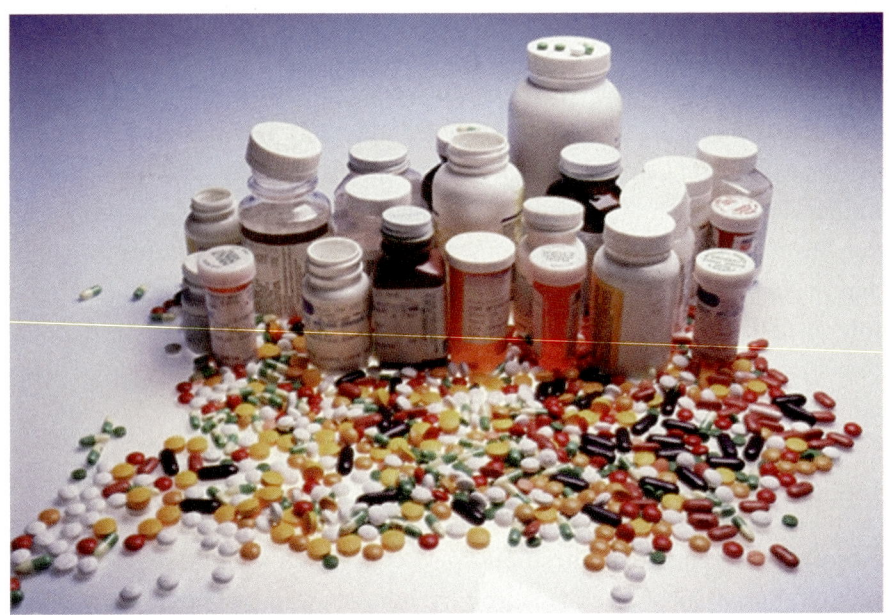

Gateway Drugs

Dr. Dupont, in his text, *Getting Tough on Gateway Drugs*, uses the term "gateway drugs" to refer to a group of psychoactive drugs that initiate drug use. These drugs are very popular and virtually all Americans who become dependent on drugs start with one or all of these substances. A misconception about gateway drugs is that they are easily controlled and dependence is unlikely. This adds to their popularity and widespread use. Gateway drugs include marijuana, cocaine and alcohol. In this text I have considered tobacco (nicotine) discussed earlier, as a gateway drug. Let's examine the health concerns of marijuana and cocaine.

Marijuana

Research has shown that severe psychological damage, which may include depression, paranoia, psychosis, and a condition known as **amotivational syndrome** (apathy), can occur when marijuana contains two percent **Tetrahydrocannabinol** (THC). Tests in the field show that most marijuana today contains four to six percent THC, at least two times the amount needed to cause serious psychological damage.

Marijuana use also has an effect on the respiratory, cardiovascular, reproductive, and immune systems. Marijuana smoke is hotter than tobacco smoke and 70 percent of the suspended particles in the smoke are retained in the lung. These factors cause lung tissue damage. Exposure to marijuana smoke impairs the functioning of alveolar macrophages (white blood cells) in the lung. These cells usually facilitate removal of debris from the respiratory system.

Chronic administration of large doses of marijuana results in increased blood volume and decreased blood pressure. The use of marijuana also speeds up heart rate relative to the amount of THC consumed. These effects are transitory and not usually significant but, for individuals with cardiovascular problems, complications could result.

Marijuana use affects sexual behavior and fertility. It can damage male and female chromosomes and adversely alter fetal growth and development. High doses over a period of time result in decreased testosterone (male sex hormone) and may lead to impotence. Also, the number of sperm per ejaculation is decreased as well as the mobility of the sperm.

Studies have shown that heavy use of marijuana may decrease the white blood cell count in the body. This impairment of the body's immune system may lower resistance to viral infections and cancer.

Cocaine

Cocaine is still a popular drug of choice in the United States. A major contributing factor is the recent availability of cocaine in a cheap but potent form called "crack." Crack is a purified form of cocaine that is ingested by smoking. A health concern of using crack is that it is far more addictive than heroin or barbiturates. This is due to the fact that when crack is smoked it is quickly absorbed into the blood stream and an extreme euphoria occurs within seconds.

Cocaine and crack are deadly drugs because they increase heart rate, blood pressure, and interrupt the brain's control over the cardiovascular and respiratory systems. Cocaine raises the body's temperature, dilates the pupils, and affects vision. The extreme danger of cocaine is that low doses are as unpredictable as higher, chronic doses.

Overdoses of cocaine can induce seizures, heart stoppage and cessation of breathing. A strong psychological dependence develops for cocaine which often destroys lives and economic well-being.

Drug Testing

It has been estimated that as many as 1 in 10 workers use psychoactive drugs on the job. This poses some significant safety hazards in certain occupations that depend greatly on mental acuity. In jobs such as air traffic controllers, truck drivers, locomotive engineers, and many more, the abililty to make rational decisions in a split-second can mean the difference between life and death.

KEY CONCEPT

COMPLICATIONS FROM MARIJUANA USE

Research has proven that marijuana smoke contains 5 to 15 times the amount of benzpyrene, (a known carcinogen) found in tobacco smoke. Further research is now being released that shows chronic exposure to marijuana damages and destroys nerve cells in the brain. The portion of the brain that is thought to be most involved is the region termed the hippocampus, which processes sensory information.

Drug testing in the workplace is a two-edge sword. On the one hand, especially for those in the types of occupations mentioned above, drug testing could prevent tragedies. On the other hand, some feel that drug testing violates a person's right to privacy. Most would ascribe to the philosophy that a person's right to swing their arm ends when their fist contacts someone else's nose. Many states are passing laws which allow employers to drug test and this trend will probably continue. **The message is this—if you use drugs, your job is at risk.**

EXPLORING WELLNESS ON THE WEB

Many resources are available on the World Wide Web. You can reinforce, expand and enhance the information presented in this chapter by accessing the following sites.

http://www.usdoj.gov/dea/pubs/abuse/contents.htm — the U.S. Drug Enforcement site contain extensive information and photographs on drugs of all types.

http://pharminfo.com/drugdb/db_mnu.html — the ParmInfoNet site which contains a drug information data base. You can access information by entering a generic or trade name.

http://www.well.com/user/woa/ — the Web of Addictions site provides information about alcohol and other drug addictions as well as information on support groups and links to other resources.

http://www.nida.nih.gov/ — the National Institute on Drug Abuse provides basic information on drug use and abuse. Covers a wide spectrum of drugs.

REFERENCES

1. American Cancer Society. (1996). Cancer Facts and Figures-1996. Atlanta, Georgia.

2. Byrd, T. (1990). *Addiction Awareness*. Dubuque, IA: Kendall Hunt Publishing Company.

3. Insel, P.M., & Roth, W.T. (1996). *Core Concepts in Health*. Mountain View, CA: Mayfield Publishing Company.

4. Lindberg, S., & Agren, G. (1988). Mortality among male and female hospitalized alcoholics in Stockholm 1962-1983. *British Journal of the Addictions*, 83, 1193-1200.

5. Schuckit,M.A. (1990). *Drugs and Alcohol Abuse, A Clinical Guide to Diagnosis and Treatment*. New York: Plenum Medical Book Company.

6. Smith, E., Cloninger, R., & Bradford, S. (1983). Predictors of mortality in alcoholic women: a prospective follow-up study. *Alcoholism: Clinical and Experimental Research*, 7(2), 237-243.

7. Staff. (1995). A link between cigarette smoking and breast cancer. *The Johns Hopkins Medical Letter*, 7,71.

8. Staff. (1991). *The Wellness Encyclopedia*. University of California, Berkeley. Boston, MA: Houghton Mifflin Company.

9. U.S. Department of Health and Human Services, Public Health Services. (1992). *Healthy People 2000 National Health Promotion and Disease Prevention Objectives*. Boston: Jones and Bartlett Publishers, Inc.

10. U.S. Department of Transportation, National Highway Traffic Safety Administration. (1994). Traffic Safety Facts. Washington, D.C.

11. Ward, D.A. (1990). *Alcoholism, Introduction to Theory and Treatment*. (2nd ed.). Dubuque, IA: Kendall/Hunt Publishing Company.

12. Wechsler, H., & Davenport, A. (1994). Health and behavioral consequences of binge drinking in college. *Journal of the American Medical Association*, 272,(21), 1672-1677.

13. Wechsler, H. & Isaac, N. (1992). Binge drinkers at massachusetts colleges: prevalence, drinking styles, time trends, and associated problems. *Journal of the American Medical Association*, 267,(21), 2929-2931.

DEFINITIONS OF KEY TERMS

amotivational syndrome — a condition in which the individual has a great deal of apathy towards tasks and life in general.

depressants — drugs that reduce the normal level of functioning of the nervous system and other physiologic systems such as the heart. In low doses, depressants may produce a mild state of euphoria.

designer drugs — drugs created by chemically modifying existing drugs to produce analogues which have effects similar to the drug mimicked.

fetal alcohol syndrome — a syndrome due to prenatal exposure to alcohol in which the baby is likely to suffer from mental retardation, low birth weight, abnormal smallness of the head, unusual facial characteristics, congenital heart defects, defective joints, and abnormal behavior patterns.

hallucinogens — group of drugs whose primary effect is to alter perception, feelings, and thoughts.

Korsakoff's psychosis — a form of amnesia often seen in chronic alcoholics, characterized by a loss of short-term memory and an inability to learn new skills. The cause of the condition can often be traced to B-complex vitamins, especially thiamine and B_{12}.

narcotics — habit-forming drugs that dull the senses, relieve pain, and induce sleep.

physical dependence — the physical state of addiction to drugs or alcohol. Physically dependent individuals must receive increasing amounts of the substance to prevent the onset of physiological trauma known as withdrawal.

psychoactive drugs — drugs that act principally on the brain, producing altered states of mood, perception, consciousness, and central nervous system activity.

psychological dependence — a situation in which an individual becomes so accustomed to a drug that he or she cannot function psychologically without it.

stimulants — drugs that activate the sympathetic division of the autonomic nervous system (i.e., amphetamines).

tetrahydrocannabinol (THC) — the chief psychoactive ingredient in marijuana and hashish.

tolerance — situation in which the body becomes adapted to a drug, so that increasingly larger doses are needed to reproduce the original desired effect.

Wernicke's syndrome — an inflammatory, hemorrhagic, degenerative condition of the brain. This syndrome is caused by a thiamine deficiency and is seen in association with chronic alcoholism.

withdrawal syndrome — an unpleasant and possibly painful condition that an individual who is physically and/or psychologically dependent on a drug experiences when deprived of the drug.

LAB 8.1

ASSESSING YOUR ALCOHOL RISK

Name _____ ID _____ Sect _____ Time _____ Date _____

Purpose

To determine your risk for alcohol abuse/addiction.

Directions

Answer **YES** or **NO** to each of the following questions. Determine your risk for alcohol addiction using the table at the end of this lab.

Y   N   1. Do you occasionally drink heavily after a disappointment or a quarrel or when your parents or boss gives you a hard time?

Y   N   2. When you have trouble or feel pressured at school or at work, do you always drink more heavily than usual?

Y   N   3. Have you noticed that you are able to handle more liquor than you did when you were first drinking?

Y   N   4. Did you ever wake up the "morning after" and discover that you could not remember part of the evening before, even though your friends tell you that you did not pass out?

Y   N   5. When drinking with other people, do you try to have a few extra drinks that others don't notice?

Y   N   6. Are there certain occasions when you feel uncomfortable if alcohol is not available?

Y   N   7. Have you recently noticed that when you begin drinking you are in more of a hurry to get the first drink than you used to be?

Y   N   8. Do you sometimes feel a little guilty about your drinking?

Y   N   9. Are you secretly irritated when your family or friends discuss your drinking?

Y   N   10. Have you recently noticed an increase in the frequency of your memory blackouts?

Y   N   11. Do you often find that you wish to continue drinking after your friends say they have had enough?

Y   N   12. Do you usually have a reason for the occasions when your drink heavily?

Y   N   13. When you are sober, do you often regret things you did or said while drinking?

Y   N   14. Have you tried switching brands or following different plans for controlling your drinking?

Y   N   15. Have you often failed to keep the promises you've made to yourself about controlling or cutting down on your drinking?

(Continued)

ASSESSING YOUR ALCOHOL RISK

Y N 16. Have you ever tried to control your drinking by changing jobs or moving to a new location?

Y N 17. Do you try to avoid family or close friends while you are drinking?

Y N 18. Are you having an increasing number of financial and academic problems?

Y N 19. Do more people seem to be treating you unfairly without good reason?

Y N 20. Do you eat very little or irregularly when you are drinking?

Y N 21. Do you sometimes have the shakes in the morning and find that it helps to have a drink?

Y N 22. Have you recently noticed that you cannot drink as much as you once did?

Y N 23. Do you sometimes stay drunk for several days at a time?

Y N 24. Do you sometimes feel very depressed and wonder whether life is worth living?

Y N 25. Sometimes after a period of drinking, do you see or hear things that aren't there?

Y N 26. Do you get terribly frightened after you have been drinking heavily?

Interpretation:

Answering **YES** to two or three questions means that you probably have the potential for more severe alcohol abuse/addiction. If you answer **YES** to several questions in each category listed below, you may be in the indicated stage of alcohol addiction.

Questions	Stage of Alcohol Abuse/Addiction	Comment
Questions 1-8	Early Stage	Drinking is a regular part of your life.
Questions 9-21	Middle Stage	You are having trouble controlling when, where, and how much you drink.
Questions 22-26	Beginning of Final Stage	You no longer can control your desire to drink.

Adapted from National Council on Alcoholism.

LAB 8.2

ASSESSING REASONS FOR SMOKING

Name _____ ID _____ Sect _____ Time _____ Date _____

Purpose

To determine factors which influence you to smoke.

Directions

Respond to each of the statements with one of the following responses:

1 - Always   2 - Frequently   3 - Occasionally   4 - Seldom   5 - Never

Place the number of the appropriate response in the blank beside each statement.

_____ A. I smoke cigarettes in order to keep myself from slowing down.

_____ B. Handling a cigarette is part of the enjoyment of smoking.

_____ C. Smoking cigarettes is pleasant and relaxing.

_____ D. I light up a cigarette when I feel angry about something.

_____ E. When I have run out of cigarettes, I find it almost unbearable until I can get more.

_____ F. I smoke cigarettes automatically without even being aware of it.

_____ G. I smoke cigarettes to stimulate me, to perk myself up.

_____ H. Part of the enjoyment of smoking a cigarette comes from the steps I take to light up.

_____ I. I find cigarettes pleasurable.

_____ J. When I feel uncomfortable or upset about something, I light up a cigarette.

_____ K. I am very much aware of the fact when I am not smoking a cigarette.

_____ L. I light up a cigarette without realizing I still have one burning in the ashtray.

_____ M. I smoke cigarettes to give me a "lift."

_____ N. When I smoke a cigarette, part of the enjoyment is watching the smoke as I exhale it.

_____ O. I want a cigarette most when I am comfortable and relaxed.

_____ P. When I feel "blue" or want to take my mind off cares and worries, I smoke cigarettes.

_____ Q. I get a real craving for a cigarette when I haven't smoked for a while.

_____ R. I've found a cigarette in my mouth and didn't remember putting it there.

(Continued)

ASSESSING REASONS FOR SMOKING

Interpretation:

1. Place the number in the blank beside each statement in the blanks below labeled with the same letter, i.e. put the score for statement **A** above in the **A** blank below, etc.

2. Sum the three scores on each line to get a total for each category. A score of 11 or greater on any category indicates that the factor is an important influence on why you smoke. A score of 7 or less indicates the factor is not an important factor to you.

_____ + _____ + _____ = _____
  (A)   (G)   (M)   Stimulation

You smoke because it gives you a lift. Substitute some form of exercise.

_____ + _____ + _____ = _____
  (B)   (H)   (N)   Handling

You like the ritual and trappings of smoking. Find other ways to keep your hands busy.

_____ + _____ + _____ = _____
  (C)   (I)   (O)   Relaxation

You get a real sense of pleasure out of smoking. Think about the damage it is doing to your lungs and heart.

_____ + _____ + _____ = _____
  (D)   (J)   (P)   Crutch

You are using smoking as a tranquilizer. In a stressful situation, use some of the techniques discussed in the chapter on stress.

_____ + _____ + _____ = _____
  (E)   (K)   (Q)   Craving

Quitting smoking is difficult for you if you feel you are psychologically dependent. Once you have stopped, you will be able to resist starting again because the withdrawal effort is too tough to face again.

_____ + _____ + _____ = _____
  (F)   (L)   (R)   Habit

If you usually smoke without even realizing you're doing it, you should find it easy to break the habit pattern.

Adapted from "Why Do You Smoke?" Washington, D.C.: NIH Publication No. 90-1822, 1990.

NOTES

Healthy Sexual Behavior

SUSAN J. KOCH

INTRODUCTION

Decisions made about sexual behavior have significant implications for the mental and emotional dimensions of wellness, as well as for present and future physical health. When we make those decisions, it is important to be operating from an informed position—that is—to be above the asymptomatic median of the wellness continuum described in Chapter 1—to be making choices based on acknowledged values and credible educational experiences, and then to grow and change in response to life's learning opportunitics.

Sexuality refers to the dimension of ourselves (based on biological and environmental factors) which concerns all aspects of sexual behavior. Although the process of learning about sexuality is a lifelong pursuit, the college years provide a particularly critical opportunity to clarify sexual values and expand knowledge. Many college students are well into the process of learning about their own sexual self and sexual behavior with others. Whatever your level of sexual experience, this chapter will help you to review basic sexual information and examine your own present and possible future sexual choices—in light of the implications for a healthy lifestyle.

SEXUAL ANATOMY AND PHYSIOLOGY

Although the sex organs of human males and females obviously appear very different, they actually originate from the same tissue during prenatal development. Your genital sex was determined at conception, depending upon whether an X (for female) or Y (for male) chromosome won the race to your mother's waiting egg in the fallopian tube. Sexual differentiation followed in a series of stages under the direction of sex hormones. Mother Nature's goal of course, for both males and females, is to produce a sexually mature adult with the necessary equipment to reproduce and continue the species.

Although the entire body participates in sexual arousal and response, the parts of the body most closely identified with sex in the male are the **testes** and the **penis** (Figure 9.1). The word testes (popular slang term—"balls") comes from the Latin "to testify." The early Romans placed their hands over their testes when taking an oath to indicate sincerity.[1] (Roman women, obviously, were not equipped for such activity. Fortunately, the placing of one's hand on the Bible as an indication of truthfulness was substituted later in many societies.)

Each testicle contains hundreds of seminiferous tubules which are responsible for the production of millions of sperm, the male reproductive cell. Ninety-five percent of testosterone (the male hormone) is also produced in the testes (the other 5% comes from the adrenal glands). The testes are suspended at the end of the spermatic cord in the sac-like structure called the scrotum. The scrotum, by virtue of being located away from the rest of the body, helps to maintain ideal temperature for viable sperm production (about $5^{1}/_{2}$ degrees lower than the body's core temperature). A muscle in the spermatic cord raises the testes closer to the body in response to sexual arousal, cold, fear, or anger.[1]

If there is any anatomical structure said to have a reputation, it surely must be the penis. When the author asked a group of university students to write down all the slang names they had heard for this structure the list extended to an amazing 43 terms! From time immemorial penile size has been associated with sexual prowess with "the bigger the better" being the mistaken belief. Women have been known to conduct mental measurements of men's thumbs, feet, and noses in the misguided belief that penile size would be proportionate to the length of those appendages.

The penis consists of three parallel cylinders, each of which is filled with tissues containing spaces. When the penis is flaccid (soft), these spaces contain only a small amount of blood. When the male becomes sexually aroused, the blood vessels which carry blood into the penis dilate and the cavities become engorged with blood. This results in the rigidity known as an erection; in slang terms—a "hard-on" or "boner." (The males of many species actually do have a bone that runs the length of the penis. Humans and whales are two exceptions.)[1]

The urethra extends through the length of the penis and carries both urine and semen to the opening at the tip. It is not possible for the urethra

FIGURE 9.1

The male genitalia.

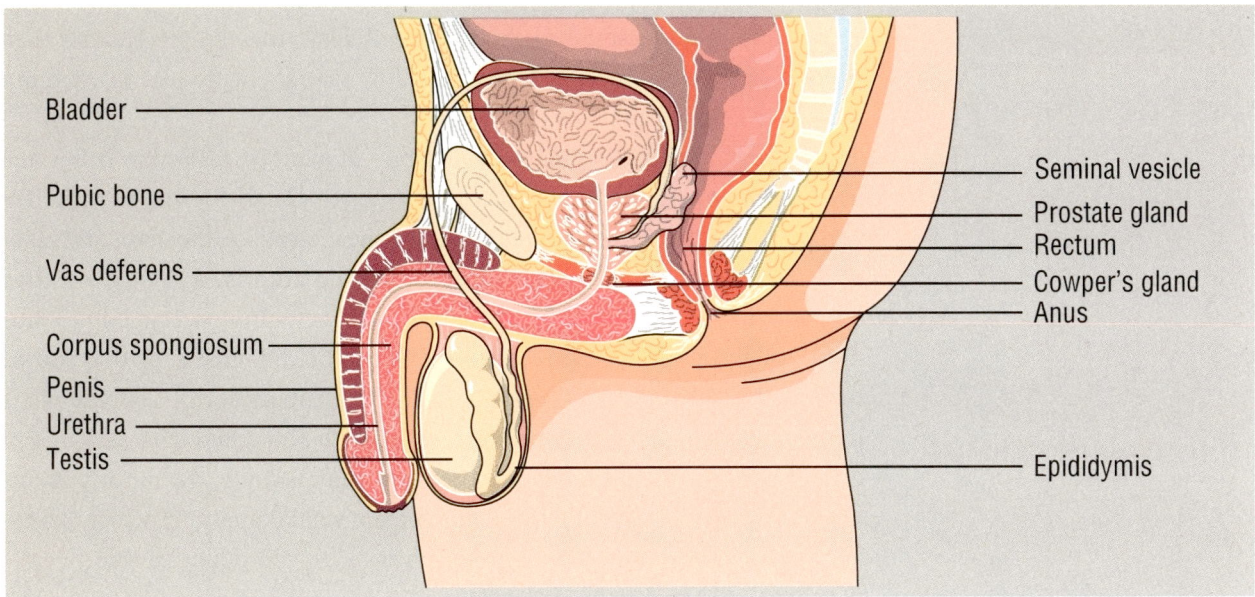

to carry urine during sexual arousal and ejaculation because muscles at the base of the penis shut off the entry of urine to the urethra.

The end of the outermost cylinder of the penis is the **glans**. Because the glans contains more receptors to pressure and touch, it is an important source of sexual arousal. The glans is partially covered by the foreskin (prepuce)—a retractable fold of skin.

Until recently, circumcision—surgical removal of part of the foreskin—was common practice for newborn males. Jews and Moslems circumcise for religious reasons, others for supposed hygienic reasons or because they want their child to look like his father or like other males his age. In 1971, the American Academy of Pediatrics stated that surgical removal of the foreskin is an unnecessary medical procedure which carries medical risks. In 1990, some medical experts again professed the belief that circumcision does have some health advantages. In any case, college students today are likely to encounter both the circumcised and uncircumcised varieties.

Some people believe that circumcision reduces the sensitivity of the penis, thus delaying orgasm (and lengthening the period of sexual pleasure) and even reducing the desire to masturbate. More recent research indicates that presence or absence of the foreskin is not a significant factor in sexual health. "Sexual sensitivity appears to be in the mind of a man, not in his foreskin."[22]

Like all other body parts, the size of the penis varies considerably. Masters and Johnson, prominent sex researchers, reported encountering penises as large as ten inches in length (when erect) and as small as one inch.[21] The average penis is about 3.5 inches long and about 3.75 inches in circumference. When erect, 6.3 inches in length and 4.85 inches in circumference are average measurements.[16] The structure of the human female makes penis length irrelevant to sexual arousal. Since the vagina is extremely elastic and is quite small in its unaroused state, males with smaller than average penis size are as capable of healthy sexual encounters as are those who have a larger than average penis.

The female sexual organs include a pair of **ovaries**, **fallopian tubes**, the **uterus**, **vagina**, **clitoris**, and the **vulva** (Figure 9.2). The term, vulva, refers to the external female genitalia; including the mos pubis, the outer and inner lips, the clitoris, and the vaginal opening. The clitoris, a highly sensitive structure of erectile tissue located just below the point where the inner lips meet at the top of the vulva, is considered to be the most sensitive part of the female body (see later mention of the Grafenberg spot). Like the penis in the male, the clitoris becomes engorged with blood and increases in size during sexual stimulation and excitement. Interestingly, the clitoris seems to be the only part of either male or female sexual anatomy which serves a purely sexual function with no accompanying reproductive role.

Like the testes in the male, the ovaries produce reproductive cells (eggs) and hormones (mostly estrogen and progesterone). Usually, one ovum or egg is secreted every month from one ovary or the other from puberty until menopause (except during pregnancy and, in some cases, during breastfeeding).

When the ovum is released from the ovary, it is conducted into the fallopian tube, where fertilization may occur if sperm is present. The fertilized egg then travels through the fallopian tube and may become implanted in the wall of the uterus—thus a pregnancy begins. If no sperm is present, the unfertilized ovum is passed out of the body through the cervix (the mouth of the uterus) and vagina, along with the lining of the uterus (containing blood, nutrients, and mucus). Menstruation, the discharge of the endometrial lining of the uterus, usually lasts about three to seven days. The entire menstrual cycle generally ranges from 21 to 35 days in length—all controlled by the hormones **estrogen** and **progesterone**.[24] (Information about conception is discussed later in this chapter.)

In 1981, sex researchers Perry and Whipple identified an erotically sensitive area, about halfway between the pubic bone and the cervix, which they named the Gräfenberg spot, in honor of the physician who first described it. There is presently conflicting evidence about the existence and location of the "G spot" with some researchers maintaining that stimulation of the area results in strong sexual pleasure and orgasmic contractions. Although research on the Grafenberg spot is not conclusive at this time, it seems to indicate that a variety of orgasmic experiences are possible.[23]

FIGURE 9.2

The female genitalia.

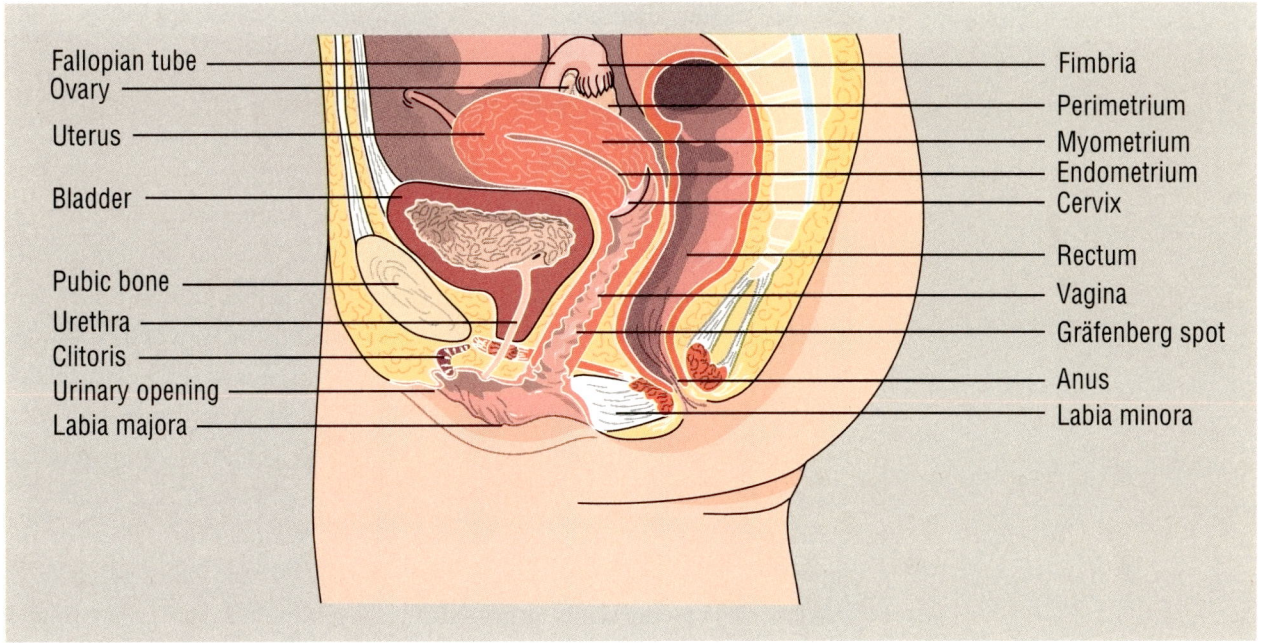

SEXUAL ORIENTATION

Each of us has a sexual orientation. Those of us who naturally feel attracted toward people of the other gender are termed heterosexual; those who feel attracted toward people of the same gender are termed homosexual; and those who are attracted to both are bisexual.[1] It is estimated that five to seven percent of the population is exclusively homosexual, with a larger percentage of people being attracted to both men and women (bisexual) to varying degrees.[14] About 80 to 90% of the population is estimated to be heterosexual.[21]

The origin of our sexual orientation, that is the reason that some of us are straight and others are gay, is not clearly understood and continues to be debated. Feelings of orientation usually emerge in early adolescence and sexual orientation appears to be fairly well established in males by age 18 and in females by age 21.[1]

Many college students are initially shocked to view more open homosexual lifestyles when they arrive on the university scene. Other students, who may have been concerned or uncertain about their own orientation, may discover, for the first time, an acceptance of their feelings. Being gay or lesbian obviously places one in a minority position and may lead to discrimination. Gay/lesbian student organizations and university counseling services often offer support for students who are gay, lesbian, or bisexual, as well as for students who are uncertain or confused about their own or others sexual orientation. Regardless of orientation, college students share common needs for acceptance, positive social interactions, academic success, and career planning.

ARE YOU READY FOR SEX?

Each of us learns about sexuality in stages, beginning when we are very young. Most adults remember occasions during childhood when they were "caught" playing doctor with siblings or neighborhood children, spent considerable time inspecting Victoria's Secret catalogs or watched forbidden television programs or videos when parents were unaware. As we proceeded through puberty and adolescence, we may have graduated to using older brothers and sisters or friends as sex "consultants" (often resulting in rather amazing bits of misinformation).

Masturbation, the most common form of sexual expression for the majority of Americans, has been experienced by 94% of males and 63% of females.[13] The media sends us graphic messages about sexual behavior and, if we are very lucky, our parents provide us with guidance and information. Often, we depend upon our own perceptions of what others in our peer group are doing.

In spite of living within the shadow of Acquired Immune Deficiency Syndrome (AIDS), an incurable sexually transmitted disease, the rate of sexual activity among American young people has increased during the past several years. When the Centers for Disease Control conducted the Youth Risk Behavior Survey in 1991, results indicated that 72% of high school seniors had experienced sexual intercourse. According to a 1990 survey of over 2000 students at Midwestern university, about 72% of students were sexually active. Thirty-five percent of the survey respondents had more than one sexual partner and one-fourth had been with three or more sexual partners.[7] Many of these sexual experiences had been alcohol-induced, unplanned, and unprotected from sexually transmitted diseases and pregnancy.

Because the possibility of contracting AIDS now looms in the background of every sexual encounter, it is more necessary than ever for every man and woman to think and plan carefully for a healthy sexual present and future. Planning carefully means either choosing to remain abstinent or taking responsibility for the prevention of both STDs and unplanned pregnancy.

Many parents have values and certain standards of conduct related to sexual behavior which they expect their children to adopt as they mature. These values and standards may be related to religious beliefs. Sex outside of marriage, living with someone before marriage, or using contraception are all issues which may cause inter-family conflict. When contemplating sexual activities, it is important to understand one's own and one's family's values and to understand the risks to family harmony which are presented when behaviors don't match family values.

Behaving in ways which do not reflect your values, something which happens not only where sexuality is concerned, but also in areas like nutrition and exercise, leads to dissonance. When your values do not match your behavior, you may feel guilty, uncomfortable, confused, angry, defensive, afraid, out of control, and stressed out! Planning to act in ways consistent with one's own values is a good way to achieve inner peace.

Regardless of your sexual past, you can exert control over your sexual future. Decisions about sexual experiences need to be considered in light of a long term plan. Sexually transmitted diseases and unplanned pregnancies can dramatically alter life intentions, including educational aspirations and opportunities, fertility, future intimate relationships, and marital commitment. Table 9.1 lists recommendations that should be considered in anticipation of any future sexual encounter.

Unplanned sexual encounters can lead to HIV or other STDs.

TABLE 9.1
You Are Ready For Sex If:
1. You feel guiltless and comfortable about your anticipated activity, in light of your own attitudes and values.
2. You are confident that you will not be humiliated and that your reputation will not be hurt.
3. Neither partner is pressuring the other for sex.
4. You are not trying to prove your love for the other person, increase your self-worth, prove that you can attract a sexual partner, get attention, love, or affection, or rebel against parents or family values.
5. It will be an expression of your current feelings rather than an attempt to hang on to a relationship that is growing old.
6. You can discuss and agree upon an effective method of contraception and, if necessary, share the responsibility and cost of using the method.
7. You have discussed and agreed upon what action you will take if conception occurs, since no contraception is 100% effective.
8. You both have honestly shared information about your sexual history as it relates to the possibility of having contracted a sexually transmitted disease.
9. You have agreed upon effective precautions for avoiding the contraction of sexually transmitted diseases.
10. Your decision is not influenced by alcohol or some other drug which affects the decision-making process.

An interesting study of situational factors at first intercourse among college students was reported in a 1996 article in the *American Journal of Health Behavior*.[25] Researchers Sawyer and Smith surveyed several hundred undergraduate students at an eastern university and found that of the 89% of sexually active respondents, 86% of the females and 59% of the males were involved in a dating relationship at the time of first intercourse. Sixty-seven percent of female and 26% of male respondents said they were "in love" when first intercourse occurred. Almost one-fourth of the women had felt pressured to have sex, compared to 5% of the men. The researchers also asked students whether they regretted, on looking back, having lost their virginity at that particular time. Mainly because they later realized that they had the "wrong partner" or that they were "too young," 38% of the women and 20% of the men in the study wished they had chosen differently.

SEXUALLY TRANSMITTED DISEASES

Sexually transmitted diseases have been reported throughout history. In recent years, however, STDs have reached epidemic proportions. As of October 31, 1995, just over half a million persons with AIDS had been reported to the Centers for Disease Control by state and territorial health departments. Sixty-two percent (311,381 people) were reported as having died.[6] According to the American Social Health Association, one in four American will contract at least one STD in their lifetime. Half of today's adolescents, many of whom are or will become members of a college community, will have had an STD by the time they are 25![1]

AIDS

In January 1992, when Magic Johnson, the idolized star of the Los Angeles Lakers professional basketball team, announced to the world that he had contracted the human immunodeficiency virus (HIV) through unprotected heterosexual sex, the "AIDS scare" became a more personal threat for many sexually active people, regardless of their sexual orientation.

Since the virus that causes AIDS was identified in France in 1983, the World Health Organization estimates that 18 million adults and 1.5 million children have been infected with HIV, resulting in approximately 4.5 million AIDS cases worldwide.[6] In the U.S. in 1993, HIV infection became the most common cause of death among persons ages 25-44 years, accounting for 19% of all deaths in that age group.[5] In 1994, an estimated 41,930 U.S. residents died from HIV infection, a 9% increase over the previous year.[5] Men who have sex with men represent the largest group of persons with AIDS in the U.S. (See Table 9.2 for AIDS cases by exposure category). The rate of HIV infection in women has been steadily increasing in the U.S. and women now constitute about 18% of reported AIDS cases.[5] Figure 9.3 illustrates the increase in the incidence of death from the disease in the U.S. through the 1980s and 90s.

The Centers for Disease Control maintains a Web Site at (http://www.cdc.gov) where the latest information about the incidence and prevalence of HIV, as well as AIDS information and advice is available. Tables 9.3, 9.4 and 9.5, which address the age and geographic distribution of AIDS cases in the U.S., provide examples of the type of AIDS information available on the world wide web.

Incidence of AIDS in the United States.

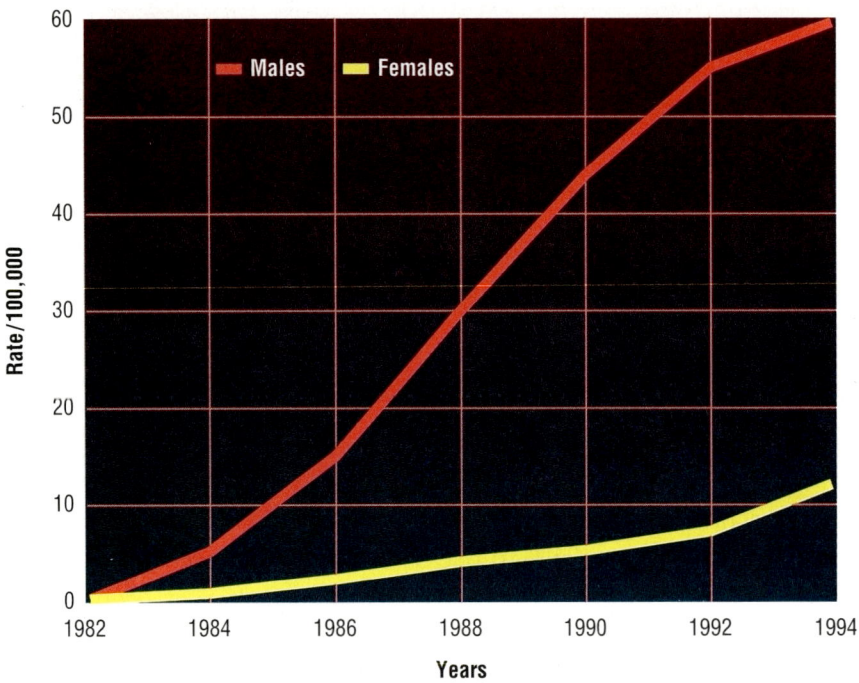

TABLE 9.2		
Aids Cases By Exposure Category[a]		
Exposure Category	**Subtotals**	**Number of AIDS Cases**
Men who have sex with men		259,672
Injecting drug use		
Male	95,245	
Female	33,452	
Total		128,696
Men who have sex with men and inject drugs		33,195
Hemophilia/coagulation disorder		
Male	3,970	
Female	137	
Total		4,107
Heterosexual Cases		
Male	13,521	
Female	26,516	
Total		40,037
Receipt of blood transfusion, blood components, or tissue		
Male	4,327	
Female	3,106	
Total		7,433
Other, including risk not reported or identified		
Male	24,790	
Female	8,607	
Total		33,397

[a]Numbers are based on AIDS cased reported to CDC through December 31, 1995.

Source: CDC semi-annual HIV/AIDS Survillance Report

TABLE 9.3

AIDS Cases by Age at Time of Diagnosis[a]

Age	Number of AIDS Cases
Under 5	5,526
5 to 12	1,422
13 to 19	2,354
20 to 24	18,955
25 to 29	73.973
30 to 34	118,898
35 to 39	114,378
40 to 44	81,000
45 to 49	44,883
50 to 54	24,031
55 to 59	13,575
60 to 64	7,720
65 and older	6,771

[a]Numbers are based on AIDS cases reported to CDC through December 31, 1995.
Source: CDC semi-annual HIV/AIDS Survillance Report

TABLE 9.4

Ten States/Territories Reporting Highest Number of Aids Cases[a]

State/Territory	Number of AIDS Cases
New York	94,751
California	88,933
Florida	51,838
Texas	35,114
New Jersey	29,327
Illinois	16,411
Puerto Rico	16,313
Pennsylvania	15,089
Georgia	14,549
Maryland	13,066

[a]Numbers are based on AIDS cases reported to CDC through December 31, 1995.
Source: CDC semi-annual HIV/AIDS Survillance Report

TABLE 9.5	
Ten Metropolitan Areas Reporting Highest Number of Aids Cases [a]	
Metropolitan Area	**Number of AIDS Cases**
New York City	81,604
Los Angeles	31,085
San Francisco	22,835
Miami	16,372
Washington, DC	14,640
Chicago	14,335
Houston	12,573
Newark	11,791
Philadelphia	11,652
Atlanta	10,439

[a]Numbers are based on AIDS cases reported to CDC through December 31, 1995.
Source: CDC semi-annual HIV/AIDS Survillance Report

The more widely accepted term for AIDS today is HIV infection. This name more clearly reflects the lengthy disease process which is initiated by transmission of the virus. The time between contraction of the virus and first symptoms can extend for several years. Thus, most HIV positive individuals do not even know that they carry the virus and are probably not receiving medical care which could extend their life and they are not likely taking any preventative measures to insure they do not pass the virus on to someone else. Additionally, it can take up to 24 months for HIV antibodies to develop in the body after the virus has been contracted. This means that an AIDS test may not show accurate results immediately after exposure, because the body has not yet had enough time to develop the antibodies being tested for. These two windows of time—one, the lengthy gap between transmission and symptoms and the other, the time between exposure and accurate test results—are among the reasons that the spread of the disease has been so insidious.[18]

HIV disease is transmitted sexually in semen and vaginal secretions and through contact with infected blood—sharing infected IV needles, across

Sharing infected needles is a primary route for HIV infection.

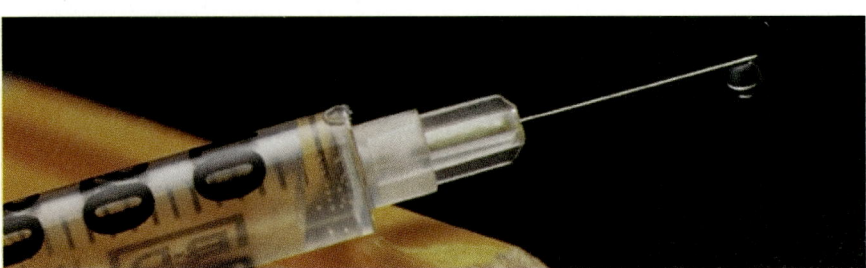

the placenta to the fetus, or transfusions of infected blood. There have also been a few cases where the virus was transmitted in a mother's milk to her baby. The virus has been detected in saliva and tears, but there are no documented cases of transmission by those routes.[20]

Thus, the primary risky behaviors for transmission of the HIV virus are unprotected sexual contact and the sharing of infected IV needles. AIDS cannot be spread through casual contact like sharing toilets, sharing eating utensils, attending school with an HIV infected person, or touching or hugging an infected person. Unlike many past epidemics when people could do very little to protect themselves because the disease agent was airborne, waterborne, or insect-borne, you can protect yourself from contracting the HIV virus! By choosing to remain sexually abstinent, engaging only in safe sexual practices, and avoiding risky sexual behaviors, you can greatly reduce the risk of acquiring the HIV virus.[18] Table 9.6 provides recommendations for reducing the risk of HIV infection and other STDs. (A discussion of ways to protect yourself from contracting the HIV virus, as well as other sexually transmitted diseases, appears later in this chapter.)

TABLE 9.6
Recommendations for Reducing the Risk of HIV Infection and Other STDs

The following suggestions may help you to make the transition from what you know to what you do:

1. If you have never had sexual contact, be assured that you have most likely avoided exposure to sexually transmitted diseases. (Be assured, too, you are not alone. Approximately 20%–25% of college students identify themselves as being abstinent.)

2. Be extremely careful about your choice of sexual partner. The days of casual sex are over! Being careful means waiting to have sex until you know your partner well and feel comfortable talking openly about your sexual health and ways to remain healthy. Obviously, this means sex with prostitutes is a very unhealthy idea.

3. Limit your sexual contacts to as few well known partners as possible. Other than abstinence—not a pleasurable lifetime prospect for most people—a long-term, monogamous relationship with one uninfected person is the healthiest choice.

4. Talk to your potential sex partner about his/her sexual past and about safe sex practices before sexual desire, alcohol, or both dim your good judgement. Although such a discussion may be difficult to initiate, its nothing compared to having to tell people you love that you have AIDS!

5. Make a commitment to use condoms during any and every sexual encounter. Latex condoms, with the spermicide nonoxynol 9, are an effective, though not perfect, way to avoid STDs, including AIDS.

6. If you are sexually active, always carry condoms with you! Condoms are now widely available and 40% are purchased by women.

7. Do not engage in anal intercourse. Anal sex is particularly risky because anal tissues tear easily, giving the HIV virus and other STD organisms a direct route to the bloodstream.

8. If you or a potential partner has engaged in unprotected sexual intercourse, shared an IV needle, observed any STD symptoms, or have any other reason to believe you may have a sexually transmitted disease, get tested before you have sex.

9. Do not share IV needles, even if you know the person well. Better yet, do not use intravenous drugs except in medically supervised situations.

10. Do not mix alcohol (or other drugs) with sexual activity. Drinking impairs good judgement and reduces the likelihood that you will follow safe sex guidelines.

The HIV virus attacks the T-cells in the immune system, causing the carrier to be vulnerable to serious infections which would not normally be a threat. The most common opportunistic infections associated with AIDS are Kaposi's sarcoma, pneumocystis carinii pneumonia, and cytomegalovirus infections. Pulmonary tuberculosis, recurrent pneumonia, and invasive cervical cancer were added to the list of AIDS related opportunistic infections in 1993.

Someone who is HIV positive may live for several years before an actual diagnosis of AIDS. According to the Centers for Disease Control, a diagnosis of full blown AIDS is made either when an individual has a T-cell count of less that 500 and an AIDS related infection or when the T-cell count is below 200 even though the individual may not have a related illness.

Drug treatments and other therapies have been developed to extend the lives and the quality of life of persons with the HIV virus. On average, people live 10 years after becoming infected with HIV. Though no cure for AIDS has yet been developed, recent developments in anti-viral drug therapies have slowed the progression of the HIV infection significantly. Using better treatments and medical strategies, physicians and persons with AIDS have developed ways to manage the infection more effectively.

About 5% of people with HIV are categorized as having "non-progressive" infection because they have remained in good health for 10 or more years. In the absence of a cure for AIDS, the best defense against this deadly disease remain prevention—this means abstinence from sexual contact, monogamous relationships, or consistent use of condoms.[18]

Because HIV disease was first identified as a disease of homosexual men, individual, community, and governmental responses to the epidemic have been, in many cases, non-existent or fraught with fear and homophobia. Persons with AIDS have been fired from their jobs, abandoned by their families, denied medical insurance benefits, and evicted from their homes. The gay community has, in many cases, been blamed for the AIDS epidemic, disregarding other forms of transmission. More recently, AIDS and human rights activists have expressed concern that, since HIV infection is now addressed more as a chronic disease, access to long-term and intensive drug therapy will be limited only to people who live in Western industrialized nations and to people who can afford the expense. This is a legitimate concern since the U.S. Public Health Service estimates the cost for treatment for one HIV positive patient is $10,000 and for a person who has full blown AIDS, $38,300. The lifetime cost of HIV disease for one individual from birth to death is estimated at $102,000.[33]

Since the HIV virus is transmitted only through body fluids, persons with HIV disease are not a threat to their family, friends, and the general population. As the likelihood increases of virtually everyone having a friend

KEY CONCEPT

SHOULD YOU GET TESTED FOR HIV?

If you are worried about the possibility of having contracted the HIV virus, discuss your concern with a health professional. If you have engaged in unsafe sex practices like intercourse without a condom or if you have shared needles, you should seriously consider getting tested. Many college student health services and county health departments offer free and confidential testing. New commercially produced home tests are also available in some states. Since testing may cause psychological consequences, get tested where both pre- and post-counseling is available. The vast majority of those who get tested find out they do not have the virus, but if HIV is present, it is important to know early in the progress of the disease so that treatment can be initiated. Table 9.7 provides telephone numbers and a website for more information on HIV and STDs.

A responsible attitude toward sex and STDs can prevent long-term complications that can significantly impact relationships. Plans for the future can be seriously disrupted by diseases like gonorrhea or chlamydia which can cause sterility.

TABLE 9.7

AIDS and STD Information Resources

Resource	Number/Location
The Centers for Disease Control Hotline	1-800-342-AIDS
Spanish Language Hotline	1-800-344-SIDA
Hotline—Deaf and Hearing Impaired	1-800-243-7889
The National AIDS Clearinghouse	1-800-458-5231
National STD Hotline	1-800-227-8922
Centers for Disease Control Website	http://www.cdc.gov

or family member who is living with AIDS, it is important that we be supportive, both personally and collectively, of persons and families who are dealing with HIV.

Chlamydia

With one in five college students estimated to have the disease, chlamydia is the most common of the 25 known types of STDs. Chlamydia is a bacterial infection which can cause permanent sterility in both men and women, mainly because its symptoms usually go unnoticed until irreversible damage to the reproductive system has been done. In males, chlamydia symptoms include a relatively clear, whitish discharge. Females may notice a mild irritation of the genitals or an itching feeling during urination. Chlamydia can be successfully treated with oral antibiotics. Between half and two-thirds of scarred fallopian tubes (and resultant infertility) has been attributed to chlamydia.[19]

Genital Herpes

More than 20 million Americans are diagnosed each year with genital herpes, another common sexually transmitted disease. Herpes Simplex II is a viral infection contracted through physical contact with an infected person during an active outbreak of lesions. In women, herpes blisters usually break out on the clitoris and labia (lips). In men, blisters tend to be located on the foreskin. The initial outbreak of herpes is usually painful enough to cause the patient to seek medical attention—thus alerting her/him to the presence of the disease. Unfortunately, no cure for herpes has yet been developed, although medications and methods for reducing discomfort and stress associated with outbreaks of the virus have been identified. Herpes II poses a significant risk to the fetus during vaginal birth. If Herpes II is active (that is, lesions are present) during labor, the baby should be delivered by cesarean section. About 6% of women with Herpes II develop cervical cancer later in life.[17]

Gonorrhea

Unlike chlamydia and herpes II, gonorrhea is a sexually transmitted disease which has been around for many years. Concern about gonorrhea diminished during the 1950's because it was so easily cured with antibiotics. During the Vietnam War in Southeast Asia, however, it was possible to acquire and use penicillin without medical supervision. The uncontrolled use of penicillin contributed to the development of resistant strains of the disease. If not diagnosed and treated quickly, gonorrhea can cause serious infections in the sexual systems of both males and females. Women can also pass the disease to their infants during childbirth, possibly causing blindness. Gonorrhea is highly infectious with over 50% of women and 25% of men contracting the bacteria after only one sexual encounter with an infected partner. As with most other STDs, symptoms in men are more likely to be noticed, with painful urination and a yellowish discharge from the urethra. Eighty percent of women notice no symptoms at all.[1]

Syphilis

Like gonorrhea, syphilis is an old disease which was feared more before the 1940s, when penicillin was developed. The incidence of syphilis is again rising, with 100,000 new cases being reported every year. A painless sore (in women, often unnoticed) on the penis, vagina, or other point of contact is the first indication of the disease. The sore, called a chancre, disappears after a few weeks regardless of treatment. Later complications include damage to the central nervous system, heart disease, blindness and death. In addition to affecting the health of the infected person and his/her sexual partner, the syphilis bacterium can also cross the placenta and cause serious damage to the fetus.[1]

Other sexually transmitted diseases include genital warts, cystitis, prostatitis, scabies, pediculous pubis, and in many cases hepatitis B (a virus that attacks the liver). Whatever the disease, safe sex practices reduce the risk of contracting the disease organism and passing it on to someone else.

STD PREVENTION

There are an estimated 14.7 million college students in the United States.[32] In general, people in this age and social group engage in exceedingly high levels of unprotected sexual intercourse, with multiple partners, in a serially monogamous pattern.[9] Although college students knowledge level about STDs is reportedly high, their corresponding preventative behaviors are not. In the same survey of 2000 college students reported earlier in this chapter, only 14% of the sexually active students said they always used a condom during sexual intercourse, even though they knew that the use of condoms is an effective STD prevention strategy.[7] A study of first year college students published in 1993 revealed that 86% of the respondents were sexually active but that fewer than 21% had always used a condom during sexual intercourse.[4] Though many university health education programs and health services have made STD and AIDS prevention education a top priority during the past several years, relatively few interventions have had a significant impact on changing behavior.[9] Some studies have reported changes in sexual practices because of the AIDS threat, but those changes are not nearly enough to reflect the enormity of the possible disease consequences.

As much as you might like to believe that sexually transmitted diseases are not a threat to you personally, the fact is that thousands of college students on campuses throughout the United States and beyond are carrying STDs. Research indicates that sexual partners, including those in long-term relationships, will not necessarily be honest with their partner when it comes to reporting infidelity or the presence of disease. According to the American College Health Association, asking a partner about past sexual experiences may be helpful, but in general, you cannot depend on that information.[2] Thus we must recognize that anyone who is sexually active is at risk. **NO SEXUALLY ACTIVE PERSON IS IMMUNE**! The only way to be absolutely safe is to be abstinent. If you are sexually active, be responsible for your own sexual health and practice safe sex procedures with every sexual encounter.

CONTRACEPTION

In this day of relatively open access to a variety of contraceptive methods, it may seem amazing to learn that over 20% of college women become pregnant during their student years.[27] It is probably safe to assume that a majority of those pregnancies are not intended. In the university study cited earlier in this chapter, only about one third of the sexually active respondents said they make consistent use of effective contraceptive methods. Another third of those who had engaged in sexual intercourse made no effort at all to avoid pregnancy.[7]

It seems that hope is still a rather popular form of birth control among college students. What happens when hope (and perhaps a dash of prayer) is your only method? A pregnancy occurs within one year for over 80% of couples! Many pregnancies result from only a few, or even one unprotected act of sexual intercourse.

According to Jaccard et. al.,[15] there are four steps in contraceptive use. First, the individual must decide whether to use a contraceptive and, if so, what method to use. Second, the contraceptive must be used consistently. Third, it must be used correctly. And fourth, there must be continuity of use—that is—the same method must be used over time or, if change is made, it is made without pregnancy risk.

Many college students who are sexually active feel guilty about their sexual feelings and behaviors. This is not surprising when we consider that very few American parents speak openly with their children about sexual issues. Research involving sexually active college students indicates that feeling guilty about sexual activity (that is, being unwilling to acknowledge one's experience) can cause you to avoid learning about contraceptive methods and avoid contraceptive use.[27] Feeling guilty will not, however, necessarily stop you from engaging in sexual intercourse. Consistent use of

KEY CONCEPT

HOW SAFE ARE CONDOMS?

Condoms are tested for leakage by the FDA. On average, 12% of condoms produced in the U.S. and 21% produced outside the U.S. fail the FDA's test. Condom breakage is also a problem. The breakage rate can be as high as 3-5%, even when used properly. Although condoms are not 100% safe and effective, when used properly they afford a significant level of protection.

The proper use of condoms can prevent STDs and unwanted pregnancies.

contraception is more likely when men and women have positive attitudes and feel open toward sexual issues and their own sexual activity.[8] If you have ever used excuses like, "we got carried away," "I was drunk," "she/he should have stopped," or, afterwards, "it will never happen again"; you need to ask yourself whether you are being honest about your sexual behavior. This important first step puts you on the road to responsible contraceptive behavior.

Contraceptive planning means that you anticipate there is at least a possibility that sexual intercourse might occur. In one study, Strassberg & Mahoney[30] asked a group of college students to report the length of time that transpired between when they actually knew they were going to have sexual intercourse and the event itself. The most common response for both men and women was "a few minutes!" Obviously, if intercourse is unanticipated, the likelihood of being prepared is greatly decreased.

If you are or may become sexually active, you need to use a contraceptive method that is most appropriate for you and your partner. Important issues to consider include effectiveness, health risks (if any), convenience, type of relationship, availability and cost of the method, relationship to STDs , and in some cases acceptability in terms of religious or philosophical beliefs. Although unintended pregnancies are experienced very differently by men and women, both have a great deal to lose when an unintended pregnancy occurs. Ideally, contraception is a shared responsibility, although each individual needs to take responsibility for his/her own health and reproductive life planning. Studies have shown that, in both married and unmarried relationships, both partner's attitudes about contraception impacts the effectiveness of contraceptive use. Studies conducted among unmarried young women have found a positive relationship between the male partner's attitude toward contraception and the woman's behavior.[15] Table 9.8 provides information about the most popular birth control methods.

TABLE 9.8

Popular Birth Control Methods

	How It Works	Effectiveness in Preventing Pregnancy*	Advantages	Disadvantages
THE PILL	"The Pill" is actually a series of pills containing one or two synthetic compounds similar to hormones that regulate the menstrual cycle. When taken as directed, the pills prevent pregnancy, primarily through blocking egg production by the ovaries.	Used correctly, the pill is the most effective, reversible single form of contraceptive. It is effective 97% of the time.	1. Easy to use and does not interrupt sex. 2. Menstrual periods may be less painful and more regular. 3. May lower the chances of getting PID, ovarian cysts, cancer of the ovaries and uterus, noncancerous breast tumors, and anemia.	1. Does not protect against any STD, including AIDS, and may make users more susceptible to chlamydia. 2. Possible side effects, especially during the first few months of use, may include: nausea, fluid retention, breast tenderness, missed periods, spotting between periods, vaginal infections, weight gain, and mood changes. 3. Other more serious health problems may develop, especially among women older than 35 who smoke cigarettes. These include blood clots, risk of heart attacks and strokes, high blood pressure, and liver tumors. 4. A medical exam and prescription are required. 5. Must be taken on a regular schedule. 6. May be difficult for some women to get pregnant for several months after stopping use.
DIAPHRAGM AND CERVICAL CAP	The cervical cap and diaphragm are both flexible rubber barriers used with spermicidal cream or jelly. The barrier and spermicide block and kill sperm moving toward the uterus. The diaphragm or cap is inserted before intercourse. However, the cap can be left in place longer and additional contraceptive cream or jelly is not needed for repeated sexual intercourse during that time.	Typically, these methods are about 80% effective.	1. Usually no serious side effects or impact on future ability to bear children. 2. Offer some protection against STDs when used with contraceptive creams and jellies. 3. The diaphragm may provide some protection against cervical cancer. 4. May be inserted ahead of time to allow for sexual spontaneity.	1. Requires a medical exam and periodic professional refitting. 2. Requires professional instruction about insertion and removal; a backup contraceptive is necessary until use is mastered. 3. May become dislodged. 4. May cause allergic reactions, urinary tract infections, and (in very rare cases) toxic shock syndrome. 5. Cannot be used for a short time after childbirth, abortion, or miscarriage, or when you are having vaginal bleeding including your periods, or any abnormal vaginal discharge. 6. Using a diaphragm may be messy because of repeated insertions of contraceptive jelly or cream. 7. Cervical cap use may lead to abnormal Pap smears and unpleasant odors (if left in too long). 8. Women uncomfortable with touching their genitals probably should consider other forms of birth control.

	How It Works	Effectiveness in Preventing Pregnancy*	Advantages	Disadvantages
INTRAUTERINE DEVICE (IUD)	The IUD is a small device inserted in the uterus by a medical practitioner. No one really knows how it works, but experts think it prevents the fertilized egg from attaching itself to the lining of the uterus.	The IUD is about 94% effective in preventing pregnancy. Effectiveness increases with continued use and if (1) the IUD placement is checked regularly, and (2) couples use condoms or spermicide during the woman's fertile days.	1. Is always in place; no special planning or preparation needed before intercourse. 2. Does not need daily attention.	1. Possible discomfort during insertion. 2. Possible heavier cramps and bleeding during periods, and spotting between periods, especially in the first few months after insertion. 3. Provides no protection against STDs including AIDS, and may make users more susceptible to chlamydia and gonorrhea. 4. In rare cases, infections associated with use may lead to PID, tubal pregnancies, and infertility. 5. Also in rare cases, may become dislodged—puncturing the uterus or become ineffective as a birth control device. 6. Must be replaced every 1–5 years, depending on the type. 7. May be expelled without being noticed, especially during menstrual periods soon after insertion. 8. A medical exam is required. 9. Many student health centers do not offer IUDs.
PERIODIC ABSTINENCE	The woman charts her menstrual cycle to learn when she is fertile and avoids unprotected intercourse during these times. Charting is done through the calendar, mucus, and temperature methods.	Typically, this method is 80% effective. It is recommended that couples use two charting methods at once to maximize effectiveness.	1. Acceptable to couples with religious and/or moral concerns about birth control. 2. No known side effects or impact on future ability to bear children.	1. Associated with a high risk of failure unless both partners cooperate in using it carefully and consistently. 2. Requires professional instruction in observing and charting fertility signs. 3. Women with irregular menstrual cycles are likely to have difficulties using this method. 4. Offers no protection against STDs. 5. Stress, fevers, and vaginal infections may make accurate observation difficult.

(Continued)

TABLE 9.8

TABLE 9.8

Popular Birth Control Methods (Continued)

	How It Works	Effectiveness in Preventing Pregnancy*	Advantages	Disadvantages
CONDOM	A protective covering made of latex (rubber) or animal membrane, the condom fits over the penis and keeps semen from entering the vagina.	Typically, condoms are less than 90% effective. However, using a spermicide with the condom boosts effectiveness to more than 99%.	1. Using latex condom with a spermicide containing nonoxynol-9 is the best protection available against AIDS and will also help prevent the transmission of other STDs. 2. Only used when needed. 3. No serious side effects or impact on future ability to bear children. 4. Easy to buy and have handy—you do not need a medical exam or prescription. They can be bought in drug stores, some supermarkets, and student health centers. They may also be available from vending machines on some campuses, and some student health centers offer them without charge. 5. They may protect against cervical cancer.	1. They are ineffective if used incorrectly or if they break. 2. Some men may report decreased sensation. 3. In rare instances, either or both partners may have allergic reactions to latex or the spermicide or lubricant used with the condom; these reactions cause genital irritation.

	How It Works	Effectiveness in Preventing Pregnancy*	Advantages	Disadvantages
SPERMICIDES	These products are inserted into the vagina shortly before sexual intercourse and are effective for a short period of time. Don't confuse creams and jellies that are spermicides with those that are only lubricants.	Typically, these methods are 80% effective. However, vaginal spermicides (possibly excepting film) used with condoms are more than 99% effective. (The data are less reliable for film because it has been available for a short period of time.)	1. Easy to buy and have handy—you don't need medical exam or prescription. They can be bought in drug stores and some supermarkets. 2. Provide some protection against STDs. Using spermicides containing nonoxynol-9 with latex condoms is the best protection available against AIDS and will also help prevent the transmission of other STDs. 3. Only used when needed. 4. No serious medical side effects or impact on future ability to bear children.	1. May cause allergic reactions (genital irritations). 2. Must be inserted before every act of sexual intercourse; this may interrupt love-making. 3. May be messy. 4. Women uncomfortable with touching their genitals probably should consider other forms of birth control.
CONTRACEPTIVE SPONGE	The sponge is a soft, synthetic round device containing the spermicide nonoxynol-9. It fits over the cervix and blocks and kills sperm moving toward the uterus. The sponge is moistened and inserted into the vagina before intercourse and may be left in place for up to 24 hours.	Generally, sponges have an 80% effectiveness rate; however, they are less effective for women who have borne children.	1. Protect against some STDs. 2. Easy to buy and have handy—you don't need a medical exam or prescription and they are available at some supermarkets as well as drugstores. 3. Usually easy to insert. 4. No separate application or spermicide is necessary. 5. May be inserted ahead of time to allow for sexual spontaneity.	1. Cannot be reused after removal. 2. May be difficult to insert or remove on occasion; you may need professional instruction to use properly. 3. Clean water must be available for insertion. 4. May cause irritation or vaginal discharge. 5. Women uncomfortable with touching their genitals probably should consider other forms of birth control. 6. Cannot be used for a short time after childbirth, abortion, or miscarriage, or when you are having vaginal bleeding (including your period) or any abnormal vaginal discharge. 7. In very rare cases may cause toxic shock syndrome.

(Continued)

TABLE 9.8

Popular Birth Control Methods *(Concluded)*

	How It Works	Effectiveness in Preventing Pregnancy*	Advantages	Disadvantages
HORMONAL IMPLANTS (Norplant is commercial name)	Hormonal implants work by releasing a constant dose of levonorgestrel, a synthetic form of progesterone, into the bloodstream. The contraceptive mechanism is the prevention of ovulation and the thickening of the cervical mucosa, interfering with the passage of sperm to the uterus.	Theoretical and actual-use effectiveness of almost 100%.	1. Provides highly effective contraception for up to 5 years. 2. Requires no compliance beyond the insertion (there is no daily need to remember to take a pill). 3. Does not interrupt sex.	1. Some menstrual irregularities, headaches, and acne have been experienced by some users. 2. May be some slight discomfort with insertion. 3. Initial cost is high ($200–$300), although for a 5-year period the cost is lower than that of oral contraceptives. 4. Contraindications for use are the same as for oral contraceptives. 5. Does not protect against STDs. 6. Medical exam and prescription are required.
STERILIZATION	Medical operations can be performed on males (vasectomies) or females (tubal ligations) to prevent future fertility. Vasectomies are safer and simpler procedures than tubal ligations.	Vasectomies and tubal ligations are about 99% effective.	1. No known long-term health effects. 2. No further concern necessary about contraception	Medical complications due to surgery may occur on rare occasions. Among males, minor complications from surgery (swelling, discoloration, discomfort, and pain) are common. Among females, complications may be more severe.

Vasectomy: The tubes through which the sperm travel from the testes to the penis are cut and blocked; ejaculation and orgasm are still possible, but fertilization is not. This is an outpatient procedure done under local anesthesia.

Tubal ligation: The fallopian tubes are closed so that the egg cannot travel from the ovaries to meet the sperm. This can be done in a variety of ways, some of which are outpatient procedures. The operation does not affect the ability to have orgasms. The likelihood of being able to reverse the procedure is very slight.

	How It Works	Effectiveness in Preventing Pregnancy*	Advantages	Disadvantages
CONTRACEPTIVE INJECTIONS	This is an injection (brandname Depo-Provera) which contains a hormone that prevents pregnancy. Women receive the injection in the buttocks or arm every 3 months.	Theoretical and actual-use effectiveness of about 97%	1. Convenient—injection is needed only 4 times per year. 2. Safe, highly effective and long-lasting. 3. No need for action before, during or after sex. 4. Can be used safely after childbirth and while breastfeeding. 5. Helps protect women from cancer of the lining of the uterus.	1. Not appropriate for women who want less than a year of protection. 2. Irregular monthly periods and spotting may occur. After a year, most women stop having periods. 3. Side effects, though uncommon, may include bloating, weight gain, headaches, depression, loss of interest in sex, and hair loss. 4. Injections do not protect against STDs.

A WORD ABOUT ALCOHOL AND SEX

The author recently noted a list of rules to live by on a female college student's T-shirt. "Drink till he's cute" and "if you're not wasted, the night is" were two recommendations. These phrases highlight an alarming trend among college women which has been a familiar behavior to college men in past years—the intention to achieve alcohol intoxication as quickly as possible.

No discussion of healthy sexual behavior during college years would be complete without consideration of the impact that the use of alcohol has on sexual behavior. Nationwide, about 50% of college students become intoxicated every two weeks with consequences ranging from academic sanctions, destruction of property and arrests to motor vehicle accidents and deaths.[31] It is estimated that about one in every five college women is sexually assaulted and 90% of those assaults are alcohol related. In a survey of students on health interests and behaviors at a mid-western university, about one-third of the respondents said they had engaged in alcohol induced intercourse.[7]

One problem with alcohol, of course, is that, even in moderate amounts, it has a tranquilizing effect, thus reducing inhibitions that may have kept you from engaging in unplanned and unhealthy sexual activity. As one college student remarked during a course activity titled "Liquor, Lust, and Latex," "If it weren't for the beers I make myself drink first, I wouldn't be having sex at all!" Brown and Munson[3] found that both men and women believe that alcohol acts to reduce inhibitions, although these effects are due more to our own psychological interpretation than to any physiological reaction. Alcohol allows us to deny responsibility for our behavior. If alcohol contained an effective contraceptive and prevented STDs, then the sex-related consequences might be minimized! Unfortunately, that is not the case.

For women, drinking alcohol poses unique risks. Women absorb about 30% more alcohol into their blood than do men of the same weight drinking the same amount. For a woman of average size, one drink will have about the same effect as two for the average size man. These unique risks for women have serious implications for social drinking when tasks like driving, judgment, and coordination are involved.[12]

Ninety percent of acquaintance rapes are related to the consumption of alcohol by either the victim, the perpetrator, or both. When one of the participants in sexual intercourse is unwilling or is unable to make an informed decision about his/her participation because of the influence of alcohol, then a possible sexual assault situation is in progress. Acquaintance rape is rape! It is a serious crime that affects thousands of college students

Don't let alcohol lead to unwanted sex.

every year and results in serious physical and emotional consequences for its victims, for the offenders, and for their families. Given that 90% of these crimes are committed after alcohol is consumed, one of the best ways to avoid becoming involved is to remain sober![26] Table 9.9 provides recommendations for preventing sexual assaults.

According to a 1990 nationwide study of alcohol use and risky sexual behavior among young adults, respondents who drank more frequently or drank heavily were more likely to have had two or more sex partners in the previous year.[11] Drinkers were also more likely to have had sex with a casual partner and were less likely to have used a condom during sexual intercourse. Another study, reported by Gordon and Carey in 1996, reported that when their male research subjects were intoxicated, they were more likely to engage in behaviors which placed them at risk for contracting sexually transmissible diseases.[10]

As if recent alcohol-related sexual assault statistics were not grim enough, a new threat has recently emerged on the college scene. The drug, Rohypnol (also known as "roofies," "roche," "rib," and "rope") is now being reported as one of the "in" drugs of the 90s, particularly in college fraternities. According to a University of Florida drug hotline, "roofies" have been added to punch and other drinks at fraternity parties and other college social gatherings and given to females to increase the chance for sexual conquest. After unknowingly ingesting the drug, some women have reported waking up hours later naked in unfamiliar surroundings and have been sexually assaulted while under the influence of the drug.[29]

Rohypnol is the brand name for a very potent tranquilizer which produces a sedative effect, amnesia, and sedation which lasts for several hours. The drug is not commonly prescribed in the U.S. and most of the Rohypnol used in this country is illegally transported across the border from Mexico. "Roofies" are relatively inexpensive—selling for only $2.00–$4.00.[29] The combination of Rohypnol and alcohol is particularly dangerous because together the effect on memory, judgment, and central nervous system depression is greater than for either drug taken alone. People who become intoxicated on a combination of both drugs typically have blackouts lasting 8 to 24 hours.[28] An overdose of the drug, particularly in combination with alcohol, can result in coma and death. Repeated use can also lead to physical dependence.

Because "Roofies" can prevent users (many of whom do not know they have ingested the drug) from remembering how they came to ingest it or what happened afterwards, investigation of sexual assault associated with use of the drug is extremely difficult. Though the physical evidence of assault may be obvious, the victim often cannot describe what happened or identify the perpetrator. Embarrassment and shame may even cause the

TABLE 9.9

Tips for Preventing Sexual Assaults

- Set sexual limits. No one has the right to force or coerce you into doing something you do not want to do.

- Be clear and consistent about your intentions. Say "Yes" when you mean "yes" and "no" when you mean "no." Make sure your body language matches what your words are saying.

- Trust your gut-level feelings. If a situation feels bad, it probably is.

- Avoid excessive use of alcohol or other drugs.

- Socialize with people who share you values. If you go out with people who are known to be more sexually permissive, others will probably think you are too.

- Be careful about dating individuals who are much older than you are. Older partners may be more sexually experienced and may expect more sooner.

- Be sensitive to your partner's intentions about sexual activity. Don't make assumptions.

- Get to know someone before you consent to a date. Do activities in groups and/or in public before going with a date to a more private place.

- Be independent and aware on your dates. Express opinions about where you would like to go and appropriate places to meet.

- Do not do something you don't want to do just to avoid making a scene or feeling embarrassed.

- Avoid attending or staying late at parties where men greatly outnumber women.

- If things start to get out of hand, be loud in protesting, leave immediately, and go for help if needed.

- Avoid secluded places where you are likely to be vulnerable. Sexual assaults usually happen on the assailant's turf—in a car, apartment or dorm room.

- Examine your attitudes about money, power and sex. If one pays for the date does that mean the other will be expected to "put out"? If that may be the case, pay your own way or suggest dates that do not involve money.

- Do not allow your behavior to be governed by social pressures from other men or women.

- Remember that being turned down for sex is not a rejection of you personally. Partners who say no are expressing their desire not to engage in a single act.

- If you partner says "no," accept the decision. If you are getting mixed messages, say so and discuss it.

- Don't assume someone who dresses a certain way or flirts wants to have sex.

- Don't allow yourself or others to take sexual advantage of someone whose judgment is impaired by alcohol or drugs. If someone is intoxicated, they cannot give consent to have sex. This behavior is sexual assault.

- Establish "buddy" plans with friends for preventing sexual assault. Plan ahead for at least one person to avoid alcohol when attending social events and watch for potentially dangerous situations among friends.

*Adapted from Friends Raping Friends: Could It Happen to You? by Jean Gorman Hughs and Bernice Sandler. Developed through the Project on the Status of Women, Association of American Colleges.

victim not to report the incident at all, simply blaming herself for getting into the situation in the first place. Administering someone a drug without their knowledge is not only insidious, it is also illegal. Having sex with someone who is under the influence of a drug, whether it is alcohol, Rohypnol, or both is also a crime because that person cannot give consent to the sexual act. Both women and men need to be aware that this drug is available and being used. The best way to avoid it is to be sure you are in surroundings with trusted friends and to know what you are drinking.

CONCLUSION

Sexual health is an aspect of wellness which demands many choices. The decisions made have both short and long term implications. The college years provide an excellent opportunity to learn more about sexual health. Colleges offer academic courses, workshops, counseling sessions, health services, support groups and library resources which can help you to expand your knowledge. If you keep in mind that the largest and most significant part of the sexual system is the brain, and we need to use this organ well before we use the others, you will be well on the way to a healthy sexual identity.

EXPLORING WELLNESS ON THE WEB

Many resources are available on the World Wide Web. You can reinforce, expand and enhance the information presented in this chapter by accessing the following sites.

http:www.siecus.org — site for Sexuality Information and Education Council of the United States (SIECUS). SIECUS is a national, private, non-profit advocacy organization which affirms that sexuality is a natural and healthy part of living.

http://www.cs.utk.edu/~bartley/saInfoPage.html — provides information on acquaintance rape, sexual abuse, assault, incest, rape, and sexual harassment.

REFERENCES

1. Allgeier, E. and Allgeier, A. (1991). *Sexual Interactions*. Lexington, MA: D.C. Heath and Company.

2. American College Health Association. (1990). *HIV Infection and AIDS: What Everyone Should Know*. Baltimore, MD: American College Health Association.

3. Brown, S. A. and Munson, E. (1987). Extroversion, anxiety, and the perceived effects of alcohol. *Journal of Studies on Alcohol*, 48, 272-276.

4. Caron, S.L., Davis, C.M., Haltleman, W.A. and Stickle, M. (1993). Predictors of condom-related behaviors among first-year college students. *Journal of Sex Research*, 30, 252-259.

5. Centers for Disease Control. (1996). *Morbidity and Mortality Weekly Report*, Atlanta, GA., February 16.

6. Centers for Disease Control. (1995). *Morbidity and Mortality Weekly Report*, Atlanta, GA., November 24.

7. Davis, T.M. and Koch, S.J. (1991). Health interests and behaviors of students enrolled in the personal wellness course at the University of Northern Iowa. *IAHPERD Journal,* Spring, 24(1), 14-16.

8. Fisher, T.D. (1988). The relationship between parent-child communication about sexuality and college students' sexual behavior and attitudes as a function of parental proximity. *The Journal of Sex Research,* 24, 305-311.

9. Fisher, J.D., Fisher, W., Misovich, S.J., Kimble, K., and Malloy, T.E. (1996). Changing AIDS risk behavior: Effects of an intervention emphasizing AIDS risk reduction information, motivation, and behavioral skills in a college student population. *Health Psychology*, 15(2), 114-123.

10. Gordon, C.M. and Carey, M.P., (1996). Alcohol's effects on requisites for sexual risk reduction in men: An initial experimental investigation. *Health Psychology,* 15(1), 56-60.

11. Graves, K.L., (1995). Risky sexual behavior and alcohol use among young adults: results from a national survey. *American Journal of Health Promotion,* 10(1), 27-37.

12. Horton, J.A. (Ed.) (1992). *The Women's Health Data Book*. Jacobs Institute of Women's Health.

13. Hunt, M. (1974). *Sexual Behavior in the 1970s*. Chicago, IL: Playboy Press.

14. Insel, P.M. and Roth, W.T. (1991). *Core Concepts in Health*. Mountain View, CA: Mayfield.

15. Jaccard, J., Helbig, D.W., Wan, C.K., Gutman, M.A., and Fritz-Silverstein, D.C. (1996). The prediction of accurate contraceptive use from attitudes and behaviors. *Health Education Quarterly*, 23(1), 17-33.

16. Jamison, P.L. and Gebhard, P.H. (1988). Penis size increase between flacid and erect states: An analysis of the Kinsey data. *The Journal of Sex Research,* 24, 177-183.

17. Kaufman, R. H. (1986). Clinical features of herpes genetalia. *The Journal of Reproductive Medicine,* 31, 5 (Supplement), 379-383.

18. Koop, C.E. (1986). Surgeon General's Report on AIDS, *Journal of the American Medical Association*, 257(November 28), 1986.

19. Lee, H. (1989). Genital chlamydial infection in female and male college students. *Journal of American College Health*, 37, 288-291.

20. Lifson, A.R. (1988). Do alternate modes of transmission of human immunodeficiency virus exist? *Journal of the American Medical Association*, 259, 1353-1356.

21. Masters, W.H. and Johnson, V.E. (1966). *Human Sexual Response*. Boston, MA: Little, Brown.

22. Paige, K.E. (1978). The ritual of circumcision. *Human Nature,* 1, 40-48.

23. Perry, J.D., and Whipple, B. (1981). Pelvic muscle strength of female ejaculators: Evidence in support of a new theory of orgasm. *The Journal of Sex Research,* 17, 22-39.

24. Rome, E. (1992). Anatomy and Physiology of Sexuality and Reproduction. *The New Our Bodies Ourselves.* New York: Simon and Schuster.

25. Sawyer, R.G. and Smith, N.G. (1996). A Survey of Situational Factors at First Intercourse Among College Students. *American Journal of Health Behavior,* 20, 208-217.

26. Sex on Campus: A special issue. (1989). *Journal of American College Health,* May, 1989.

27. Smith, S.F. and Smith, C.M. (1990). *Personal Health Choices.* Boston: Jones and Bartlett.

28. Smith, D., Wesson, D., and Calhoun, S. (1997). *Rohypnol (Flunitrazepam) Fact Sheet.* Available at www.lec.org/DrugSearch/Documents/Rohypnol.

29. Staten, C. (1997). *Roofies, The New "Date Rape" Drug of Choice.* Available at www.emergency.com/roofies.html.

30. Strassberg, D.L. and Mahoney, J.M. (1988). Correlates of the contraceptive behavior of adolescents/young adults. *The Journal of Sex Research,* 25, 531-536.

31. Students, alcohol, and college health: A special issue. (1987). *Journal of American College Health,* 36, 2.

32. U.S. National Center for Health Education Statistics. (1994). *Digest of Educational Statistics* (USDE Publication No. NCS94115). Washington, DC: Office of Educational Research and Improvement.

33. U.S. Public Health Service. (1992). The Agency for Health Care and Policy Research, Report no. 93-0006.

DEFINITIONS OF KEY TERMS

abstinence — the practice of refraining from sexual activity.

AIDS — Acquired Immune Deficiency Syndrome, a fatal disease caused by the Human Immunodeficiency virus (HIV), causes severe suppression of the immune system, reducing the body's ability to resist disease.

bisexual — the capacity to feel sexual attraction toward both males and females.

chlamydia — an STD caused by the bacterium, Chlamydia trachomatis, frequently without symptoms in women, chlamydia is the most common sexually transmitted disease in the U.S.

circumcision — the surgical removal of the foreskin from the penis of the male or the hood from the clitoris of the female.

clitoris — the highly sensitive erectile tissue located at the point where minor lips converge at the top of the vulva, only known function is to provide female sexual pleasure.

condom — a sheath, usually made of latex, placed over the erect penis before sexual activity, used for the prevention of pregnancy and protection from sexually transmitted diseases, also called a rubber.

contraception — the practice of using a technique, a drug, or a device to prevent contraception.

erection — the engorgement and hardening of the penis during sexual response.

fallopian tube — tubes through which eggs (ova) are transported from the ovaries to the uterus, fertilization normally takes place here.

genital herpes — a viral infection (herpes simplex II) contracted through physical contact with an infected person during an active outbreak of the sores, almost 100 million Americans are estimated to have this incurable STD.

glans — the sensitive tip of the penis or clitoris.

gonorrhea — an STD caused by the bacterium Neisseria gonorrhoeae, people 20–24 are at highest risk for contracting this disease.

Gräfenberg spot — also known as the G spot, an area of sensitivity in the vagina accessed through the upper wall, about two inches from the vaginal entrance.

heterosexual — erotic attraction toward the other gender.

HIV infection — carrying the human immunodeficiency virus.

homosexual — erotic attraction toward the same gender.

masturbation — self-simulation of the genitals.

menstruation — the sloughing off of the uterus' endometrial lining and accompanying discharge through the vaginal opening, often referred to as a woman's period.

ovaries — the two small organs which lie above and beside the uterus and produce eggs and hormones.

ovum — the human egg, the female reproductive cell

penis — the male sex organ.

rape — sexual intercourse without consent and under actual or threatened force.

scrotum — the sac which contains the testes.

sexual assault — coercion of a nonconsenting victim to have sexual contact.

sexual orientation — refers to erotic attraction toward one gender or the other, or both. Kinsey proposes that individuals can be placed on a seven-point continuum from exclusively heterosexual to exclusively homosexual, based on sexual behaviors and erotic feelings.

sexuality — the dimension of ourselves, based on biological and environmental factors, which concerns all aspects of sexual behavior.

sperm — the male reproductive cell.

syphilis — an STD caused by the bacterium Treponema pallidum, once a major health problem in the U.S., incidence is again on the rise.

testes — the small organs located in the scrotum which produce sperm and hormones.

testosterone — the masculinizing sex hormone.

vulva — the external female genitals.

LAB 9.1

SEXUAL DECISIONS

Name _____ ID _____ Sect _____ Time _____ Date _____

Purpose

To identify and ponder reasons to engage in and not to engage in sexual intercourse.

Directions

Listed below are reasons why you might or might not engage in sexual intercourse in any particular situation. Identify the relative importance each reason plays in your decision to engage or not engage in sexual activity by checking the appropriate column listing the degrees of importance.

Reasons	Not Important	Slightly Important	Important	Very Important	Extremely Important
Risk of Aids	☐	☐	☐	☐	☐
Risk of other STD	☐	☐	☐	☐	☐
Risk of Pregnancy	☐	☐	☐	☐	☐
Sexual history of partner	☐	☐	☐	☐	☐
Partner not an IV drug user	☐	☐	☐	☐	☐
Biological gratification	☐	☐	☐	☐	☐
Peer-influence	☐	☐	☐	☐	☐
Desire to be accepted by partner	☐	☐	☐	☐	☐
Dissipation of stress	☐	☐	☐	☐	☐
Need to feel loved/cared for	☐	☐	☐	☐	☐
Sign of commitment in a relationship	☐	☐	☐	☐	☐
Expression of love for partner	☐	☐	☐	☐	☐
Desire for a variety of partners	☐	☐	☐	☐	☐
Evidence of desirability	☐	☐	☐	☐	☐
Proof of sexual prowess	☐	☐	☐	☐	☐
Moral/ethical/religious prohibition	☐	☐	☐	☐	☐
Improves self-esteem	☐	☐	☐	☐	☐
Determination of sexual compatibility before marriage	☐	☐	☐	☐	☐
Feelings of regret the day after	☐	☐	☐	☐	☐
Want to remain a virgin until marriage	☐	☐	☐	☐	☐
Influence of alcohol	☐	☐	☐	☐	☐

(Continued)

SEXUAL DECISIONS

Self-Evaluation

Think about your responses to the above checklist. Are the reasons checked above for engaging in sexual intercourse related to your personal desires/feelings/gratifications or to considerations of your partners desires/feelings/gratifications? Are the reasons checked above for not engaging in sexual intercourse related to your fear of consequences or to your moral/ethical/religious standards?

NOTES

10

Coping with Stress

Susan J. Koch

INTRODUCTION

For most people, college is a time of stress. New living arrangements, changes in nutritional habits, new relationships, unscheduled time, financial pressures, interpersonal conflicts, and academic adjustments are all experiences common to college life which require substantial accommodation or readjustment.

Although many students make the transition to university life easily, most experience a period of at least minor difficulty. For some students, collegiate stress has resulted in anxiety, depression or burnout. According to an October, 1987 *Newsweek on Campus* special report, burnout—emotional and physical exhaustion—is the single most common reason students give for leaving school before graduation.

On the other hand, stress can also be viewed as a positive force. When managed properly, stress can be a powerful ally for growth and accomplishment.

Establishing a personal strategy for coping with collegiate stress early in your college career can help reduce anxiety and increase academic and social progress. Managing stress appropriately also enhances overall physical, mental, and emotional health by minimizing the negative effects. This chapter will help you to examine your current level of stress and will assist you in planning personal strategies for stress management and reduction.

UNDERSTANDING STRESS

During the past decade, the word stress has become a common part of our vocabulary. For most of us, stress means tension, uneasiness, and a sense of urgency. Dr. Hans Selye, a world-renowned Canadian endocrinologist often referred to as the "father of stress research," has defined **stress** as "the nonspecific response of the body to any demand made on it."[30] Nonspecific means that your body will respond in the same way regardless of whether the cause of the stress (the **stressor**) is positive or negative. The demand might be physical (running across campus with only a few minutes between classes) or it might be psychological (you and your roommate disagree on the level of noise that is acceptable in your room).

Researcher Dr. Walter B. Cannon, a distinguished American physiologist, described the human reaction to stress as the **fight-or-flight** mechanism. This innate characteristic has allowed the human race to survive.[3] Physiological responses to the fight-or-flight mechanism are illustrated in Figure 10.1. Modern humans have the same stress response that cave dwellers experienced when faced with a saber-toothed tiger. This response may

FIGURE 10.1

Physiological Responses to the "Fight-or-Flight Mechanism." There are many potential physiological responses to the "Fight-or-Flight Mechanism."

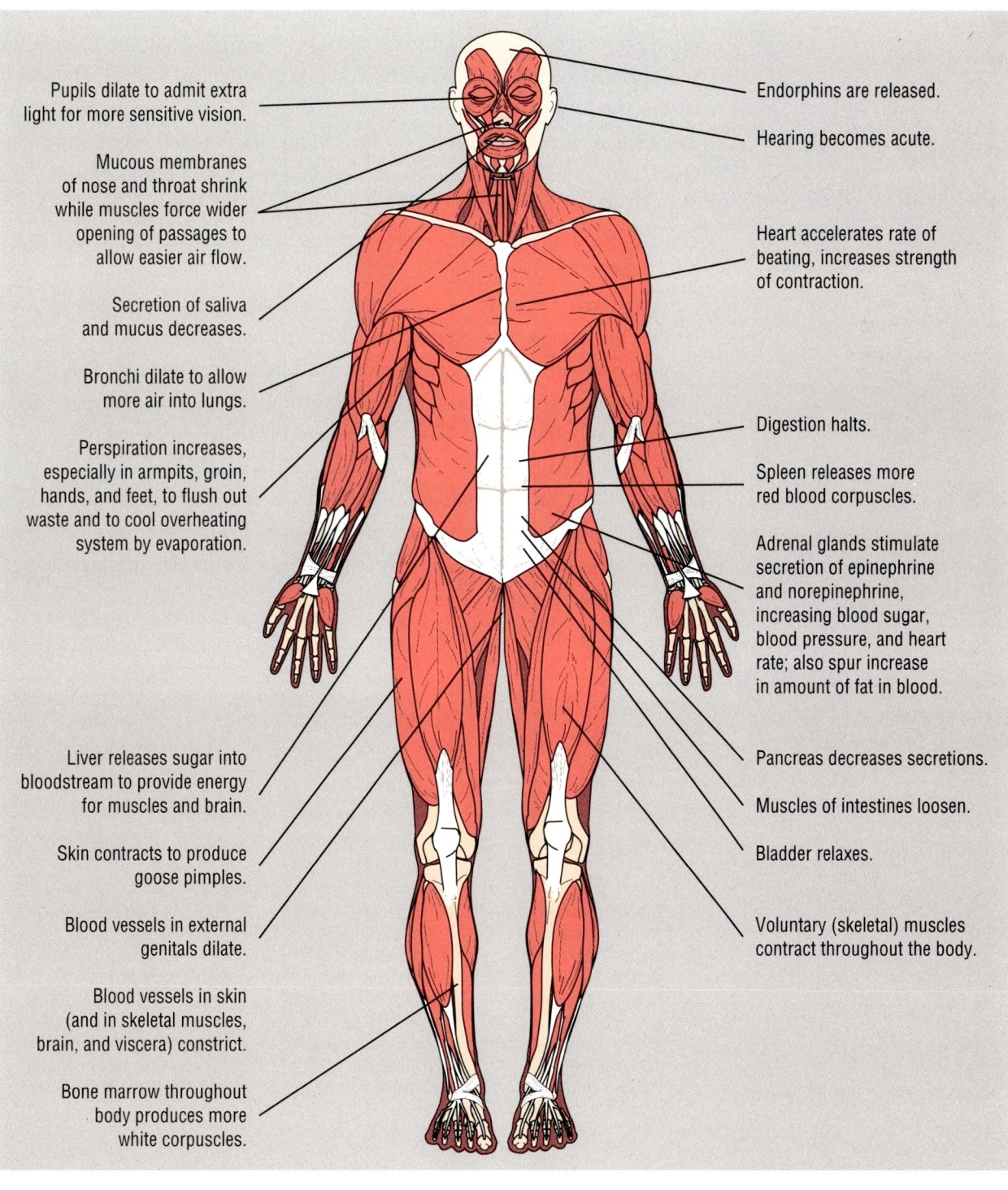

Pupils dilate to admit extra light for more sensitive vision.

Mucous membranes of nose and throat shrink while muscles force wider opening of passages to allow easier air flow.

Secretion of saliva and mucus decreases.

Bronchi dilate to allow more air into lungs.

Perspiration increases, especially in armpits, groin, hands, and feet, to flush out waste and to cool overheating system by evaporation.

Liver releases sugar into bloodstream to provide energy for muscles and brain.

Skin contracts to produce goose pimples.

Blood vessels in external genitals dilate.

Blood vessels in skin (and in skeletal muscles, brain, and viscera) constrict.

Bone marrow throughout body produces more white corpuscles.

Endorphins are released.

Hearing becomes acute.

Heart accelerates rate of beating, increases strength of contraction.

Digestion halts.

Spleen releases more red blood corpuscles.

Adrenal glands stimulate secretion of epinephrine and norepinephrine, increasing blood sugar, blood pressure, and heart rate; also spur increase in amount of fat in blood.

Pancreas decreases secretions.

Muscles of intestines loosen.

Bladder relaxes.

Voluntary (skeletal) muscles contract throughout the body.

be triggered hundreds of times each day, with stress and its effects accumulating over days, weeks, and months. Since the triggering of the flight-or-flight response is often involuntary, learning to control and direct it is a major objective of stress management training.[30]

Selye classified reactions to stress as the **General Adaptation Syndrome.** As shown in Figure 10.2, during the alarm reaction the stressor (stress producing factor) activates the body for fight-or-flight. During the resistance stage, the signs of alarm reaction are reduced as the body adapts to the stress. Finally, in the exhaustion stage, if the stressful stimuli are not diminished, your adaptive energy is used up, alarm reactions become constant, resistance is decreased, and illness or even death may follow. It is important to remember that adaptation energy is finite! Stress over time will deplete your body of the resources it needs to defend itself and you. Illness, physical and/or mental, is the likely result.[30]

An alternative, and far more positive, ending to the given example could be that the person described makes decisions and takes appropriate action to reduce or eliminate the stress before the third stage is reached. This results in the body returning to a state of equilibrium, wherein the body's systems function smoothly again. This phenomenon is called **homeostasis.**

Selye called positive stress reactions **eustress** and assigned the term **distress** to describe negative responses to stress. Eustress is viewed as a reaction which increases health and performance, but when the physiological limitations are exceeded; distress, with its accompanying negative effects is experienced.[30]

FIGURE 10.2

The Three Phases of the General Adaptation Syndrome (G.A.S.)

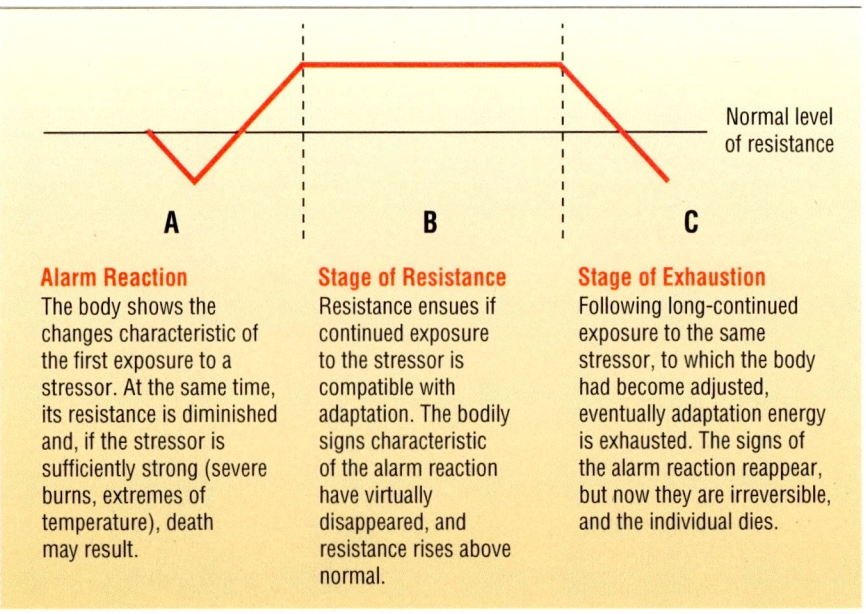

A

Alarm Reaction
The body shows the changes characteristic of the first exposure to a stressor. At the same time, its resistance is diminished and, if the stressor is sufficiently strong (severe burns, extremes of temperature), death may result.

B

Stage of Resistance
Resistance ensues if continued exposure to the stressor is compatible with adaptation. The bodily signs characteristic of the alarm reaction have virtually disappeared, and resistance rises above normal.

C

Stage of Exhaustion
Following long-continued exposure to the same stressor, to which the body had become adjusted, eventually adaptation energy is exhausted. The signs of the alarm reaction reappear, but now they are irreversible, and the individual dies.

Stressors in Collegiate Life

Every environment, including the college campus, has its own set of stressors. Additionally, individuals react to the same stressor in different ways.

According to *The College Student's Health Guide* by Sandra Smith and Christopher Smith,[32] sources of stress most frequently named by college students can be grouped in three areas; academic and social situations, environment, and lifestyle. Richard Lazarus, a noted stress researcher, stated in *The College Student's Health Guide* that students feel most anxious about wasting time, meeting high standards, and being lonely.[32]

Davis, Eshelmena and McKay[7] group stressors into four major categories:

1. Environmental stress including noise, the weather, pollution and the like;

2. Social stress including financial problems, deadlines, demands on your time and the loss of loved ones;

3. Physiological stressors like illness, lack of exercise, poor nutrition and sleep disturbances;

4. Your thoughts—that is—the way your brain interprets changes around you and "decides" the degree of stress response you will make to various stressors.

When a group of 200 students in a college wellness class were asked to generate a list of college stressors they most often named interpersonal relationships, with academic issues and money close behind. When the same group was asked to name pleasurable college experiences, socializing was most often mentioned. It is interesting to note how similar the sources of stress and the sources of pleasure are in the same group.

Professional preparation for a future career is a fundamental reason for college attendance. Thus academic achievement and pressures which accompany course work are commonly cited stressors in the collegiate environment. Declaring a major, maintaining an acceptable grade point average, fulfilling your own and your parents expectations, dealing with professors, managing a variety of academic assignments, and competition are all sources of academic stress.

Since stress is experienced very individually, as you begin to make a plan for reducing and managing stress, it is useful to spend some time thinking about the events in your life that you find most stressful. The exercise illustrated in Table 1 will help guide your thinking.

You may find that the study skills which were adequate for your high school work are inadequate for more challenging college courses. If you recognize the difficulty early, you can take action to correct the deficiency

---

TABLE 10.1

Identifying Stressful Events

Step 1: Make a list of the situations you experience (or expect to experience in the near future) which trigger anxiety. In your description name the setting, the action, and the people involved. List at least 20 different situations including minor to most serious.

Step 2: Make a second list, rank ordering the listed experiences in order from least stressful to most stressful.

Step 3: Review your list and consider, for each situation, whether it is possible or advisable for you to simply avoid the situation or whether you need to work on managing the situation better to reduce associated stress. Place an "A" next to the situations best avoided and a "M" next to those which need stress management.

---

before serious damage is done. Most colleges have student assistance centers where strengths and weaknesses can be assessed and specific skills, like note-taking, listening, and test-preparation strategies are taught. Talking with your professor or academic advisor about a problem, finding a tutor, or having a friend with good writing skills edit your work are also positive strategies. Asking for help is often viewed by students as admitting defeat; but recognizing when help is needed is far more healthy than leaving the issue unresolved. As academic skills are improved, your confidence will increase and anxiety about academic success will be diminished.

Most students experience some degree of concern before college exams. A certain amount of anxiety or stress can be a powerful motivator. However, when anxiety gets out of control, it can lead to poor concentration, postponed study sessions, inadequate planning, and even panic. **Test anxiety** can cause you to lose valuable study time and make incorrect assumptions both about your own academic ability and about appropriate preparation.

Test anxiety has been defined as a state marked by heightened self-awareness and perceived helplessness. According to Insel and Roth[18], students with test anxiety view themselves as being unprepared and view the testing situation as threatening. They become preoccupied with perceived inadequacy to the point where it interferes with their ability to prepare for the exam. Finally they expect failure, which leads to a self-fulfilling prophecy.

Research has resulted in the development of effective techniques for overcoming test anxiety. These techniques include education about the stress response, self-talk scripts which emphasize one's ability to succeed, positive visualization, rehearsal techniques for tests, and specific strategies for defusing anxiety immediately before and during an exam. It is important to keep in mind that adequate preparation, often over an extended period of

TABLE 10.2	
Causes and Prevention of Test Anxiety	
Causes	**Prevention**
1. Inadequate preparation	1. Pacing and planning
2. Negative self talk	2. Using realistic and positive self-talk
3. Negative mental images	3. Using mental rehearsal
4. Physical tension	4. Practicing daily deep relaxation and using Six-Second Quieting Response
5. Inadequate exercise, nutrition, sleep	5. Maintaining a wellness lifestyle, especially during exams

time, is a necessary element in preventing test anxiety. If you don't know the material, test anxiety is completely understandable.[27] Table 10.2 illustrates causes and preventative strategies for test anxiety.

Stress within the family back home becomes an on-campus stressor for many college students. Family financial difficulties, parents' marital problems, and illness are all possibilities. In one survey of 300 college students, 14% of the respondents said they had experienced a significant loss within the past year. These losses included the deaths of parents and grandparents, death of a sibling, breakups of significant relationships, and miscarriage.[17]

In addition to the common stressors already described, many students are challenged by special circumstances. The nontraditional student (often described as one beyond the typical college age) may have parental responsibilities and more difficult than usual financial limitations. An international student may be struggling with the language barrier, culture shock, and extended separation from family. The student with a physical disability may have difficulty with note-taking or transportation.

A key issue in stress management is to recognize the stressors in your environment. You can then take action to remove those that you can and manage those that cannot be removed.

ASSESSING YOUR VULNERABILITY TO COLLEGIATE STRESS

Do your recent past experiences predispose you to stress-related illness? Are you setting yourself up for negative stress effects by your lifestyle? Is your body trying to tell you something by exhibiting stress symptoms? Is your personality type pushing you toward stress-related problems? In recent years, a number of assessment instruments have been developed which can help you to answer these questions and identify the factors that contribute to your own stress reactions. This is the fundamental first step in stress management.

Do your recent past experiences predispose you to stress-related illness? Preliminary studies seem to indicate that there is at least some relationship between life events and disease. In 1967 Drs. Thomas Holmes and Richard Rahe published the *Social Readjustment Rating Scale* .[16] In examining the medical charts of 5000 patients, Holmes and Rahe noticed that many stressful events occurred at about the same time as disease onset. They postulated that significant events in one's life—some of which are negative, like death of a close family member and some of which are positive, like outstanding personal achievement— require readjustment. These readjustments, particularly when a number of them are required in a short time frame, may place you at greater risk for illness.

Recent studies have somewhat altered the original hypothesis, as other researchers have suggested that individuals are affected differently by significant life events. Factors like personality type, whether the event is negative or positive, and the amount of social support the individual has available seem to moderate the effects.[11]

Since change is endemic to collegiate life, particularly for the first year student, the likelihood of your having experienced significant events is high. If you have experienced or expect to experience a number of changes, it is particularly important for you to make a stress management plan. In addition, where delay or avoiding a stressful event is possible, you may be able to reduce your risk of stress-related illness.

Are you setting yourself up for negative stress effects by your lifestyle? Many people fail to recognize that the simplest, daily health-related behaviors either increase or decrease one's vulnerability to stress. Factors like fatigue, noise, the quality and quantity of the food you eat, and the amount of caffeine you consume influence the body's susceptibility to negative stress effects.

According to Smith and Smith,[33] caffeine consumption can be particularly troublesome because caffeine increases the amount of adrenaline in your bloodstream. Since the stress response also triggers the secretion of adrenaline, the stress effects are compounded. With heavy caffeine use, behavioral symptoms are often similar to those of someone having an anxiety attack.

The good news about stress vulnerability factors is that they are usually within your power to change! Making a commitment to exercise regularly, reduce caffeine consumption, and/or improve your diet are all great ideas for reducing your vulnerability to stress. By so doing, you can inoculate yourself against the negative effects of stress and reduce your vulnerability to illness. Anticipating high-stress time periods like midterm and final exam week by building stress resistance with positive health behaviors is an important step in stress management.

Reducing caffeine intake can reduce the effects of stress.

Is your body trying to tell you something by exhibiting symptoms of stress? An important part of a stress assessment is to identify your own symptoms, the level of their severity, and the events which seem to trigger them. Table 10.3 lists common physical, behavioral and emotional symptoms of stress which have been cited by college students. As you examine this list, ask yourself when, during recent weeks, you have experienced any of these symptoms. Establishing the linkage between symptom(s) and events will help you to eliminate some causes of stress and manage or modify others.

It is sometimes difficult to determine the connection between symptoms of stress and a particular event. If the cause remains elusive, it may be helpful to keep a written log for several days of the times when the symptoms occur and any events that happen before, during and after the symptoms. Write down where you are, with whom, and a description of the environment, including factors like temperature and noise level. For example, you may experience headaches every evening around 9:00 at about the same time you initiate some serious studying. It may soon become clear, from reviewing your log, that your study environment could be the cause of your headache. (Perhaps you have been studying in your room, which is on a usually noisy residence hall floor.) By changing locations and making plans to study at the library instead of in your room, you eliminate the stressor and the symptom. Exerting control over at least some of the stressors in your life, will provide substantial stress relief and leave you less vulnerable to negative effects.

TABLE 10.3		
Symptoms of Stress		
Physical	**Behavioral**	**Emotional**
sweating	increased drinking	feeling scared
rapid heart rate	increased smoking	feeling angry
tenseness	increased use of OTC drugs	
headache		feeling depressed
stomach ache	insomnia	
diarrhea	excessive sleeping	lack of concentration
allergy problems	accident proneness	aggressiveness
trembling		
dry mouth	overeating	unstable
pimples	undereating	
coldsores	poor eating	edgy
colds		
vomiting	sexual problems	impulsive
stiff neck	overreacting to minor problems	loneliness
fatigue	isolation	feeling anxious

Personality characteristics also influence how we handle stress and negative stress effects. Psychologist Suzanne Kobasa has identified traits of what she terms the "**hardy personality.**" According to Kobasa, people with a hardly personality have developed the "three C's of health," **challenge**, **commitment**, and **control** . They view challenge, not as a threat to be avoided, but as a stimulating opportunity for growth. They feel a strong commitment to their activities and they recognize that they have the power to control their own lives. Although to some extent, we begin to learn these personality traits during childhood, these characteristics can also be cultivated in the adult years. Practicing the three C's is another way to inoculate yourself against negative stress effects.[22]

The relationship between personality type and heart disease has been the subject of research since the early 1950s. When cardiologists Rosenman and Friedman, at Mt. Zion Hospital in San Francisco, studied several thousand cardiac patients, they noted that those patients who seemed to be extremely hard-driving, impatient, and aggressive (the Type A personalities) had a significantly greater number of heart attacks than did patients who were more laid back and relaxed (the Type Bs). Rosenman and Friedman found their theory to be so predictable that they even offered to pay the funeral expenses of any Type B in their practice who died of a heart attack at an early age.[9]

The risk of heart attack, and other types of coronary heart disease, for the Type A personalities was believed to be higher because Type As were more likely to involve themselves in stressful situations like intense competition and high-stress jobs. They were also more likely to exhibit explosive behavior in high-stress situations—resulting in increases in blood pressure and stress hormones. As is explained further in Chapter 7, high blood pressure causes damage to blood vessels and is often a precursor to circulatory problems.

More recent research on the Type A—Type B personality type has suggested that more specific characteristics increase the risk of heart disease. Rather than implicating the entire Type A personality type, many researchers now believe that the truly lethal personality trait is **hostility**. In one report from Yale University, presented at the 1990 American Heart Association annual meeting, researchers found that men who react to situations with strong emotions, particularly anger, are especially likely to die of cardiac arrest.

Another study conducted by Dr. Redford Williams at Duke University indicated that people with high hostility at age 19 tend to have high cholesterol at age 40. Williams study followed 830 people who took personality tests while enrolled at the University of North Carolina in the 1960s. Those who scored high on a hostility scale tended to have high levels of total

TABLE 10.4

Suggestions for Altering Type A Responses

- Recognize your imperfections.
- Recognize that life is always unfinished.
- Do one thing at a time
- Avoid overscheduling.
- Maintain as much flexibility in your schedule as possible.
- Plan relaxation breaks.
- Plan for some time alone.
- Listen quietly when others are speaking.
- Smile at people!
- Let someone else go first.
- Use self-talk
  "You are not upsetting me. I am allowing you to upset me."

cholesterol and low amounts of HDL (the so-called good cholesterol). Chapter 7 details the strong link between these two factors and cardiovascular disease.

Hostility may harm health in other ways, too. Other Duke research found that alumni who were especially rebellious and hostile were more likely to smoke cigarettes. This suggests that hostile people may be less likely to practice good health habits.

Type A/Type B self-assessments give you a general idea of which personality type you more closely resemble. Keep in mind that many Type A characteristics are positive and contribute to success. Your reactions in stressful situations, particularly if you consistently exhibit anger and/or hostility, are the key concern. Dr. Meyer Friedman, author of *Type A Behavior and Your Heart*,[10] believes that Type A's can significantly reduce their health risk through behavior modification. Friedman's suggestions for modifying Type A behavior are found in Table 10.4.

Anxiety

Though most college students cope well with the everyday pressures and changes of college life, sometimes long-term stress can lead to anxiety. According to Smith and Smith,[33] anxiety is particularly common among college-age people. One study they cited found that 65% of all panic disorders (a severe form of anxiety) began between the ages of 15 and 29 years.

Anxiety can be perfectly normal and healthy, as when you feel some anxiety about leaving your car unlocked in the parking lot. However, if you find yourself regularly experiencing intense "fight-or-flight" responses in situations that most people find only mildly stressful, you may be experiencing anxiety. Chronic feelings of anxiety can inhibit school performance, social relationships and the overall satisfaction you feel with your life. If you find that anxiety is increasing, that you are having difficulty sleeping, that you are in a constant state of tension, or that you are closing yourself off from normal interactions with other people or situations, its time to seek help. There is no need to suffer unacknowledged with an anxiety disorder! Counseling, along with behavior modification activities, is usually an effective treatment.[12]

Depression

Stress can lead to depression.

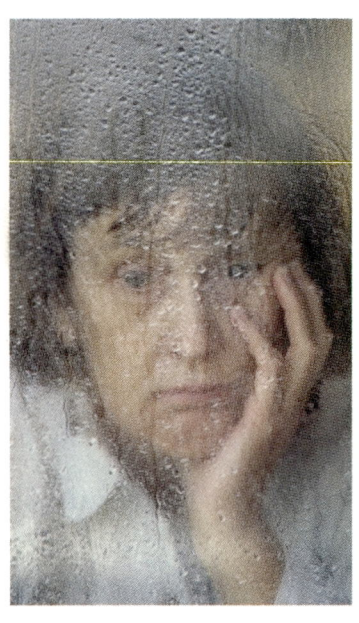

Unresolved stress can lead to depression. Researchers believe that between 10% and 25% of people in the U.S. will experience a major depression at some point in their lives.[20] Factors which appear related to depression include an accumulation of stressful events within a relatively short space in time, lack of social support and having a family history of depression. There can also be chemical imbalances in the body and other physical causes which contribute to depression. Depression is much more than normal "sadness;" it is a debilitating condition which can lead to serious health consequences, including suicide.

The questionnaire in Lab 10.2 at the end of this chapter, known as the **Wakefield Questionnaire**, is designed to help you become familiar with the symptoms of depression and begin to assess whether depression might be a health problem for you or someone you know. Though clinical depression can only be diagnosed by a trained health professional, the Wakefield Questionnaire is useful for beginning to learn more about this condition.

CONSEQUENCES OF STRESS

Stress, especially distress, has many short and long term effects on physical, mental, and emotional health. Short term effects include fatigue, digestive disturbances, headache, acne, amenorrhea (absence of menstrual period), and sexual difficulties. Anxiety, loss of memory and concentration, impatience, and anger are other common short term stress effects.

Far more serious long-term health problems have been recognized as having a stress-related component. Stress researchers estimate that between 70 and 80% of health problems are either caused by or made worse by stress.[24] A link between stress and heart disease has been recognized for many years and researchers are presently examining the relationship between stress and asthma, arthritis, ulcers, colitis, headaches, and cancer.[13]

Stress has also been implicated as a factor in a diminished immune response—leaving the individual more susceptible to infectious diseases. In one study, for example, medical students had a decreased immune response during times of increased academic pressure. Other studies have shown a relationship between emotional stress and the number of helper T-cells (white blood cells which fight disease) available at a given time.

In their book, *Stress Management: A Comprehensive Guide to Wellness*,[4] Charlesworth and Nathan categorize long term stress effects as the three D's; disorders, drugs, and dollars. Stress related disorders among Americans include: 1 million heart attacks per year, 25 million cases of high blood pressure, and 8 million Americans with ulcers.

There are about 5 billion doses of tranquilizers, 3 billion doses of amphetamines, and 5 billion doses of barbiturates prescribed in the U.S. each year and 12 million Americans are alcoholics. Premature employee death costs American industry $19.4 billion per year with another $15 billion lost because of stress-related absenteeism.[4]

Poor management of stress, in combination with other negative health-related decisions, is even more debilitating. In his book, *High Level Wellness; An Alternative to Drugs, Doctors, and Disease,* Donald Ardell states "if you combine poor management of stress factors with reckless nutrition, disregard for exercise, dependence on the medical system, and an adverse environment, you get a lifestyle guaranteed to produce disease and premature death.[2] When the abuse of drugs (particularly alcohol) , so common in the collegiate environment, is added to the list, the health risks are further compounded.

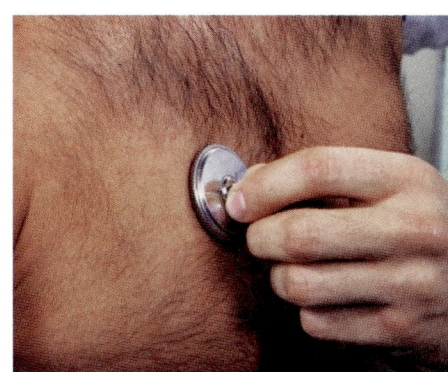

Unmanaged stress can lead to more serious health consequences.

STRATEGIES FOR STRESS REDUCTION AND MANAGEMENT

Assessing your stress vulnerability and identifying personal stressors is the fundamental first step in stress reduction/management. If you recognize that stress is a problem, either all of the time or during particular times in the semester, there are several effective strategies for stress reduction and stress management which will produce positive results.

Just as the effects of stress vary from one individual to another, you will find that some of the strategies described are more useful than others for you. The important action you can take is to assemble a variety of strategies which work for you in a variety of situations. Stress management, to be effective, needs to be a natural part of your lifestyle—something you engage in every day—often without even thinking about it.

Stress Reduction

Some stressors are better eliminated than managed. Charlesworth and Nathan[4] noted that the majority of environmental stressors are more amenable to reduction than to management. They suggest that thinking of yourself as an environmental engineer is a helpful approach. As your own environment engineer, your goal is to eliminate as many stressors as possible from your environment.

This may require some long-range planning as you request a residence hall or off-campus apartment which has a "quiet reputation." A student commuter might plan to arrive on campus a few hours before class to avoid traffic and parking problems.

Other ways to eliminate stressors include substituting water or caffeine-free drinks for coffee and other caffeinated beverages, reducing other chemical stressors like alcohol and nicotine, keeping television viewing and video game playing at a minimum, and using earplugs to block out noise.

Stress Management

Learning how to live with your personal stressors, without letting them interfere with the quality of your life, is the goal of an effective stress management program. As is the case with many behavior change goals, however, you may find that there are barriers to your actively engaging in stress management. Problems students most often encounter at this stage include lack of support from friends, skepticism as to whether the techniques will really be effective, difficulty in finding a quiet place, and not reserving enough time to practice the techniques.

You can increase your chances of success by discussing your personal reasons for beginning stress management training and the potential obstacles that you may encounter with friends or relatives. A public commitment is often more difficult to break and others may offer valuable suggestions. Finding a partner to work with may also be a helpful motivator. Finally, if you think there is a possibility that the symptoms you have identified as stress-related could be caused by serious physical, mental, or emotional illness, visit you campus health center, family physician, or public health clinic before you engage in stress management activities. Misinterpretation of symptoms could lead to you delay medical treatment for serious illness.

Resolving Conflict

Conflict is a normal part of every individual's life and certainly a significant part of the lives of most college students. Disagreements and/or misunderstandings between roommates, friends, lovers, students and professors, parents and students, and members of college organizations can lead to severe stress and negative consequences, if they are not dealt with in a positive manner. Developing skills for resolving conflicts in creative ways is an important component in stress management and will result in a safer and healthier environment for you, as well as for those around you. If approached skillfully, conflict offers an opportunity to learn, grow, communicate more effectively, increase sensitivity to others, and reduce, rather than increase, stress.[23]

Conflict resolution refers to the process of resolving disagreements within a specified framework with the use of specific conflict resolution skills. These skills—active and reflective listening, expressing feeling and thoughts clearly with the use of I-messages, restating the thoughts and feelings of others, and creative lateral thinking for identifying solutions—can be applied in a variety of interpersonal as well as academic situations.

When two individuals work together using the skills above, we call the process negotiation. When a third party is involved, to guide the disputants through the conflict resolution process, the process is called mediation. The mediator does not provide solutions, but does provide a managed opportunity for resolution. Unlike the more directed processes of arbitration and the judicial system, in negotiation and mediation the disputants are responsible and in control of the future solution.

Everyone has their own style of dealing with conflict. We develop that style over the years as we observe how conflict is handled in our families, as we try out and discard methods of dealing with conflict, and as we learn conflict resolution methods from our culture and from the media. Three conflict resolution styles which are easily identified are avoidance (denial), aggression (confrontation), and problem solving (talking it out). None of these methods is necessarily negative in itself and each method might be appropriate in certain circumstances. For example, if someone shows you a gun and demands your wallet, avoiding conflict by handing the wallet over is probably a very wise action.

Avoidance is the most common style of dealing with conflict. Unfortunately, avoidance often results in a conflict which only gets bigger with neglect, and is often accompanied by a buildup of anger and frustration. Aggression, whether verbal or physical, usually escalates conflict and, although it may resolve the disagreement temporarily, is extremely damaging to relationships. Problem solving, particularly when at least one of the two disputants has learned conflict resolution skills, most often results in a solution where both individuals feel they have won, where dignity and self-esteem are enhanced, and where the relationship between the two disputants is preserved.

Although some conflicts may require some form of arbitration for resolution, most do not.

In any conflict, certain behaviors will escalate the conflict while other behaviors will de-escalate the conflict and make positive resolution more likely. Escalation behaviors include standing up, raising your voice, stepping closer to the other disputant, name-calling, using the "silent treatment", raising past events or issues, bringing other people into the dispute, and losing self-control. Making a conscious effort to use de-escalation behaviors is a significant step in managing conflicts in a positive way. De-escalation behavior includes sitting down, lowering your voice, allowing comfortable physical distance, keeping confidentiality, and expressing emotions directly, without losing control.

The use of I-messages offers a strategy for clearly communicating problems and how your feel about them. The following situation offers an I-message example. You have an 8:00 a.m. class. You try hard not to wake your roommate, but a certain amount of noise is really unavoidable. Your roommate is getting angrier and angrier at being awakened before his or her preferred time. You need to say: "I feel... frustrated (or hurt, or angry, or whatever you feel). when... you get mad about my early morning noise level, because... I am trying hard to be as quiet as possible, but I must get ready for class, and I need... to get ready for class without having to feel as if I don't belong here.

The four steps of the I-message: I feel..., when..., because..., and I need..., allow you to say exactly what is on your mind and why. Your roommate could respond with an I-message: I feel...angry, when...you make noise while you are getting ready for class, because...I work until midnight every night, and I need...my sleep. Obviously, the problem is not resolved as a result of these statements, but the two roommates can now discuss several different ways they could resolve the problem. Along with active listening (non-verbal attention, no interrupting, no judging), I-messages allow for a rational discussion of real problems.

The conflict resolution process is the application of conflict resolution skills in a specified framework. A framework which works well for resolving interpersonal conflict is the six step process presented in Table 10.5.

Journaling

In his book, *Opening Up: The Healing Power of Confiding in Others*, author Jamie Pennebaker advocates journaling as a means of self-exploration and self-expression.[25] Where stress management is concerned, journals do not replace more specific coping techniques, but they can contribute significantly to greater self-awareness and self-recollection. According to Seaward reporting in a 1986 study in *Managing Stress*,[29] individuals who kept a journal along with practicing relaxation techniques, were more successful in reducing the physical manifestations of stress. Journal writing gives the

TABLE 10.5
Resolving Interpersonal Conflict

Step 1: Agree on a convenient time to talk together. Make a request like "I'd like to talk to you about our early morning problem" or "Can you have a Coke with me in the lounge about 4:00 today?"

Step 2: State what the problem is and how you feel about it. Be careful to express the situation carefully, respecting the other person's dignity and feelings. Make a conscious use of de-escalation behaviors and I-messages.

Step 3: Listen to the other disputant do the same thing. As you listen, try to see the issue from their point of view.

Step 4: Talk together about what each of you can do to solve the problem. Make a mental list of all the possibilities you can think of.

Step 5: Agree on what each of you will do.

Step 6: Identify a time when you can check in with each other and see how things are working.

"author" an opportunity to let go of feelings and thoughts and work through recent experiences. Rereading journal entries, especially if a journal is kept over a long period of time, can provide a personal history of stress in one's life and creates valuable awareness of behavior patterns which are both helpful and harmful where stress is concerned.

If you decide to keep a journal, you'll need a notebook exclusively for that purpose. Some people find using their personal computer for journaling to be more effective than writing by hand. Make a commitment to write at least three times each week for 15-20 minutes each entry, for a period of at least six weeks. It is also useful to find a designated private space where you will do your journal writing each time. Though there are no hard and fast rules for a stress journal, you will want to include descriptions of both stressful and unstressful experiences, as well as details about the event and thoughts and feelings you had about the experience. You may also want to include drawings, poetry, or other forms of expression. Ideally, since a journal is meant to teach you more about yourself, a journal should be confidential.[29]

Seaward has the following additional recommendations for making your stress journal an effective stress management tool:

1. Identify and write about those concerns that cause the most frustration, grief, and tension.

2. Described the emotions that are elicited when the stressors are encountered.

3. Use the writing process to develop creative resolutions to the problems described.

Journaling can be a method of stress reduction.

Kathleen Adams in *Journal to the Self*,[1] suggests using "unsent letters" as part of the journaling experience. Unsent letters to people with whom we have experienced conflict or some other type of stress provide opportunity to release suppressed emotion, clarify how you feel, and begin to bring unresolved issues to closure.

Exercise

Exercise is one of the simplest, most effective forms of stress management and is probably used by more college students than any other technique. When you are in good physical condition, you have a greater capacity to absorb stress and a greater resistance to fatigue. The fact that exercise, particularly aerobic exercise, has the additional benefits of cardiovascular system improvement, weight control, recreation, and self-esteem enhancement makes this choice an appealing one for many students.

Exercise is an effective stress management strategy for most people for a number of reasons. The key one, perhaps, is its simplicity. Most individuals can take a vigorous 15-minute walk every day without any instruction or sophisticated gear. Exercise does not usually require a great deal of advance planning, coordination with other people's schedules, or financial investment. Since most college campuses have organized wellness programs, recreational facilities and informal exercise activities on campus are often targeted for student use.

Exercise is a particularly appropriate stress reducer in the academic environment because it is a diversion from intellectual activity. Hans Selye, in *Stress Without Distress*,[30] maintains that diversion from one activity to another is almost always more relaxing than complete rest! This sends a clear message to the student "napper" that a walk, a bike ride, a game of basketball or a swim would be more helpful than sleep in most circumstances.

When the "fight-or-flight" response is activated, muscles become tense. As is the case with most mental stress, there is no opportunity to reduce than tension and it continues to build throughout the day as stress responses accumulate. Vigorous physical activity releases the tension and diverts the mental strain to the muscle system. After exercise, body muscles are not only fatigued, but relaxed.

Exercise also reduces stress by clearing your mind. Researchers have measured brain wave activity of individuals engaged in aerobic activity and have found an increase in alpha-waves. The same reaction has been recorded during deep relaxation and meditation. Additionally, during extended exercise periods, opiate-like chemical substances called **endorphins** are produced in the brain. These chemicals are believed to produce feelings of euphoria and calmness. Exercise has also been shown to induce the release of neurotransmitters in the brain which increase alertness, creativity, and

Exercise is a significant means of reducing stress.

imagination. These effects extend for some time after the exercise has stopped, thus, a late afternoon workout may help you to approach evening study time with more alertness, confidence, and energy.[29]

The benefits of exercise for stress reduction are attainable by most college students. However, fitness activities have the opposite effect if you go overboard. Overemphasizing the competitive nature of some activities or consistently pushing yourself to work out faster, harder, or for longer periods of time will eliminate the stress reducing benefits of exercise and can lead to injury, increased negative stress effects, and academic difficulties.

It is also important to remember that simply incorporating exercise into your daily life will improve overall health and reduce stress. Use your car less and your bicycle more, park at the far end of the parking lot, use the stairs instead of the elevator, go dancing (but skip the alcohol), and explore your college community on foot.

Managing Time

One of the most exciting discoveries you may have made as you began your college career is that you have large amounts of unscheduled time during each week. Paul A. Grayson, Ph.D., of Weslyn University noted that "no other environment, not high school beforehand or the conventional workplace afterwards, poses quite the same challenging set of time conditions." Choices you make regarding your use of unscheduled time will not only have a dramatic effect on your academic work, but will also either reduce or intensify stress.[32]

Most effective time managers keep a graphic representation of their semester posted prominently on a wall and/or in a portable academic planner. Creating a visual picture of your quarter, semester, or year will immediately show you where your unscheduled time is during the week. You can then make plans to use that time to your best advantage.

A written schedule will also help you to keep track of important events including exams, due dates for papers, meetings, lectures, and activities. Every academic time period builds to peak workload periods. Identify those times at the outset and work on major assignments at least for a short time each week. This will minimize the need for the infamous caffeine-fueled all night sessions at the end of the term.[28]

As you plan your time, keep in mind your social and personal goals, as well as your academic ones. If you would like to meet more people this semester—commit time to joining a campus organization or working on the campus newspaper. Perhaps enhancing your spiritual wellness is a personal goal which can be nurtured by committing time to a campus ministry group or volunteering at the local homeless shelter, food pantry, or crisis hotline. Pencil in, too, time to take care of yourself including regular meals, adequate sleep, exercise, and time to be alone.

Managing time is often a balancing act.

Many college seniors look back on their academic careers and are amazed at the amount of time they wasted. Identifying your own time wasters and eliminating at least some of them is a significant component of managing your time. Common time-wasters include telephone interruptions, TV, too much socializing, lack of organizations for academic work, and inadequate study skills. As you consider the time wasters, ask yourself which are the major problems for you and what action you can take to eliminate the problem.

Unexpected visitors, telephone calls, excessive noise, idle socializing, and fatigue may be related to your study location. For most students, the residence hall, home, or fraternity/sorority house is the worst place to study! Some creative sleuthing can lead to discovery of an ideal study site in an empty classroom, a library conference room, or a deserted lounge. If your room is your main study location, take time to set up your work space with good lighting, plenty of surface area, storage space, and study supplies. Increasing your computer literacy and study skills are also helpful steps.

As Abraham Lincoln said, "You can't escape the responsibility of tomorrow by evading it today." Procrastination, the bane of many student's existence, is a major cause of stress, which leads to more procrastination, which leads to more stress. Sticking to a written plan or schedule, as previously described, helps to reduce the procrastination problem. Setting up a series of rewards for yourself, to be awarded after particular sub-tasks are accomplished, may be helpful.

Begin your work with the most difficult, burdensome, or boring part first. Focus on one step at a time and don't permit distractions. (One chronic procrastinator found it useful to follow a "Not Do List." She included specific things she would not do during a two-hour work session including not answering the phone, not accepting visitors, and not snacking.)

If your task is a writing project, get something onto the paper! Very often the primary obstacle is the first paragraph. Finally, don't wait for "divine inspiration" or "until you feel like it." Chances are, neither will occur before the end of the term.[26]

Relaxation Techniques

Advice often provided to persons in distress is to "just relax." Most individuals, however, need more than just encouragement. A number of relaxation techniques have been developed in recent years which have proven effective in a variety of situations. The goal of relaxation techniques is to counteract the stress response described early in the chapter. Relaxation techniques are designed to trigger the relaxation response which is characterized by slowed respiration and heart rate, decreased blood pressure, reduced oxygen consumption, and muscle relaxation.

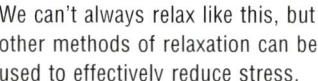
We can't always relax like this, but other methods of relaxation can be used to effectively reduce stress.

Relaxation exercises need to be practiced in a comfortable place. A quiet environment will reduce distractions and enhance the opportunity to achieve relaxation. Assume a relaxed sitting position wherein all parts of your body are fully supported. Lying on your bed is usually not recommended for early practice sessions because you are likely to fall asleep—which is not the primary goal. (If you are using relaxation techniques to help you fall asleep, obviously, the bed is where you belong.) Do not cross your arms or legs. After several practice sessions and as skill increases, you will find that you can achieve a conscious, relaxed state almost anywhere, even in a lecture hall during an exam.

Breathing exercises have been used for centuries as a relaxation technique. Because breathing exercises are simple and require only short periods of time, you may find this relaxation technique an appropriate beginning one. Consciously focusing on and slowing down the breathing process has a profound calming effect on the body and mind. Curtis and Detert, in their book, *Learn to Relax*,[6] describe the following four basic criteria for breathing exercises:

- Breathe normally, that is, let the body breathe by itself and observe the process passively.

- Disregard the inhalation phase of the breathing cycle, simply allow it to occur without any awareness.

- Concentrate on the exhalations.

- Experience a sense of heaviness and letting go as you focus exclusively on the exhalation phase.

KEY CONCEPT

BREATHING EXERCISES

Breathing exercises should be performed at least twice each day for 5 to 10 minutes. Exhalation breathing establishes a cue for relaxation by instructing the body to relax. It is important to breathe normally during this exercise. Follow the steps below.

- Assume a comfortable relaxed position with as much support as possible. Do not cross the arms or legs. During the exercise, maintain a passive attitude and simply allow relaxation to occur.

- When ready, allow your eyes to close and for several breaths quietly be aware of the air entering and leaving your nose.

- Then, for the next several breaths, focus only on the exhalation part of your breathing, noticing the warmth of the air as it leaves your nose, relaxing further and further each time you exhale.

- Continue to focus on your exhalations as you feel your body sinking down into the supporting environment. Notice the body sinking down and relaxing with each exhalation.

- Continue the relaxation and exhalation breathing and remain in a relaxed state for several minutes.

- When you are ready to end the exercise, open your eyes, stretch, and take a deep breath. Notice how alert and relaxed you feel after only a few minutes.

Progressive muscle relaxation is a technique which was developed by Dr. Edmund Jacobsen.[19] Physiological research has demonstrated that the procedure, based on the premise that after tensing, a muscle will relax more completely when released, produces a profound relaxation. Tensing and relaxing muscles helps you to become more aware of your body's muscular response to stress and which muscles tend to stay tense even after the stress response has dissipated. Progressive muscle relaxation works best when used for 20 to 30 minutes each day. Try the technique for at least a week to determine its usefulness for you. Lab 10.3 at the end of this chapter provides practice in muscle relaxation. If you exercise on a regular basis, use progressive muscle relaxation as part of your cool-down.

Meditation is a form of mental exercise which originated in Eastern cultures and has become popular in Western countries in recent years. The purpose of meditation is to gain control of your attention, so that you can choose what to focus on rather that being constantly distracted by internal and external stressors. Meditators experience a number of health benefits including reduced anxiety, a more positive attitude, healthier sleep patterns, decreased muscle tension, and slower respiration and heart rate. In one study, school children decreased their test anxiety after 18 weeks of meditation instruction.

Although there are many forms of meditation (Transcendental Meditation, Chakra Yoga, Zen), there are two basic approaches; the meditator either uses an exercise to focus attention (on an object, phrase, or word) or to open up attention.

For your initial meditation experiences, it is important to choose a relaxed, quiet environment. Since caffeine and nicotine both stimulate the nervous system, do not ingest these substances before meditating. It is best to meditate before eating. Sitting in a comfortable, straight-backed chair will help you to remain erect and keep you from falling asleep. (You will not gain the benefits of meditation by sleeping through the exercise.) It is recommended that you meditate twice each day for about 20 minutes each session. Instructions for meditating are in Table 10.6.

Imagery is a relaxation technique which employs mental images to achieve both physical and mental relaxation. Imagery training reduces mental anxiety by blocking out disturbing and upsetting ideas. Imagery is daydreaming—with a few embellishments![4]

There are several commercially available audio tapes and video tapes which utilize imagery techniques. Some tapes offer descriptions and images of beautiful mountains, the ocean, or a peaceful meadow. Others feature nature's sounds—the ocean surf, a backyard stream, or the wind in the trees.

Periodic meditation can help focus your energies.

TABLE 10.6

Instructions for Meditating[14]

The object of meditation is to induce a hypometabolic state, that is, one wherein the body systems are slowed down. This state is thought to have beneficial effects upon both physical and mental health. The meditation process is entirely controlled by you at all times. You can open your eyes and stop whenever you want.

- Be seated in your chair with your buttocks pushed against the back of the chair. Place your feet slightly forward of your knees, and rest your hands on the arms of the chair or in your lap.

- Don't try to relax—simply assume a passive attitude and allow relaxation to occur without effort.

- Close your eyes and repeat in your mind the word "one" every time you inhale and the word "two" every time you exhale. Breathe regularly without attempting to control your breathing.

- Mentally focus, in a passive way, on your breathing. You will probably not be able to keep problems and thoughts out of your mind for very long—this is natural. However, when you do notice your thoughts straying from your breathing, gently refocus and continue to repeat in your mind "one" on each inhalation and "two" on each exhalation.

- Continue the exercise for about 20 minutes. Relax and enjoy it! When you think the time has passed, simply check your watch. Do not set an alarm. If you feel pressured for time or anticipate the end of the session, the benefits of meditation will be lost.

- When you stop meditating, give your body a few minutes to become readjusted. Open your eyes slowly, stretch, and take several deep breaths.

KEY CONCEPT

DESIGNING YOUR IMAGE

To develop images that are tailored to you, use the following questions to help:

1. Where are you?
2. Who is there?
3. What colors do you see?
4. What images are nearby? In the distance?
5. What sounds are present?
6. What is the temperature?
7. What sensations can you feel? Heat? Cool? Wind? Soft grass?
8. What can you smell? Flowers? Ocean?
9. What can you taste?
10. What movement is happening?
11. How are you feeling?

Creating peaceful and relaxing images can help reduce stress.

Since you have your own ideas about images which are relaxing, you may wish to design your own imagery. Designing at least one personally relaxing scene that you can use for relaxation will increase the benefits of the exercise and will enhance your commitment to stress management. To develop your own scene, try to include all five of your senses; consider what you can see, hear, touch, taste, and feel. The Key Concept "Designing Your Image" will help you create a personal image.

Forgiveness

In his famous Essay on Criticism, Alexander Pope wrote, "To err is human, to forgive, divine." More to the point for our consideration of stress and coping, Simon and Simon, in *Forgiveness: How To Make Peace With Your Past and Get On With Your Life,*[31] suggest that forgiveness is an essential step in the resolution of major life stressors. Holding a grudge or harboring resentment for a long time really does hurt you more than it hurts the person who seems to have wronged you. Over time, anger and feelings of having been victimized can contribute to a negative outlook on life in general and cause you to feel unhappy and resentful.

Simon and Simon suggest that forgiveness is a process, albeit not an easy one, of working through and letting go of toxic thoughts and emotions. Forgiving involves 3 steps—recognizing and acknowledging that you have, indeed, been violated in some way; feeling justifiably angry about it and eventually coming to terms with what happened; and, accepting it and moving on with your life. Forgiveness leads to reduced stress because you no longer carry the feelings of resentment and victimization which were occupying your mind at an earlier time. Simon and Simon call forgiveness a "healing process" where self esteem is restored.[31]

Biofeedback

Biofeedback refers to the use of instruments to mirror information about mental states and body physiology back to an individual. Biofeedback instruments can present data about muscle tension, blood flow, changes in skin temperature, and even brainwave activity. Recent technological advancements have linked biofeedback measurement devices with computers to provide ongoing information via video monitor and a printout about the impact of relaxation exercises on specific body processes.[29]

Biofeedback illustrates the interaction between mind and body and shows the participant that the stress response can be consciously controlled. You can use biofeedback as an assessment tool to evaluate your ability to relax and to chart your progress as you proceed through relaxation training.

Biofeedback is also used, in the clinical setting, for the treatment of hypertension, insomnia, stuttering, panic attacks, and other disorders.

Biofeedback works by providing the participant a feedback loop wherein the biological response (increased heart rate, muscle tension, skin temperature) to stress is measured by the biofeedback device and fed back to the individual. The participant then uses this input to voluntarily change the physiological response. A variety of relaxation techniques are used in conjunction with biofeedback training including meditation, imagery, and progressive muscle relaxation.

There are several types of biofeedback systems including thermal instruments, electromyographic instruments (for measuring muscle tension), galvanic skin response measuring devices (for electrical conductivity) and heart rate monitors. The stress management card, a simple, inexpensive device based on the principle that tension causes constriction of the blood vessels and, thus, cold hands, is another type of biofeedback device.[29]

The goal of biofeedback training is to teach you to self-regulate stress and relaxation responses—ultimately, *without* the assistance of biofeedback equipment. Biofeedback training is usually supervised by trained personnel and may be available through campus counseling and health centers, local hospitals, or mental health centers.

Humor

You may have noticed that during predictably high stress times of the academic year, your school's entertainment committee sponsors a stand-up comedy program, a slap-stick performer, or some other humorous event. If this is the case, you can be sure that someone on your campus recognizes that **laughter** is an excellent stress reliever. Laughing stimulates a rush of endorphins to the brain and results (afterwards) in greater muscle relaxation. Laughing helps you to keep things in perspective and helps you to keep a positive attitude.

Laughing can reduce stress and encourage a positive attitude.

Therapeutic humor has even proved useful in the treatment of disease. Former *Saturday Review* editor Norman Cousins reported that he overcame a degenerative spinal condition partly by designing his own humor therapy regime which included reading funny books, watching Marx Brothers films and viewing old episodes of *Candid Camera* .[5]

Arranging "humor breaks" for yourself by using joke books, watching *Saturday Night Live* re-runs, attending comedy shows, and/or simply being able to laugh at yourself provides a stress reliever that takes very little rehearsal. Keep in mind that humor at the expense of others—ridiculing, sarcasm, and ethnic or racist jokes—is not therapeutic and reflects an unconscious effort to express fear or anxiety.[8]

Music

Listening to music is a popular form of stress management. You can use music while doing breathing exercises, practicing imagery, or as a stress reliever by itself. Quiet music causes the listener to breath more slowly and deeply, reduces the stress response, and exhibits a calming effect on mental processes. Most people have specific preferences in music, but certain types of music have been shown to be especially useful for relaxation. In general, music without lyrics is more relaxing than music with words and slow music (that is music with a rhythm which is slower than the heart rate) is more relaxing than fast.[29]

Leisure

"It is from leisure that one constructs the true fabric of self." So wrote Agnes Repplier in her 1893 *Essays on Idleness*. Americans, in particular, as they continue in the 1990s to work more and more hours with increased levels of stress-related health problems, would do well to contemplate her words. One of the best ways to relieve stress is to plan for and enjoy leisure time.

The word leisure comes from the Latin, "licere," which means "to be free." J.R. Kelly described leisure as having three characteristics: the element of necessity is absent, leisure is freely chosen, and leisure is enjoyed for its own sake.[21] Indeed, an essential element of leisure is experiencing a sense of timelessness, i.e. a feeling of being so absorbed and so relaxed that, for a while at least, you forgot all about the passage of time.

People engage in leisure activities for many reasons and may gain benefits or even experience negative consequences from participation in leisure. A true leisure experience is one that contributes to your total

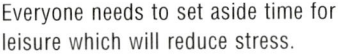

Everyone needs to set aside time for leisure which will reduce stress.

well-being. Thus, allowing most of your leisure time to be spent drinking beer or watching television may seem relaxing, but it does not, over time, provide stress relief or an overall enhancement in well-being.

Participation in leisure is influenced by knowledge, skills and resources. Leisure traditions established by families and what our friends do with their unscheduled time are also powerful factors which affect use of leisure time. In this day of millions of dollars worth of leisure-product advertising—from leisure clothing to leisure vehicles to exotic leisure vacations—it is well also to consider the impact of advertising on our decisions about use of leisure time.

Making choices about the use of leisure time is an important aspect of an overall stress management strategy. Leisure can be a time to be completely idle, a time to play, a time for enjoyable exercise, a time for solitude, or a time for spending time with people who are important to you. Whatever leisure activities you pursue, the important thing is to value yourself enough to give yourself the gift of healthy leisure activities on a regular basis.

GETTING PROFESSIONAL HELP FOR PROBLEMS RELATED TO STRESS

There are times when stress associated with social and/or academic problems moves beyond one's capability to reduce or manage it. It is extremely important, both for yourself and for fellow students, to be able to recognize the signs of severe stress and to understand that part of living a wellness lifestyle is being able to recognize those signs of difficulty and get help when help is needed.

Informal support systems including friends, roommates, residence hall assistants, professors, and family members can help. Most colleges have health services and counseling centers where trained professionals as well as peer counselors are available. Additionally, academic support programs are often available through the student services program. These services offer confidential support for students experiencing a variety of difficulties.

Each year, about 100,000 people in the U.S. between the ages of 15 and 24 attempt suicide—about 5000 succeed. Suicide is the second leading cause of death in the 15-19 age group and over 1000 college students commit suicide every year. Significantly more females than males attempt suicide, but more males actually succeed.

Table 10.7 cites suicide rates in the U.S. for persons 15-24 years old for the past several decades. Note that the suicide rate for young adults is substantially higher than the rate for adolescents.

Depression, the abuse of alcohol and other drugs, and feelings of being overwhelmed by academic and/or personal circumstances are contributors to suicide in the college environment. Since 8 of 10 people contemplating suicide give warnings of their intentions, classmates, friends, and others need to intervene promptly if the signals in Table 10.8 are observed.[15, 32]

If you observe the signals in Table 10.8, take action. Tell your friend of your concern, ask if you can help, and contact your campus health service at once. If you find yourself having thoughts of suicide, call your local crisis services center (most have hotlines which are staffed 24 hours a day) or seek help at your campus health or counseling center. Keep in mind that the circumstances which may have contributed to suicidal thoughts will pass and that, with help, you can get past them and live in a brighter tomorrow. Suicide is a disastrous and irrevocable event, not only for the person who no longer has a future, but also for family and friends who will never completely recover from the loss.

TABLE 10.7
Suicide Rates* for Persons 15-24 Years of Age in the U.S., 1950-1990

Age Group and Gender	Year				
	1950	1960	1970	1980	1990
15-19 yr					
Male	3.5	5.6	8.8	13.8	18.1
Female	1.8	1.6	2.9	3.0	3.7
Total	**2.7**	**3.6**	**5.9**	**8.5**	**11.1**
20-24 yr					
Male	9.3	11.5	19.2	26.8	25.7
Female	3.3	2.9	5.6	5.5	4.1
Total	**6.2**	**7.1**	**12.2**	**16.1**	**15.1**
15-24 yr					
Male	6.5	8.2	13.5	20.2	22.0
Female	2.6	2.2	4.2	4.3	3.9
Total	**4.5**	**5.2**	**8.8**	**12.3**	**13.2**

* Rate per 100,000
Source: National Center for Health Statistics, CDC.

TABLE 10.8
Suicide Warning Signals

- Verbal expression centering around depressing thoughts
- Withdrawal and/or isolation
- Loss of interest in others, in activities, in school work
- No experience of joy or fun
- Neglect of personal hygiene
- Loss of appetite

CONCLUSIONS

Stress is a part of the collegiate experience, but how you choose to deal with stress is within your control. Stress has both short- and long-term negative health implications. Managing stress effectively by using stress management techniques can help reduce anxiety, increase academic progress and social satisfaction, and enhance overall good health.

Engineering your environment to remove stress and employing the described strategies to control and reduce stress in your daily life are positive actions which can be freely chosen. Unfortunately, engaging in **negative strategies** to reduce stress is also a choice often made. Negative strategies— including overuse of alcohol, nicotine, and other drugs; unhealthy sexual activity; driving too fast; involvement in unhealthy relationships; and other behaviors—may seem to reduce stress temporarily, but usually result in more intense distress and impaired health and performance over the long term.

EXPLORING WELLNESS ON THE WEB

Many resources are available on the World Wide Web. You can reinforce, expand and enhance the information presented in this chapter by accessing the following sites.

http://www.imt.net/~randolfi/StressPage.html — the Stress Management and Emotional Wellness Page. Provides many links to other stress-related resources.

http://www.stressfree.com — provides many resources on stress assessment and management.

http://www.siec.ca — Suicide Information and Education Center (SIEC) that contains expansive suicide resource material including crisis training, related organizations, and a list of crisis centers in the U.S.

REFERENCES

1. Adams, K. (1990). *Journal to the Self*. New York: Warner Books.
2. Ardell, D.B. (1986). *High Level Wellness: An Alternative to Doctors, Drugs, and Disease*. Berkeley, CA: Ten Speed Press.
3. Cannon, W.B. (1953). *Bodily Changes in Pain, Hunger, Fear, and Rage*. Boston: Charles T. Branford Co.
4. Charlesworth, E.A. and Nathan, R.G. (1984). *Stress Management: A Comprehensive Guide to Wellness*. New York: Ballantine.
5. Cousins, N. (1981). *Anatomy of an Illness as Perceived by the Patient; Reflections on Healing and Regeneration* . New York: Bantam.
6. Curtis, J.D. and Detert, R.A. (1985). *Learn To Relax: A 14-Day Program*. LaCrosse, WI: Coulee Press.

7. Davis, M., Eshelman, E., and McKay, M. (1995) *The Relaxation and Stress Reduction Workbook*. Oakland, New Harbinger Publishers.

8. Dixon, N.F. (1980). Humor: A cognitive alternative to stress? In Sarason, I.G. and Speilberger, C.D. (eds.), *In Stress and Anxiety* (7). Washington, D.C.: Hemisphere.

9. Friedman, M. and Rosenman, R.H. (1959). Association of specific overt behavior pattern with blood and cardiovascular findings. *Journal of the American Medical Association*, 169, 1286-1296.

10. Friedman, M. and Rosenman, R.H. (1974). *Type A Behavior and Your Heart*. New York: Fawcett.

11. Friedman, M. and Ulmer, D. (1984). *Treating Type A Behavior and Your Heart*. New York: Alfred A. Knopf.

12. Goodwin, D. (1986). Anxiety. New York: Ballatine Books.

13. Graham-Bonnalie, F.E. (1972). *The Doctor's Guide to Living With Stress*. New York: Drake.

14. Greenberg, J.S. (1987). *Comprehensive Stress Management*. Dubuque, IA: W.C. Brown.

15. Hatton, C.L. and Valente, S.M., (eds). (1984). *Suicide: Assessment and Intervention*. Norwalk, CN: Appleton, Century, and Crofts.

16. Holmes, T.H. and Rahe, R. H. (1967). The social readjustment rating scale. *Journal of Psychosomatic Research*, 11. 213.

17. Horowitz, M.J. (1976). *Stress Response Syndromes*. New York: Jason Aronson.

18. Insel, P.M. and Roth, W.T. (1991). *Core Concepts in Health*. Mountain View, CA, Mayfield.

19. Jacobsen, E. (1974). *Progressive Relaxation*. Chicago: University of Chicago Press.

20. Jefferson, J. and Greist, J.H. . (1996). *Unmasking Depression: Seeing Things in a Different Light.*. Pfizer, Inc.

21. Kelly, J. R. (1982). *Leisure*. Englewood Cliffs, NJ.: Prentice-Hall.

22. Kobasa, S. O. (1982). The hardy personality: Toward a social psychology of health. In G.S. Sanders and J. Suls eds. *Social Psychology of Health and Illness*. Hillsdale, N.J.: Lawrence Erlbaum Associates.

23. Koch, S. (1995). *Teaching Educators About Conflict Resolution*. Washington, D.C.: National Institute for Dispute Resolution Publishing.

24. Pelletier, K. (1972). *Mind as Healer, Mind as Slayer*. New York: Dell Publishing.

25. Pennebaker, J. (1990). *Opening Up: The Healing Power of Confiding in Others*. New York: William Morrow.

26. Rutherford, R.D. (1981). *Just in Time: Immediate Help for the Time-Pressured*. New York: Wiley.

27. Schafer, W. (1992). *Stress Management for Wellness*. Fort Worth, TX: Harcourt, Brace, Jovanovich College Publishers.

28. Scott, D. (1980). *How To Put More Time in Your Life*. New York: Rawson/ Wade.

29. Seaward, B. (1994). *Managing Stress: Principles and Strategies for Health and Well Being*. Boston: Jones and Bartlett.

30. Selye, H. (1974). *Stress Without Distress*. New York: Harper and Row.

31. Simon, S. B. and Simon S. (1990). *Forgiveness: How to Make Peace With Your past and Get On With Your Life*. New York: Warner Books.

32. Smith, S. and Smith, C. (1988). *The College Student's Health Guide*. Los Altos, CA: Westchester.

33. Smith, S.F. and Smith, C.M. (1990). *Personal Health Choices*. Boston: Jones and Bartlett.

DEFINITIONS OF KEY TERMS

biofeedback — the use of instruments to mirror information about mental states and body physiology back to an individual. Biofeedback is used in stress management training to teach conscious control of stress and relaxation responses.

conflict resolution — a spectrum of processes, including negotiation and meditation, which utilize communication skills and creative thinking to address conflicts and cooperatively develop voluntary solutions which are acceptable to those concerned in a dispute.

distress — damaging or unpleasant stress, negative responses to stress. Distress is linked to illness.

endorphins — chemicals produced by the brain and released during periods of stress. Endorphins reduce anxiety, tension, and depression and are sometimes referred to as the "runner's high," a feeling of euphoria reported by some individuals during intense periods of exercise.

eustress — stress that is beneficial; stimulation that keeps the mind and body functioning in a healthy way.

fight-or-flight — theory describing the human survival mechanism for responding to threats; a defense reaction that prepares the body and mind for conflict.

General Adaptation Syndrome (G.A.S.) — Selye's three-stage explanation of the response to stress. The G.A.S. includes alarm, resistance, and exhaustion.

hardy personality — a personality type characterized by a view of challenge as an opportunity for growth, commitment to activities, and recognition of personal power to control one's own life. According to Kobasa,[22] individuals with hardy personalities are more able to handle stress in a positive way.

hostility — a feeling of deep anger, considered to be the lethal personality trait where stress is concerned. Person's who develop a hostile attitude are more likely to experience stress related illnesses.

imagery — a relaxation technique employing mental images to achieve physical and mental relaxation.

journaling — keeping a journal of experiences, situations, and feelings.

mediation — the intervention into a conflict of an impartial third party who assists the participants to negotiate and develop an acceptable solution to their problem.

meditation — a stress management technique used to bring the mind to a state of peace and stillness. Based on traditional Eastern cultures, the object of meditation is to produce a hypometabolic state.

negotiation — a voluntary dialogue between two or more participants in a dispute. In a negotiation, participants educate each other about their needs and interests, exchange information, and work together to create a solution which meets the needs of both parties.

progressive muscle relaxation — a stress management technique based on the premise that after tensing, a muscle will relax more completely when released. Progressive muscle relaxation techniques guide the participant through a series of tensing/relaxing exercises with a goal of achieving profound whole-body relaxation.

stress — the nonspecific response of the body to any demand that is made on it.

stress management — the process of assessing life stressors, learning about stress, developing an array of stress management skills, and implementing a plan for reducing stress in daily life. Stress management is an essential element of personal wellness.

stress response — the physiological response of an organism to a stressor.

stress vulnerability — personal health behaviors which predispose one to experience negative stress effects. Stress vulnerability is affected by one's nutritional practices, use of alcohol, consumption of caffeine, sleep patterns, etc.

stressor — a cause of stress.

test anxiety — an extreme state of concern which has a negative effect on test performance; a state marked by heightened self awareness and perceived helplessness.

Type A personality — personality type linked with increased risk for negative stress effects, particularly cardiovascular disease. Type A behavior is characterized by intensity, impatience, and unremitting attempts to achieve more and more things or participate in more and more events in less and less time.

Type B personality — personality type characterized by a calm, relaxed, "laid back" attitude.

ASSESSING STRESS IN YOUR LIFE

Name _____ ID _____ Sect _____ Time _____ Date _____

Purposes

1. To determine the level of stress you experience.

2. To identify areas of stress that can be reduced.

Directions

Below is a list of potential stressors that students often encounter. Check each one that has occurred to you in the **past 12 months**. Total the number of points from all the stressors checked. Use the interpretation at the bottom to assess your stress level and potential health consequences.

Death of a close family member	____ 100	Increase in workload at school	____	37
Death of a close friend	____ 73	Outstanding personal achievement	____	36
Divorce between parents	____ 65	First quarter/semester in college	____	36
Jail term	____ 63	Change in living conditions	____	31
Major personal injury or illness	____ 63	Serious argument with instructor	____	30
Marriage	____ 58	Lower grades than expected	____	29
Getting fired from a job	____ 50	Change in sleeping habits	____	29
Failing an important course	____ 47	Change in social activities	____	29
Change in health of family member	____ 45	Change in eating habits	____	28
Pregnancy	____ 45	Chronic car trouble	____	26
Sex problems	____ 44	Change in family social interaction	____	26
Serious argument with close friend	____ 40	Too many missed classes	____	25
Change in financial status	____ 39	Change of college	____	24
Change of major	____ 39	Dropping of more than one class	____	23
Trouble with parents	____ 39	Minor traffic violations	____	20
New girl or boyfriend	____ 37		**Total**____	

(Continued)

ASSESSING STRESS IN YOUR LIFE

Interpretation:

Score	Risk Level for Developing Health Problems
>300	Very High Risk (>50% chance)
150 -300	High Risk (50% chance)
50-149	Moderate Risk (33% chance)
<50	Low Risk

Adapted from Sarason, I.G., et al. "Stressful Life Events: Measurement, moderators, and adaptation," in Susan R. Burchfield, ed., *Stress.* Washington D.C.: Hemisphere, 1985.

ASSESSING SYMPTOMS OF DEPRESSION

Name _____ ID _____ Sect _____ Time _____ Date _____

Purpose

To increase awareness of symptoms of depression by using the Wakefield Questionnaire.

Directions

Carefully read each group of statements and circle the number in front of the statement that best describes how you are feeling. Make sure you pick the statement that describes how you are feeling **now**, not how you were feeling or how you hope to feel in the future.

1. I feel miserable and sad.

   (0) No, not at all

   (1) No, not much

   (2) Yes, sometimes

   (3) Yes, definitely

2. I find it easy to do the things I used to do.

   (0) Yes, definitely

   (1) Yes, sometimes

   (2) No, not much

   (3) No, not at all

3. I get very frightened or panicky feeling for apparently no reason at all.

   (0) No, not at all

   (1) No, not much

   (2) Yes, sometimes

   (3) Yes, definitely

4. I have weeping spells, or feel like it.

   (0) No, not at all

   (1) No, not much

   (2) Yes, sometimes

   (3) Yes, definitely

5. I still enjoy the things I used to.

   (0) Yes, definitely

   (1) Yes, sometimes

   (2) No, not much

   (3) No, not at all

6. I am restless and can't keep still.

   (0) No, not at all

   (1) No, not much

   (2) Yes, sometimes

   (3) Yes, definitely

(Continued)

7. I get off to sleep easily without sleeping tablets.

   (0)   Yes, definitely

   (1)   Yes, sometimes

   (2)   No, not much

   (3)   No, not at all

8. I feel anxious when I go out of the house on my own.

   (0)   No, not at all

   (1)   No, not much

   (2)   Yes, sometimes

   (3)   Yes, definitely.

9. I have lost interest in things.

   (0)   No, not at all

   (1)   No, not much

   (2)   Yes, sometimes

   (3)   Yes, definitely

10. I get tired for no reason.

   (0)   No, not at all

   (1)   No, not much

   (2)   Yes, sometimes

   (3)   Yes, definitely

11. I am more irritable than usual.

   (0)   No, not at all

   (1)   No, not much

   (2)   Yes, sometimes

   (3)   Yes, definitely

12. I wake early and then sleep badly for the rest of the night.

   (0)   No, not at all

   (1)   No, not much

   (2)   Yes, sometimes

   (3)   Yes, definitely

Interpretation:

Add up the circled numbers for all twelve questions. If your score is 15 or higher, it is recommended that you show the test to a health professional and ask him/her to evaluate you for depression. Even if you did not score 15 or higher and still suspect you are depressed, tell you doctor. Some people with normal scores on depression questionnaires are actually severely depressed and benefit dramatically from a treatment program. **If you develop thoughts of harming yourself or others, call a crisis center or tell someone immediately.**

LAB 10.3

PROGRESSIVE MUSCLE RELAXATION

Name _____ ID _____ Sect _____ Time _____ Date _____

Purpose

To learn and practice muscle relaxation technique.

Directions

The following outline for progressive muscle relaxation describes the basic technique. After you have assumed a comfortable position, tighten individual muscle groups as described in the outline, while leaving other parts of your body limp. Keep the muscle tensed for a few seconds and then relax. Using a mental script (that is, silently saying to yourself) "Relax and let go" for each muscle group will further encourage relaxation. Coordinate relaxed breathing with the exercise by exhaling as you relax. You may want to record the instructions on a tape, have someone read them for you, or make use of a commercially available tape. Some people use relaxing music in conjunction with PMR to further enhance relaxation.

1. Find a quite place where you can recline or sit comfortably. Assume a relaxed position with as much support as possible. Do not cross the arms or legs.

2. Begin the exercise with a long, deep breath. Hold the breath for two or three seconds and then release the air slowly through your nose and mouth. As you exhale, let your face relax, allow your shoulders to relax and feel relaxation flowing into your arms and hands.

3. Beginning at the top of your head, tighten each of the body parts listed below. Hold the tenseness for about 10 seconds. Pay attention to how the tenseness feels. Then release the tension and draw a deep breath, moving on the next body part. Notice for each body part the difference in feeling between tenseness and relaxation and become aware of your ability to control the relaxation and tension of your muscles.

Body Parts:

Head and face	Left forearm	Right knee and calf
Neck and shoulders	Left fist	Right foot and ankle
Right upper arm	Chest	Left thigh
Right fist	Abdomen and hips	Left knee and calf
Left upper arm	Right thigh	Left foot and ankle

(Continued)

Answer the following questions:

1. Which body parts, if any, were difficult to make tense? Why?

2. Which three body parts felt the best when they were relaxed following the tension?

3. Describe your overall feeling after completing all the body parts. Did you feel relaxed? Explain.

Glossary

abstinence — the practice of refraining from sexual activity.

adenosine triphosphate (ATP) — a high-energy chemical compound that supplies the energy the cells of the body need to function.

adipose cells or fat cells – cells in the body that contain the body's storage fat.

aerobic — literally means with oxygen. Usually refers to energy systems in the body which use oxygen to make ATP.

AIDS — Acquired Immune Deficiency Syndrome, a fatal disease caused by the Human Immunodeficiency virus (HIV), causes severe suppression of the immune system, reducing the body's ability to resist disease.

amino acids — building blocks of proteins; categorized by source — from the diet or manufactured in the body (non-essential), or diet only (essential).

amotivational syndrome — a condition in which the individual has a great deal of apathy towards tasks and life in general.

anabolic steroids — illegal drugs used to enhance muscle size and strength.

anaerobic — literally means without oxygen. Usually refers to energy systems in the body which make ATP without using oxygen.

android-type obesity — the type of obesity most commonly seen in males. It is characterized by greater fat deposition in the abdominal area.

angina pectoris — chest pains resulting from insufficient oxygen supply to the heart muscle.

anorexia nervosa — an eating disorder characterized by an aversion to eating caused by a distorted self-image.

antioxidants — substances, mostly vitamins and minerals, that help to defend the body against cellular damage produced by free radicals.

aspartame — (Nutrasweet™) sugar substitute.

asymptomatic — the absence of indicators that suggest the individual may need to seek medical care.

atherosclerosis — the process whereby the inner layers of artery walls become blocked due to deposits of fat, cholesterol and other substances, collectively referred to as "plaque."

atria — the upper two chambers of the heart that act as temporary holding reservoirs for blood coming back to the heart from the body.

B

benign — non-cancerous.

bioavailability — the measure of how efficiently the body is able to absorb minerals.

bioelectrical impedance analysis (BIA) — relatively new method for estimation of body composition that measures the resistance to a small current passed through the body. Body fat increases the resistance to the current.

biofeedback — the use of instruments to mirror information about mental states and body physiology back to an individual. Biofeedback is used in stress management training to teach conscious control of stress and relaxation responses.

bisexual — the capacity to feel sexual attraction toward both males and females.

blood glucose — ingested carbohydrates broken down in the digestive tract and absorbed into the bloodstream. Also called blood sugar.

body mass index — an index of the weight to height relationship used to evaluate how overweight or underweight a person is.

bulimia nervosa — an eating disorder characterized by binge eating following by purging the stomach contents by self-induced vomiting.

C

caffeine — central nervous system stimulant.

carbohydrates — most efficient energy source for the body (4 kcal/g).

cardiac output — the volume of blood pumped out of the heart in one minute.

cardiorespiratory endurance — the ability of the heart and lungs to supply oxygen to the skeletal muscles. Interchangeable terms are aerobic endurance and cardiovascular endurance.

chlamydia — an STD caused by the bacterium, Chlamydia trachomatis, frequently without symptoms in women, chlamydia is the most common sexually transmitted disease in the U.S.

cholesterol — a type of lipid found in animal tissues. High cholesterol is related to formation of plaque in the arteries.

circuit weight training — a method of resistance training characterized by multiple stations or exercises, performed in sequence with little or no rest between each exercise. The general objective is to maintain rhythmical contractions for an extended duration in order to gain some aerobic benefit.

circumcision — the surgical removal of the foreskin from the penis of the male or the hood from the clitoris of the female.

clitoris — the highly sensitive erectile tissue located at the point where minor lips converge at the top of the vulva, only known function is to provide female sexual pleasure.

complete proteins — dietary proteins that contain all essential amino acids; animal sources.

complex carbohydrates — multiple sugar molecules (polysaccharides).

condom — a sheath, usually made of latex, placed over the erect penis before sexual activity, used for the prevention of pregnancy and protection from sexually transmitted diseases, also called a rubber.

concentric contraction — developing muscular tension during which the muscle shortens

conflict resolution — a spectrum of processes, including negotiation and meditation, which utilize communication skills and creative thinking to address conflicts and cooperatively develop voluntary solutions which are acceptable to those concerned in a dispute.

contraception — the practice of using a technique, a drug, or a device to prevent contraception.

coronary arteries — two arteries arising from the aorta that provide blood to the heart muscle. When these arteries become clogged with plaque, it is called coronary heart disease.

coronary heart disease — a disease process whereby the arteries that supply the heart with blood, the coronary arteries, get narrowed by a build-up of a fatty material called plaque. This narrowing of the arteries reduces blood flow and oxygen delivery to the heart muscle.

D

depressants — drugs that reduce the normal level of functioning of the nervous system and other physiologic systems such as the heart. In low doses, depressants may produce a mild state of euphoria.

designer drugs — drugs created by chemically modifying existing drugs to produce analogues which have similar effects as the drug mimicked.

diabetes mellitus — a disease of abnormal glucose metabolism. As a result of the inability of glucose to enter cells, glucose levels in the blood rise to high values.

diastolic blood pressure — the low reading for blood pressure. It is the pressure of the blood in the arteries when the heart is resting between pumps.

dietary fiber — carbohydrate that does not provide nutrient value, but acts as a natural laxative.

disaccharide — a simple carbohydrate compose of two sugars.

distress — damaging or unpleasant stress, negative responses to stress. Distress is linked to illness.

duration — how long you exercise in a single exercise session.

eccentric contraction — developing muscular tension during which the muscle lengthens.

enabling factors — skills, resources, or access to resources that make it possible for a person to act out health related behaviors

energy balance difference between energy intake and energy expenditure. Any change in either of these will change the energy balance and, thus, body weight.

energy system — a series of biochemical reactions in the cells that produce ATP.

endorphins — chemicals produced by the brain and released during periods of stress. Endorphins reduce anxiety, tension, and depression, sometimes referred to as the "runner's high," a feeling of euphoria reported by some individuals during intense periods of exercise.

erection — the engorgement and hardening of the penis during sexual response.

ergogenic aids — substances or procedures used to improve athletic performance.

essential fat — amount of fat utilized by the body in such areas as the brain, cell membranes, and reproductive organs. Loss of these fats would result in physiological damage.

eustress — stress that is beneficial; stimulation that keeps the mind and body functioning in a healthy way.

exercise prescription — the amount of exercise that it is appropriate for an individual to perform. The exercise prescription usually identifies the mode, frequency, duration, and intensity of exercise

extrinsic decisions — decisions motivated primarily by forces outside of one's self. Advertising or the persuasiveness of others are examples.

fallopian tube — tubes through which eggs (ova) are transported from the ovaries to the uterus, fertilization normally takes place here.

fat component — component of a body composition model that contains all of the body's fat. The fat component has a density less than water and makes a person weigh less underwater.

fat-free component — component of a body composition model that includes everything but the fat. The fat-free component has a density greater than water and makes a person weigh more underwater.

fats (lipids) — concentrated energy source for the body (9 kcal/g).

fat-soluble vitamins — Vitamins A, D, E, and K; absorbed in the body with the help of fat; stored in the liver and fatty tissues.

fatty acids — chains of carbon and hydrogen atoms; one component of fats; categorized by saturation level of molecule.

fetal alcohol syndrome — a syndrome due to prenatal exposure to alcohol in which the baby is likely to suffer from mental retardation, low birth weight, abnormal smallness of the head, unusual facial characteristics, congenital heart defects, defective joints, and abnormal behavior patterns.

fight-or-flight — theory describing the human survival mechanism for responding to threats; a defense reaction that prepares the body and mind for conflict.

food additives — materials deliberately added to food to help manufacture and preserve food.

frequency — how many times per week you exercise.

General Adaptation Syndrome (GAS) — Selye's three stage explanation of the response to stress. The G.A.S. includes alarm, resistance, and exhaustion.

generalized equations — equations that use skinfold measurements to estimate body composition. These equations are most accurate in adolescent to middle-aged populations that are not extremely thin or obese.

genital herpes — a viral infection (herpes simplex II) contracted through physical contact with an infected person during an active outbreak of the sores; almost 100 million Americans are estimated to have this incurable STD.

glans — the sensitive tip of the penis or clitoris.

gonorrhea — an STD caused by the bacterium Neisseria gonorrhoeae, people 20–24 are at highest risk for contracting this disease.

Gräfenberg spot — also known as the G spot, an area of sensitivity in the vagina accessed through the upper wall, about two inches from the vaginal entrance.

gynoid-type obesity — the type of obesity most commonly seen in females. It is characterized by greater fat deposition in the buttocks and thighs.

hallucinogens- group of drugs whose primary effect is to alter perception, feelings, and thoughts.

hardy personality — a personality type characterized by a view of challenge as an opportunity for growth, commitment to activities, and recognition of personal power to control one's own life.

HDL cholesterol (HDL-C) — high density lipoprotein cholesterol. HDL-C is the "good" cholesterol because it is involved in reducing the level of cholesterol in vascular cells.

heart attack — the result of insufficient oxygen supply to the heart muscle. The heart muscle cells die as a result.

hemoglobin — an iron-containing protein in the blood that attaches to oxygen to facilitate oxygen transport.

heterosexual — erotic attraction toward the other gender.

high level wellness — an optimal level of health; a dynamic, not static state.

HIV infection — carrying the human immunodeficiency virus.

homosexual — erotic attraction toward the same gender.

hostility — a feeling of deep anger, considered to be the lethal personality trait where stress is concerned. Person's who develop a hostile attitude are more likely to experience stress related illnesses.

hydrogenated fat — a unsaturated fat that has been changed into a saturated fat by chemical means.

hypertrophy — an increase in muscle size due to an increase in the size of individual muscle fibers.

hyperplasia — an increase in the number of muscle fibers.

hypoglycemia — low blood glucose.

I

ideal body weight – body weight that falls within a weight range that is neither too low or high and minimizes chronic health risks. This weight is determined based on an ideal percent fat.

imagery — a relaxation technique employing mental images to achieve physical and metal relaxation.

incomplete proteins — dietary proteins that do not contain all essential amino acids; plant sources.

insulin — hormone, secreted by the pancreas, that allows blood glucose to enter working cells.

intensity — how hard you exercise. Intensity may be measured by heart rate or rate of perceived exertion.

intrinsic decisions — decisions made to meet one's personal needs and provide personal satisfaction

isometric contraction — developing muscular tension without the muscle shortening, resulting in no movement. Sometimes referred to as a static contraction.

isotonic contraction — developing muscular tension with either a shortening or lengthening of the muscle which results in movement.

J

journaling — keeping a journal of experiences, situations, and feelings.

Korsakoff's psychosis — a form of amnesia often seen in chronic alcoholics, characterized by a loss of short-term memory and an inability to learn new skills. The cause of the condition can often be traced to B-complex vitamins, especially thiamin and B_{12}.

kilocalorie – unit of energy which is used to quantify the amount of energy in food.

lactic acid — a by-product of anaerobic energy production which interferes with muscle contraction.

lactovegetarian — dairy products such as milk, cheese and butter are included in vegetarian diet.

LDL Cholesterol (LDL-C) — low density lipoprotein cholesterol, the so called "bad" cholesterol which is found in the plaque clogging the arteries.

malignant — cancerous.

masturbation — self-simulation of the genitals.

maximal oxygen uptake (VO_2max) — the maximal volume of oxygen that can be utilized by the body.

mediation — the intervention into a conflict of an impartial third party who assists the participants to negotiate and develop an acceptable solution to their problem.

meditation — a stress management technique used to bring the mind to a state of peace and stillness. Based on traditional Eastern cultures, the object of meditation is to produce a hypometabolic state.

melanoma — a deadly and virulent form of skin cancer.

menstruation — the sloughing off of the uterus' endometrial lining and accompanying discharge through the vaginal opening, often referred to as a woman's period.

metastasized — spreading cancer.

minerals — inorganic compounds that are catalysts of several vital physiologic functions in the body.

mode — the type of exercise performed, such as bicycling, running, walking, or swimming.

monosaccharides — the simplest form of sugar molecules. Glucose and fructose are the primary monosaccharides in foods.

monounsaturated fats — one of the "healthy" types of fatty acids in which there is one double bond between carbon atoms.

muscular strength — the ability of a muscle to develop maximal tension one time.

muscular endurance — the ability of a muscle to repeat or maintain tension development.

N

narcotics — habit-forming drugs that dull the senses, relieve pain, and induce sleep.

near-infrared interactance — a method of body composition assessment based on the way a light beam is reflected and absorbed by tissue.

negative energy balance — when the calories consumed are less than the calories expended. This would result in a weight loss.

negotiation — a voluntary dialogue between two or more participants in a dispute. In a negotiation, participants educate each other about their needs and interests, exchange information, and work together to create a solution which meets the needs of both parties.

O

osteoporosis — a complex disease process resulting in a decrease in the strength of the skeletal system and characterized by bone fractures and skeletal deformity.

ovaries — the two small organs which lie above and beside the uterus and produce eggs and hormones.

overload principle — a basic principle of physiologic training that states if an overload is placed on a physiologic system (like the cardiorespiratory system or muscular system) in a systematic manner, the system will adapt and get better at performing its task.

overuse injuries — exercise injuries caused by repetitive motion and accumulated trauma.

ovum — the human egg, the female reproductive cell

ovolactovegetarian — eggs and dairy products are included in vegetarian diet.

P

penis — the male sex organ.

percent fat – the percentage of the total body weight that is fat. This includes both the essential fat and the storage fat.

physical dependence — the physical state of one's being addicted to drugs or alcohol. Physically dependent individuals must receive increasing amounts of the substance to prevent the onset of physiological trauma known as withdrawal.

physical fitness — the ability to perform one's daily task without becoming fatigued while having enough energy reserve for situations requiring higher levels of energy, such as exercise.

plaque — a fatty material that forms on the inside lining of arteries. Cholesterol is a major component of the fatty material.

PNF Stretching — a method of stretching that utilizes static stretching combined with isometric contractions of the muscles being stretched.

polysaccharides — molecules containing more than two sugars. The primary polysaccharides in foods are starch, dextrin, cellulose, and glycogen.

polyunsaturated fats — one of the "healthy" types of fatty acids in which there are more than one double bond between carbon atoms.

progressive muscle relaxation — a stress management technique based on the premise that after tensing, a muscle will relax more deeply when released. Progressive muscle relaxation techniques guide the participant through a series of tensing/relaxing exercises with a goal of achieving profound whole-body relaxation.

progressive resistance — the application of systematic increases in resistance as a person becomes stronger.

protein — primarily used to build new tissue and repair muscle tissue.

positive energy balance- when the calories consumed are greater than the calories expended. This would result in a weight gain.

positive self-concept — a positive view of self

premature death — death that occurs before the average age of death, roughly 75 years of age for American men and 80 years of age for American women.

predisposing factors — knowledge, attitudes, beliefs, values, perceptions that underpin behavioral desires

progressive resistance — a method of continuing to overload the muscular system as the muscles get stronger.

psychoactive drugs — drugs that act principally on the brain, producing altered states of mood, perception, consciousness, and central nervous system activity.

psychological dependence — a situation in which an individual becomes so accustomed to a drug that he or she cannot function psychologically without it.

rape — sexual intercourse without consent and under actual or threatened force.

rating of perceived exertion (RPE) — a rating of how hard you are exercising. Usually a scale of 1–10 is used to indicate no work (1) to maximal work (10).

reinforcing factors — support (organizational, cultural, social) to adopt or continue certain behaviors

repetition maximum — the greatest weight than can be lifted in a specific movement one time.

resting metabolic rate (RMR) – rate of energy used by the body to maintain body functioning during resting conditions. RMR can be influenced by both energy intake and expenditure.

risk ratio — a ratio of total cholesterol to HDL-cholesterol (TC/HDL-C). It is a measure of how much of the total cholesterol is HDL-C or good cholesterol. The lower the ratio the better. Ratios less than 3.5 are considered low risk.

S **satiety** — the feeling of fullness after consuming a meal.

saturated fat — animal fat. Saturated fat consumption causes the body to produce more cholesterol than the body needs resulting in high cholesterol values.

scrotum — the sac which contains the testes.

set — a series of repetitions of an exercise without rest between repetitions.

set-point theory — theory which suggests that the body has a predetermined weight or amount of fat that it attempts to maintain in spite of small changes in energy intake or expenditure. However, prolonged changes in either intake or expenditure may readjust the set-point.

sexual assault — coercion of a nonconsenting victim to have sexual contact.

sexuality — the dimension of ourselves, based on biological and environmental factors, which concerns all aspects of sexual behavior.

sexual orientation — refers to erotic attraction toward one gender or the other, or both. Kinsey proposes that individuals can be placed on a seven-point continuum from exclusively heterosexual to exclusively homosexual, based on sexual behaviors and erotic feelings.

simple carbohydrates — single sugar molecules (monosaccharides) or double sugar molecules (disaccharides).

skeletal muscle — the type of muscle that attaches to the bones and causes movement when the muscle shortens or lengthens.

specificity principle — a basic principle of physiologic training that states the effects of overload are specific to the system being overloaded.

sperm — the male reproductive cell.

standard error of estimate (SEE) — a measure of accuracy of prediction formula. The SEE identifies how close you can expect the predicted value to be to the true value.

stimulants — drugs that activate the sympathetic division of the autonomic nervous system (i.e., amphetamines).

storage fat — fat on the body that is in excess of the essential fat. This is the type of fat that is intended to be lost through a weight reduction program.

stress — the nonspecific response of the body to any demand that is made on it.

stress management — the process of assessing life stressors, learning about stress, developing an array of stress management skills, and implementing a plan for reducing stress in daily life. Stress management is an essential element of personal wellness.

stressor — a cause of stress.

stress response — the physiological response of an organism to a stressor.

stress vulnerability — personal health behaviors which predispose one to experience negative stress effects. Stress vulnerability is affected by one's nutritional practices, use of alcohol, consumption of caffeine, sleep patterns, etc.

stroke volume — the volume of blood pumped out of the heart each heart beat.

syphilis — an STD caused by the bacterium Treponema pallidum, once a major health problem in the U.S.; incidence is again on the rise.

systolic blood pressure — the high reading for blood pressure. It is the pressure of the blood in the arteries when the heart is pumping.

T

test anxiety — an extreme state of concern which has a negative effect on test performance; a state marked by heightened self-awareness and perceived helplessness.

testes — the small organs located in the scrotum which produce sperm and hormones.

testosterone — a male sex hormone which promotes the increase in muscle size and strength during puberty.

tetrahydrocannabinol (THC) — the chief psychoactive ingredient in marijuana and hashish.

tolerance — situation in which the body becomes adapted to a drug, so that increasingly larger doses are needed to reproduce the original desired effect.

triglycerides — primary form of fat stored in the body.

tropical oils — plant sources of saturated fats.

Type A personality — personality type linked with increased risk for negative stress effects, particularly cardiovascular disease. Type A behavior is characterized by intensity, impatience, and unremitting attempts to achieve more and more things or participate in more and more events in less and less time.

Type B personality — personality type characterized by a calm, relaxed, "laid back" attitude.

U

underwater weighing — method of body composition assessment based on differences in density between the body's fat weight and fat-free weight. It is considered as one of the most accurate methods to estimate body composition.

unsaturated fats — the "unhealthy" type of fatty acids in which there are no double bonds between carbon atoms.

vegan — strict vegetarian; no animal products of any kind are consumed.

vitamins — organic compounds involved in almost every metabolic process in the body.

valsalva — an increase in intrathoracic pressure by forcible exhalation against the closed glottis.

ventricles — the two lower chambers if the heart that are responsible for pumping blood around the circulatory system.

vulva — the external female genitals.

water-soluble vitamins — Vitamins C and the B complex; transported in the body in water.

wellness — a standard of health based on the interaction of physical fitness, nutrition, stress management, sexual decision making substance use patterns, emotional health, safety, environmental considerations, and other factors.

wellness continuum — a scale for assessing fulfillment of one's wellness potential.

Wernicke's syndrome — an inflammatory, hemorrhagic, degenerative condition of the brain. This syndrome is caused by a thiamin deficiency and is seen in association with chronic alcoholism.

wholistic — (also spelled "holistic") identifies the potential influence on health of integrating the multiple dimensions of physical fitness, nutrition, stress management, sexual decision making, substance abuse patterns, emotional health, safety, environmental considerations, and other factors.

withdrawal syndrome — an unpleasant and possibly painful condition that an individual who is physically and/or psychologically dependent on a drug experiences when deprived of the drug.

Index